BALAAM'S PROPHECY

BALAAM'S PROPHECY

Eyewitness to History: 1939-1989

By

Naphtali Lau-Lavie

Cornwall Books
New York - London

Cornwall Books
440 Forsgate Drive
Cranbury, NJ 08512

Cornwall Books
16 Barter Street
London WC1A 2AH, England

Cornwall Books
P.O. Box 338, Port Credit
Mississauga, Ontario
Canada L5G 4L8

The paper used in this publication meets the requirements of the American National Standard for Permanence of Paper for Printed Library Materials Z39.48-1984.

Library of Congress Cataloging-in-Publication Data

Lau-Lavie, Naphtali, 1926–
    Balaam's prophecy : eyewitness to history, 1939–1989 / by Naphtali Lau-Lavie.
        p.   cm.
    Includes index.
    ISBN 0-8453-4860-4 (alk. paper)
    1. Lau-Lavie, Naphtali, 1926–   2. Statesmen—Israel—Biography.
3. Holocaust, Jewish (1939–1945)—Poland—Personal narratives.
4. Holocaust survivors—Israel—Biography.   5. Israel—Politics and government.   I. Title.
DS126.6.L373A3   1998
940.53'18—dc21   97-20946
                                                                                       CIP

Dedicated to my parents and brother
whose ashes are strewn on the fields
of Poland and Germany

Translated from the Hebrew

AM K'LAVIE

by Professor Avraham Greenfield,
Bar-Ilan University, Israel

Jacket design: Rafi Dayagi

Illustration: Meravi Geffen

Courtesy of Ma'ariv Book Guild, Tel Aviv

CONTENTS

BALAAM'S PROPHECY

A PRE-TEXT

Saturday morning, June 29,1996. I am sitting in a small hotel room converted into a synagogue, on the slopes of Mount Hermon, watching my father as he chants aloud from the Bible.

He is standing in the middle of the room, draped in his prayer shawl, his family flanked around him like young olive saplings surrounding an ancient olive tree.[1] We are celebrating his seventieth birthday, fifty-seven years after his bar mitzvah. He chants from his *haftarah*, chapters 5-6 from the prophet Micah. As a young boy of thirteen, he recited the same chapter. Watching him now, I can see him in Cracow in June 1939, a mere sapling himself, flanked by his father and grandfather in the ancient synagogue of their ancestors. My father chants in his deep, quiet voice, intoning the special melody of these familiar verses, which he has read aloud, every year, on the Sabbath of his birthday:

> O my people, remember what Balak, king of Moab
> devised, and what Balaam, the son of Beor answered
> him; So that you may know God's righteous acts.[2]

The words of the prophet, the cry for remembrance, and my father's voice echo in my ears as we leave the synagogue. My mother, my sister and her husband, my brothers and sisters-in-law join us for *kiddush* while the children play on the lawn. Father and I discuss the topic that has been preoccupying him for a few weeks – the title for the English translation of this book. The Hebrew title, *A Nation as a Lion*, is taken from the words of the Aramean prophet Balaam, whose story is told in the Book of Numbers, which chronicles the wandering of the Israelites in the Sinai Desert before entering the Promised Land. Balak, king of Moab, hires Balaam, the prophet and sorcerer of the time, to curse the tribes of Israel, his enemies.

The Bible narrates Balaam's journey in minute detail – his hesitation, his encounters with God, even a talking donkey – only to reach the story's highlight: As the prophet views the tents of Israel, his mouth utters praises where curses had been intended.

> It is a people that shall dwell alone, and not be reckoned among the nations. . . . No enchantment can be against Jacob, and no divination against Israel. . . . This is a nation that rises like a great lion and lifts itself up as a young lion.[3]

My father's memories tell of the curse of the Holocaust and the blessing of the renewal of the Jewish State. Our family name, Lavie, means lion, and the story of my father's life is Balaam's prophecy fulfilled. Father wanted to name the English version of the book *Balaam's Prophecy*, but hesitated, concerned that its meaning might not be understood. In our conversation that Saturday morning on the slopes of Mount Hermon, I explained to him why I thought the title was good, its meaning and power extending far beyond our reach. As we walked together, I was reminded of the last portion of Genesis, as Jacob blesses his son Judah: "Young lion, Judah, you have risen from prey, my son. He stooped down like a lion, who shall raise him up?"[4]

That morning, I came to understand how, through the story of my father, I can remember all the ancient stories, weaving them into my life, blessed with the gift of personal meaning.

I suggested writing these thoughts as a form of introduction, a pretext for presenting my father with an offering of appreciation, gratitude, and the love of a young cub.

Amichai Yehuda Lau-Lavie

1. Psalms 128:3
2. Micah 6:5
3. Numbers 23: 9, 24-28
4. Genesis 49:9

INTRODUCTION

ACCIDENT IN NEW YORK

On a fateful day in January 1990, as Natan Sharansky and I were returning from a meeting in New York, engrossed in our conversation about past experiences - his under the KGB, mine under the Nazis - we were suddenly jolted into a new harrowing ordeal.

I had been in New York just a few days, having come to attend an executive meeting of the United Jewish Appeal to raise funds for the absorption of Soviet Jewish immigrants into Israel. Scheduled to open the meeting January 15, on a Monday, I spent the preceding Sabbath with friends, George and Adele Klein, where Natan Sharansky, the noted Russian dissident, joined us for lunch. Our discussion dealt with immigrant needs and George offered a substantial contribution.

The following day, Sunday, George, Natan, and I met again, this time in the home of our mutual friend, Professor Yaacov Ne'eman, a prominent Israeli lawyer and guest lecturer at New York University. Over a pleasant dinner with Yaacov and Hadassa Ne'eman, we talked about every conceivable topic on Israel's agenda at the time. George authorized me to handle his donation, which would be set aside as a loan fund for Soviet immigrants. Yaacov and Natan agreed to serve on the board of directors of the fund.

Around 10:00 P. M., we left the Ne'emans' apartment on 54th Street and Second Avenue. It was a cold, dry night. George headed north to his own apartment, and Sharansky and I walked south toward our hotels. We were so absorbed in our discussion that we paid no attention to the distance we had covered. Natan spoke of the effort he had invested in writing a book about his experiences in Soviet prisons and urged me to write about mine under the Nazi regime. We passed the Israeli consulate at 800 Second Avenue, where I had spent four years as consul general, and turned into 40th Street. We stopped at a traffic light on the corner of the exit of the Queens-Manhattan tunnel.

Suddenly, two cars raced into the intersection and collided violently a few feet from where we were standing. One of them, a yellow cab, was thrown toward us and knocked down the pole. I was victim number two. I was knocked down and pinned under part of the cab. Natan, who had not been hurt, was panic-stricken. He called for help, shouting, "He's dead, he's dead."

Natan tried to pull me out from under the taxi, without success. Finally I grabbed hold of the bumper above my head and, using all my strength, pulled myself free. I got to my feet, but could not move. Leaning against one of the cars, I passed out.

I came to, and felt myself being lifted onto a stretcher and into an ambulance. Natan rode with me, using his handkerchief to wipe the blood trickling from my nose and forehead. A policeman kept asking questions, but I was too dazed to talk. Within ten minutes, the ambulance arrived at Bellevue City Hospital in East Manhattan.

In the emergency room, two young Jewish doctors were so excited by Sharansky's presence that they hardly paid any attention to me. Fortunately, a third Jewish doctor recognized me from my time as consul general in New York, and summoned the chief physician on duty. The whole team sprang into action, trying to determine the extent of my injuries, halt the internal bleeding, and relieve the pain.

The medical team did their best to make me comfortable. They placed ice packs beneath my hip and bandaged my knee, ankle, and nose, which had finally stopped bleeding. It was now about one o'clock in the morning. Natan was due to catch an early morning flight for Los Angeles, and I urged him to go back to his hotel to get some sleep. Before he left, he phoned George Klein to tell him about the accident.

Within a short while George was at my side. He looked ashen. Whether his shock was caused by my condition or by the condition of some of the other patients in the emergency room, I was not sure. Next to me lay a giant of a man holding his nose in his hand - his nose had been bitten off in a fight. The man on my other side was lying on his stomach, the handle of a long knife protruding from his back.

George asked the doctors about my injuries. While I worried that I would now be unable to attend the meeting of the executive council of the UJA, George was told that I might need emergency surgery, and that I would need to undergo a battery of X rays and CAT scans.

At 3 A.M., two nurses pushed my bed into the X-ray room and gently lifted me onto the X-ray table. When the X rays had been taken, they asked me to get down from the table and stand behind another X-ray machine so that they could photograph my chest and abdomen. A male nurse helped me walk over to the machine, and then stepped away. I felt myself passing out even as I held on to the machine, and collapsed to the floor. An hour later I was taken for a CAT scan, and lay motionless for about forty minutes.

Back in the emergency room, George told me that my condition was not as serious as had originally been feared. But the pains in my stomach and, more so, in my back, were getting worse, and I felt an unbearable pressure in my bladder. Fortunately, one of the nurses remembered that I was supposed to empty the eight liters of liquid I had drunk before the scan.

George remained by my side, trying to keep my spirits up and ensuring that I was given the appropriate treatment. He left at dawn and came back a short while later with an electric shaver and a pair of *tefillin*.

I was hooked up to a drip but was not allowed to drink anything. In the meantime, the ice packs I had been given to prevent clotting had melted, and my sheets, blankets, and mattress were soaked. A young doctor saw that I was shivering and ordered that my sheets be changed. I was then moved from the emergency room into the ICU, and began to feel better. I was further cheered by a visit from my good friend, Rafi Rothstein, vice president of the UJA. I asked him to write down some of the points I had intended to make at the executive council regarding the responsibility of Diaspora Jewry to contribute to the absorption of Soviet immigrants.

The clock on the wall showed eight o'clock; a calendar next to it showed January 15. My accident and the date took me back forty-five years to January 15, 1945, in Czestochowa, Poland, the night I was evacuated by the Germans to Germany. Twice on January 15, my life had hung in the balance, and twice it was given back to me as a gift.

In the evening, Dr. Leon Pechter, head of the ICU, decided that I didn't need an operation after all, and moved me to a private room under round-the-clock observation. The doctors ordered me to lie flat on my back, and not to move. Exhausted and heavily sedated, I fell asleep. In my dreams I saw several vaguely familiar figures: A man dressed in black said over and over again, in Yiddish, "Write! Write!" Suddenly, I heard someone ask in Hebrew, "How are you feeling?" I opened my eyes and saw two figures standing over me, and recognized my friends: Rabbi Shaul Roth of the Fifth Avenue Synagogue and Dr. Chaim Reich of University Hospital.

They stayed a while, and after they left, I went back to sleep. In the middle of the night, a big, buxom nurse shook me awake and told me to get out of bed and follow her. It was almost four in the morning and I could not imagine why I needed to be examined at that hour. She wheeled me into an examining room and told me to step onto a scale to be weighed. I joked that I was not for sale and that, in any case, at four o'clock in the morning, I didn't care how much I weighed. She took no notice. With the help of another, equally strapping nurse, she sat me in a wheelchair and wheeled me to the scales.

The next morning I mentioned the incident, while being examined by a group of doctors making their rounds. At first they did not believe me and said that I had probably been hallucinating. When they heard that I was telling the truth, they burst out laughing.

I told Dr. Pechter that I wanted to go back to Israel as soon as possible. He agreed, but insisted that I be accompanied by a doctor. I was released the following day and went to stay with the Kleins for a few days until I was fit enough to travel.

In the El Al lounge at Kennedy Airport, I was greeted by my friends Ellis and Israel Krakowski. Israel and I had gone through the Holocaust together, and we got together whenever I was in New York. They rushed to the airport as soon as they heard about my accident to make sure that I was well enough to make the long trip.

I was lifted onto the plane in a wheelchair. The flight attendants did their best to make me comfortable, but I could not leave my seat nor could I sleep. I spent the entire flight remembering scenes I had lived through in the distant and not-so-distant past. I recalled Sharansky's encouragement to record my experiences, and the figure in my dream at the hospital urging "Write!"

When I got back to Israel, I was housebound for a month. I used the time to reflect on my own personal fate and that of my people. I have been privileged to be an eyewitness, sometimes a participant, in the turbulent history of modern Israel, both in times of war and in the effort to achieve a lasting peace. I also thought about my younger brother, Yisrael, then chief rabbi of Tel Aviv. The experiences we had endured together have created a bond between us far stronger than that between ordinary brothers. Each of us, "brands snatched from the fire" (Zechariah *3:2*), ultimately chose his own path.

It was the Gulf War in January 1991 that diverted me from routine affairs. The nights in our sealed rooms, the sirens, the alarm brought back the sensation of the many past perils in my life. Scenes, emotions, memories that had been buried deep in my subconscious for so many years surfaced with a vehemence I could no longer ignore, a compulsion I could no longer suppress. They demanded voicing, recording. Feverishly I began writing my testimony for the coming generations.

A Personal Note

The material in this book covers over fifty years of personal experience and involvement in historic events of the Jewish people, and is based on memory and notes.

The people, sites and dates mentioned in the book are all authentic. For any occasional misspellings, misplaced locations or incorrect names in the Holocaust chapters only – the failing of human memory – I sincerely apologize. Inconsistencies in transliteration of names or organizations and geographic sites reflect the way various sources anglicize their names

I owe a debt of thanks to my wife Joan, our children and close friends who convinced me to record my testimony for future generations. In particular, I am deeply indebted to my good friends in New York City – Sam Bloch, Adele and George Klein, Israel Krakowski, and Ira Leon Rennert for their encouragement to publish the English version of the book.

My thanks to Professor Avraham Greenfield of Bar-Ilan University for his diligent work in translating this book from its original Hebrew. Special thanks to Ayala Ida Myers for her skillful editing of the manuscript, and to my wife, Joan, for her tireless efforts in preparing the manuscript for print. My appreciation also to my numerous friends for their valuable comments.

Naphtali Lau-Lavie

1

PROLOGUE

FORTY DAYS IN AUSCHWITZ

Witnesses to a historic turning point often misread its significance, even when it affects them directly and can ultimately seal their fate. Certainly I, as a boy of fifteen, did not read the political upheavals in Europe as portents of a looming cataclysm. But on Friday morning, June 27, 1941, five days after Hitler attacked the Soviet Union, the reality of World War II exploded around me, changing my life forever.

The forces of the *Wehrmacht* had already smashed through the Russian fortifications to the east of the Bug River, which runs from north to south and divides Poland in two. (According to the Ribbentrop-Molotov Pact signed in 1939 by the foreign ministers of Germany and Russia, eastern Poland was annexed by Russia, and the area west of the Bug River was annexed by Germany.) The German invasion into Russian territory considerably expanded the scope and nature of the war. The front line was now about two hundred miles east of my home town of Piotrkow, a third of the way between Warsaw and Cracow. It was in Piotrkow that the Nazis established the first ghetto in occupied Poland, and it was in that ghetto that we were now enclosed. Some people were sure that Hitler would be defeated in the wide Russian Steppes, as Napoleon had been. Others, stunned by the speed of Germany's lightning advance into Russia, were deeply worried. Germany's supremacy had been established on the eastern front as well. That morning, we had seen Red Army prisoners being marched through our streets, beaten and humiliated. It was a bright summer day.

I walked through the ghetto, carrying my notebooks, on my way home from a lesson with a private tutor. As I passed the city prison on our street, I noticed an unusually large number of police cars marked with the letters POL, short for "Polizei." The cars drove into the prison yard to unload their captives and drove out empty.

About an hour later, when I was alone at home, there was a pounding on the door. Before I could open it, two *SS* officers burst in, dressed in black uniforms with red ribbons and swastikas on their sleeves. "Where's the rabbi?" they shouted. Without waiting for an answer, they raced from room to room, slamming doors. One of our rooms had been given over to an elderly, white-bearded man, Moshe Warshaver, who walked with crutches. Assuming that he was the rabbi, one of the officers shouted, "On your feet, old pig. Quickly!" Moshe tried to stutter a reply. The officer grabbed a crutch and slammed it down on Moshe's back. "He's not the rabbi," said the other Nazi.

The first officer grabbed me by the ear, dragged me down the stairway, and forced me into the back seat of a gray Volkswagen. He got in next to me, shoving me against the window with his elbow to create some distance between us. The other sat next to the driver, who was also wearing a black *SS* uniform. Not a word was exchanged between the three, and I did not dare open my mouth. The car stopped at a gray building on 14 Bankowa Street, named Legionow Street before the war. "Out!" cried one of my captors, kicking me in the buttocks. They marched me into the lobby of a public building, city headquarters of the Gestapo and the *SS*. I stood in the middle of the lobby, paralyzed with fear, while the two talked in whispers. One of them grabbed me by my collar, marched me to a closed door, opened it, and kicked me down a flight of stairs. I got up in a daze and looked around me. I was in a cellar. Light filtered dimly through small latticed windows. About thirty men, evidently respectable upper-class Poles, were sitting against the walls. I did not know any of them. They looked at me with astonishment.

"How did you get here, child?" one of them asked.

I had no reply.

"They just grabbed you off the street and brought you here?" asked another.

They seemed somewhat offended that a Jewish boy should be thrust into a group of Polish Christians. Later, I found out that they were local dignitaries who had been arrested by the Nazis upon the outbreak of the war on the Russian front, in order to prevent disturbances in the city.

I found a space against the wall and sat down, next to a well-dressed man in his sixties. He asked me where I was from, and I told him what had happened. "They were looking for your father," he said. "When they find him, they'll let you go." Suddenly, light flooded the cellar and we heard footsteps coming down the stairs. Four *SS* men with drawn pistols stationed themselves in the middle of the room, each facing a different wall. Without being ordered to, the prisoners all raised their hands above their heads. I copied them. The Germans bade three of the prisoners to follow them. They came back a few minutes later, carrying a container of water and two baskets of bread – one loaf of bread for every four prisoners. The man who had been sitting next to me offered me a quarter of a loaf, but I was too anxious to eat. I drank some water from a tin cup.

The man told me that he was a manager at the town brewery and that he knew my father. He was sure that I would soon be released. Toward evening, he suggested that I try to get some sleep. I lay down on the filthy floor and shut my eyes, but I could not sleep. My head was filled with frightening scenarios. I thought about my family, now sitting around the Sabbat table, worrying about me. The following day in synagogue, I was due to have been called up to the Torah to mark the second anniversary of my bar mitzvah, and my parents had prepared a *Kiddush* at home after the services. I was sure that my parents were doing everything they could to get me out of there and was convinced that by the following Friday night I would be home with them. I told myself that I was with a distinguished group of people and that it was only a matter of time until we would all be released.

At 5:00 A.M., the cellar was again bathed in light. Six *SS* men came in and ordered us to stand against the wall, our hands crossed behind us. The commandant and one of his deputies passed down the line, looking us up and down. He then ordered us to clean up the cellar and to line up in single file. He inspected every cranny of the cell to be sure that we had cleaned up properly. We went up the stairs, carrying our slop buckets, and went out of the cellar.

On the street, we were told to get on a waiting truck and were taken to the courtyard of the town prison, not five minutes away.

Screaming and kicking us, the German soldiers marched us into a fenced compound that already held some twenty prisoners.

The prison was only a few minutes' walk from my house. I prayed that my family would find out where I was and would get me released. I was also greatly bothered that I had been forced to desecrate the Sabbath, for the first time in my life. I was sitting on the ground with my head in my hands, when I felt a tap on my shoulder. It was my neighbor from the cellar. "Don't worry," he said. "They'll get you out of here."

In the evening, we were ordered to get up. A truck drove into the empty yard, which was intermittently lit by the beam of a revolving searchlight in the guard tower. We got on the truck and sat on the floor against the sides. I stayed close to my friend from the cellar. He was also terrified. "Don't tell them that you're Jewish," he advised me. I realized that being Jewish made me different from the other prisoners, and knew that I would have to be very careful. An *SS* sentry sat behind a guardrail on the roof of the driver's cabin, a loaded machine gun aimed at us. The prison gate opened and the truck drove out, flanked by three German escort cars in front and three behind, into Pilsudski Street, where I lived.

Some of the prisoners tried to guess where we were headed. Some thought we were being taken to the Rakow forest, where the Germans had recently executed a group of Poles suspected of underground activities. Actually they were mostly Jews caught outside the ghetto for violating the curfew.

After about an hour, the convoy stopped. The guards got out, had a drink, and relieved themselves. They got back into their cars and resumed the journey. The sentry on the cabin roof cursed us. "Polish pigs," he said. "We'll finish you off one by one!" The prisoners ignored him. Fortunately, the German did not know that besides being a "Polish pig," I was also Jewish.

Sometime after midnight, the convoy stopped outside a large building. We got off the truck and were herded into the courtyard. The building was heavily guarded by Germans in green uniforms. At first I thought that we were being handed over to a regular army unit, but it soon became clear that the soldiers were part of an *SS* field unit, which wore *Wehrmacht* uniforms with *SS* emblems on their helmets and lapels.

We were lined up for inspection and counted again and again. The commander of the convoy reported that he was delivering forty-six prisoners from Piotrkow and the surrounding areas, had accomplished his mission, and was transferring us to another commandant. None of us had any idea where we were. The following morning we found out that we were in Radom, the district capital.

We were forced to relieve ourselves in the compound. By afternoon we had had nothing to drink for almost twenty-four hours, and one of our group approached the sentry at the gate and asked for some water. He got no response. A few minutes later, German soldiers burst into the compound and began beating us with their clubs. After that, no one complained again.

At sunset, about twenty Germans came into the courtyard and ordered us to line up in single file. They tied our hands behind our backs, arranged us in rows of five, and marched us out of the compound. We walked for about an hour, guarded by soldiers with machine guns, until we reached a railway depot where a train consisting of an engine and four cattle wagons was waiting. From the train, people peered out through the barred slits. The Germans made us line up next to the fourth wagon, untied our hands, and ordered us to get on. About ten people were already inside. As the last of us got on, the sliding door was slammed shut and bolted.

Starving, thirsty, exhausted, and miserable, we lay on the floor of the wagon, waiting for the train to move. One of the prisoners tried to reassure the rest of us: "If they didn't shoot us in Rakow forest or finish us off along the way, there's a good chance that we'll eventually get out." He could never have imagined where the train was headed. I cried quietly, for myself and for what my parents must have been going through. I knew that it would now be almost impossible for them to find me.

Next to me lay a Polish Christian boy who had been on the train when we got on. He looked about two years older than I, the only other person on the train of about my age. He told me that his name was Bronislaw Kaczmarek, Bronek for short, and that he was a high school student from Radom. My full Hebrew name was complicated, so I introduced myself as Tulek, my family nickname. He told me that he had been arrested in the street during a German search for underground activists, and although his parents could not have known what had happened to him, he hoped that they would get him out. A kind of comradeship developed between us, two young prisoners on their way to the unknown. Crying silently, I tried to pray. "Pray for me too," said Bronek, crossing himself.

Toward evening, the train began to move. We looked through the barred slits to try and see where we were going; one of the prisoners deduced that we were traveling south. A few hours later, the train stopped at its final destination – Auschwitz, or Oswiecim in Polish. The prisoners were aghast. I realized that the place must be notorious, although I knew little about it.

The train had barely come to a stop when I saw the gates of hell open in front of me. *SS* guards with hunting dogs dragged us from the wagon, shouting, beating us, and making us lie on the ground. When the wagons were empty, the guards stood us up to be counted. Two hundred and fifty-seven people. Barefoot (many of us had lost our shoes while being dragged from the train), bleeding, and exhausted, we marched half a mile to the camp. (The track was later extended to connect the station directly to the camp.) I could not believe what was happening to me and convinced myself that this was a passing nightmare. Ferocious dogs, barking wildly, raced around us frighteningly close. Bringing up the rear were *SS* sentries. I could not fathom their faces. To me they appeared like faceless robots. Only their black jackboots and gray-green uniforms convinced me that they were real.

We were made to sit on the ground in an empty lot at the edge of the camp with our hands on our shoulders. We sat for a long time, in the dark of the night. To ensure compliance, we were awakened from time to time by the bright glare of searchlights installed on all the guard towers along the fence. Shortly before dawn, we were made to run to the inspection ground, where we advanced in four columns toward a row of clerks, veteran prisoners, who recorded our personal details. One clerk wrote down "Lauer" instead of "Lau"; another wrote "Blau." I did not correct them.

We were marched to the barbers, who shaved our heads. We were told to throw all our clothes and personal possessions onto a pile in the middle of the yard. A few veteran prisoners who served as *kapos* took us to the showers. We came back to the inspection ground naked, and were given prison uniforms and wooden clogs.

We were assembled for another inspection in front of Block 11. The commander gave a short speech on camp regulations. From then on, we were told, we were to identify ourselves only by the numbers we would receive. On June 30, 1941, my name was eradicated. Pointing to the electrified fence, the commander warned us what would happen if we attempted to escape. "The only way out is through there," he said, pointing to the crematorium chimney.

I stood next to Bronek, hoping that we would be kept together. An officer passed between the columns, indicating where each of us was to go. A large group of prisoners was detached and was taken to Block 11. Bronek was among them, much to my regret. The remaining fifty prisoners, myself included, were taken toward Block 23. It was already almost light.

Block 23 was a rectangular two-story building. We were met at the entrance by two Austrian *kapos* whom we came to know as Bruno and Ernst. Bruno was tall and lean, with a fierce scar across his right cheek, from ear to mouth. Ernst was short, with a flat nose and hairline mustache. They were both veteran criminal prisoners, and rumor had it that they had been brought to Auschwitz to maintain discipline. They led us into a long, narrow hall on one side of the building, in which around three hundred and fifty prisoners were asleep on the floor. There were no beds. A few moldy sacks scattered on the bare wooden floor served as mattresses. We were allowed to lie down for what remained of the night, but I doubt that anyone slept. The area was so cramped that there was hardly room to change position during the night.

I thought about a story I had learned the previous week, in which Abraham is thrown into a furnace by Nimrod, ruler of Ur Casdim, for having smashed his idols. The Talmud relates that the angel Gabriel offered to save Abraham by descending to earth and cooling the furnace. God replied that He would save Abraham Himself. "I am unique in my world," He said, "and Abraham is unique in his. It is fitting that the unique should save the unique." I was hoping for a similar miracle and prayed that someone, not necessarily the Almighty Himself, would rescue me from this furnace. I lay there half-awake, until the *kapos* burst into the room shouting *Raus! Raus!* ("Out! Out!"). We staggered to our feet and stumbled out of the block.

Veteran prisoners from the other side of the block were already lining up against the wall of the block. They looked at us with compassion. The last prisoners to come out of the building dragged four bodies behind them, prisoners who had died during the night, and laid them alongside the group of prisoners. The dead bodies distressed me greatly, even though I had seen corpses before, when Piotrkow had been bombed in September 1939. But this time I could actually see their faces. One was lying near me, his eyes staring at me, his fist clenched threateningly.

I was still reeling from the shock of my arrest and imprisonment in the Gestapo cellar, and the journey to Radom and then to Auschwitz, here in hell itself. I could picture my father, running from place to place, trying to get me out, and I was sure that any minute my name would be called and I would be released. Only last week I had turned fifteen, and here I was, in a group of political and other prisoners, most of whom were at least ten years older than I. What was I doing in this hell, I asked myself, and how could I get out?

After roll call, the *kapos* assigned us to *kommandos* (work groups). Bruno looked at me with his blue eyes and signaled for me to remain. I hoped he would take pity on me and make my life easier. He sent me to work as an assistant to the block clerk, a young and kindly Pole named Heniek.

That day I swept and cleaned the rooms of the block staff – the *Blockaeltester* (block chief), the *kapos*, and the clerk. I was also sent to help the two prisoners who were assigned to clean the latrines. This was a horrible job, considering the total absence of sanitation. When I had finished, the cleaners gave me two slices of bread from the extra ration they received. I lay down on the floor and slept. In the evening, the work groups returned. They waited outside for evening roll call and for their daily food ration before being allowed to enter the block.

My presence as "houseboy" in a block at which I had arrived only the previous night aroused the suspicion of some of the veterans. "Who is that child?" I overheard one of them ask. A Pole called Mietek, who had arrived in the same transport as I, told him who I was and where I was from. "You'd better not leave him alone with the *kapos*," the veteran cautioned Mietek. "There aren't any women here and they look for boys like him." I had no idea what they were talking about.

After roll call we were allowed to stay outside for about an hour. Mietek took me aside and suggested that I stay close to him during the night and at morning roll call. He advised me to join a *kommando* in the morning and not stay in the block under the *kapos'* "protection."

"They're animals. They use boys like you for their own gratification," he said. "If you have any trouble, tell Krist, the block elder, or Heniek, the clerk. He's a decent man." I learned that Heniek was trusted by the political prisoners as well as by the *SS* and was responsible for recording the roll. I was relieved to know that he was around should I need his help.

That night I was too scared to close my eyes. Mietek, lying beside me, reassured me. "We've warned them not to come near you," he said. After the morning count, I stayed with Mietek and went out with his work group to the *Baustelle* (construction site).

While we were walking to our workplace, a group of Poles gathered around Mietek. They turned out to be the leaders of the group of political prisoners, which had united against the criminal elements. In some blocks the political prisoners had already driven out the criminal elements and gained control. In my block this showdown was still to come, although the political prisoners had already gained the upper hand. There seemed to be great solidarity among the political inmates; I was envious. They belonged to a group and looked out for one another, while I was the only Jew. At least I had gained the protection of Mietek.

We arrived at our worksite, a muddy field a few hundred yards from a miserable-looking village called Brzezinka, or Birkenau in German, consisting mostly of thatch-roofed farmhouses and huts. Cattle, chickens, and geese roamed in the yards.

We laid out narrow metal tracks across the large field, over which we pushed carts of gravel to marked areas. We poured the gravel onto the swampiest areas of the field and spread it around with a spade. Others dug drainage ditches across the field. Albert, the French-speaking *kapo* attached to our group, said that a large camp was being built for Russian POWs. Albert never raised a hand against anyone, except when *SS* soldiers were near and he had to demonstrate his ruthlessness.

None of us could have imagined that we were laying the foundations for a factory of death.

Pushing the carts was relatively easy work, easier than unloading and spreading the gravel. We all took turns at both. When my turn came to spread the gravel, my feet sank deep into the mud. With every step I took, my clogs sank deeper. I worked barefoot until I got used to the stiff clogs.

It was July, and the days were hot. At the end of the day I was sweaty, filthy, and exhausted. Albert told us to line up according to the foreman's instructions. The foremen, mostly veteran prisoners as well as a few foreign workers, were all *Volksdeutsche*, Poles of German origin. The foremen were authorized to set the pace of our work and could make our lives either easier or harder, according to their whim. They treated most of us cruelly, especially those they identified as Jews.

There were eight groups in our *kommando*. My group led the way on the march back to camp; Albert marched with us, club in hand. Walking up to Sme, he thrust two squares of chocolate into my hand, and resumed his position. From a few rows back, I heard Mietek's voice: "Careful of him. He's also a son of a bitch." A mile from the camp, I could not walk any further in my mud-caked clogs and continued barefoot, carrying my clogs. Others followed suit. At least this problem was not mine alone.

It was dark by the time we got back to the block and lined up for evening roll call. We then waited until nine o'clock until our evening rations of soup and bread were delivered. I was starving. The prisoner who was serving the soup fished around for scraps of vegetables or potatoes. We all clamored around him, mouths watering, hoping to be the recipients of his largesse. Most of us were left with our stomachs rumbling.

Terrified of coming face to face with Bruno or Ernst, I sneaked back to my "bedroom." The floor was already covered with sleeping prisoners. I looked for Mietek, my protector of the previous night, but could not find him. One of the other prisoners told me that he was outside in the fenced-off area between the two blocks. I went outside, and there he was, whispering in Polish in the midst of a group of prisoners. They seemed to be speaking in a sort of code. I stood to the side, sensing that it would be unwise to get too close. Mietek saw me and called me over. Standing next to him, I heard that the leaders of the Polish Workers' Party had arrived in the camp that afternoon. "By evening," reported one of the prisoners, "all that was left of them was ashes." They had apparently been the first victims of the experimental gas chamber that had been built next to the crematorium.

We went back into the block. I lay down next to Mietek, who told me that he had been the public prosecutor in one of the cities in Silesia, northern Poland, where he had been active in the Polish Socialist Party. He never told me his surname. (I once heard someone call him "Czorny"; when I asked him if that was his name, he just smiled.) Mietek was a natural leader and was treated with respect by all the other prisoners, including the camp veterans. The *kapos* must have seen that I was under his protection, and kept their distance.

On the way to work the following morning, Mietek sneaked into the ranks of a work group from another block. When he returned to our group, he reported that the Germans had advanced on Moscow. This exchange of information between groups took place under the watchful eyes of the Germans, and by the time we reached our workplaces, everyone knew about the German successes on the Russian front. The mood became even grimmer, as the prospect of the Germans being quickly defeated grew slim. Only one person remained hopeful, Nudelman, a middle-aged man who had been in the transport from Radom with me. He cursed the Germans frequently, in Yiddish spiced with Hebrew. He was in a parallel work group, and until that morning I did not know that he was Jewish.

A sadistic German foreman named Kunz bragged about the tremendous victories of the *Wehrmacht,* which had captured city after city during its advance through the Steppes of Russia. He assured us that the course of Germany's victory would proceed at the same pace. Nudelman displayed amazement at these victories and asked Kunz in all seriousness whether the Germans had captured "Misa Meshuna" ("death in agony," a Yiddish curse). Kunz wanted to hear all about that important city. Nudelman answered that it was deep in the eastern Ukraine. "If it's on the map," said Kunz, "we'll get to it." Nudelman almost choked with laughter; this was the one and only time in Auschwitz that I ever had the urge to laugh.

Nudelman was the only other Jew I had met in the camp. We talked about whether anyone outside the camp knew where we were. "Don't expect anyone except your family to help," said Nudelman.

"The Jews in the ghettos, and certainly the ones in the world at large, will not do anything. They're all too worried about their own skins."

One Friday, we finished work unusually early. Some prisoners guessed that there would be a "selection" in the camp, by which some of us would be sent to work in factories or coal mines. Others thought that the weakest prisoners would be taken away and eliminated. I was still sure that my parents were trying to find me and that I would be released any moment. In order to help them, I wanted to play my part. The only way I could pray was by heart; I had no prayer book or *tefillin*. That Friday, on my way back to the block, I recited Psalm 130, which I knew by heart. Over and over, I said to myself, "From out of the depths, I called upon you, O Lord..." I was sure that my prayers would reach heaven. Tears ran down my cheeks, and one of the older Polish prisoners tried to comfort me.

At about four o'clock, we were ordered to run to the *Appelplatz* near the commander's office. We were lined up according to blocks, unlike morning and evening roll call. Dozens of *SS* soldiers faced us, their rifles aimed. The *kapos* were told to watch their groups. Word got around that prisoners who had been caught trying to run away or who had been involved in activities would be summarily executed.

In front of us stood a gallows, which had been made of a long iron bar attached to two poles. Underneath the bar, on wooden boxes, stood five prisoners, their hands tied behind their backs. Their eyes begged for mercy. Overcome with terror, I wet my pants. My whole body shook. Five *SS* officers stood next to the victims, awaiting the command of the head executioner. I did not hear the actual command. I saw each hangman place a noose around the neck of his victim and kick away the box, leaving the victim dangling in agony until he died.

The *Sonderkommandos*, the units for removing the dead, took down the bodies, placed them on a cart, and wheeled them to the crematorium. No one knew, and no one asked, why these prisoners had been executed. We were all terrified that we might be next.

That evening, after roll call, I did not bother to take my rations. I had lost the will to live. I could neither eat nor drink. During the two weeks I had been at Auschwitz, I had seen death all around me. That very morning we had brought eighteen bodies out to roll call. Men died from hunger, from disease, and from beatings. In spite of the constant fear, I was slowly getting used to living like that. But the hangings of that afternoon were a new horror.

In the days that followed I walked around in a daze. I stopped counting the days and lost all hope that I would ever leave that hell. I worked like a robot. One evening on the way back to camp, Mietek encouraged me to keep my spirits up. "You never know where help might come from," he said. I doubt that he knew he was quoting Psalm 121, one of my favorites. The words sparked new hope. I recalled the first line of the psalm: "I will lift up my eyes to the hills, from whence will come my help." As Mietek talked on, I recited the rest of the verse to myself. "Do not allow your feet to falter, your Guardian will not slumber." That was all I could do.

I had discovered that it was best to remain part of a group, both in the block and at work; loners were more vulnerable to the whims of the *kapos*, foremen, and *SS* sentries. For several days I looked unsuccessfully for Nudelman, as I was still uncomfortable about being the only Jew among non-Jews. My sole remaining hope was the protection of Mietek.

One day I received orders to clean the wagon tracks. Scraping off the upper layer of gravel from the rails, I inadvertently dislodged a wooden tie under the track. Luckily, there were no wagons nearby that might have caused an accident. Stefan, one of the cruelest of the *kapos*, saw me trying to put the tie back in place. He pounced on me, with his tongue hanging out like a hunting dog falling on its prey. The first blow landed on my back before I could manage to straighten up. He continued to beat me with his wooden club right and left. I tried to protect my head with my hands, but he did not let up until he saw me lying on the ground writhing in pain. All this time, I did not utter a sound, just bit my tongue and my lips. My daily prayer "From whence will come my help?" was still unanswered. My face was untouched by the flogging, but I could barely drag myself back to camp.

An elderly man walking next to me tried to help me. He was a Czech by the name of Bendarcek, a high school teacher by profession, who had been in Auschwitz for six months. "We won't be freed for a long time," he said. "But we mustn't lose hope. You're young and you mustn't give up."

Overcome with pain, I turned and twisted that night on my bit of floor in the block, trying to fall asleep, in order to face another day of hell. The words of Bendarcek heartened me. I told Mietek about him, and he too added words of support.

The following day I stayed as far away as possible from Stefan. I joined a team pushing the wagons and kept my nose to the grindstone all day. This was my thirty-seventh day in Auschwitz.

After evening roll call, Mietek called me aside. We walked to the area between the blocks and he whispered that contact had been made with my family. "Tomorrow morning," he said, "don't join a work group. Stay behind to help Heniek, who will take you to the clinic and hand you over to a Polish doctor called Kazik. He'll look after you. Do whatever he tells you. If all goes well, we'll meet again on the outside."

I was very excited. In the middle of the night, Mietek tapped me on the back and whispered, "Be brave and you'll be all right." I could not believe that this might be my last night in the block.

The next morning, Heniek took me to the clinic and handed me over to Kazik. Several *SS* doctors were walking around, but Kazik ignored them. My stomach was churning from anxiety. Kazik put me on a camp cot and pretended to give me an injection in my backside. He called an orderly to help me wash and put on a patient's gown. Dressed as a patient, I followed Kazik outside, ostensibly toward another building for an "examination." We passed the inspection grounds where the gallows awaited their next victims. Kazik pointed to a brown van parked next to the camp kitchen, about two hundred yards away. "Take a good look at that car," he said. "Pay attention and remember every detail." We slowed down and watched the driver of the van open the door of the van and take out racks of baked goods. We passed close by and I got a good look at the driver's face. He was the owner of a nearby bakery who came to the camp twice a week to deliver bread and cakes for the Germans. He had become a familiar face, and his van was only rarely checked.

We returned to the clinic and Kazik told me to get onto one of the bunks in the quarantine area. Twice I heard him report to the German doctors, who seemed satisfied with his explanations. For two days I enjoyed being "sick," and the rest did me a world of good. On the third day, my fortieth in Auschwitz, Kazik gave me a pair of pants, a vest, and a jacket which had a personal number sewn above the pocket. Kazik had taken the jacket from a corpse which was being wheeled to the crematorium, putting my jacket in its place. He gave me a pill to swallow, probably a tranquilizer, and sent me on my way. I was carrying a cardboard box full of lab bottles, that I was to take to the building in which I had supposedly been examined two days earlier.

I was shaking, and Kazik tried to reassure me. "When the driver opens both back doors, go over to him, put the box in the car, and help him with the empty racks. When he taps you on the back, jump in and he'll close the door. Lie down inside until he tells you to come out."

Trembling, I walked toward the van. I could see the driver putting the racks into the van. One of the back doors was still closed. When I was about twenty yards from the van, the driver opened the other door. Quick as a flash, I ran to the van and placed my box inside. I felt a tap on my back and jumped in. The door closed behind me.

The van began to move. I lay down on the floor and breathed in the aroma of freshly baked goods. My heart was still pounding, even though the car was already traveling at a good speed. Encased in the moving cage which, with luck, would bring me to freedom, I had no idea where I was. After about an hour, we turned into a bumpy, rocky road and the van came to a halt. The door opened and the driver called me to come out.

I found myself in the yard of a small country farm. Several pigs and chickens were running free, and I followed the driver into a wooden hut. The single large room served as kitchen, dining room, and bedroom. A fat white cat stared at me, and an old woman handed me a mug of warm milk and a slice of black peasant bread, which I devoured. To this day I can vividly recall the taste of that bread. She smiled at me with friendliness, and I wondered if she knew who I was. The driver, whom she called Bolek, was apparently her son. Seeing how hungry I was, she offered me another slice of bread, this time spread with butter. "Eat, eat," she said, smiling from under the brightly colored kerchief that covered her head and half her face.

Bolek ran a bakery in the nearby town of Sosnowiec. He was about fifty, and had a stern face, a thin mustache, and light blue eyes. He said very little to me. He removed the prison numbers from my jacket, and gave me a pair of boots and a peaked cap which concealed most of my bald head. Bolek told me that I was to travel with him to the nearby railway station at Zawiercie, and gave me a train ticket to Koluszki, a station between Warsaw, Lodz, and Piotrkow. He told me to change trains at Czestochowa. At Piotrkow, I was to cross the main road in the direction of the fields and walk from there to my house, bypassing the ghetto boundary.

Fortunately, there were no uniformed Germans at the station. On the train, I huddled in my seat, afraid that any Pole who recognized me might turn me in. A middle-aged Pole wearing a felt hat and carrying a raincoat was sitting opposite me and looked up at me from time to time. I was terrified that he had been following me. I pretended to be asleep but could not relax. When I got off the train at Czestochowa, he followed me. On the platform, he came up to me and whispered, "Don't be frightened. I'm with you." I got on the train to Piotrkow. I looked around for him and smiled when I caught his eye. He positioned himself in the corridor by the door of my compartment. When the train arrived in Piotrkow, he told me to stay close to him. He took off his hat and draped his coat over his arm. We walked together like old friends until we got to the fields behind the houses on Pilsudski Street where a young Pole was waiting for us. We carried on walking. The young Pole walked ahead, serving as a guide until we neared the ghetto.

"This is the most dangerous stretch," said my companion from the train. "They could recognize you here." His presence was very reassuring, even though I knew the area well. I just wanted to get home as quickly as possible. We walked for about half an hour on a footpath through the fields, parallel to the road that led to the town's Christian cemetery. The young guide left us. We continued on our way until we reached the "Jewish Ghetto."

I led the way to the back entrance to the courtyard of our house. The gate had been blocked by order of the authorities, and I would have to climb the wall of the courtyard to get in. I thanked my companion for taking care of me. We shook hands and he wished me luck. He helped me over the wall, tipped his hat, and was gone. I jumped down into the cobblestone courtyard. Crossing the courtyard toward the stairwell of our house, I encountered Regina, the fourteen-year-old daughter of our neighbors. Her parents, the Gomolinskis, lived in the apartment opposite ours. She asked me where I had been for the last few weeks. "In Cracow," I answered, "visiting family." I decided that this hastily fabricated lie might be useful in the coming days.

I walked up the stairs to our apartment and gently opened the door. My father's study, which had become the most important room in the house, was empty. I walked toward the kitchen. Mother was standing at the table, her back to me.

She turned. The knife she was holding fell from her hand and dropped to the floor. She froze. I forced myself to smile and ran into her arms. She held me close, her tears wetting her face and mine.

Holding me by the hand, she led me into the dining room, where my two brothers and I would sleep. Father was sitting at the table with my twelve-year-old brother Milek, studying the weekly Torah portion. Lulek was sitting on the floor, building a tower out of wooden blocks. Milek saw me and nudged Father. Father's face lit up and I ran to him. He pressed me tightly to him and I leaned on his shoulder. I felt his empty right sleeve; since the accident in which he had lost his right arm, he usually wore an artificial limb, using his left hand to write. He stroked the back of my neck. How many times, in the darkness of Auschwitz, had I imagined this reunion.

Despite the emotion with which my parents welcomed me, I realized that my sudden entrance had not surprised them. They had never given up hope that I would come back. Lulek abandoned his game and jumped on me, squealing with joy. Milek begged me to tell him where I had been. Mother quietly raised a finger to her lips, signaling me not to speak.

I stuck with the lie invented for Regina, and told them that I had been with our relatives in Cracow. Milek knew these cousins and wanted to hear all about them, so I made up the answers as I went along. Father asked when I had last eaten. Mother had already prepared tea and cake, offering me my favorite cup. Sitting with my brothers on either side of me, I heard all that had happened in the ghetto in recent weeks, including the death of Regina's mother from a typhus epidemic that had raged through the ghetto. Father glanced at his watch, remembering that a dozen or so men would be waiting for him for afternoon prayers in his study. My brothers and I got up to go with him, but he told me to stay with Mother.

While I was alone with Mother, she gave me strict instructions: "Forget all about the last few weeks. You were not in Auschwitz. You have never heard of such a place." Seeing my surprise, she said that everything would be explained in due course. Meanwhile, and only when asked, I should say that I had been with relatives in Cracow, exactly as I had told Regina.

Much later, after Father and Milek had been taken to Treblinka, and I remained with Mother and Lulek, she told me of the efforts she and Father had made to find me and bring me home. She described the despair and frustration of the first days after I had disappeared, and how they spoke to every person of influence in the town who might be able to help. My parents learned that the operation in which I had been taken to the Gestapo cellar had been carried out by a special unit from district headquarters in Radom. In Piotrkow, neither the Gestapo nor the *SS* knew of my arrest. Through a family friend, Rabbi Yehiel Kestenberg, rabbi of Radom, they succeeded in locating the group from Radom to which our transport from Piotrkow had been added and then taken to Auschwitz. Following up on this information, Mother's younger brother, Rabbi Mordechai Frankel-Teomim, rabbi of Jaworzno, contacted Polish acquaintances in his town; many Auschwitz inmates worked in the Jaworzno coal mines, supervised by local miners. Through these contacts, my parents learned that I was alive in Auschwitz. My uncle then arranged for my escape in exchange for a very considerable sum of money. My uncle's contacts even managed to have the card with my personal name removed from the Auschwitz files. This card was handed over to my parents as proof of the faultless execution of the operation.

Late that night, after my brothers had gone to sleep, I told my parents everything that had happened to me. They were horrified. Every so often Mother interrupted, "Are you sure you're not exaggerating?" They especially wanted to know if mass executions were taking place in Auschwitz, having apparently heard rumors about what was happening. They were relieved to hear that, aside from a few hangings and killings in the experimental gas chamber, there were no mass killings. They were surprised to learn that most of my fellow inmates were Poles and other gentiles, that Jews were only a small minority. This encouraged them to believe that the Nazis were not targeting Jews exclusively. They were convinced that as long as Jews were not the only group singled out by the Nazis, our situation was less desperate.

When I was alone with Father, I hesitantly mentioned that for six weeks I had had no opportunity to pray or observe any commandments. He was not surprised, and asked me whether my faith had remained strong. I could not assure him that it had. Sensing my discomfort, he dropped the subject.

My parents kept me under "house arrest" for ten days, making sure that I ate well and slept a lot. They were also worried that I would be snatched again, since the Germans had already begun seizing people from the ghetto for forced labor. I stayed off the streets in consideration of my parents' wishes, as well as to avoid bumping into friends and having to answer questions. My experiences at Auschwitz were indelibly engraved in my consciousness. I had terrible nightmares every night.

Three weeks after I got home, the Germans "celebrated" September 1, the second anniversary of the outbreak of war. Several *SS* units burst into the ghetto and fanned out over several streets and alleys. I was on my way home from the house of a friend with whom I had studied before the war. A short distance away, I saw a group of people being rounded up and loaded onto a truck. I backed into an alley and walked straight into a patrol of four Germans leading a group of Jews to the truck. Within a minute, I had been forced into the truck. Salek Greenstein, a friend and classmate from before the war, was already inside. Seeing my terror, he tried to reassure me. "It'll only be for a few hours," he said. "With a bit of luck, we'll be home soon." We were taken to an empty lot near the Phoenix glass factory, then used as an improvised gas station for army vehicles, and were ordered to shift a pile of gasoline barrels. We set to work. When we had finished, three or four hours later, we reassembled for the trip back to the ghetto, but there was no truck in sight. I thought that we would be allowed to walk home, but the German soldiers guarding us ordered us to stay where we were. Suddenly, twenty more Germans appeared out of nowhere and began clubbing some of us with their rifle butts. Our screams only encouraged them. Eventually they ordered us to line up and march back to the ghetto. Luck was with me that day and I was not hurt.

My parents were deeply troubled by such events. They knew that they could not keep me at home forever. They considered some of the invitations they had received from friends and former students of my father in Slovakia. From there it would be possible to continue through Hungary, Romania, Turkey, and eventually to Palestine.

Mother was now in favor of this plan, but Father was against. "A captain may not abandon a sinking ship," he would say. Even though he was powerless to help his people, he felt that, as a leader of the community, he had a responsibility to stay with them. The evening after I had been snatched off the streets of the ghetto, he suggested smuggling Milek and me into Slovakia, so that we at least would be able to reach Eretz Yisrael. I overheard my father say to my mother, "With all that he's been through, he'll be able to take care of Milek." Milek and I never left, for Slovakia was soon in the same situation as Poland, and the route through Hungary, and Romania was blocked.

The jaws of the trap snapped shut around the ghetto, leaving us no way out. We heard nothing from friends and Jewish organizations in Britain and the United States. Cut off from the outside world and at the mercy of the Nazis, we could only hope for help from Heaven, which was not forthcoming.

Father retreated into silence. Although he had many Jewish friends in the West, whom he often met at conferences and with whom he corresponded regularly, he did not think that they could be able to help us. The only people who showed interest in our plight were former students of Father in Slovakia, Hungary, and Romania who were now also under Nazi rule, especially Rabbi Yosef Zvi Carlebach of Hamburg-Altona. They sent *etrogim* for Succoth and matzoth for Passover, as well as frequent letters of encouragement. That was all that they could do. Occasionally I overhead my parents regretting that they had not been sufficiently aware of the danger we were in. The writing on the wall had been clear for over three years, and no one had bothered to read the words. Now it was too late.

Before Auschwitz I had been a boy who had never tasted the personal struggle for existence. But those forty days had changed me totally. I returned steeped in horrendous experiences and was consumed with suspicion, fear, caution, and determination. Father tried to reassure me: "God's salvation can come in the blink of an eye." To me that indicated his despair of salvation by the hand of man. I was seized with worry about the future and doubt that anyone in the free world was concerned about our fate. Why, I asked him, had the Jews always been singled out for such cruelty, and why were the Jews always victims of war between other nations?

He fixed his gaze on me, tears in his beautiful blue eyes. Then he pulled me to him, hugged me, and kissed me on my forehead. "There are Jews who live in anxiety," he said, "and others who live in tranquillity." I did not understand what he was trying to tell me. I could not imagine that there were Jews living in security who would be indifferent to the fate of less fortunate Jews. "Aren't we one nation?" I asked. "Don't the Poles in London worry about their compatriots here?" My wise and knowledgeable father had no answer. He was as helpless as I.

Momentarily, I forgot about the present. Perhaps it was no more than a prolonged nightmare from which we would shortly wake. Thinking back, I saw myself as I had been two years ago, in our peaceful home, before the flood had engulfed us.

2

HOME

By the time I was ten years old, I had already lived in three different countries: Poland, Romania, and Czechoslovakia. In 1926 my parents were living in Suceava, Romania, where Father was serving as chief rabbi. In anticipation of my birth, Mother returned to her parents' home in Cracow, Poland, where we remained until I was two months old. My grandparents lived in a spacious house with a large communal courtyard, which was used by all the other families.

My grandparents, Rabbi Simcha and Miriam Frankel-Teomim, were well known all over Poland. Grandmother Miriam traced her ancestry back to the eleventh century. Her illustrious ancestors included Rashi (Rabbi Shlomo Yitzhaki, 1040-1105), one of the greatest commentators of the Bible and the Talmud; the Maharam of Padua (Rabbi Meir Katznellenbogen, 1482-1565), who lived in Italy in the sixteenth century; Rabbi Shaul Wahl-Katznellenbogen, whose grandson is said to have been king of Poland for one night in 1587; Hacham Zvi (Rabbi Zvi Ashkenazi, 1658-1718), well-known rabbi of Istanbul, Sarajevo, Lwow, Hamburg-Altona, and Amsterdam; and his son, the Ya'avetz (Rabbi Yaacov Emden, 1697-1776), who served as rabbi of Hamburg and Emden. Rabbi Baruch Frankel-Teomim (1760-1828), author of *Baruch Ta'am,* and Rabbi Haim Halberstam of Sanz (1793-1876), author of *Divrei Haim,* were Mother's paternal and maternal grandfathers.

My father, Moshe Chaim Lau, was born in 1892 in Lwow, capital of East Galicia, then part of Ukraine in the Austro-Hungarian Empire. He too came from an eminent family of scholars and intellectuals. His mother's ancestors included famous *poskim* (halachic authorities) such as Bach (Rabbi Yoel Sirkis, 1561-1640), rabbi of Brest and Cracow, as well as a number of other cities, and author of *Bayit Hadash* and many other commentaries; Taz (Rabbi David Halevy Segal, 1584-1662), author of *Turei Zahav*, one of the most important commentaries on the *Shulhan Aruch*; and Rabbi Efraim Zalman Shorr, author of *Tevuot Shorr*.

Father was a known scholar, author, and orator. I remember him as an imposing figure, with his tall, athletic physique and trim, light-brown beard. He had been ordained at the age of eighteen by some of the greatest rabbis of his generation. During World War I, when Ukrainian gangs led by Petlura staged pogroms against the Jews of Lwow, his parents' house was burned down and the family fled to Vienna. The Austrian capital presented Father with many cultural and academic opportunities. In Vienna he made the acquaintance of rabbis, philosophers, and intellectuals, including Dr. Natan Birenbaum, the Jewish philosopher whose ideas on modern Zionism preceded those of Theodor Herzl. Father became his close friend, guiding him through his first steps in Jewish practice.

A charismatic leader, Father was much in demand throughout the communities of eastern and central Europe. He gave his closest allegiance to Agudat Yisrael, a party that came into being in order to counter the Zionist Organization and the Socialist Bund, secular movements established after the Emancipation. In the early 1930s he was among the founders of Beth Ya'acov, a network of religious schools for girls, which went on to revolutionize ultraorthodox education for girls.

His political activities gravitated toward the religious labor wing, Poalei Agudat Yisrael, which was involved in settling and repopulating Eretz Yisrael, then under British rule and called Palestine. Father became the spokesman for Poalei Agudat Yisrael in its confrontation with the more conservative Agudat Yisrael which, because of the antireligious stance of many of the early pioneers, wanted no part in settling Eretz Yisrael. Father spoke fervently in favor of religious pioneers, emigrating and building new Jewish settlements in Eretz Yisrael. I was sure that one day we would find our place in the Holy Land, even though practical plans were never discussed.

In 1928, at one of the world conferences of Agudat Yisrael in Vienna, the leaders of the Jewish community in Presov, Czechoslovakia, invited Father to become their rabbi and he accepted. At the age of two, when I had just begun to mouth my first words in Romanian, I was forced to switch to another language. However, the transition to Slovakian was facilitated by German which, in time, became a very useful tongue. During the four years that I studied at the Jewish school, German enjoyed equal status with Slovakian as the language of instruction for secular topics. Jewish studies were taught in German and occupied a half day. At home we spoke a mixture of Yiddish and Polish.

My childhood in Presov was happy and carefree. I had many friends with whom I played for hours in the big fruit orchards that surrounded our house. One of my most vivid memories is of the *brith milah* of my brother, Shmuel Yitzhak, born in September 1929, when I was three. Many of Mother's relatives came from Poland to join the celebration. The pathway through the orchard to the gate of the synagogue next door was decorated with flowers, and the main entrance to the synagogue was carpeted in blue. I sneaked in between the adults and found a vantage point near my mother's empty seat in the ladies' gallery. Looking down, I could see the podium in the center of the synagogue on which all the distinguished guests stood around Father, who was draped in a striped *tallit* with an elaborate silver border. Grandfather sat in the chair of Elijah, an ornate chair used only at circumcisions, the baby in his lap.

When the ceremony was over, I ran outside to wait for the nurse, who was supposed to take my new brother home. I stood at the foot of the stairs that led to the ladies' gallery, when Elsa, our Jewish maid, caught sight of me. "We've been looking everywhere for you," she said. "Your mother is worried. Where have you been all this time?" She burst out laughing when I told her. She took my hand and led me home. My mother could also not help laughing when she heard where I had been.

I went in to see the baby, whom I had seen only once since his birth, eight days earlier. He returned from the ceremony bearing the name Shmuel Yitzhak, in memory of Father's grandfather, Rabbi Shmuel Yitzhak Shorr, a prominent rabbi in eastern Galicia, author of *Minchat Shai*. His name was far too much of a mouthful for me. I decided to call him Milek, which went well with my own nickname, Tulek. No one voiced any objections, and he remained Milek until his dying day.

My mother, Chaya, or Helena as her Polish friends called her, was a wise, well-educated woman. She had learned Polish and German in school, and had also been given extra tutoring by private teachers. Although her family's rabbinic, hassidic traditions had precluded her going to university, she was extremely knowledgeable and well read. Her beauty, regality, and elegant attire, which was fully in keeping with the laws of modesty prescribed by orthodox Judaism, attracted many an eye. Her charm and friendliness gave her a special status in the community.

She was a warm and caring mother, instilling in us children a love of people and a zest for life. She was rarely angry, and when she was, her anger was usually tinged with humor. Mother was the dominant influence on my education and the molding of my personality throughout my early childhood.

In addition to being a devoted and loving wife, mother, and housewife, she was also active in community affairs. She devoted a great deal of time to looking after the needy and to counseling and comforting the many who turned to her for help. I remember her as someone who quietly influenced everyone about her.

My mother taught me the Hebrew and the Latin alphabets by the time I was four. When I entered preschool at the age of five, I could already read the Hebrew morning prayers fluently, as well as the opening verses of Leviticus. On my fifth birthday, in recognition of my scholastic achievements, my parents held a festive meal to which they invited many community leaders. Extra chairs and tables were brought into the library, which also served as Father's study and was filled with bookshelves from floor to ceiling. I was placed on a chair next to Father at the head of the table, from which I gave a short speech, which Father had written for me. He presented me with a set of the Five Books of Moses and put the gold chain from his pocket watch around my neck. I was very proud. The guests, I suspect, enjoyed Mother's pastries more than my sermon.

Even the rigors of school did not mar the happiness of my childhood. Jewish studies were taught to my class of over fifty six year olds by Mr. Guttman, a short, elderly man with a small, pointed beard.

Prayers, Bible, and Jewish laws were taught by rote, in German. We memorized the passages verse by verse, repeating them in a sing-song fashion. I already knew most of the material, but since my parents did not want me to skip a grade, I stayed in grades one and two for the two full years. Reading, writing, and arithmetic were taught in Slovakian by Mr. Brill, a thickset man who walked with a limp. He also taught us physical education, and was more like an older friend than a teacher.

Although my parents were satisfied with my grades, they arranged for additional tutoring in Bible and Mishnah. My tutor was a student in a yeshiva that had been established by Father. The extra lessons did not affect my boyish high spirits nor did they prevent me from playing with my friends.

Reward for my many hours of study came in the long summer vacations, which we spent in the Tatra Mountains or at Bardejov, near Presov. We spent two summer holidays at Zakopane, on one of the Tatra peaks, together with relatives from Cracow.

On these vacations I discovered a different facet of Father's personality. He loved walking in the mountains; discarding his long, black coat, he hiked with us in his shirtsleeves, cane in hand. Occasionally he would borrow a horse-drawn cart from one of the farmers and we would go on outings to far-off places. Sometimes he disappeared at daybreak to go swimming in the river outside the village. Vacations allowed him to escape from his responsibilities and to spend time with his family.

Mother enjoyed not having to worry about household chores, exchanging the dark silk scarves that covered her fashionably combed wig for brighter colors. She always wore a wig in the presence of others, since, according to orthodox Jewish tradition, a married woman may not show her hair to any man except her husband.

In August 1933, my older brother, Yehoshua, known as Shiko, from Father's first marriage, left for Wizhnitz to study in the yeshiva of his uncles, the Wizhnitz rabbis. He stayed with them until he left for Palestine in 1944.

Prior to his leaving for Wizhnitz, Romania, we spent that summer in Krynica, a beautiful spa resort on the Polish-Czech border. The rabbis of Ger, Bobov, Wizhnitz, and Belz – the greatest rabbis of Poland, Hungary, and Romania – were also in Krynica, accompanied by hundreds of their *hassidim*. Although I was only seven, Father took me in to introduce me to these luminaries. To me, Rabbi Benzion Halberstam of Bobov seemed the most impressive. Hearing my name, he told me about the ancestors whose name I bore, reminding me that I was also descended from Rashi. He bent down and kissed my forehead, then shook my hand and pressed a Polish zloty into my palm.

As I was leaving, a boy of about my own age wearing a hassidic-style peaked cap asked me for the coin, offering me ten times its worth. I hesitated, but he persisted. I told Father about the offer, pointing out the young trader. Father told me that the boy was the son of a famous hassidic rabbi from Poland. "Do as you please," he told me, "but if it's worth so much to him, it should be to you too." The boy again asked that I sell him my coin. I could not understand how it could be so valuable to him, and eventually sold it for the ten zlotys. Neither of us got rich from the transaction. The little boy went on to become the rabbi of Ger. Years later, Rabbi Pinchas Menachem Alter became one of the most prominent rabbis in Israel. Under his influence, Israeli governments were formed and brought down.

It was in Krynica, in the summer of 1933, that I first heard the name Hitler, when the rabbis and some of their disciples were discussing developments in Germany following the Nazis' rise to power. Some were worried; others not. Overhearing a conversation between Father and Rabbi Meir Shapira, his cousin and good friend, I began to understand the possible consequences of Hitler's ascendance. Rabbi Shapira, who had just returned from a fund-raising trip to the U.S., told Father about his experiences in the New World. He was concerned that Jewish immigrants in America might not survive as Jews.

He also spoke about Eretz Yisrael - the first time that I heard Palestine discussed as a place in which Jews actually live. Even though he had never been to Eretz Yisrael, Rabbi Shapira described the holy places vividly. I was mesmerized by his portrayals of the Western Wall, Rachel's Tomb, and the Dead Sea. I pictured myself walking in these places, though thoughts about Eretz Yisrael as a place where one could live in the near future were remote from our reality.

On the train back to Presov, I asked Father about Hitler. "The Lord will help," he replied. He then mentioned to Mother that Rabbi Shapira had suggested that he submit his candidacy for the position of rabbi of Piotrkow, a post that Rabbi Shapira had resigned two years earlier to become rabbi of Lublin and head of the famous Hachmei Lublin Yeshiva. Mother was enthusiastic about going back to Poland, where she would be closer to her family, thus obviating the need to cross frontiers between countries constantly at odds. My parents' decision centered solely on whether Poland or Czechoslovakia would be more suitable for setting up their permanent home.

Two months after we saw him in Krynica, Rabbi Shapira passed away suddenly at the age of forty-six. Father was deeply affected and delivered the eulogy at the funeral, which was attended by thousands of people from all over Europe.

An emergency committee that had been set up on behalf of the Hachmei Lublin Yeshiva asked Father to go on a fund-raising mission for the yeshiva. One of his stops was Piotrkow, the city in which Rabbi Shapira had been chief rabbi. Father was now offered the position. He accepted, and his installation was set for December 1934, on Hanukkah.

He continued to Cracow on his fund-raising trip. At the Cracow station he had a serious accident, as a result of which his right arm was amputated. He was in a hospital in Cracow for a month, and then went to stay with one of my uncles to recuperate. Mother made arrangements for the family to join Father in Cracow, without telling us children about the accident. Thus we left Presov, to return nine months later for a final farewell before proceeding to our next destination, Piotrkow.

We arrived in Cracow just before Hanukkah. One of my cousins told me about my father's accident. I was very upset and asked to be allowed to see him. I went into his room, where he lay in bed propped up on two pillows, a clipboard on his lap. Naturally I was horrified at the sight of his bandaged stump. Gently, my father explained what had happened. "I had just boarded the train," he said. "As I was about to go into the corridor, the train suddenly lurched forward. I lost my balance and was thrown out of the train door and under the carriage between the rails. As the train passed over me, I tried to protect my head with my right arm. My elbow got caught under one of the wheels and was crushed. After the train passed, I was pulled up onto the platform and was taken to the hospital. The doctor said that he had no choice but to amputate. I must thank the Almighty for bringing me through alive, and will just have to get used to it."

Father asked me to place his *tefillin* on his left arm, telling me that when the stump healed he would use his left hand to put his *tefillin* on the stump of his right arm. He showed me the clipboard on which he was already learning to write with his left hand. He was clearly in great pain and I began to cry. Mother comforted me, saying we must be grateful for having a "new father."

Mother saw to it that I did not waste a single day of our stay in Cracow. The day after our arrival, she took me across the River Vistula to Yesodei Hatorah, a private Jewish school. Because I spoke Polish, I was accepted into third grade, together with pupils around my own age. I quickly got used to the new curriculum and made friends, including boys I had met on our vacations in the Tatras. I fell in love with the city of Cracow, and enjoyed playing in Grandfather's courtyard with my many cousins. I would have been happy to stay in Cracow permanently, as would my mother. But at the end of the summer, when Father returned from Vienna, where he had been fitted with an artificial limb, we went back to Presov to wind up our affairs before moving to Piotrkow.

We spent Rosh Hashanah of 1935 in Presov. Father took leave of the congregation with an emotional sermon, which reduced some of the men to tears. Two days later, a huge crowd escorted us to the railway station. About twenty friends came with us on the train as far as the Czech border at Orlov. They waved good-bye from the platform as the train rolled slowly toward the Polish checkpoint at Muszyna.

After a ten-hour journey, we arrived in Piotrkow a few days before Yom Kippur. Hundreds of people were waiting at the station, and they greeted Father with singing and dancing. We were taken to our temporary apartment in horse-drawn carriages decorated with flowers.

Father's first appearance as rabbi in this town of sixty thousand people – one-third of them Jews – was on *Kol Nidrei*, Yom Kippur eve. Many people who usually prayed in other synagogues came to hear the new rabbi's sermon, and the huge synagogue, including both levels of the ladies' galleries, was packed. Father sat on the right of the Holy Ark, in the chief rabbi's seat, which had been vacant since the departure of Rabbi Shapira. Next to him was the podium on which the cantor and choir stood. Two chairs facing the congregation had been placed behind Father for Milek and me.

When Cantor Baruch Kaminecki and his choir had finished *Kol Nidrei*, Father rose to deliver his sermon. While he spoke, the congregation sat in absolute silence, hanging on his every word. He was a thrilling speaker. Even people who did not entirely understand the meaning of his words were captivated by his appearance and resonant voice. From my seat I could clearly see the members of this large congregation and could sense the impact upon them.

After the High Holidays, we moved to our permanent home at 21 Pilsudski Street, the main east-west thoroughfare of the city. I made new friends in school, particularly those living nearby. Pilsudski Street was in the heart of a vibrant Jewish neighborhood. Shops were closed on the Sabbath and on Jewish holidays – except for barbershops that catered to non-Jews wanting to get their hair cut before Sunday. The communal institutions were controlled by the Socialist Bund, which had won the recent community elections, defeating the religious factions led by Agudat Yisrael. The Jews lived mostly in the area between the Great Synagogue and Plac Trybunalski, known locally as Trybunalski Rynek. This square had been the focal point of Jewish communal life in Piotrkow for centuries. At the center stood a water pump, at which wagon drivers watered their horses on market days.

In 1663, a Jewish pharmacist from Cracow named Matityahu Kalhora was accused of insulting a Catholic priest. He was condemned to death and was burned at the stake in Plac Trybunalski. His ashes were returned to Cracow, where a tombstone still stands on his grave in the old cemetery, next to the ancient synagogue where the famous Rema had prayed.

Piotrkow had been an important city in Polish governmental affairs, housing the parliament and the supreme court of Poland, the tribunal, from the fifteenth until the end of the seventeenth century. Piotrkow was proud of its rich history. The Jews, for their part, were proud of the great rabbis who had served the city for four hundred of the seven hundred years in which there had been a Jewish community in Piotrkow. Gradually, I became caught up in this local patriotism, though I have always felt a greater attachment to Cracow, the place of my birth.

Our years in Piotrkow were marked by periodic outbreaks of anti-Semitism in Poland. In 1934 a decree designed to prohibit, or at least restrict, the ritual slaughter of beef for Jewish consumption, was passed on the grounds of cruelty to animals. This was followed by anti-Semitic statements from several Polish politicians. Prime Minister Slawoj Skladkowski, for example, condemned a pogrom against Jews in Pshitik, but when asked about the boycott of Jews in business and the unwillingness of Polish employers to employ them, replied: "Oh, that's all right." The anti-Semitic sentiments of government leaders further encouraged the masses, already imbued with a hatred of the Jews. Popular anti-Semitism was expressed in graffiti on the walls of houses and fences, and especially on Jewish public buildings and institutions. During Christian holidays we were fair game for attacks by Polish youths, and on the nights of Christmas and Easter we did not dare go out into the streets. The rest of the time, however, relations were neighborly; Jewish boys studied in the public schools alongside Christian children and played in the same public parks and sports fields.

I sensed the growing unease in the Jewish community. Young people came to consult Father about whether they should go to pioneer training farms to prepare for emigration to Eretz Yisrael as farmers. There were many who wanted his help in acquiring immigration certificates from the British mandatory authority in Eretz Yisrael. Others simply came to say good-bye before leaving. "Why don't we go to Eretz Yisrael?" I asked Mother. At first she tried to ignore the question, then she said that some go to Eretz Yisrael, some go to America, but we will stay here with our family. I got the feeling that she was not at peace with her answer.

On June 1, 1937, when I was eleven years old, my youngest brother was born. Eight days later, the Great Synagogue was festively decorated with flowers. Since early morning, horse-drawn carriages had been lined up near the house. The one decked out with an arch of flowers was to take my new brother to his *brith milah* in the synagogue. All the dignitaries of the congregation were there, along with Mother's family from Cracow and Father's from Lwow and Katowice. My younger brother Milek and I got to ride in the decorated carriage of honor, together with Mother's brother Shmuel and his fiancée Hannah, daughter of Rabbi Elimelech Perlov of Stolin-Karlin in Pinsk. To symbolize fertility, the couple was honored with carrying the baby to the ceremony, where he would be given a name. Since Shmuel and his fiancée were not yet married, they needed chaperones, an honor given to Milek and me.

The baby was to be named after at least four prominent people whom Father greatly admired. His first name, Yisrael, was the name of Rabbi Yisrael Hager, Grand Rabbi of Wizhnitz, as well as the name of Rabbi Yisrael Friedman, grand rabbi of Chortkov, revered by many, including Father. The second name, Meir, was in memory of Father's cousin, head of the Hachmei Lublin Yeshiva, Rabbi Meir Shapira, whom Father now followed as rabbi of Piotrkow. The two names together, Yisrael Meir, carried on the name of Rabbi Yisrael Meir Hacohen of Radin, one of the greatest Torah scholars, regarded as one of the most righteous of his generation. He was the author of the *Hafetz Haim*, a major contribution to the rabbinical literature of the twentieth century.

Hundreds of guests from far and near came to the celebration. There were speeches, greetings, and songs. As the elder brothers, Milek and I were also happy to receive gifts. We chose to nickname him "Lulek." He was a beautiful baby and we loved to rock him in his cradle and walk him in his carriage. I never imagined in my wildest dreams that a day would come when he would be entrusted to me, to be father, mother, and mentor to him.

Meanwhile I continued to enjoy the ordinary pursuits of children my age. The weekdays were long, with little opportunity for youthful mischief. Letting off steam from the tension of school days had to be deferred to the Sabbath. On Saturday afternoons when the parents in every Jewish household were enjoying a nap, we roamed the Jewish Quarter.

Like many other cities, Piotrkow had its share of homeless people, some of whom should probably have been institutionalized. They lived a sad life, shuffling between the synagogues and the doorways of Jewish homes, looking for shelter. The Jewish housewives gave them food and clothing.

One of these unfortunates was known as Yaacov *Kav veNaki* (Concise and Clear) because of his knowledge of a Bible commentary by that name. Others claimed that he acquired the nickname for his deft exploits. He was in his thirties, with a thick beard and a large potbelly. He always wore a battered cap with a visor that hid his eyes. He spoke as a man of the world, spicing his words with wise sayings from scholarly sources, spurning offers of bread or food, inventing his own method of staying well fed. Lurking in the shadows, he would wait for a householder to leave the kitchen, then slip in with the grace of a cat, extract some dish from the oven, and sneak away to eat his meal. True to his name, he always returned the pot, empty and clean, to the doorway of the house.

Yaacov knew all the homes and chose his "suppliers" by the savor of that day's menu. On the Sabbath, he scouted around the bakeries where Jews had delivered pots of *cholent* on Friday. *Cholent* is a traditional Sabbath stew cooked overnight. Rather than have every home keep a fire going all night and morning, the bakery ovens were used for that purpose. Poor people made do with potatoes and beans in a gravy. The well-to-do included pieces of beef, chicken legs and wings. The rich even put legs of veal into the pot. Yaacov would select "his" *cholent* on the basis of aroma. On Sabbath morning all the pots of *cholent* were brought back piping hot to their owners. He would wait until the families left for morning prayers in the synagogue, then snatch the pot of his choice. One Sabbath some of us children organized a cruel trap for Yaacov. We got up earlier than usual and went to the early services of the Ger *hassidim*. Then we fanned out over the streets, tracking Yaacov's footsteps. One of our groups spotted him near the house of Shmuel Zebrowicz on Szewska Street. We set a well-planned ambush and caught Yaacov fleeing from the doorway, hot pot in hand. He panicked and threw the contents of the pot at us. The wonderful aroma of *cholent* wafted all around us as the contents spilled out over the street. It was Yaacov's last exploit in our neighborhood. He vanished from Piotrkow and was never seen again. We looked for him for several weeks but he never returned. My conscience bothers me to this day for my participation in trapping him and banishing him from our little world.

During the next two years the shadow cast by Hitler began to approach us. The threats against Austria, and later against Czechoslovakia, aroused alarm, but in spite of everything life continued as usual. In the summer of 1937, as in 1938, we spent our vacation in the foothills of the Tatra Mountains. We children were involved with our games but it was impossible to ignore the concern on the faces of our parents and their friends.

Hitler demanded the annexation of all territories with a majority of German-speaking people. In 1938 he annexed Austria to the German Reich and received a hero's triumphal welcome in Vienna. Then he demanded the Sudetenland, the German-speaking part of Czechoslovakia. Prime Minister Neville Chamberlain of Britain forced Czechoslovakia to yield, and Hitler took control of the Sudetenland where Germany faces the Czech border, a mountainous region with excellent military defenses. The thirty-five-division Czech army, well trained and well armed, could have put up an excellent defense. The German occupation left the remaining part of Czechoslovakia defenseless and gave Germany one of the largest arms factories in Europe, the Skoda Works. This classic appeasement policy set the stage for the Nazi takeover of the remainder of Czechoslovakia in March 1939. This was the first time Hitler violated his oft-repeated assertion that he had no interest in non-German-speaking lands. Chamberlain now realized, too late, that Hitler had deceived him.

The Poles, feeling threatened, asked for a defense treaty with Britain and France. However, neither of them had any practical way of coming to the aid of Poland, now surrounded by Germany and Czechoslovakia. The Soviets offered Britain and France a treaty to open a two-front war in case Hitler should attack Poland, with Russian troops entering Polish territory in order to fight the Germans. The paranoid Polish suspicion of Soviet motives led to rejection of such a treaty. The consequent refusal of Russia's offer by Britain and France and their shabby treatment of the Soviets in subsequent talks on joint action against Hitler, the common enemy, finally convinced Russia that she could put no trust in Britain or France. In the summer of 1939, the two implacable enemies, the Nazis and the Soviets, found it expedient to sign a treaty of friendship, dividing Poland between them in case of war. This freed the Nazis from the threat of a two-front war and set the stage for their invasion of Poland in September 1939. After numerous demands that Germany return to her own borders, World War II broke out when Britain and France finally declared war on Germany.

3

WORLD WAR TWO

On June 23, 1939, I was to graduate from eighth grade. Like all my schoolmates, I waited impatiently for this happy day, although I would be leaving dozens of friends with whom I had studied over the last three years. I knew that I would not be continuing with the rigid regime of the Yesodei Hatorah school. The new school would have an integrated curriculum, prepared by Father for a small group of boys my age, taught by highly qualified private teachers. Studies from morning until evening would take place in a small classroom in the Talmud Torah school opposite the Great Synagogue.

I especially looked forward to getting my report card on graduation day, confident that my grades would not embarrass the family. However, on the day when the report cards were to be handed out, I was to be in Cracow with the family for my bar mitzvah. As was customary, the date of my bar mitzvah was set for the first Sabbath after my birth date on the Jewish calendar. By coincidence, this date turned out to be a few days before graduation.

In Poland at that time, a bar mitzvah was a small family affair, not entailing the large-scale festivities that characterized the public celebration of a *brith milah* or a wedding. Most of Mother's family lived in Cracow under the patronage of my grandfather, Rabbi Simcha Frankel-Teomim, in his spacious home. Mother was the second of three daughters, and her father's favorite. She would not consider celebrating my bar mitzvah without him. Since his coming would entail moving a huge entourage of family, synagogue functionaries, and servants, she opted for us to travel to her childhood home at 3 Yozefinska Street, in the Cracow suburb of Podgorze.

Grandfather's house, with its tall, stucco facade and three stories around a large inner courtyard, was home to three of his sons and his youngest daughter, a home that radiated family warmth, comfort, and security. On Sabbaths and festivals, dozens of worshipers came to pray in Grandfather's private study hall and partake of cake and wine for *Kiddush* after the service. This was the place and the atmosphere in which Mother wished to celebrate my bar mitzvah.

There was another reason for an early departure for Cracow. As a youth about to enter into the rights and obligations of Jewish manhood and as one about to qualify for being counted in the *minyan* (ten-man quorum required for congregational prayers), I needed suitable clothes. For her, as well as for her brothers and sisters, there was only one tailor in all of Poland capable of sewing a garment fit for a young man on such an occasion. Only Klamka, whose shop on 13 Krakowska Street was in the heart of the Jewish Quarter of Cracow, would do. This section was named Kazimierz, in honor of the Polish King Kazimir the Great, who had permitted the Jews to settle in Poland in the fourteenth century. In order for Klamka to prepare my suit in time, we had to leave Piotrkow early - another reason to forgo the ceremony at school. However, the trip to Cracow and the anticipated celebrations with family made up for my disappointment at not attending the graduation. Furthermore, I knew that after my bar mitzvah my two younger brothers, some cousins, and I would be going on vacation to the north slope of the Tatras, the mountains that divide Czechoslovakia from Poland.

When we pulled into the Cracow railroad station, we were greeted by a large family delegation, which escorted us home in two horse-drawn carriages. Cracow is a beautiful city. I always missed it when I was away, and not just because I was born there. I spent several happy summer vacations there and studied a whole year in the local school. Each and every street, square, and place of interest was well preserved in my memory. Now, sitting in the carriage next to Father, with the family dancing attendance around me, I felt like a prince.

That same evening Mother took me to Klamka the tailor. Very few were privileged to be received by him after regular hours. But Mother, as daughter of the Skavin rabbi and the wife of the chief rabbi of Piotrkow, had special status. Klamka inspected me from every possible angle, took measurements, decided what kind of suit he would sew, and chose the color and cloth. I had no say in the matter. Mother went along with all his decisions but pressed hard for an early fitting. As a reward for my cooperation, she took me to Rosenbaum's shop for a large ice-cream cone.

That year my birthday fell on a Thursday. In the morning, Father took me to the old fifteenth-century Rema Synagogue, named after Rabbi Moshe Isserles, a famous expositor of Jewish law, who had served as chief rabbi of Cracow. He took me there for initiation in putting on the *tefillin*, one strapped to my forearm and the other to my head, thus qualifying me to join the congregation as an "adult," privileged to read from the Torah for the first time. After prayers we went to the cemetery alongside the synagogue, resting place of some distinguished forebears. Facing the windows of the women's gallery were the still-standing tombstones of Rabbi Isserles and his family. Nearby were the graves of other Jewish sages from as far back as five hundred years. Standing next to Rabbi Isserles' grave, Father drew a tiny volume of Psalms from his pocket and recited a few verses. Then he passed the book to me, pointing out the verses I was to recite.

On our return, we walked through the narrow streets and alleys of the old Jewish Quarter. Here and there, old acquaintances greeted Father. Upon hearing the reason for his visit, they showered blessings and good wishes on me. I relished the attention and began to feel important. Father must have sensed that. Instead of continuing to the Vistula bridge and Grandfather's house, he turned off the main street and led me along the river bank, his left arm resting around my shoulder in a gesture of paternal affection.

For the first time in my life I heard him speak of his past as a young man, of his studies, his relationship with family, rabbis, and teachers. Finally he told me about his marriage to my mother and, before that, to his first wife, mother of my brother Yehoshua, Shiko.

Gradually he opened a window before me into the world of men. In reserved language he described the problems of adolescence, apparently trying to forestall the acquisition of this knowledge elsewhere, preferring to enlighten me in his own fashion regarding the sexual desires of adolescents. It was a marvelous educational presentation, in which Father proceeded from the down-to-earth plane of my reality. There was no attempt to make a saint out of me. He outlined realistically the unfolding challenges and dangers confronting nascent adulthood.

As the Sabbath approached, the activity in Grandfather's courtyard intensified. Barrels of beer were placed around the yard. Every corner was filled with pans of baked goods, pots of cooked dishes, and trays of gefilte fish. While preparations were under way, I slipped away with some friends to a nearby public park where we played volleyball, until one of the boys accidentally hit a pair of lovers sitting on a distant bench. Within minutes, the young man summoned some hooligan friends from the end of the park and they began to chase us. One of my friends, Shimon Weinberger, could not keep up with us. The hooligans, shouting wild cries against the Jewish "lepers," threw him to the ground and pelted him with blows. When I reached our yard, I alerted my two young uncles, Shlomo and Shmuel, both strong and ever ready for a fracas. They returned with me and my friends, now outnumbering the hooligans. Seeing reinforcements on the way, they fled.

Some eighty people gathered around the tables on Sabbath eve. Grandfather, looking majestic with his white beard, sat at the head of the main table. I was privileged to sit between him and Father. Most of the eighty were family members, several were regular weekly guests, and some were guests invited specially for the occasion. Father was the speaker of the evening. He spoke about the weekly Torah portion, the story of Balaam, who had been hired by Balak, king of Moab, to curse the Children of Israel on their way to the Promised Land, but wound up blessing them instead.

I listened very carefully so as not to repeat Father's ideas in the speech I had prepared for delivery at the *Kiddush* the following morning. I worked hard on that speech, using my own ideas, with only minimal guidance from Father. I had chosen to speak about Balaam's impression of the camp of the Children of Israel, and his words, "How goodly are thy tents, O Jacob, thy dwellings, O Israel." To my great joy and relief, Father did not refer to this passage. He explained why Balaam's utterance, "They shall be a people living alone and among the nations they shall not be considered" (Numbers 23:9), was indeed a blessing.

By Saturday afternoon, I felt much more relaxed and went into town with friends. The bar mitzvah ceremony, though a family affair, had been a heavy burden. I was called up to the reading of the Torah, followed by the traditional downpour of candies and nuts aimed at me from all over the synagogue, while the smaller children scampered to retrieve the treats. The greatest challenge was the delivery of my short speech. With all this behind me, I felt as if a millstone had been lifted off my back.

Two days later, Father went to Lublin. As a board member of the Lublin Yeshiva, he had to participate in a week of discussions. Mother and her younger sister took the three of us and cousin Sonia to a resort village at the foot of the Tatra Mountains. During a previous six-week vacation in Rabka and the nearby village, Jordanow, we lived in a rented farmhouse and had the run of the meadows with grazing cows and sheep, surrounded by groves of trees, green open fields, and a river in which we enjoyed swimming. To the south towered the Carpathian peaks with the famous resort town of Zakopane. Many Jewish families from Cracow and its surroundings came there for the summer, and their children were my friends from previous years. The reunion was a joy for all of us, creating an atmosphere suited for youthful mischief.

A favorite pastime was to jump onto the back of a cart taking farm produce to market. We would jump, grab the rear pole, and cling to it for dear life, until the driver spotted us and waved his whip in our direction. Then we would jump off quickly and wait by the side of the dirt road for the next cart to come along. On one occasion the driver turned as if to attack us, roaring, "Just wait, Hitler is on his way, and he will finish you!"

We related this incident over dinner and could feel a heavy cloud hanging over us. No one referred to it, but the anxiety about what lay ahead affected everyone. The adults talked among themselves about the growing threat of war and the need to return home early. Some phone calls to Grandfather's house in Cracow restored a little calm and we stayed on, returning to our everyday vacation routine.

One morning I went with cousin Aharon to the cowshed to watch the milking and bring back a jug of fresh milk. Jewish law requires that a Jew be present during the milking, to be sure that nothing unkosher is added. On this morning, the milkmaid was Stashka, our landlord's wife. She could not stop cursing the "Zhids" (Jews) who had brought upon Poland its troubles with Hitler. She also had a personal grievance against Hitler and cursed him as well. Her only solace was that he would settle Poland's score with the Jews. When we brought Mother the milk and gave her an account of Stashka's outburst of curses, which she dispensed at no charge after exacting full price for the milk, Mother just waved it aside as if to say, "We've heard all that before."

During the third week of our stay in Rabka, I joined a summer camp of youngsters my age at a nearby village. Mother remained with the family and my two younger brothers, Milek, aged ten, and two-year-old Lulek. We did not talk about war at the camp. We were too busy playing games and having fun. At the end of the second week in August, we lit a huge campfire and held a farewell party attended by all the campers. I parted from my many new friends and returned to the family in Rabka. Then we went back to Cracow to say good-bye to Grandfather and receive his blessing for the new school year and Rosh Hashanah, the Jewish New Year. I took leave of the city with a heavy heart, in hopes of returning the following year to family and friends, little realizing what was actually in store for us.

On board the train to Piotrkow, we could feel the tension in the air. The cars were packed to capacity, mostly with young men carrying cheap suitcases, wooden boxes, backpacks, or bags. It was only with difficulty that we held on to the reserved seats in our compartment. The journey took nine hours instead of the usual five. At each station more young men boarded, after scenes of tearful farewells. Wives parted from husbands, children from fathers, and old people from grandsons. Mother whispered to me that these were mobilized soldiers and that it seemed war would soon break out.

I had read about wars and heard stories from men who fought in World War I. I also read newspaper reports of Hitler's threats to Poland after the occupation of Czech Sudetenland. I knew about the Nazi takeover of Austria. But the Nazis also demanded the elimination of the Polish corridor to the Baltic Sea, including the port city of Gdansk (Danzig), which separated East Prussia from Germany. This brought all the international tension and insecurity to our own doorstep. Still, it did not seem real to me and I was unable to fathom its ultimate dimension or devastation.

Father was waiting at Piotrkow station together with David Zacks, a young man who was staying at our house, studying *Halachah* (Jewish law). Edzia, our maid who had been working for us for two years, waited at the side. She had been looking after Lulek since his birth, in addition to her other household duties. It took two carriages to transport us and our belongings to the house, which was immaculate, as if prepared for the Passover holiday. It felt good to be reunited. Mother directed the unpacking, making occasional asides to Father. Though he heard what she was saying, his only comment was, "The smell of gunpowder is in the air."

The date was August 29, 1939. The school term was to open three days later, Friday, September 1, with a one-hour orientation session for students to meet their teachers. Actual instruction was to begin on Sunday. I had arranged to meet two classmates on Friday at 7:45 A.M. next to the Talmud Torah school, a dilapidated building Father had decided to renovate. To give the new school a boost, he chose six graduates from the Yesodei Hatorah primary, which I had attended, and built a class around them, choosing the brilliant Rabbi Moshe Zicher, a superb teacher, as our tutor. For general high school subjects we had another instructor.

Exactly on time, I waited at the corner of Jerozolimska and Pilsudski Streets until my friends arrived. We were just about to cross over to the schoolhouse when the blasting of sirens pierced the air. We froze on the spot, not knowing what was happening. The sight of two trucks racing down the street in the direction of our house, headed for the front, with soldiers shouting *"Wojna!"* (War!) soon hit us with grim reality.

The wife of the *dayan* (religious judge) Rabbi Mendel Weiss, who lived in the corner house, saw us standing and waiting. "Children, go home quickly! War has started and you should not be in the street," she called out.

This marked the end of my schoolboy days.

4

GERMAN OCCUPATION

The house was enveloped in gloom when I returned from school – the school I never entered. Our only radio had two earphones. I found Mother listening on one and Father on the other. Both looked worried. They did not see me enter and did not share the news with me. Only later did I learn that the Germans had bombed Wielun in western Poland, inflicting many casualties and heavy damage.

Panic pervaded Piotrkow. Many people packed their belongings and fled east, hoping that the Germans would not attack areas close to the Soviet frontier. Actually few, if any, ever got near the border. They tried to seek shelter in small towns and villages around Piotrkow, reasoning that the Germans would not bother with strategically unimportant places. Discussing the new turn of events, my parents decided to stay in the city, considering the absence of security elsewhere.

We prepared for the Sabbath as usual. On Saturday morning, we went to pray in the Great Synagogue, less than a ten-minute walk from home. Very few people attended because many were afraid to leave home. At about 10:30 A.M., as the weekly Torah portion was being read, the building shook from a nearby explosion. There had been no prior alert. Only after a series of explosions did the sirens begin to function. We hastily concluded our prayers and hurried home. It was in the short distance between the Great Synagogue and our house that I saw the first victims of the war.

Scores of wounded, some with inner organs spilling out, were being carried to the municipal hospital a few hundred feet east of the Great Synagogue. One of the first fatalities was Romek Zaks, scion of a well-known family, who had stepped onto the porch at the first sound of aircraft. The moment he opened the door to look out, he was fatally hit by flying shrapnel.

"We must continue with our routine as long as we can," said Father, as he prepared the wine and cups for the Sabbath midday *kiddush* (sanctification of the Sabbath over wine). Some visitors from out of town had been invited for Sabbath lunch. One was Avraham Namirovsky, whom Father had met in the local prison while visiting Jewish inmates. He had introduced himself as a Muscovite living in Warsaw since the Bolshevik Revolution, now serving a four-year sentence for a financial transgression. Our prison held convicts from all over Poland (including Namirovsky). When the bombing began that morning, many of the prisoners were released. Since the only person Namirovsky knew in Piotrkow was the rabbi who had visited the prison, he approached Mother and introduced himself as an acquaintance of her husband's, whereupon she promptly invited him for lunch.

By midday, there was only an occasional rattle of antiaircraft machine guns to break the silence. While we were sitting at the table, trying to overcome our gloom, a youngster in army uniform burst in, shouting hysterically, "Save me! They want to kill me!" Namirovsky firmly placed his hands on the youngster's shoulders and sat him down. "Tell me who you are and what happened to you," he said. The boy started to stammer something about Polish soldiers chasing him and accusing him of treason. Slowly, Namirovsky managed to extract his name, where he lived (a small town called Opoczno), and what brought him to us. He had been attached to an antiaircraft gun unit positioned on the roof of the Jewish bathhouse. During the morning, a Polish reconnaissance plane was shot down in the area. His teammates in the gun crew all pointed to him as the one who fired at the plane. Realizing that the Poles were simply using this opportunity to rid themselves of the unwelcome lone Jew among them, he ran for his life.

By afternoon, the streets were crowded with people pushing carts full of possessions, heading eastward. The two subsequent alerts that day proved to be false alarms. We held evening prayers at home. No sooner was *Havdalah* (the ceremony that marks the end of the Sabbath) over, than Jews began to flock to our house seeking advice from Father where to flee. He counseled them with a quote from Isaiah (26:20):

"Hide thyself for a little moment, until the indignation be overpast."
Many chose nearby towns, on the assumption that they would return
when the "indignation be overpast."

That night the blackout was almost total. Only faint lights could be
seen from the houses and none from the street. The traffic was heavy
on main roads and city streets. Infantry units and cavalry marched
westward through the city, while an onrush of refugees fleeing for their
lives kept running in the opposite direction. Nearby destinations were
Pszyglow and Wlodzymierzow, villages where we had spent summer
holidays. Sulejow was a small town farther away, where refugees,
mainly Jews, were congregating. Sulejow's accommodations were very
limited and hundreds of families slept in the forest or in open areas at
the edge of town.

Our house had no cellar and no air-raid shelter. When our friend
and neighbor, Rabbi Yitzhak Finkler, the Radoshitz rabbi, invited us to
share his improvised shelter, we gratefully accepted and moved in at
midnight.

There were about forty people, including infants, sitting along the
concrete walls among sacks of potatoes and piles of coal for heating.
Despite the musty smell and dampness, these walls became our
protection against the bombing, which could resume at any time during
the day. When darkness fell, we went home, assuming the Germans
were unlikely to bomb at night or, as some wags claimed, "They're not
going to give up their comfortable night's sleep in bed." Indeed the
preceding two nights had passed quietly.

Within the stifling atmosphere of the cellar, the discussions went
on about German war strategy, Polish helplessness, and the treachery
of the Western allies. Most barbs were directed at British Prime
Minister Neville Chamberlain, with the French government taking
second place. President Roosevelt was deemed our last hope, although
as the long hours passed, that too began to fade.

Mother prepared snacks for us and our new neighbors. For the
most part they were leftover portions from the ample Sabbath dinner.
She also looked after a young woman with a two-month-old baby and
three other children, whose husband had been mobilized. The care of
Lulek, now two years old, was left to our maid Edzia and me. She
spent most of the time crying and worrying about her family.

Father sat in a remote corner studying one of the books piled in front of his armchair. Occasionally, he would exchange learned words with our host, Rabbi Finkler. Avraham Namirovsky, who considered himself an expert on the Soviet Union, prayed that we be spared the greater danger, the arrival of the Russians. News of a possible division of Poland between Germany and Russia terrified him, lest we fall into the dangerous Russian zone. "It's easier to get along with the Germans," he claimed. In an attempt to be lighthearted, he voiced the fond wish that Hitler would commit suicide while mourning the death of Stalin. I do not remember anyone laughing at his jest.

On Monday afternoon, waves of German bombers and fighters attacked the village of Sulejow, mercilessly bombing and strafing with machine-gun fire the thousands of refugees seeking cover in the village and nearby forests. Hundreds of Piotrkow residents were among the casualties, including the aged judge, Rabbi Yaacov Glaser, his daughter, and grandson. His wife and son-in-law, Rabbi Shimon Huberbrand, a learned young *hassid*, escaped the bombing. They returned to Piotrkow but left for Warsaw as soon as the former was captured by the Germans, only to be deported later. They perished in one of the transports to Treblinka. We had not yet recovered from the shocking news of the Sulejow carnage when rumors spread that the Germans were approaching. The Polish Army's resistance in the sector adjacent to ours had completely collapsed.

I was appointed to serve as runner for the block civil-defense commander, a local bank manager with the appearance of a Polish aristocrat. On Tuesday, September 5, we stood in the doorway of the building where we had taken shelter, together with the commander's deputy, a Jew who also lived there. Around four in the afternoon we saw motorcycles with sidecars followed by a gray military vehicle, approaching from the west. The column stopped next to the prison building and one motorcycle turned into the nearby square. The block commander smiled. "At last they are here," he beamed.

"Who are they?" asked his Jewish deputy.

"The English or the French," the commander responded confidently.

I ran with the joyous news to the cellar, and announced from the top of the steps: "The English and French have arrived!"

A skeptical silence followed my announcement. I could see the absolute mistrust in Father's eyes. I told him about the motorcycles and the commander's happy reaction. "Sit here by me," he said, "the Germans are closer." Father kept me by his side.

Across from me sat Zvi Hirsch Eichenstein, son-in-law of the Radoshitz rabbi. He and his bride Sara were still on their honeymoon. He sat on a square brown case that he never let out of his sight. Apparently it contained all of the young couple's jewelry and wedding presents. He wanted to know about the news that the English and French had arrived. Before I could answer, I heard the commander summoning me from the cellar, "*Goniec! Goniec!* (Messenger!) Come here!"

As I reached the doorway, I saw a long convoy of motorcycles with sidecars about 300 meters away. In every sidecar sat a soldier, holding a circular symbol on a baton with which he was signaling to the motorcycle behind. We heard indistinct words exchanged between them. The deputy said they were speaking German. The convoy moved past us to the corner of Pilsudski and Jerozolimska streets, stopped at the intersection, then returned in our direction. The soldiers wore gray-green uniforms and steel helmets that looked unfamiliar. Once we saw the swastika, there was no doubt about their identity. Within a minute, they were opposite 17 Pilsudski, close to our house. Suddenly we heard bursts of shooting. I ran to the gatekeeper's apartment by the entrance to take cover. One overly curious tenant, a Jewish house painter, peeped out of the doorway, got hit by several bullets, and dropped to the ground.

Terrified by the German invasion, we spent that night in the cellar of the rabbi. We did not yet know any specifics, but simple caution demanded that we stay put and not stick our heads out.

Next morning, Wednesday, the Germans gave us an introduction to what we could expect from them. Toward noon, a number of military vehicles pulled up outside the house. Soldiers poured out and stationed themselves on the four corners of a residential block populated exclusively by Jews, between Zamkova, Wspolna, Stara-Warszawska, and Jerozolimska Streets. A few shots into the houses quickly brought most of the tenants outside. People fled in every direction as the soldiers pumped gunfire into the buildings. In that first action, six Jews were killed and twenty injured. All of the houses were burned down.

We could still see the smoldering remains of the Jewish homes. After completing their murderous mission intended as a warning signal, the Germans withdrew. Only then could we return home to 21 Pilsudski Street.

For the next two days we were confined to the house. An evening-to-morning six-to-six curfew was imposed and strictly enforced. Violators were shot as a deterrent. I had to go out twice a day on Mother's instructions to buy bread and other food supplies. At Koenigstein's bakery on 9 Pilsudski Street there was a long line. A Polish policeman maintained order from a distance, without getting involved with the shoppers. I was last in line when I heard some Polish women calling to the policeman that a Jewess had grabbed a place at the head of the line. They pointed to an attractive young girl. "There, that's the *zhidovka* (Jewess) who did not wait her turn. Throw her out!" The Polish policeman looked embarrassed, apparently not deeming it his job to discriminate against a Jewish girl. But the women persisted until the girl left her rightful place and moved behind me. I now learned a new chapter in neighborly relations – how good neighbors of yesterday could turn overnight into today's preying wolves. I almost forgot who fought with whom as I saw us, the Jews, victims of both the conquering Germans and the conquered Poles.

Saturday, September 9, 1939, Elul 26 on the Jewish calendar, was Milek's tenth birthday. We did not normally celebrate birthdays in the family, but something had to be done to mark this round number of ten. Some of his classmates came over after Sabbath morning prayers. They made so much noise, getting on everyone's nerves, that the improvised party had to be moved to the courtyard. When two German officers appeared and asked for the rabbi, the boys became frightened and ran away. Only Milek stayed and guided the Germans to our guest room. They were *Wehrmacht* officers, who had brought Father a summons to appear that same day before Oberst (Colonel) Brandt, military governor of Piotrkow.

Father, dressed in full Sabbath splendor, invited the officers to sit down. They politely complied but refused to partake of any refreshments. They continued chatting and asked where he had acquired such excellent diction and command of the German language. Father inquired whether the summons was urgent or could be deferred until the following day. One of the officers wanted to know why there was need for a delay. "Today is our Sabbath, which limits what I am permitted to do," explained Father. "Tomorrow is our Sabbath, so we will hold the meeting on Monday," said one of the officers.

This relaxed and polite conversation with the two army officers gave rise to some hope for the future. It was reinforced at Monday's meeting with the military governor in his office on May Third Avenue. David Zaks, Father's acting secretary, accompanied him to the meeting and was very impressed by the German officer's courtesy and businesslike manner. Colonel Brandt wanted to inform the leader of the Jewish community, Father, that he would not tolerate disruptions by elements hostile to the military authorities, and would prevent outbreaks among different sections of the population. His only demand at that meeting was that every morning the Jews provide 200 men for various tasks required by the city garrison.

Father explained that, as the rabbi, he could not mobilize workers. This would have to await the reorganization of communal institutions, which would then take care of it. "It would be a pity to leave labor mobilization in the hands of the authorities, who would snatch people off the streets. It would cause unpleasantness," replied Brandt – a threat carried out the very next morning.

The streets inhabited by the Jews were cordoned off by dozens of soldiers assisted by Polish police. They began a house-to-house search to find men fit for labor, prodding them on with blows and insults. This procedure was repeated the following day, September 13, the eve of Rosh Hashanah (Jewish New Year). This time it involved illegal entry and looting of Jewish stores and shops.

For the first time since the war began, I scouted around streets farther away from home. Here and there lay murdered bodies. Entire families were pushing handcarts with corpses for burial. The destruction around the block in the Jewish Quarter that had been burned was distressing and terrifying. Outside the communal offices at 27 Pilsudski Street, Jews were standing in line to check the possibility of receiving any compensation for the damage they had sustained. People had not yet adjusted to the new situation and were slow to come to terms with the grim reality.

Upon returning home I found a gray Volkswagen parked by the gate. Shlomo Besser, a watchmaker living on the ground floor of our building, told me that three German officers had come in this car and gone up to our apartment. The only identification I could see on the car was "POL," police.

When I went upstairs, Mother said that Gestapo officers were sitting in the guest room waiting for Father to end a meeting in the library. I walked into the library and told Father that, according to the markings on the car, these were policemen, not soldiers, adding that I had not yet seen their uniforms. There was a knock on the door. When I opened it, I found myself facing three men in black uniforms and red bands with swastikas in the center tied to their left arms. I recoiled. One of them tried to reassure me with a smile, "Is the *Herr Oberrabbiner* (chief rabbi) here?" When I nodded, they entered the room and saluted Father.

They introduced themselves as the Radom District Security Police, which included Piotrkow. They knew about Father's meeting with the military governor but informed him that dealings with the Jewish population had now been turned over to the security police and their various branches. They spoke politely and again brought up the request of the military governor for Jewish workers. They addressed Father with the term used by Colonel Brandt, *Aeltester der Juden* (Elder of the Jews). Father thanked them for the flattering title and pointed out that he was chosen by the community to serve as its spiritual leader only. Communal affairs were managed by a community council. They wanted the names of the council members and directors. When Father told them that the communal offices were only three doors away, they said they had already been there and found the offices closed. Father explained that many residents had fled during the bombing and had not yet returned.

The senior officer presented a list of demands: a map of the city marked with the concentrations of Jewish residents; names of communal council members and functionaries; a list of community property, including synagogues, schools, and welfare and cultural institutions. There was absolute silence in the room as Father stated with deliberate emphasis, that a rabbi could not serve as an emissary of the authorities to his congregation. The Germans smiled. Apart from compliments for Father's flowing and polished German, they said nothing more and rose to leave. Father asked whether it would be permissible to hold public prayers that night and on the two days thereafter, our Rosh Hashanah holiday. They exchanged glances. The senior policeman ruled, "Of course! No one will disturb your prayers."

On the first night of Rosh Hashanah most people preferred to pray in neighboring places, small synagogues, classrooms, and even private homes. In spite of the curfew, they could move from place to place via internal courtyards. The Great Synagogue, with its adjoining seminary building, was closed that evening because of the curfew. The following morning, only about thirty people showed up at the Great Synagogue for the New Year morning prayers, instead of the hundreds that normally attended even on an ordinary Sabbath. A larger gathering of worshipers, numbering about three hundred, was organized in the orphanage, part of the communal building near our house. The city cantor, Baruch Kaminecki, led the congregation with his deep, resonant voice.

Though the first day passed uneventfully, Father decided to pray in the improvised orphanage synagogue on the second day. At several of the small services, consternation took hold as word spread that a German unit had attacked the synagogue of the Amshinov *hassidim*. Several dozen men, still in their prayer shawls, were loaded on trucks and driven around the streets of the city, forced to violate the sanctity of Rosh Hashanah. They were beaten and humiliated, some were even put to work cleaning public toilets while still wearing their prayer shawls. After being totally demoralized, they were finally sent home.

In our makeshift synagogue there were two Torah scrolls that we wished to adorn with the requisite ritual ornaments before removing them from the Ark: silver Torah crowns encrusted with precious stones, etc., which had been sent to us for safekeeping by the congregation of Lipno, Silesia. They feared imminent attack, never dreaming that our town would fall the same day as theirs. Three of us went down to the cellar to borrow the religious items from the treasure trove of Judaica. As we carried the bells and silver Torah crowns up the stairs, we encountered two Gestapo officers in black uniforms with red swastika armbands. Taking note of our valuable items, they wanted to know, "Are these for religious rites? What time will the service be over?" they asked. They left, only to return later in the afternoon, this time to our home.

"We would prefer order in our relationship with the Jews. We need one thousand workers every day. If the community will supply that number, there will be no need for the forced levy or disruptions in the regular life of the city," said one of them – a tempting offer, since the forced labor caused no end of distress and fear. Sometimes the work details were given murderous beatings. At least two men were already dead as a result of the work and the accompanying brutality. Father's response disappointed them.

"I do not serve as a representative of the authorities to the Jews," he said. "Then act as a representative of the community to the authorities," came the response. After a half hour, the conversation ended inconclusively.

The morning after Rosh Hashanah, a number of Jews living near the Great Synagogue came to our house to report that large quantities of wood had been stacked in the adjacent courtyard during the night. There could be little doubt that the Germans intended to burn the building. Our visitors were frightened and began planning a way to save the Torah scrolls and other holy articles. While they were still talking, a Polish policeman brought a summons for Father to appear before the newly appointed mayor of the city, Hans Drecksel, a Nazi appointee whom we did not know. Before Father left for the meeting, he suggested organizing the neighbors to remove the holy articles from the synagogue and distribute them to houses nearby.

The meeting with Drecksel took place at the mayor's office on Slowackiego Street. He introduced himself as *Oberbuergermeister*, with the responsibility of running the city, including contacts with the Jewish community. Then he addressed Father as the "Rabbi and Elder of the Jews," and demanded a special group levy of 25,000 German marks to compensate the *Wehrmacht* for damages suffered during the first days of the occupation of the city. Father was stunned by the demand, no less by the pretext given. He explained that the community was not yet functioning and that most of the Jews still had not returned to Piotrkow. Drecksel dispensed with polite niceties and immediately lowered the sum by about half – 25,000 Polish zloty, each worth half of one German mark.

He wanted the money delivered within one week but agreed to postpone the due date by fourteen days, until the middle of the Feast of Tabernacles. Father asked what the authorities intended to do with the

Great Synagogue. Drecksel replied that he knew nothing about it, and referred Father to the military governor, Colonel Brandt. Leaving the mayor, Father proceeded to *Wehrmacht* headquarters.

To save the synagogue from being burned down, Father proposed to Brandt that, by removing the furniture and equipment, the building could be used to house Polish prisoners of war, who at that time were dispersed in temporary camps around town. Brandt accepted the proposal, adding that he had also thought of it. In fact, wood had already been prepared to install latrines in and around the building. Now Father understood the purpose of the timber stacked in the adjacent square.

That evening, we organized the rescue of the Torah scrolls from the Holy Ark in the Great Synagogue. Toward evening, eight youths and two adults gathered under cover of darkness in a Jewish apartment facing the synagogue on Jerozolimska Street. At nightfall we slipped across the street in pairs, entering the synagogue via the main entrance which had already been forced open. The first pair found only six scrolls in their place in the Ark. We searched every possible corner of the building but found nothing more. Finally someone stumbled across the wooden rollers, used to roll up the parchment of a Torah scroll, sticking out from under a pile of tables and benches. This furniture had been moved outside, between the synagogue and the nearby seminary of the Yeshiva Beth Yosef. Poles from the neighborhood had removed some pews to prepare firewood for the winter. Inside this pile, we found many sacred books and, even more important, twenty-two precious, sacred handwritten Torah-scroll parchments.

We distributed the scrolls among a number of apartments in the two facing buildings. The following morning we loaded them into the black hearse used by the Jewish Burial Society to transport the dead to the cemetery. The undertaker, David Nutkievitz, took charge of the operation, supervising us youngsters in conveying the hearse with its sacred contents for burial.

Since we had no horses, we hitched ourselves to the hearse and set off, some pulling, others pushing from behind. The undertaker guided us to two crypts near the entrance of the cemetery, graves of the rabbi of Rospsza and the rabbi of Wolborz, where we hid the scrolls temporarily. The permanent burial was deferred until the following day, when we planned to bring glass and wooden panels to line the casket against dampness and rot. The casket would be interred in the grave that David was preparing between the existing crypts. Nobody thought that the scrolls would stay buried for more than a few weeks at most.

Fifty-one years later, I arrived in Piotrkow together with eighty young leaders of American Jewry who had heard of the buried scrolls and insisted on going to Piotrkow to search for them. We found the ruined crypts and began to dig, but found nothing. An old woman wandered over and asked what we were looking for. Upon hearing the story, she pointed to a man in his seventies, whom she introduced as her brother. Their father had been the Polish watchman guarding the cemetery and, according to the son, had witnessed the burial of the scrolls. It seemed to the old watchman that silver artifacts were included with the scrolls. After digging and finding only the hand-written parchments, he had stored them in his apartment and, after the war, early in 1950, delivered them to the Jewish Council of Lodz.

September 17, the day after the meeting with Drecksel, Father launched a campaign, "Soul Redemption," to raise the levy required by Drecksel. The heads of the Spielfogel and Szereszewski families, who owned rural estates and factories in the village of Wola Krzysztoporska, donated the first 4,000 zloty toward the levy. By September 21, two days before Yom Kippur (the Day of Atonement), Father had succeeded in raising close to 15,000 zloty. He was hoping that many Jews would attend *Kol Nidrei* services and make it possible to raise the rest.

I recruited some friends to prepare the *Kol Nidrei* appeal. We prepared pieces of paper in two colors. On the white paper we marked "Soul Redemption, 10 zloty, for the family head," and on the blue one, "Soul Redemption, 5 zloty, for every additional family member." This contribution was to be in place of the *kapparot* (remembrance for the sacrificial atonement in the Temple), money that Jews generally offered before the afternoon services of Yom Kippur eve. We distributed the pieces of paper to all the synagogues, with the hope that they would be redeemed. The outcome was disappointing.

Yom Kippur services were held in small synagogues, meeting places of *hassidim,* and private homes. The day passed relatively quietly. Here and there, people were snatched off the street for various jobs but released fairly quickly. That evening, after the fast, the peace in the Jewish Quarter was disrupted again. Scores of uniformed

Germans spread throughout the Jewish streets, broke into houses, and took men, whom they brought to an empty lot in the Jewish area next to the River Strawa, subjecting them to beatings and demonic sadism. One of the officers in charge screamed incessantly, "Where is your rabbi?" From time to time he picked a victim, placed him by the wall, and threatened him with a more severe beating unless he pointed out the whereabouts of the rabbi.

That same night the Nazis invaded our building and took four neighbors. That they passed over our apartment could be viewed either as an oversight or as a deliberate signal to Father. By midnight, everyone returned home, including the many bruised and wounded in need of medical attention.

Monday morning, September 25, Father was again summoned to Drecksel's office. The mayor decided not to wait until the Feast of Tabernacles. He wanted the levy immediately. In vain Father repeated that he had been given until the following Monday, the first of October, during *hol hamoed* Succoth (the intermediary days of the Feast of Tabernacles). "Today is Monday, and today you pay the levy," insisted Drecksel. Father said he did not yet have the full amount. The mayor was willing to accept what had already been collected. Father had to go home to fetch the money and turn it over to Drecksel. As before, David Zaks accompanied him, and this time so did I, carrying the large leather briefcase with the money.

When Drecksel saw the briefcase in my hand, he welcomed us cordially. He invited Father and David to sit and offered them cigars. Father refused and once again explained that he had not yet collected the entire amount. Drecksel grimaced and turned to me for the briefcase. He placed it on the table and emptied the contents. A smile of satisfaction spread over his face when he saw the golden bracelets, earrings, jeweled brooches, and rings amid the pile of coins and banknotes. With both hands, he swept the entire pile into his desk drawer. Then he asked whether the holidays were over, and was it possible to start discussing important matters on the agenda.

"The festivals will end in ten days, but some things can be discussed without delay," said Father.

"Such as what?"

"We would like to shorten the curfew hours and avoid labor levies. We would also like to guarantee the safety of public institutions such as synagogues, hospitals, and schools."

"Good, good," commented Drecksel, but first there must be a "*Juedisches Wohnviertel*" (a Jewish residential area), he added. He did not use the term "ghetto," but Father understood. Within less than two weeks, Piotrkow became the first ghetto in all of the occupied territory, officially established on October 28, 1939, its borders marked by sign posts erected at all the surrounding junctions, with the word "GHETTO" in German letters above the skull and crossbones.

5

FIRST GHETTO

On October 10, 1939, two days after the proclamation of establishing a ghetto, the first in German-occupied Europe, control of the city was transferred from the military government to the mayor, Commissar Hans Drecksel, who now became the final arbiter of Jewish fate. He could rely on the backing of the security police, the Gestapo, the *SS*, and independent gangs of Polish *Volksdeutsche* (Poles of German origin). The latter instilled fear by random brutality perpetrated against Jews, though it soon became evident that they could be bought off relatively cheaply.

Before establishing the ghetto, Drecksel selected twelve members of the Community Council, and appointed them to the newly established *Aeltestenrat* (Council of Elders), commonly known as *Judenrat* (Jewish Council). It functioned until the abolishment of the ghetto in October 1942. Zalman Tannenberg, a Jewish leader active in the Socialist Party, which opposed both the Zionist and religious parties, was appointed chairman of the council. Tannenberg, a carpentry teacher in the ORT Technical School, displayed leadership qualities and ability to circumvent most of the Nazis. He manned the council with friends from the Socialist Bund leadership but included a few active Zionists and religious representatives.

With the appointment of the council, Father was greatly relieved, feeling a heavy load lifted from his shoulders. Until then, he had been the permanent address for every German demand and whim. As chief rabbi of Piotrkow, he was required to be a member of the Jewish council and to participate in their discussions and decisions. He served on the council for some time, but when Tannenberg began to act imprudently, Father resigned.

The specific issue that triggered Father's resignation was Tannenberg's decision to set up a Jewish police force (*Juedischer Ordnungs Dienst*) in the ghetto. Father objected adamantly to such a unit on the grounds that it would become a tool used by the Nazis against Jews. There was support for his point of view, but Tannenberg controlled a majority and announced the establishment of a Jewish police force. Father stormed out of the meeting, followed by some members, who tried to persuade him to remain. He refused, but admonished his friends on the council to be particularly vigilant to ensure that only men of integrity were to be appointed to the Jewish police, and to prevent infiltration by negative elements.

A number of community leaders, members of the Council of Elders, shared Father's standpoint, including Moshe Nordman, Baruch Zilberschatz, Fischel Lubliner, and Bunim Kaminsky. Dr. Stanislaw Zilberstein, a prominent lawyer (son of Wilhelm Zilberstein, a former communal head) and a supporter of Tannenberg, was appointed commander of the Jewish police force.

Father's resignation from the council did not release him from the onerous task of communal leader. Displaced Jews coming to the ghetto found a sympathetic ear in him. Some came as refugees, others as deportees dispersed by the German systematic "cleansing" of Jewish areas. He set up a system to locate housing for displaced Jews. Volunteers strove to place them in apartments and public buildings still in Jewish hands. Complementing Father's activities, Mother initiated a public soup kitchen for the needy, aided by some of her friends, including Mrs. Henya Greenberg, presently living in Ramat Gan, Israel; Malvina Tannenbaum, currently a resident of Warsaw; and Mrs. Kaminska, who later perished in Treblinka. This project was located in the courtyard of the Jewish orphanage. With the help of food supplied by the American Jewish Joint Distribution Committee in Warsaw, the women cooked and served lunches to more than a thousand people every day.

Father established a rabbinical court in our house to deal with the problems of *agunot* (widows unable to remarry after the disappearance of their husbands, without clear proof of death). He tried to find ways to free them from their uncertain status, so they could remarry.

Frequently, marriages and divorces took place in Father's study, with us as witnesses. Jews with disputes over money matters that would ordinarily have been referred to civil courts now came to the chief rabbi for adjudication. Father's study served as a courtroom, while the adjacent kitchen became the waiting room for litigants.

Our privacy was subordinated to the needs of the community during the day, but after six o'clock, the strict curfew afforded us a degree of family life. Left alone in our apartment, Father would use the time for writing his book and for study. He had me join him in analyzing cases involving *agunot* (discussed in Chapter 17 of section *Even Haezer* of the *Shulhan Aruch* – Code of Laws). I had to prepare myself by studying the background material on this topic in tractate *Yebamoth* in the Babylonian Talmud.

Learning alone was difficult, so I recruited a few school friends to join me, making us a group of four. We were lucky to find a remarkable teacher in the person of Rabbi Raphael Blaustein, highly erudite not only in hassidic lore but in secular disciplines as well. He and his wife were childless refugees from a town annexed by the Third Reich. He was the son of the rabbi of Glowno, a student of one of the most famous hassidic spearheads of the nineteenth century, Rabbi Mendel Morgenstern of Kotzk. He imbued us with hassidic knowledge and also gave us a taste of the teachings of the *maskilim* (intellectuals who rejected many fundamentals of traditional Jewish thought) and philosophers, both Jewish and non-Jewish. It was he who introduced me to Kant, Hegel, and Spinoza, along with such exegetes of traditional Judaism as Maimonides, Sa'adia Gaon, and Moshe Chaim Luzatto.

He also introduced me to the Zionist ideas that preceded those of Theodor Herzl, founder of modern Zionism, and exposed me to political Zionism that developed prior to the outbreak of World War I. Blaustein was the only teacher to give me a glimpse of such a wide vista of worldly knowledge.

On the last night of Hanukkah 1940, a Polish farmer knocked on our door. He had a sealed envelope for the rabbi. I took the envelope to the study, where Father was engaged in a discussion with a number of people. He gestured for me to leave, but upon hearing that someone was waiting for a reply, he read the message and went with me to the door. He asked the farmer the whereabouts of the woman who had sent the message. The farmer replied that she was in his house in a village, afraid to enter the ghetto. Father told me to fetch David Nutkiewicz, the grave digger of the city burial society, who lived four houses away. I found David, unsuccessfully trying to light a heater. The cold outside was fierce and the twigs would not catch fire. He returned with me to our house. Father told him that the body of an important man lay in the field close to our house and needed a Jewish burial. David said that he could not dig a grave by himself in the frozen ground. He would need a few men to help him. He also wanted a Jewish policeman to escort the burial party to the cemetery, which was outside the ghetto. Then he went home to change and to enlist the help of two or three men. He returned in boots and a thick overcoat, accompanied by Leibel Miller, a neighbor who had agreed to help with the burial. Since there were not enough men, Father asked me to join the funeral and to take along one or two friends.

The dead man was engineer Maurycy Bossak, son-in-law of Asher (Oscar) Cohen, a Jewish millionaire, owner of the largest textile factory in Lodz. Bossak's wife reported that she, her husband, and two small daughters had been hiding in a village near Piotrkow, waiting for someone who was to smuggle them into Switzerland, where her father was expecting them. Her husband had been chopping firewood for a heater and developed blood poisoning from a rusty nail. He died shortly thereafter. She wanted to give him a proper Jewish burial.

The body, covered with a rough woolen blanket, lay on a horse-drawn sled at the back gate of our courtyard leading out to the fields. The only marks on the snow were those made by the horse. No Jew dared venture out in this area outside the ghetto. The farmer sat himself at the foot of the corpse and spurred the horse to move. We were four Jewish escorts, two of us under sixteen, recruited as grave diggers. We plodded through deep snow behind the sled for two miles. At the cemetery, we could not find the Polish watchman, who usually helped with the digging.

David chose a plot, marked the corners of the grave, and told us to start clearing the snow and begin digging with the pickaxes and shovels he gave us. He and Leibel Miller began preparing the body for burial.

My friend Meir Lewartowski repeatedly hit the frozen ground with his pick, but could not make a dent. I turned to David for help. He sent Meir and me back to the ghetto to get a shroud for the body, while David and Leibel lit a fire on the plot to thaw the ground. When we got home, I told Father of the difficulty in digging and the need for a shroud. Father walked into the bedroom and said to Mother, "Imagine! The son-in-law of the king of textiles, Asher Cohen, doesn't even have a shroud." Mother opened the linen cupboard and took out a white sheet to serve as a shroud. On the way back to the cemetery, we were joined by Landau, the policeman. Now we had both an escort and another pair of helping hands to dig the grave. By the time we arrived, David and Leibel had dug half the depth of the grave after melting the frozen upper layer. Upon completion of the digging, the four of us struggled to lower the corpse. David arranged the grave in accordance with the traditional customs and recited the prayer for laying the dead to rest. That evening I heard Mother remark to Father that I was too young for such experiences. His response was that I would have to become accustomed to them sooner or later.

The German victories in Holland, Belgium, and France depressed us. People began to despair. There was no hope for a quick defeat of the Nazis. Father worried about the supply of *matzoth* mandatory for the spring Passover festival. Religious observances became a challenge of logistics. Before the *Succoth* festival in the fall, Father had gone to great lengths to obtain at least one set of the four varieties of plants (citron, palm sheath, branches of myrtle, willow) required for the ritual. It was passed from worshiper to worshiper for recitation of the appropriate blessing. A friend in Presov sent us one set. There were only a few *succoth* (temporary outdoor huts commemorating the Exodus from Egypt during the eight-day festival of Tabernacles) in the entire area, instead of one for every home, as was customary. Ours was a small one that we shared with neighbors in a hidden corner of our courtyard. However, procuring *matzoth* for Passover was more complex: There was no distribution of flour in the ghetto.

One winter's day in 1940, Father received greetings from Hans Kristmann, an acquaintance from before the war. They had known each other from the time of Father's studies in Vienna and his service in the Austrian army during World War I. Kristmann was Father's age. Before the war, they used to meet occasionally. He now lived in Piotrkow, where he managed two factories. When the Germans began to seize men off the street for forced labor, Father tried to arrange permanent jobs at Kristmann's plants for the Jews in the ghetto. The initiative did not bear fruit, but the relationship with Kristmann continued. Now Father again turned to him in the hope that he could help obtain a permit to acquire flour to bake *matzoth*.

Kristmann received the message and came to the ghetto unannounced. The two friends spent a long time together, but Father came away dejected. He told Mother that Kristmann believed the war would last at least two more years unless the United States came to the aid of the Allies right away. He did, however, promise to make an effort to resolve the *matzoth* problem, and kept his promise. The authorities allotted a quantity of flour based on the number of residents in the ghetto. One of the bakeries was thoroughly cleaned for Passover and the *matzoth* were baked. In addition, gift packages came from Father's friends. There was a small one from Rabbi Yosef Carlebach in Hamburg, Germany; another one from Rabbi Schoenfeld in Zagreb, Yugoslavia; and a bigger one from Rabbi David Grunwald in Lucerne, Switzerland, who had been one of Father's students in Presov.

The ghetto in Piotrkow was relatively bearable. Many refugees came from Lodz and the surrounding areas after annexation to the German Reich. Streams of refugees also came from Warsaw, where people were starving. In Piotrkow, the Jews and the Poles still mingled freely outside the ghetto. Trade between the two parts of the city continued to be the major source of income for ghetto residents. Traffic back and forth continued almost without restriction until mid-1941. However, the Nazi authorities reduced the space in the ghetto, removing areas that bordered on the central prison and other public buildings. As a result, the availability of living quarters decreased, creating even greater population density.

In July 1940, the Germans demanded a census of males over fifteen, to be taken by the council. Many feared that the men would be mobilized for forced labor outside the city, and opposed the census. Zalman Tannenberg, the head of the council, was compelled to take the census. Upon its completion, the Germans demanded that he supply a thousand young men for urgent work. He took some from the census data; others were simply seized off the ghetto streets by a German unit. The mobilized men were taken more than a hundred miles away for forced labor along the banks of the River Bug, which separated the German and Soviet armies. The men were imprisoned in four labor camps: at Plazow, Cieszanow, Hrubieszow, and Belzec. The Nazi commander, Dolf, in charge of these camps, was especially tyrannical.

Many were permanently injured and maimed from beatings. Some crossed the river to seek sanctuary on the Soviet side, but the Red Army drove them back into the hands of the *Wehrmacht.*

Solomon Gomberg from Piotrkow was among the laborers in the "Lublin Camps," as they were called by the prisoners. Born in Lodz, he had come to the ghetto as a refugee and quickly became involved in communal life. A natural leader, he gathered the Piotrkow men around him into a coordinated group. On Rosh Hashanah eve, he succeeded in reaching Piotrkow to report on the four camps. He related that of the thousand men taken, almost one hundred had already died. The community leaders were at a loss. Tannenberg was wary of taking any independent action uncoordinated with the local authorities. Gomberg came to seek Father's help. He described Dolf's behavior and claimed that the man could be bribed to let the Piotrkow contingent go home. The price would be 100,000 Polish zloty, four times the sum Drecksel had demanded the year before. Nevertheless, Father promised to raise the full amount, and gave Gomberg the names of friends in Lublin who would help organize the release of the forced laborers and their return home.

In preparation for Yom Kippur, Father again organized a major fund-raising campaign, "Soul Redemption." He stressed that this was a Jewish initiative to save our local men from torture and death, and not just a response to German greed. Accordingly, the contributions were greater and the full amount was raised. Immediately after Succoth, the forced laborers from the Lublin camps began to return by truck, in groups of forty. One hundred and twelve did not come back. They were buried next to the Lublin camps. Sixty of them had been deliberately murdered by Dolf and his men.

In October 1940, a typhus epidemic broke out in the ghetto. Since the Jewish hospital was outside the ghetto, the community doctors improvised a temporary hospital in the Jewish high school. To contain the spread of the plague, a sanitary service was set up, to isolate affected families. Their apartments were placed under strict quarantine, enforced by ghetto youth recruited for this purpose. Solomon Gomberg took charge of the sanitary service. I was one of the youths enforcing the quarantine. Apartments lacking toilets were given special containers for the inhabitants to relieve themselves. We, the enforcing youth, had to collect the full containers and take them to sewage points or septic tanks. It was a horrendous task, which lasted all through the winter months of 1940-41. With the coming of spring, the situation improved and the death toll dropped, but the typhus epidemic persisted until the end of 1941.

During the months that I was busy enforcing the quarantine, I did not participate in private lessons. The hours I spent in a stairwell of a quarantined apartment were used to do lessons on the subjects I was studying: Torah, Prophets, mathematics, chemistry, and Latin. Little of what I read during those months got absorbed; however, my daily contact with afflicted families gave me an understanding of people and real-life experiences that I would not find in any book.

As Passover approached, the authorities gave us permission to bake *matzoth*, as in the previous year. The ghetto population continued to grow, with refugees pouring into Piotrkow. Our ghetto had absorbed more than two thousand refugees from the province of Pomerania and the cities of Poznan and Gniezno. Typically, there were about ten people crowded into a two-room apartment; twenty thousand people crowded into 4,178 rooms, in two hundred apartment buildings. Many were forced to live in synagogues, schools, and public institutions. The health situation became acute. Children suffered from malnutrition. Dysentery replaced the typhus epidemic.

In spite of the dire economic situation, relentless German harassment, and crucial health situation, the Jews obstinately observed the festivals, educated their children, and retained their humanity in an inhuman atmosphere. In private apartments, study groups of four to eight children were taught, under the most difficult physical conditions. Here and there, the children staged plays and participated in other cultural and educational projects. The heads of the community distributed basic needs to the many people without means of survival. Before Passover, Father organized operation "Beth Lehem" (Bread for the House), to obtain *matzoth* for the festival. After hard bargaining with the supply department of the Council, he obtained enough flour to bake *matzoth* for Passover for every resident of the Piotrkow ghetto.

6

TERROR

In the summer of 1941, while I was in Auschwitz, the Gestapo raided the homes of all Bund leaders, among them Zalman Tannenberg, head of the Council of Elders. Following the arrest of a young Jewess caught with subversive propaganda she had brought from Warsaw to Piotrkow, the Bund leaders were accused of belonging to an anti-Nazi underground. The young woman had acted for the Polish underground *Armja Ludowa* (Popular Army) which, like the Bund, was under the influence of the Polish Socialist Party. Tannenberg and all the other Piotrkow Bund leaders were arrested and held in the same Gestapo cellar where I had been imprisoned before being sent to Auschwitz. They were interrogated and tortured for ten weeks, until their deportation to Auschwitz in September. Their families received containers with their purported ashes.

Tannenberg's place as head of the *Judenrat* was taken over by Szymon Warszawski, a wealthy merchant, member of the congregation board, and representative of the nonaligned traders. Warszawski established good contacts with the authorities and, like his predecessor, successfully eased some harsh decrees by the payment of bribes.

Thanks to his efforts, the Germans institutionalized forced Jewish labor, ending the random seizure of workers. Three German-owned industrial plants engaged in war work were permitted to employ hundreds of Jews, who thereby acquired papers that kept them safe from seizure for forced labor. The largest of these was Dietrich und Fischer, a woodworking plant on the banks of the river Bugaj.

Two other German-owned companies were registered in Belgium by Emil Hoebler and Sons. One was called Kara, which made plate glass; the other, Hortensja, which produced bottles, cups, electric and kerosene lamps, among other products earmarked mainly for the *Wehrmacht*. These two glass plants were managed by Hans Kristmann, a friend of Father's, whom Father had approached in 1940 with the idea of employing Jews from the ghetto to avoid seizure for forced labor. Kristmann attempted to get official German recognition for the factories as essential to the war effort, but at first did not succeed. At Warszawski's request, Father interceded once again, and Kristmann promised to reapply for the coveted status.

In October 1941, he informed Father that his plants would absorb 500 Jewish workers. Most went to work at Kara; less than one hundred to Hortensja. Within a few months the number steadily increased, until eventually over one thousand Jews were employed at the two plants.

As Hanukkah approached in late 1941, rumors reached the ghetto of massacres perpetrated by the SS in captured areas in the east, on the Russian front. Murder squads, known as *Einsatz Gruppen* (Special Squads), wiped out entire Jewish communities. These were the first reports of methodical mass killing of Jews by SS formations. Father's younger brother, Yaacov, reported from Lwow, capital of East Galicia, that the Nazis first murdered women, children, and the aged, keeping the men for last, so that they could dig the mass graves. Later, my uncle, his wife, and two small daughters were also murdered.

The horror stories followed one after another and the ghetto was gripped by terror. One rumor told of the mass deportation of German Jews to the east. Mention was made of a small town near Riga, capital of Latvia, while others spoke of an area near Lublin for the resettlement of those deported. We received confirmation of the deportation from a postcard, postmarked December 1941 and delivered by regular mail in February 1942. Yosef Carlebach, chief rabbi of Altona, Hamburg, and Wandsbeck, wrote in Hebrew: "To my dear friend Rabbi Moshe Chaim, Our congregation was uprooted and sent east with myself at their head. God have mercy. Yosef-Zvi Carlebach."

The letters and postcards were scrutinized for confirmation that the deportees were in fact being resettled. No one wanted to believe that entire transports could be dispatched to their death. An actual report of systematic mass murder reached us only in March 1942, and even then many doubted its credibility.

This information was brought by two young men in their twenties who came to the ghetto seeking shelter. Chaim Yerachmiel Widawski and Yitzhak Justmann told a horror story that was beyond belief: On the way to Piotrkow, they were followed by a Gestapo agent, Emering, a Pole of German *Volksdeutsche* extraction. As they approached our neighborhood, the two decided to split up in order to shake off the agent. Justmann ran in the direction of the Great Synagogue, with Emering hot on his heels. But Justmann eluded him and found sanctuary in the Weissberg home, where he was well hidden. Widawski ran in the opposite direction and circled around to our door, arriving breathless, followed by a Jewish policeman, Checinski, dispatched by Emering. Checinski caught Widawski as he entered the hallway to our house and tried to drag him away. His screams brought Father to the stairwell. He demanded the release of the young man and told Checinski to return to his post. Distraught and weeping, Widawski asked for water and the opportunity to tell his story.

According to Widawski, both he and his friend, Justmann, had escaped from a *kommando* assigned to bury murdered victims at Chelmno. None of us had ever heard of this place.

Father shut the door to his room, remaining alone with Widawski. After about one hour, he came out and asked me to assemble a few of his friends as quickly as possible, among them prewar members of the Communal Council such as Moshe Nordman, Meir Abramson, Boruch Zilberschatz, Hirsch-Leib Krakowski, Fischel Lubliner, Mordechai Michelson, Bunim Kaminski, Rabbi Moshe Temkin, and Dr. Stein. Within the hour, they were all in Father's study. I was also permitted to remain and heard Widawski repeat his story. He spoke, and Father transcribed all that he said, and thoroughly cross-examined him.

All those present in the room were horrified by the eyewitness account of systematic, cold-blooded mass murder. Widawski described how dozens of Jews, taken from the masses imprisoned at the Chelmno Palace, were squeezed into a special chamber built into the back of a large truck. During the half-hour ride from the palace to a forest clearing outside the city, the victims slowly suffocated by fumes piped into the chamber from the engine exhaust. Muffled blood-curdling sounds could be heard from the chamber. When the trucks arrived in the forest, the dead bodies were dumped into prepared burial trenches. Widawski and his friend were among the grave diggers. Widawski was standing by when, among the bodies that spilled out from one of the trucks, he recognized the members of his family and his fiancée. At that, he broke down and fainted. Justmann supported him until he recovered. At the end of the day they returned to the camp at the Chelmno Palace, where they were kept separated from those doomed to be murdered. They decided to escape, no matter what the consequences. That very night they managed to flee and, after four days on the road, reached Piotrkow.

Naively, I believed that nothing could horrify me after my own experiences at Auschwitz. But Widawski's story, halted by sobs, dispelled that illusion. He talked compulsively, with Father writing everything in his notebook, pressing him for further details. The others listened, petrified. No one moved or spoke. Father gestured for me to take Widawski to our dining room, where Mother had already prepared a hot meal for him. He was soaked with sweat, his face stained with tears. While he ate, the group in the study made arrangements for a safe place for him and his comrade. Both were in desperate mental and emotional states, but the threat of discovery by the Gestapo agent meant that they had to leave as soon as possible.

Because of the curfew, I had to go through the courtyards to bring Widawski and Justmann to the Goldring's apartment, a few houses away. There the two were dressed as Polish railroad workers, and given identity papers and money. Widawski clung to me and would not let me leave, his tears wetting my cheeks. Thirty years later he visited my home in Ramat Gan, Israel, just a few houses away from his daughter, Chaya, and her Israeli husband. He became a wealthy businessman in Belgium, with a family, several children, and grandchildren. At one point in our conversation, our eyes met and he suddenly burst into loud sobs, transporting me back to the courtyard of the Goldring apartment in Piotrkow in March 1942, moments before his departure in the guise of a Polish railway worker on his way to Germany. Widawski died several years ago. Yitzhak Justmann, his partner in the escape from Chelmno, died a few years earlier.

I read Widawski's testimony the day after he left the Piotrkow ghetto, when Father gave me his notebook and asked me to type the Yiddish transcript on a Hebrew typewriter. I can never forget the story that I heard, read, and typed. The litany of atrocities seared the soul: the heinous, slow suffocation; the dumping of still-warm bodies into trenches, layer upon layer to save valuable space, with little children squeezed into gaps between the corpses; and finally the murder of the eight grave diggers upon completion of their grisly task, forced to lie on top of the pile of their brothers' bodies to await the final burst of gunfire from the *SS* murderers – I still have nightmares of these scenes.

When we met in my home in Ramat Gan before the Passover festival of 1972, Widawski wanted to know why so many people refused to believe his story of March 1942. I explained how inconceivable it seemed that a cultured nation like Germany could embark on a diabolic program of annihilation for no conceivable reason other than the Jewish origin of their victims. I told him of Father's notebook, where his ordeal had been recorded, and I recounted his own words as I had typed them and as they remain preserved in my memory. He sat listening in an armchair, his face paled. I noticed that he looked unsteady and seemed about to faint. A glass of cold water revived him.

The bitter message left by Widawski and Justmann underscored the danger for every Jew. Within days the news spread throughout the ghetto, causing great trepidation. Many came to ask Father's advice. There were young men who decided to escape to forests or seek a hiding place in the town outside the ghetto, where the Germans stalked. There were couples who wanted to marry and escape together. Few placed faith in the ultimate safety of hiding inside the ghetto.

In May, the two glass factories, Kara and Hortensja, announced that they would accept six hundred more Jewish workers from the ghetto. Many believed that the documents held by workers in an industry essential to the Germans would serve as an insurance policy against deportation. More and more people began to realize that the Unknown was in fact a death camp. Three such camps were already known: Chelmno, Belzec, and a village near Malkinia, later identified as Treblinka. The stories that filtered back from these camps were hair-raising and people refused to believe them. As for me, after Widawski's testimony, I was prepared to believe anything.

Mother pleaded with me to register for work in one of the glass factories, hoping that this would grant me immunity from deportation. When I asked her what would happen to the rest of the family, she replied, "Each of us will have to find his own solution. For you, the

most practical solution is to sign up for work in an essential war plant."
I turned to Felek Poznanski, director of the *Judenrat* labor bureau
responsible for supplying manpower in accordance with the German
demands. He advised me to register for Hortensja. He even took the
trouble to accompany me to the registration office, making sure that I
was in a shift where the foreman was Edelman, a Pole of German
origin, but one of the more benign overseers.

The plant worked round the clock, with three eight-hour shifts,
starting at eight in the morning, four in the afternoon, and midnight. We
left the ghetto under guard two hours before work time, returning one
hour after the shift ended. The job was in the area where molten glass
was blown and cast. The blowers stood on scaffolding around the hot
ovens. My job was to open and close the molds into which they blew
the glass. The searing heat at the oven openings on hot summer days
and the constant harassment by Polish workers, who looked for every
opportunity to goad the Jews, made this work close to intolerable.
Despite the decent foreman, I asked to be transferred to a group that
unloaded raw material – coal, soda, and sand – from freight railroad
cars. Doing piecework, like any jobber, one could finish early. Each
team of four men was required to unload a freight-train carload in six
hours.

I quickly learned that I had jumped from the frying pan into the
fire. The work was physically exhausting. The men there were strong
and healthy, in their twenties, thirties, and forties. Alongside them, I
felt like a puny weakling.

The easier part was to shovel the sand into bins. The harder part
was to unload the coal and the hardest of all was unloading the sacks of
soda. When my turn came to unload the coal, I was required to push a
wheelbarrow containing up to 330 pounds of coal up a series of
wooden planks sixteen inches wide to the top of the ten-foot-high pile
of coal, while my partner would pull from above by an attached rope.
We had to unload about one hundred such wheelbarrows per day. It
was essential to keep the load balanced and to make sure that the
wheelbarrow's single wheel stayed on the plank. The first time I tried
it, I lost control of the handles and unbalanced the heavy load even
before I reached the plank. The wheelbarrow, coal, and I all tumbled
over. I was sure that that would be the end of my assignment in this
group. Fortunately, a guardian angel came to my rescue. A well-built

man in his forties helped me reload the spilled coal and taught me the trick of keeping the wheelbarrow on its narrow path. From that day on, Elkana Liebeskind became my mentor, treating me as his protégé, and guarding me like an angel.

Then came my turn to unload the soda. Every sack contained one hundred and sixty-five pounds of soda. I had to carry these sacks of soda on my back about one hundred times per shift, up a three-story makeshift ramp composed of a pile of torn sacks. The spilled contents made the "stairway" slippery and dangerous. At the end of every day, I returned home completely drained, unable to move a muscle until morning, when it started all over again. My parents tried to bolster my spirits with the hope that the situation would not last long. Deep in their hearts, they wanted to believe that a miracle would happen and we would be spared the bitter fate that now appeared inevitable.

At the end of August, about three weeks before Rosh Hashanah, we quietly celebrated Milek's bar mitzvah without public fanfare. He was called up to the Torah in an improvised synagogue, followed by a *Kiddush* in his honor. The atmosphere was dismal. Almost all the guests were whispering about rumors of mass deportations from the Warsaw ghetto to some unspecified destination. Some mentioned Malkinia as the place where the trains of deportees were heading. Nobody mentioned the possibility of annihilation in that place.

Milek was a handsome boy, with a shock of blond hair and lively blue eyes. I watched him as he delivered a short speech, and saw a young adult with whom I could feel comfortable and secure. That afternoon, I suggested to my parents that he also be registered for work in the glass factory where I worked, promising to keep an eye on him. I was only three years older, but felt that I had the experience to take on such a responsibility. Father mentioned my suggestion to Milek. At first he hesitated, but then agreed to join me. I promised that he would be given the job of carrying cold drinks to the glass blowers, rather than unloading railroad cars.

Two weeks later he came to work with me, confident that he would receive the prized documents which would serve as his life insurance. For almost one month we were together in the plant and I kept in close touch with him, watching over him, though my workplace was some distance away. He began to feel confident. We hoped his safety was assured. However, at the crucial moment, dawn of October 14, 1942, when we were supposed to report for work, he chose to stay home. That was the day deportations of ghetto residents began. He broke down, afraid to leave our parents.

7

DEPORTATION TO TREBLINKA

In October 1942 I was a lad of sixteen, in my fourth year under Nazi tyranny, with forty days of Auschwitz behind me. With a valid workcard in an essential plant – allegedly a permit to live – in my possession, I should have felt relatively secure. However, the black clouds looming over the fall sky forebode disaster. People packed necessities, warm clothing, and food for a journey of indefinite duration and destination. Others prepared hiding places in cellars, attics, or concealed storerooms. Both the "packers" and the "hiders" sensed something disastrous was about to happen. On the way to and from work in the glass plant, I witnessed the same disquieting, ominous scenes.

On the morning of October 13, I went to work along with about four hundred others who, like me, were supposedly privileged to stay alive. When we came to the gate, we were admitted by Foerster, one of the *Volksdeutsche*, who delighted in tyrannizing us. His sharp facial features and the cold, steely eyes boded evil. On that morning, he was the supervisor of the Polish security guards. The regular stream of imprecations with which he greeted us every morning on arrival and every night upon departure took on an even more strident tone that morning. Apparently he must already have known that, beginning the following day, we would be at his mercy.

That morning I was assigned to a group working with Wojdala, a scurrilous, brutal Polish foreman who could neither read nor write. He had a special, perhaps justifiable, dislike for me. At one roll call when he "read" our names from a register, I noticed that he was holding the book upside down. I stepped out of the front line to point that out. Wojdala, the gigantic boor with the menacing face, gave me a murderous look as the blood rose to his head. Though I survived this confrontation unscathed, he never forgot. Our task during the shift was to feed the furnaces with the raw material for making glass: white sand, soda, and broken glass. Cursing and bullying us on with "Faster, faster, *Zhidi* (Jews)!" Wojdala evoked the biblical image of Egyptian taskmasters embittering the lives of our enslaved ancestors, making the crushing labor all the more unbearable.

Another wicked but craftier taskmaster was Slomko. He affected culture, etiquette, and good manners while inciting Wojdala against us. Slomko was excessive in his elegant dress and highly polished leather riding boots. I became the butt of his malicious barbs, not least because I was "the rabbi's son." We pushed the sand-laden wheelbarrow to the rhythm of curses from Wojdala and Slomko. Slomko pointed to the railroad track, twenty yards beyond the plant fence, reminding us that the "black train" would again pass by soon; we'd better be grateful to him and his friends for their protection, saving us from the fate of the deported. Two weeks earlier, my partner, Meir Zilber, had identified familiar faces peeking from the slats of one wagon of the death train carrying deportees from his home town of Czestochowa to Treblinka. Ever since the day after Yom Kippur, Czestochowa had been supplying deportees for the black train, which passed by every third day on this very track in front of our eyes.

After liquidating the ghetto of Czestochowa, the Germans turned to the Radomsko ghetto. The last train of sixty closed cattle cars, transporting the remaining six thousand Jews, had passed in front of us two days earlier. The next was Piotrkow, our city. Counting the refugees who had found refuge with us, close to thirty thousand people were now facing deportation.

As I was returning the empty barrow to the railroad siding for a new load, I noticed Wojdala and Slomko standing by the storage pile of soda, engaged in what struck me as plotting. Indeed, as I approached, Wojdala called out to me. Leading me into a deserted storehouse, he kicked me viciously, threw me onto a stack of soda sacks, then began beating me systematically with the wooden pole used to help place the sacks on our backs. He beat me first on my back, then my rear and thighs, and finally my chest, not touching my head. Neither of us uttered a sound. Finally, he brushed off the caked soda that had stuck to his hands, ordered me back to work, and stalked out.

During the half-hour lunch break we were left unattended by the guards and foremen. We sat on top of the pile of coal by the rail siding, where we could watch the death train passing on its way to Treblinka. Though we all knew the purpose of this trek, we did not say a word about it, each one of us struggling with the monstrous reality that was beyond words. Amid stories of atrocities in neighboring towns, and macabre jokes about our own destiny, no one came up with a practical alternative, a way to save ourselves. It was inevitable that all too soon, while sitting here on this same ten-foot pile of coal, many of us would see our own loved ones passing before us in the death train deporting the Jews of Piotrkow.

We ended our shift at four in the afternoon and reported to the open area by the plant gate. As our names were called, we formed a file, three abreast, with the guards already in position alongside, ready to march us out the gate. Suddenly, the plant manager of Hortensja, Kuczamer, ran up and ordered us to stop. "Beginning tomorrow morning, you will live within the plant compound until further notice. Bring essential personal belongings with you, and report here by five in the morning," he announced.

We paid no attention to the Polish children along the roadside, who usually sold us loaves of bread and bags of sugar. No one felt the need to stock up on anything. The only thought was how to escape our approaching doom without abandoning our families at home, a home about to disintegrate.

When I got home, I found Father sitting in his study reading a small book. He noticed my arrival but continued perusing the faded pages, though he seemed more absorbed in his thoughts than in the book. Finally, he sighed, "That's it." We exchanged glances without a word. I sank into the deep armchair beside him, bursting into tears. We were alone in the room; there was no sound in the house. Father did not try to calm me, but began to talk, as if edifying his eldest son. He spoke quietly and with restraint, but not a word of what he was saying penetrated. He stopped when friends and neighbors arrived, as usual, for evening prayers. Abraham Dessau, one of our neighbors in mourning for his mother, led the prayers. He stood by the small Holy

Ark, with its ancient miniature scroll of the Law, of inestimable historical value, and concluded with *Kaddish* in memory of his mother. Someone said: "And who will say *Kaddish* for us?" No response. The people left and quiet reigned once more in the study, lined with thousands of books.

Mother prepared backpacks, as though for an outing in the countryside. Each pack contained cakes, candies, dried fruit, underwear, socks and sweaters, and, of course, such essentials as a pocket-size prayer book, scriptures, and the Mishnah. From force of habit, she wrote the name and address on each pack.

Mother, with self-enforced composure, spoke to me of the need to keep an eye on Milek, my brother Shmuel, whose bar mitzvah we had celebrated just two months earlier. In spite of his youth, he had been accepted for work at the glass factory, essential to the German war effort. This provided Milek with an insurance policy against deportation – so we thought.

Blond and blue-eyed Shmuel, charming and determined, hearing Mother's request, just looked into my eyes and shook his head. He would not go to work with me. He would stay with the family. His adamant stand put an end to my own quandary about whether to return to work or remain with the family. I decided to stay with the family, wherever fate would lead us.

Father came over to me as I sat on the couch, and kissed me on the forehead. His warm tears fell onto my cheek. "We need to act as our patriarch Jacob did in preparation for his confrontation with his hostile brother Esau. He divided his family into three camps, in the hope that at least one of the camps would survive." He went on to explain his plan. Mother and five-year-old Yisrael, Lulek, would hide in a neighboring house, until the wave of deportations was over. Shmuel and I would go to the glass factory. As for himself, Father would go with his congregation, come what may. "A shepherd does not abandon his flock in the face of a pack of wolves. I will not seek to save my own skin and abandon my flock," he said with resolve. He would remain in the ghetto and report for deportation at the *Umschlagplatz* (transfer place), as ordered.

Milek, in tears, did not want to leave them. As the oldest brother, I finally accepted Father's decision. There was no point arguing. Mother pulled a few things from Milek's backpack and put them into mine.

That evening we gathered to share the last meal in our home. Together, the family and some regular guests sat around the perfectly set rectangular table. As always, no detail was missing from the full complement of flatware and china, from the elegant manner of serving that was standard at our table. The menu, however, was sparse, consisting of potatoes and slices of bread.

A little after eight in the evening, the silence was shattered by deafening bursts of gunfire from various weapons. We could hear cries of the wounded from the neighboring building, which housed the Council of Elders, long since renamed *Judenrat*. Since our windows were blacked out, there was no way of seeing what was happening in the street. Shlomo Besser, the watchmaker who lived in an apartment on the ground floor of our building, with an attached storefront, burst into our apartment panic-stricken. The short and shriveled Besser, hardly able to breathe, had just seen the special deportation unit.

The men of this unit were Ukrainians, Latvians, and Lithuanians under German command. They were murderers who took professional pride in their work. Some of them now roamed the streets, firing indiscriminately to induce terror in the inhabitants, while their comrades tightened the noose around the ghetto.

I do not remember whether any of those seated around the table on that night tasted the food in front of them. We sat frozen in our chairs, not uttering a sound. Here and there someone toyed nervously with a fork, knife, or spoon. The food remained untouched. When Father invited Rabbi Raphael to say grace, he burst into loud sobs. Seventy-year-old Rabbi Raphael Blaustein, a refugee from Glowno, north of Lodz, had become a member of our household and my teacher for the last two years. He was unique in being both a disciple of the famous rabbi of Kotzk and a scholar in secular disciplines. His clear thinking, sharp insight, and *Weltanschauung* had been an invaluable asset to me during these agonizing times. There was always a sparkle of humor in his eyes, no visible trace of sadness or gloom, despite the fact that he was childless and impoverished. Now, at this last meal, even he broke down and his bitter tears started a chain reaction for the rest of us around the table. By 11:00 P.M, our family was alone in the house. I was to report at the gate of the ghetto at four in the morning

Father, at age fifty, was in the prime of life. He reviewed his life with us, his accomplishments and failures. He talked about his rabbinical education, received from rabbis who were the greatest authorities of that generation - including Rabbi Sholom Mordechai Hacohen Shvadron, the rabbi of Brezhan, and Rabbi Meir Arik of Tarnow-Butchatch - culminating in his ordination as a rabbi and judge of *Halachah* (Jewish Law) while still a very young man. His secular education included a doctorate in philosophy and theology. His wisdom, understanding, and charisma made him the unquestioned authority and leader of every community he ever served, yet in no way did it detract from his innate sensitivity and warmth as a human being and loving father.

In his short lifetime, he served as spiritual leader and chief rabbi in three countries: Suceava, Romania, 1920-28; Presov, Czechoslovakia, 1928-35; Piotrkow, Poland, 1935-42. He excelled in every aspect of his office as chief rabbi: scholarship, oratory, writing, and leadership – a remarkable blend of talent, compassion, and integrity, leaving an indelible imprint wherever he served. He trained hundreds of students, who themselves became rabbis in far off cities around the world. In recent years he had written a book on the laws of martyrdom and the conditions under which a Jew may give up his life to save another or to prevent sacrilege. The manuscript was ready, but every day he kept adding more detailed comments and explanations, in the light of the catastrophe around us. During our last night together he seemed to be preparing himself for his ultimate personal test, the very test about which he had so prophetically written.

Mother also came from an illustrious background: the Halberstam and Frankel-Teomim families. Attractive, aristocratic, in her early forties, she was a well-known figure in the ghetto, as she stood every day in the courtyard of the Jewish Orphans' Home, along with her friends, Mrs. Kaminska, Malvina Tannenbaum, and Henya Greenberg, cooking and distributing free lunches to about a thousand needy people. Henya Greenberg was saved and came to Israel with her husband, Dr. Greenberg, and their son. Mother, who devoted her efforts to feed the needy, was deported to Ravensbrueck concentration camp, where, on the very threshold of liberation, she died of hunger and typhus at the age of forty-five..

A person with a mind of her own, Mother was uneasy about splitting up the family, but accepted Father's decision. I was to head one of the "three family camps" that Father had referred to in the Jacob and Esau story. Mother worried about getting me to the ghetto gate in time to reach my "sanctuary." I parted from her and my two brothers, biting my lips for composure. While we hugged and kissed, the rumble of gunfire kept growing louder. We could feel time running out. Mother admonished me to walk carefully to the gate, hugging the walls to avoid being seen and shot by the murderers on the streets below. She tucked anything in sight that might be of use to me inside my coat pocket and my backpack. She held me tight – a hug that was to last me a lifetime. Only with great effort did I manage to move my feet to the stairwell hall. Once outside the apartment, I found myself face to face with Father.

We stood there, just the two of us, a sixteen-year-old boy heading into the maelstrom alone, and Father, a communal leader and rabbi with a wealth of experience, who would not abandon his flock, who valued loyalty and responsibility above his own life. He placed his left hand upon my head and, like parents blessing their children on Yom Kippur eve before the *Kol Nidrei* prayer, gave me his blessing.

I was too distraught to absorb and understand all that he said in that unforgettable scene of our last two hours together. But over the years, from time to time, segments of that final discourse in the hall outside the door of our home keep surfacing in my memory. Speaking of the tragic end of European Jewry, he quoted from Jeremiah (16:6,7): "Both the great and the small shall die in this land; they shall not be buried, neither shall men lament them, nor cut themselves, nor make themselves bald for them: Nor shall they break bread for them at their mourning, to comfort them for the dead; neither shall men give them the cup of consolation to drink for their father or for their mother."

His intuition told him that his elder brother, Yisrael Yosef Lau, chief rabbi of Kolomyja, and his younger brother, Yaacov of Lwow, had already perished. He hoped that his two sisters, who had fled Europe in good time, managed to reach the safe shores of Israel. He spoke at length of his close relations with his parents, brothers, sisters; and especially of his own personal family, of the future of his sons. He named several generations of distinguished rabbis from his and from Mother's side, as if to emphasize the responsibility devolving on any surviving son to continue the heritage of an unbroken chain of thirty-seven generations of officiating rabbis into the thirty-eighth generation. "Take special care of Lulek," he said, as though it was in my power to protect him. He had faith that my youngest brother, Yisrael, would come through this hell intact in body and soul, to continue the legacy of generations faced with the threat of extinction.

This was a difficult and emotional talk, the first and last of its kind that I ever heard from him. I was gripped by his words, as though hypnotized by the intensity of his blue eyes penetrating my very psyche. Not even the sounds of shots, screams, and rumbling vehicles could distract me from his exhortation. In his heart Father believed that I would come out alive from this inferno, and, by his parting words, was transmitting to me his values and guidelines for my future.

His face did not reflect his inner tension and turmoil. He was pale but composed, even when he voiced the possibility that this might be our very last meeting. Even now he was immaculately dressed, his beard neat – only the prosthesis was missing from his empty right sleeve.

His words were clear, concise, articulate: "No one volunteers to give up his life, but when it is decreed from Above, there is no alternative but to entrust one's personal fate to the Almighty. Acceptance of the decree is not the same as giving up hope, for faith is always capable of surprises." Thus he spoke at our final parting under the dim light suffused by a small blue electric bulb. To underscore his resolute belief in such a reality, he spoke of the way his life had been saved at the Cracow railroad station seven years earlier, when he fell between the tracks and lay there helpless as the coaches flashed by overhead. Resisting the instinctive urge to get up, he did not move. His faith that divine intervention was protecting him precluded any initiative of his own; faith saved his life, albeit his arm was crushed by the wheels.

He did not attempt to counsel me how to behave in the face of unforeseen future challenges, but stressed that whatever I do should be in the firm knowledge that there was an overriding factor, watching over us. If I am so privileged, I too will be granted help from above, said Father. Then he read more from Jeremiah (31:17): "And there is hope in thine end, saith the Lord, that thy children shall return to their own border." He quoted additional verses from Jeremiah that I can no longer remember, and added, "You are young and must not despair. Jeremiah's prophecy is not just a figure of speech, but a recommendation to those who come out of this. God willing, if you come safely through this scourge, you will know how to find your home, not here, and not on any alien and hostile soil. Your home will be in Eretz Yisrael, the Land of Israel. Even if it has to be acquired at the cost of great pain and suffering, they will be pains of love."

We were both overcome with emotion. I heard footsteps beyond the door. Apparently Mother had not moved from the door and stood there listening. I did not dare open the door. I could not bear the thought of another parting. Had there been a choice, I would have stayed there forever clasping my Father's warm hand, but the inexorable ticking of the clock meant the last chance for me to leave the ghetto.

There was nothing left to do except one last, strong hug. It was Father who finally pushed me away and led me to the stairs. His brimming eyes looking straight at me, he again put his hand to my head, then sent me on my way.

As soon as I left the gate, I felt my legs failing me. The tension and emotion of the parting – our final parting – with the straps of my backpack digging into my welts from Wojdala's beating, had drained me physically and emotionally. It took all my resolve and strength to walk the one-third mile from the house to the ghetto gate. Many of my fellow workers were already there, also having just parted from their families. They stood there, stricken, weeping, trying to catch one last glimpse of home and family.

Facing the Doomed

We were called up for roll call even before the break of dawn, to be marched out of the ghetto gate. The blue-uniformed Polish guards and the Jewish ghetto police, with their armbands and caps, had been reinforced. Alongside them stood the men of the special unit for carrying out the "Final Solution," consisting of Ukrainians, Latvians, and Lithuanians in Red Army uniforms, and *SS* commanders in their gray uniforms, with rifles pointed at us.

We marched in silence down Pilsudski Street, renamed Ostland Strasse, in the direction of the plant. Polish passersby seemed surprised at the sight of us surrounded by the heavy multinational guard. Sioma Pikus, marching to my right, was a tall, strong young refugee from Lodz, who had come to our ghetto two years earlier. When I saw

The author with his family

The author`s father,
Rabbi Moshe Chaim Lau,
who died in Treblinka, 1942

The author`s mother,
Chaya Lau, who died
in Ravensbrueck, 1944

The author and his younger brother, Lulek,
after their liberation from Buchenwald

The two brothers forty years later; the author
and Rabbi Israel Meir Lau, Chief Rabbi of Israel

Age two with mother

Age 27 during reserve duty
in the Israeli navy

The author in front of block 27 in Auschwitz,
where he was detained in 1941

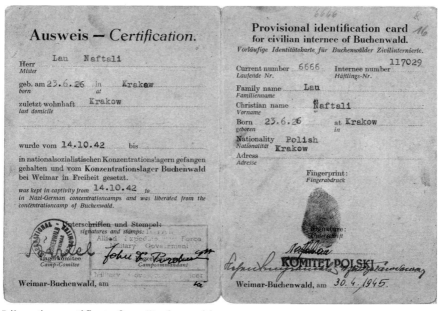

Liberation certificate from Buchenwald

The two brothers arriving at Haifa Port in July 1945. The younger, Lulek, age 8, is holding the flag. The author stands behind the flag on the left .

Guiding General Thomas Kelly, of "Desert Storm" operation
in 1991, through the Holocaust Museum Yad Vashem in Jerusalem,1992

With Natan Sharansky, 1991

Interviewing Prime Minister David Ben Gurion, 1962

Meeting with Pope John Paul II, 1995

Sioma walking alongside me, crying like a child, I could no longer hold back my own tears. Suddenly the floodgate burst, the façade cracked. Weeping and marching, we constituted a procession of a few hundred mourners returning from the funeral of our loved ones. Behind us the streets of the ghetto were deserted; within its walls the imprisoned inhabitants waited for their execution; before us stretched a path with no exit.

Seeman, the security overseer stationed at the plant gate, was a *Volksdeutscher*, like Foerster. His trademarks were distorted facial features and a huge Mauser pistol strapped to his waist. As he supervised the head count, he began taunting us: "Where have you left your Sarahs, Rivkas, and Rachels? Don't worry, the *wschodnie bydlo* (eastern cattle, the Polish nickname for deserters from the Red Army, and prisoners of war who volunteered to help the *SS*) will take care of them."

For the next two hours we stood in the plant yard, waiting for housing arrangements, while the foremen prepared work schedules. This time I fell into the group where I had previously worked, unloading freight cars of coal, sand, and heavy sacks of cement and soda.

It is difficult to say which distressed me more, the physical or emotional stress. During the five hours of work on the pile of coal, we did not even get a sip of water. To increase the availability of these urgently needed wagons for the war effort, we had to unload a full wagon within six hours. In the race against time and growing physical exhaustion, we almost forgot the drama taking place around us. The rumors traveled from person to person. The *akcja* (operation) had begun in the ghetto. Wojdala arrived to check on the pace of work and made sure to apprise us of what was going on at home. "They're throwing a party for you," he announced. From a distance he noticed me and came over to check that I was indeed working along with the adults. He smiled mockingly: "Look, the rabbi's son is trying to be a man!" But Elkana walked over to show he was with me. Apparently he enjoyed some status among the foremen.

Toward evening, at five o'clock, a lone locomotive arrived for the empty wagons. While we were cleaning out the last of the coal dust, the locomotive driver urged us to hurry, claiming that in another half hour the siding to the main line would be blocked. By way of a "special treat," he gave us the news that in the coming hour, a freight train would be leaving the rail station with a cargo of Jews. The news quickly spread and within minutes hundreds of Jewish workers were running to the coal pile.

At 6:00 P.M. we were to get our daily ration of food, a thin unidentifiable "soup" and one slice of bread. However, we were all sitting on the pile of coal, waiting in horror for what would soon come into view. At a quarter past six we could see a pair of joined locomotives slowly progressing northward. And then, about twenty seconds later, we saw the closed cattle wagons. In the twilight, it was difficult to recognize faces, But some of the voices reaching us were only too familiar. Some threw postcards, photos, and personal mementos, some of which reached us. Others were collected by the Polish youngsters on the path between us and the main line. We remained there a long time, watching the train vanish over the horizon. The anguished voices echoing around us, and the names of those who identified themselves by sending a last greeting to their loved ones here, haunted us for many days.

That first night away from home, I barely closed my eyes. Though physically only a couple of miles away, I felt I was on a different planet. I was housed in one of the empty cement stores with twenty others, all of us tossing and turning or walking around. In the dark of night, I got up from my straw mattress and walked out, seeking I knew not what. I was not alone. Men were wandering around aimlessly, saying not a word to one another. I finally found refuge in the white-sand store, where incoming cargo was cleaned and dried. I stretched out near the oven, on a vacant patch of warm sand. At some point I fell into a deep sleep, but only for a short time. Terrible nightmares brought me to my feet again. The sights of the preceding twenty-four hours flashed before my eyes. Cold sweat poured off my brow. I noticed Sioma staring at me silently. Thrusting a hand into his inside coat pocket, he retrieved an envelope with pictures to show me. One was a photo of two beautiful girls, one about seventeen, the other a few years younger, both with blond hair tumbling over their shoulders. Holding out another, smaller photo of an attractive, smiling woman, he said: "That is all I have left – only the picture." He spoke in Polish, not knowing Yiddish.

The Pikus children had been born into an assimilated Jewish family in Lodz. Sioma had received a Polish education and knew nothing of Judaism. The sorry fate that brought us together strengthened our relationship, despite the differences between us. In some ways, I was able to open a window for him into a world that was strange to him. We were to become firm friends in the next few months, a friendship that helped both of us, though in different ways. Sioma was taller and stronger than I and we worked together as a pair in freight-offloading work. He was sensitive and cultured. Under the circumstances, I could not have hoped for a closer friend, especially since we now had much in common.

While I was sitting and talking to Sioma, I heard the sounds of praying. Entering a nearby storehouse, I saw some twenty men, wrapped in prayer shawls, reciting *shacharit* (the morning prayer). Among them were familiar faces from home: Elazar Sheinfeld, Leibel Boimgold, Moshe Shapira, Arieh Eizner, and other frequent visitors to our home. All were married men with children, trying to hold on to a spark of Judaism – a spark of faith – even under these conditions. I joined in the prayers and became a part of this small group.

I remembered Elazar Sheinfeld from before the war as a handsome man with a well-trimmed beard, always well dressed from a family of bankers and Gerer *hassidim*. He was learned in his own right. Elazar left behind him in the ghetto his parents; his wife, Tzila, of the Englard family from Bendin; and a three-year-old daughter. The mother and daughter found a hiding place, but were caught and imprisoned with hundreds of others in the Great Synagogue. Before the Germans could transport all their prisoners to Treblinka, Tzila climbed to the second floor and jumped to her death, with the child in her arms.

Bit by bit, day by day, we heard news of the atrocities in the ghetto. Every other evening we gathered on the pile of coal to take leave of the deportees, as they passed by in the cattle wagons. Piotrkow supplied four trainloads to Treblinka, twenty-four thousand Jews, taken to their death.

On the last day of deportation from Piotrkow, October 21, 1942 (the eleventh of Marheshvan 5703 on the Jewish calendar), there were two empty wagons. The *SS* needed two hundred additional victims to make up the train's quota of six thousand.

Around noon we were informed that a roll call was to be held in our camp. We knew only too well what that meant. I realized that I needed to vanish for a few hours. Four of us found a hiding place under the glass-melting furnaces. The heat and smoke were suffocating, but we escaped the lineup that furnished eighty men to *SS* Commander Hermann as the contribution of our camp to the quota for Treblinka.

We saw the last train pass by on that same Wednesday, October 21, 1942, at about seven in the evening. Again we heard familiar voices, as in previous transports. This one included the heads of the community, among them my father, "the rabbi," as the cries from the wagons informed us.

"The whole town is here, even the rabbi is with us," a female voice shouted from the wagon. For one short moment, I could not believe my ears. But when I noticed several people turning their eyes on me, it hit me. Stunned, I sat down on the coal and fainted. After a time, I came to on a pile of warm sand in the drying store, where I had been carried.

On the following day, some of the few who had succeeded in escaping deportation began to arrive in the glass factory. Felek Poznanski was one of them. Seeing me in the yard, he confirmed what I had heard the day before from the wagons. He could not tell me anything about Mother and my two brothers.

Every day at the end of the work shift, laborers were conscripted from among us to clear out the vacated ghetto apartments. Furniture and household goods of any value were brought to a central storehouse in Plac Trybunalski, at the center of the liquidated ghetto, always under close guard to ensure that we did not approach the "Little Ghetto," a block of houses on Jews' Street – nicknamed the "Block"– where the laborers at the three plants were soon to be housed. In all, there were two-thousand four hundred Jewish slave workers at the glass factories and the Dietrich und Fischer wood workshop along the Bugaj River.

A week after the final transport, the Germans finished their liquidation of the last of the hiding places and bunkers. The Jews they found were transferred to the Great Synagogue to be loaded into trucks and taken to the nearby town of Tomaszow for deportation. Those who were too late for the Tomaszow deportation were taken to the Rakow forest outside Piotrkow and shot.

While still in the Hortensja camp, I heard a rumor that Mother and Lulek were safe in one of the Little Ghetto apartments. There was no way to check the story until we, the workers, were moved into the Little Ghetto, early in November. With quaking knees, I climbed the steps at 12 Jerozolimska Street, where they were reported to be. Lulek greeted me on the first floor and told me what had been happening in the bunker, their hiding place, and that Father and Shmuel were indeed gone. I had no idea how I would face Mother.

She seemed calm, restraining her emotions, but only for a short time. Seeing me brush away tears, she too burst out crying, apologizing, "This is the first time that I have been able to cry."

8

GHOSTS

The trauma of the deportation of Father and Milek paralyzed me and prevented me from going to work at the Hortensja plant. Mother tried hard to persuade me to return to work lest I lose my "lease on life" - a very real threat. Without the essential work immunity, we were all liable to be included in one of the groups in the Great Synagogue, destined for deportation. Mother had already had a taste of this jail. On October 18 she had been taken there from the Umschlagplatz with Milek and Lulek, since the train transport to Treblinka was already full and she was among three hundred deportees consigned to wait for the next train. Father was still free then and, with his ingenuity, managed to get her out. When she was called to the synagogue exit to be released, she held her two sons close by her. She hoped to smuggle them past the *SS* sentries, under cover of darkness. Little Lulek walked right out in front of her and found himself safely outside. Milek, close behind her, was torn from her grasp and pushed back into the synagogue. Her pleas were of no avail. The Ukrainians beat her on the back with rifle butts, forcing her out into the street, while Milek remained inside.

Father ran around like a caged lion, attempting to get Milek released, but was restrained by his fear for Mother and Lulek. He sent them to a hiding place at the house of neighbors outside the Little Ghetto. He despaired of getting Milek out but on the day of his own deportation, October 21, was reunited with him on the fourth and last transport to Treblinka.

For four days I refused to go back to work. I sat for many hours trying to comfort Mother. The first day, it had been the other way around. Then, she was doing the comforting, speaking soothingly to me, trying to raise my spirits. With Father gone, I became aware of my new status in our truncated family. Not only was I responsible for my own fate, but also for the fate of the remaining family, since I was the holder of essential work papers. Dr. Leon Weinziger, a surgeon who lived next door, supplied me with a medical certificate attesting that, after being laid up for a few days with a sprained ankle, I was now fit to work. The following morning I reported for work at the plant.

Upon our return, at 5:00 P.M., we were stopped at the entrance to the Little Ghetto, on orders from Meister Klette, a particularly ruthless *SS* officer whom we had met earlier. We were put to work clearing out the now vacant houses of deported Jews. This time we were split into teams of four, each team guarded by a blue-uniformed Polish policeman.

My team was assigned to clearing a group of newly vacated houses near Plac Trybunalski (Supreme Court Plaza). We were supposed to proceed from building to building and from room to room, collecting and packing furniture and household goods already marked by previous teams. What was left over had to be tossed onto piles in front of the houses. The "blues" guarding us took items that were found here and there, but the most valuable ones were taken by the Germans for themselves, particularly Klette. A laborer walked behind him with a big suitcase, to hold everything that found favor in the eyes of his Meister.

There was another team working on the floor above us in the home of a well-to-do family, clearing out the valuables that still remained after the initial looting by the Ukrainians and others. The sound of breaking glass from upstairs boded ill. Klette came running from the street below and took in the incriminating scene. A glass or crystal ball had fallen from a dangling chandelier and lay smashed on the floor. Bloomstein, trying to dismantle the chandelier, was still standing on a table. Klette ordered him to get down and stand against the wall. Then he put a pistol to the man's temple and fired point-blank. "Sabotage!" he shrieked. He placed the gun in its holster and returned to the street.

After four hours of work we returned to the Little Ghetto. Mother was worried about the long delay. She was standing in the courtyard of the central building, 12 Jerozolimska Street, distributing soup to the workers returning from the plants. She already knew about our overtime occupation and was even able to tell me that a "blue" policeman guarding another clearing team had discovered a mother and baby hiding in a kitchen pantry and called the Germans. The young woman, whose husband had been murdered earlier and whose nerves were frayed, ran to a window and jumped from the third floor with the baby in her arms. She was one of the girls of the well-known Lipschitz family.

At least four German murderers in *SS* uniforms constantly traversed the ghetto, terrorizing us. The names of Lockner, Klette, Leonarchek, and Weiland (Wilhelm), with his black dog, made us shudder. Wilhelm, the most brutal, sicked his dog on anyone who did not suit his fancy. He and his hound roamed the outer ghetto, searching for hidden Jews. He had been seen working with a Jewish policeman who teamed up with him to help find hiding places of Jews. Hundreds of Wilhelm's victims were imprisoned in the Great Synagogue, to be taken to the nearby Rakow forest to be killed. The Great Synagogue became a Gehenna on earth for the Jews waiting to be sent to their death. In addition to being subjected to the abuse of the sadistic Ukrainian guards helping the *SS*, they were deprived of the most elementary needs; no food and no water for days at a time. One night, a baby was born to one of the women prisoners. The Ukrainian guards heard the cries of the newborn, burst into the synagogue, and grabbed the baby. Running around like in a drunken orgy, they tossed the infant back and forth like a football. Finally, tiring of their sport, they brought a large metal bowl salvaged from the nearby pile of Jewish possessions, filled it with water, and put it on the bonfire they had built to warm themselves. When the bowl of boiling water was white hot, they threw the newborn baby inside it.

In December 1942, almost six hundred people, mostly women and children, were caged in the synagogue. The *SS* picked out forty-two men and made them walk for a half hour to the forest, where they were given spades and ordered to dig pits. The men began their task, but immediately rebelled, attacking the Germans and their helpers with the spades and stones. Then they ran in every direction, fanning out through the forest. Most were shot and killed but a few did manage to get away. Some of them slipped back into the Little Ghetto to report on the latest incident. The following morning the Germans took five hundred and fifty people from the Great Synagogue into the forest under heavy guard, shot them, and dumped the bodies into pits. Not all of them were shot dead. A handful clawed their way through the corpses, threw off the layer of dirt above them, and fled.

Mother worried about Lulek's safety, begging me to keep an eye on him when she was busy in the soup kitchen ladling soup to the ghetto inhabitants. A lively child, Lulek refused to hide at home, even when *SS* men stalked through the ghetto. We had to keep him under constant guard, lest he be caught by the murderers or their dogs. Even in the courtyard of our house, he was twice saved from Weiland's dog only by a hair's breadth. Our courtyard had been converted to a ghetto center, housing the Jewish police headquarters, a health clinic, and the *Judenrat* headed by Szymon Warszawski. Prayer services and classes for the young were held in private rooms within the Little Ghetto.

One day in November 1942, a number of *SS* vehicles drove into the courtyard. Many suspected the start of another deportation. But this time Lockner appeared with a list of three Jewish people of Turkish and Iranian citizenship. Two of them, Vitorz and Kam, had vanished with their families from the Large Ghetto before deportations began. Now the Germans wanted to take them to Vienna, to be traded against Germans held by the Allies. The third one was found in the Little Ghetto. It was Yaacov Kurtz, a Piotrkow man who had emigrated to the Land of Israel (then Palestine) in the twenties and became a British citizen by virtue of his residence in mandated Palestine. Lockner gave him five minutes to pack and take leave of his friends. Kurtz, quivering with terror, blew kisses to us and promised to tell the world what was going on. He did indeed get to Haifa, via Turkey, and there told his story about what was happening to the Jews in the ghettos and the extermination camps. No one believed him. As a loyal party man of the dominant Israel Workers Party (Mapai), he was given the chance to tell his story to Berl Katznelson, a party leader, who assigned a young writer to record the tale. Within two months, Kurtz and his writer produced a manuscript of his book, *Sefer Aidoot* (*The Book of Evidence*), which was printed by the Am Oved publishing house in Tel Aviv. It was the first eyewitness account of the systematic mass extermination. However, it was a lone voice in the wilderness. It did not ruffle the complacency of fellow Jews.

Kurtz's departure aroused faint hopes in the ghetto. To some, it suggested the possibility of large-scale exchanges. Many spoke of efforts by the Jews of the world to rescue us from the Nazi trap. We could not accept that we were alone and abandoned by all our brothers.

In March 1943, another spark of hope flickered. On March 21 (Adar 14), the date of Purim, an *SS* convoy again entered the courtyard, this time with an ambulance marked in the red and white of the Red Cross. Word spread like wildfire that another exchange was about to take place. A senior *SS* officer whom we did not recognize strode into the office of Szymon Warszawski, the *Judenrat* chairman, while Lockner and Leonarchek remained below with the convoy.

The officer presented Chairman Warszawski with a list of names of ten prominent people to be traded for Germans held by the British in Palestine. The first name was Rabbi Moshe Chaim Lau, my father, followed by two doctors, Brahms and Glater. With their families, that came to ten people. Warszawski told the officer that Chief Rabbi Lau was no longer in the Little Ghetto. The *SS* man immediately replaced the name with that of Stanislaw Zylbersztajn, head of the ghetto police force. Short of one person, they added the name of a young lawyer, Shimon Stein. The convoy moved off, as many of the ghetto inhabitants watched with envious eyes. On that same date, the Jews in Persia were saved from annihilation at the hands of Haman, circa 500 B.C.E.

By evening of the following day, we heard of the bitter fate of the ten selected for "exchange." The Nazis had decided to celebrate our Purim, but in their own way. The ten men were taken to the Jewish cemetery outside town. It was a Sunday afternoon. Scores of Germans were gathered there with their families, mostly *Volksdeutsche*, with a small band. The ambulance drew up to the cemetery gate. The ten Jews were ordered to run up the hill on a path between groups of graves until they reached an open pit waiting for them. To the sound of bursts of rifle fire and the noise of drumbeats from the band, the crowd celebrated Purim by watching the execution of ten Jews in retaliation for the hanging of Haman's ten sons two thousand five hundred years ago, as told in the Book of Esther.

The aged Polish watchman of the cemetery, who witnessed this horrendous scene, brought scraps of clothing and shoes to the Little Ghetto, identified as belonging to Dr. Brahms' children. The Nazis called this exchange "Operation Purim." Among our Polish slave drivers in the glass plant where I worked, one could sense their glee at this demonic massacre with its obvious religious overtones. At a burial ceremony for Jews murdered in the Little Ghetto, the mourners bribed the escorting Polish policeman to allow them to tidy the burial place of the Purim victims and lay some wildflowers on the grave.

In early summer 1943, we were informed of the impending liquidation of the Little Ghetto. Piotrkow was being declared *judenrein* (cleansed of Jews). The last two-thousand three hundred Jews were compelled to vacate the "Street of the Jews" (originally called Stara Warszawska), the street that had been a center of Jewish life for hundreds of years and which, for the ten months since the start of mass deportation, comprised the entire ghetto. The workers were to be moved back within the confines of the German industrial plants where they worked. At the town railway station, alongside the placard bearing the name of the city, now hung an additional sign declaring in large German lettering: PETRIKAU IST JUDENREIN (Piotrkow is cleansed of Jews).

A few hundred Jews were sent to labor camps at Skarzysko. Families with children were taken to the Blizin camp near Kielce, where the children were separated from their parents by trickery and then murdered in cold blood. Eight hundred of us, including Mother, Lulek, and me, were housed near the glass plant; and eleven hundred, at the Dietrich und Fischer wood factory.

9

PARTING FROM MOTHER

bout a month before Hanukkah, on November 22, 1944, the rumor spread that the Kara-Hortensja camp would be liquidated and its captive laborers would be sent to Germany. I was unloading wagons of soda as one of a foursome consisting of the muscular Elkana Liebeskind, who lost his wife and all three children at Treblinka; Chaim Ritterband, a twenty-two year old filling in for our regular teammate Sioma Pikus; twenty-one-year-old Aharon Rosenzweig, nicknamed "Horse" because of his strength; and myself. Our savage Polish overseer, Wojdala, hovered over us, taunting, "They're taking you to Palestine," and then muttering audibly, "as soap." On days when we unloaded coal, he would change his tune to "They're sending you to the gas converters." To the gentile workers it meant being sent to work at hard labor in the stifling hot plant, which produced gas for the glass furnaces. But for Jews, as Wojdala well knew, the threat had a more sinister connotation, which he spitefully emphasized by stressing the word "gas."

While we were cleaning out the empty wagon, Solomon Gomberg came by and, in a whisper, confirmed that the liquidation of the camp was imminent. He had been head of the ghetto sanitary service and was now leader of the Hortensja camp. He had no idea where we would be sent. Each of us was to be on his own. Chaim and Aharon talked of escaping that very night, and invited me to join them. Elkana pointed out something I already knew: Mother and Lulek, my seven-year-old brother, were my responsibility to take into consideration.

At six in the evening we returned to our compound, the two stone buildings that had previously housed the workers' families. Now they were enclosed in barbed wire, under constant guard. Mother already knew the latest news, and had prepared two backpacks for a dawn departure. The large one held blankets, some food, books, and shoes. The smaller one held clothes, towels, eating utensils, and some toiletry items. We hoped to remain together as a family unit, whatever our destination.

The backpacks reminded me of a valuable package I had hidden in the cellar under the floor of the room in which we lived. We kept our food reserves in the cellar, in a cooling compartment lined with wooden panels. I had also found a corner there to hide the package containing the manuscript of *Kiddush Hashem* (*Sanctification of the Name*), the book on which Father had worked until the very last day before deportation to Treblinka. There were hundreds of typed and handwritten pages and responses from Torah sages who corresponded with him on this topic. Some of our more learned friends, Moshe Shapiro, Elazar Scheinfeld, Aryeh Eizner, and others who knew of my possession of the manuscript would borrow a few pages at a time, study them, and then exchange them for new pages. I guarded this manuscript like a priceless treasure. On the night before leaving the camp I went down to the cellar, removed the manuscript, wrapped it carefully, and put it into the larger backpack.

The SS guards from a special unit were already in place around the compound, even before dawn, to take us we knew not where. Screaming like madmen and firing warning shots into the air, they burst into the courtyard of the camp, pulled us out of the buildings, and lined us up for roll call by the exit gate. Mother took out my *tefillin* from her sack and handed them to me without a word. Apparently she had a premonition that we would be separated. The SS guards made us march to the railway siding at the Kara glass factory and stand next to the cattle wagons of the "death train," as we named it after witnessing the many transports to Treblinka.

Lulek clung to Mother, afraid of being separated. Clearly, if they were going to separate men from women, he would go with her. There was no time for us to consider the various options open to us, as the SS began to chase us into the wagons.

In a split second, Mother hugged both of us and thrust Lulek into my arms. "He stands a better chance with the men," she said. There was no time for discussion. She hugged us again, kissed each of us and, with brimming eyes, parted from us – forever.

For what seemed to be an endless time, Lulek and I stood there, clinging to each other amid about one hundred men crammed into the wagon. Lulek cried incessantly; I couldn't calm him. Finally, after hours of standing in a crowded, rocking train, the two of us, at the end of our strength, slid to the floor. Lulek dozed off in my arms.

The train rattled on through the night, frequently switching back and forth between the main line and spurs. From the long hours, we surmised that our destination must be far inside Germany. To our surprise, we heard Polish voices at a depot when we stopped. Evidently we had not traveled that far. The sliding door was jerked open and a blinding beam of light penetrated the interior of the wagon. An SS guard climbed aboard, muttering the usual curses and crudities. Someone outside slammed the wagon door shut. The gun barrel of the guard's submachine swung from side to side every time he changed position. "Soon you'll all be in Palestine," he taunted us. Nobody responded. The cattle wagon remained totally silent until, in the afternoon of the following day, Friday, November 24, we stopped at an industrial plant, which still showed traces of Polish signs. This was a plant in Czestochowa that the Germans had converted into a munitions plant called Hasag Werke.

Within minutes we were out of the train, lined up along the siding, facing the commandant of the neighboring Warta Camp, who had come to meet us. The size of this giant, named Battenschlaeger, was enough to strike us with dread. He delivered the routine speech on what we could expect in the camp, provided we obeyed the guards and overseers. Surveying our ranks with piercing eyes, he spotted Lulek, who stood out because of his size and puny look. He called the boy to him and asked, "Which is your father?" Lulek, in terror, pointed to me. Battenschlaeger came up to me and knocked my cap to the ground with his cane.

"When did you start making children?" he roared with laughter.

"He is my young brother," I answered.

"And what do you do?"

"I worked as a mechanic and metal fitter," I lied. He returned Lulek to my side and let us be. At nightfall we found ourselves in a large hut with an unpaved floor. Everyone found a place to lie down. I chose a place next to the living quarters of the commander of the hut, Pantel, the policeman. Pulling out a woolen blanket from my backpack, I spread it on the damp floor and put Lulek down to sleep, covering him with a feather quilt that was to serve both of us. He fell asleep without having eaten. He had been given a ration of bitter coffee, which he spat out. One of the old-timers had offered him a slice of bread, but he pushed it away. His bitterness and anger were aimed at me; I was the one who had taken him from Mother's hands.

With aching heart, hungry and chilled, the damp cold penetrating my bones, I lay down next to Lulek so that we could warm each other. Annka, companion of Pantel, the policeman in charge of our hut, noticed the child and brought him a hot drink. This time he accepted it, drank it, and even ate the piece of bread that I was still holding in my hand. Then he once again burst into tears. With difficulty I finally calmed him. Once he fell asleep, I tried to do the same. Gradually I became aware of a faint melodic sound coming from the other end of the hut - a comforting voice singing a familiar tune. It seemed like an echo from the past. I didn't place it at first; then it came to me. I recognized the voice of Yossel Mandelbaum, the cantor who had sung "*Mikdash Melech*" from the "*Lecha Dodi*" prayer, at the Friday evening service to greet the Sabbath. This particular melody was popular among the Bobow *hassidim,* which I used to hear in Cracow. As a child of nine, I used to go to the Bobow synagogue, where Yossel Mandelbaum led prayers in honor of Ben-Zion Halberstam, the Bobow rabbi, whenever he would visit the city.

I got up and crawled the length of the hut, to come upon a group of Jews quietly singing the well-known melodies, led by Yossel Mandelbaum. It was Friday night, and the songs celebrated the coming of Sabbath. All that remained of Mandelbaum's erstwhile impressive appearance and rich black beard was a straggly mustache over his thin lips, extending over his sunken face. However, his deep melodious voice was unchanged. It remained soothing and unforgettable. One of the men invited me: "Come, sit with us." They were all from Cracow, via the camps at Plaszow and Skarzysko, where they worked in the Hasag munitions plant. In the morning, by daylight, I could see that almost all of them were emaciated. Their skin had changed to a yellowish color. They had been filling shells with gunpowder by hand, in Plant C. As a result of the direct contact with the hazardous chemicals, many sickened and died.

Someone asked where I was from. Hearing my family name and that I came from Cracow, they immediately welcomed me as one of them. They all knew my wealthy and influential grandfather, the rabbi of Scavin. Some of them volunteered news of the fate of my uncles and cousins, who had been shot to death in the Plaszow camp. A couple of them knew my mother well, and asked about her fate. Yossel Mandelbaum especially wanted to know which of his melodies that I had heard only once, ten years back, I could still hum. I spent a long while with this group.

One of the men, Yehezkel, used to be a regular member of Grandfather's household. He told me an amazing story about Grandfather's death: Grandfather, Rabbi Simcha Frankel-Teomim, had been very active in the Cracow ghetto, collecting money for those who had lost their wealth and were reduced to abject poverty. Day after day, escorted by a communal functionary, he would go from door to door, taking from the rich and discreetly distributing to the newly poor. In December 1941, he contracted blood poisoning. Sensing that his end was near, he summoned his sons and the members of his household, and asked them to give him *taharah* (purification for burial by washing the dead body) immersed in snow. They looked at one another in astonishment. It was Thursday, with the sun shining brightly, no hint of snow in the offing. Grandfather died at midnight and, as customary with pious Jews, burial had to take place as soon as possible. Preparations were made for the funeral to take place the following day, Friday. For some unknown reason, on that particular Friday the Germans would not allow access to the cemetery, beyond the ghetto walls. The funeral had to be postponed to Sunday. On Saturday night there was a snowstorm. The drifts piled up to a height of almost two feet, and the burial society could hold the *taharah* in a pile of snow, as Grandfather had requested. Thousands of mourners accompanied him on his last journey to Plaszow cemetery, the very place where, one year later, the Nazis murdered the rest of his family in the ghetto.

I left the group and crawled back to my blanket with the good feeling that I had found valuable new friends. This, especially under the present circumstances, might be very helpful. I lay down next to Lulek and tried to fall asleep. But the story about Grandfather, who had been only sixty-five, and the details about his funeral gave me no rest. I had no one with whom to share my thoughts and feelings. I tossed and turned on the cold, damp floor until I heard the police whistles. There was no time to go to the water faucet to rinse my face. The Polish police were shoving us out of the hut. Hundreds from the other huts were already standing in line in the assembly area, waiting for work assignments. Because of Lulek, who clung to my hand and never moved from my side, I was left alone for the morning and allowed to return to the hut. A policeman introduced himself as Kornheuzer from Wieliczka, a townlet near Cracow. He was a former yeshiva student who had been well acquainted with both my father and grandfather. He said he would make sure that Lulek would be safe in the hut, as long as he did not go out and the SS did not notice him.

My first day in camp, which I spent in the hut, was a Sabbath. To my surprise quite a few other Jews had not gone to work, for various reasons. Among them was Yossel Mandelbaum and some of his group. They put together a *minyan* for the Sabbath prayers, which I joined. Seeing only one prayer book among them, I fetched the Bible I had been carrying for so long in my backpack. It was a one-volume copy of the Five Books of Moses, published as *Mikraot Gedolot* (text plus several commentaries), part of the library of my uncle, Rabbi Mordechai Vogelman of Katowice. He had sent it to us in Piotrkow just before the war in September 1939. I brought it so that we could read the weekly selection from the Bible. After the service, Yossel Mandelbaum asked me to leave him the book for a while. He wanted to study from it.

On a December evening, two days before Christmas, Yossel Mandelbaum lit the first candle of Hanukkah, using an empty rifle cartridge as his candlestick. The whole group sang the traditional *"Maoz Tzur Yeshuati"* ("My Fortress, My Rock, and My Salvation") with special empathy. Someone saw to it that everyone got baked potatoes, to approximate the traditional potato pancakes. It must have been one of the strangest Hanukkah celebrations ever. Here we were, celebrating our ancestors' deliverance from religious oppression two thousand years ago, while we ourselves were facing death for the very same reason – Jews serving God: two millennia, same experience.

The members of the group – professionals, merchants, scholars, all at least twenty years older than I – were united by a deep religious faith and determination to observe the *mitzvoth* (commandments) as far as possible. I marveled at their steadfast faith after all they had gone through. Each and every one of them had lost a wife and children two years earlier. I was puzzled and perturbed, but tried not to show it. One of the members, Itzikel, apparently surmised my perplexity and tried to reproach me and test my faith in God. I told him, without overly considering my words, that it had been some time since I last sensed God near me. I even expressed my view that maybe he was on the other side, the side of the murderers, giving them his protection. Itzikel, who had lost a wife and four children, was shocked by my heresy. He stroked my face, laid his head on my shoulder, and burst into tears.

I spent time almost every day with Mandelbaum's group. He was very introverted, keeping to himself. He saw in Lulek, and to some degree in me as well, his own sons, who had died with their mother. He knew about my doubts, discerned my confusion, and tried to bolster my faith. "You don't need to search for God. He's here with us. Without him we wouldn't be here." Thus he tried to restore my trust and faith in divine providence. From time to time he described the personal tragedy that had befallen him and his friends, emphasizing that it was not for us to question the workings of divine providence. One time, he fervently sang "Rabbi Ishmael purified himself," a selection from the Yom Kippur prayers describing how the ten greatest sages of their generation were tortured to death by the Romans, eighteen centuries earlier, with God refusing to intercede. The pretext of the Romans was that the sages had to be punished for the guilt of Joseph's brothers, who had sold him into slavery sixteen centuries before that time. It was remarkably similar to the Nazi "decree" of their "Operation Purim" in the ghetto of Piotrkow. Mandelbaum seemed to be saying that there was nothing new under the sun. I cannot remember whether he succeeded in restoring my shaken faith, but the conversations with him were a source of spiritual calm and succor for me in those first days without Mother.

In January 1945, a transport bearing Yossel Mandelbaum and his Cracow friends left our camp, reportedly for Germany. Once again I experienced the bitterness of parting. I returned to the elderly friends from Piotrkow who had come to the Hasag Werke with me. But I keenly felt the loss of the bond with Yossel Mandelbaum, who had

succeeded in reminding me of my happy childhood. Also gone was the
Bible I had lent him for his studies.

A week later, when we arrived in Buchenwald, I found a trace of
Yossel Mandelbaum. In the compound where we waited our turn to be
disinfected and showered, a familiar book stuck out from under the
heap of personal items that prisoners were forced to leave on the
assembly ground. I later retrieved it. It was the Bible of my uncle,
Rabbi Vogelman of Katowice. Thus I now knew that Mandelbaum was
in Buchenwald. But all my attempts to find him were to no avail.

Forty years later, as consul general of Israel in New York, I was
invited to the study hall of Rabbi Shlomo Halberstam, the rabbi of
Bobow, to participate in the *brith milah* of the grandson of a relative
who was very close to the rabbi. This was on Hanukkah in 1985; the
enormous study hall in Borough Park, Brooklyn, was crowded with
hundreds of *hassidim* in their holiday finery. Shlomo Halberstam knew
me both as a representative of the State of Israel and as a relative. My
appearance, clean-shaven and in ordinary, non-hassidic clothes, did not
deter him from inviting me to sit next to him at the head of the table. He
inquired about affairs in Israel and about my family. He particularly
wanted to know about the chance of my brother, then chief rabbi of
Netanya, to be chosen as chief rabbi of Tel Aviv. I related some of the
experiences that same little brother, Lulek, and I had gone through
during the Holocaust.

As we talked, the rabbi raised his hand for silence. A chill ran
down my spine as I heard the familiar voice that had haunted me from
Cracow to Czestochowa. I didn't dare believe that this could be the
voice of Mandelbaum. By my estimate, if he was alive, he had to be in
his eighties. It seemed unrealistic that he might still be alive and
singing. My pondering was halted when the rabbi directed further
questions to me. But the voice continued to echo in my ears. I told
Rabbi Halberstam about meeting Cantor Yossel Mandelbaum, who
used to sing for his late father, Rabbi Ben-Zion Halberstam, in
Czestochowa. I also told him of our camp conversations and of the last
parting. He smiled and again raised his hand. This time, a young
attendant materialized at the rabbi's side for some whispered
instruction. Minutes later, a man with a flowing white beard came
alongside the rabbi, and respectfully waited for him to speak. Rabbi

Halberstam stood up, brought the old man to me, and said: "This is Yossel Mandelbaum."

The rabbi, seeking to ease the tension, joked: "His beard has turned white, but his voice has become stronger." I tried to get Yossel to talk about all that had transpired since we last parted in Czestochowa. He only kept repeating: "I don't remember when and where I was liberated." I could not tell whether he had genuinely forgotten or whether he had made an effort to forget his experiences.

Yossel Mandelbaum returned to his seat and, at the rabbi's request, sang *"Mikdash Melech"*, which, as I told the rabbi, had so moved me in Czestochowa. Hundreds of *hassidim*, in their festive fur hats, all crowded round me. I felt transplanted, the faces suddenly blurred: I was once again seeing the hundreds of emaciated fellow Jews with whom I had shared the miserable plot of damp earth in captivity, again shivering from the same penetrating cold. Only when Yossel Mandelbaum softly sang *"Maoz Tzur Yeshuati"*, as on that first night of Hanukkah in December 1944, could I feel an easing of the vise that gripped my heart.

10

IN A SACK TO BUCHENWALD

We had been in the Czestochowa camp of Hasag Werke for almost two months. To ensure my survival in this camp, upon arrival on November 24, 1944, I claimed that I was a metal fitter and mechanic, hoping that there would be a demand for skilled labor in the shops for fixing tanks and other vehicles. Indeed, within three days I was assigned to repair and maintenance of tanks and armored vehicles at the *Reparatur Werke*, where we enjoyed preferred status because of the vital importance of our work.

Luckily my professed skill was never put to any real test. Failing such a test might have drastically shortened my life expectancy. There was one occasion when I barely escaped from such a catastrophe, which could have sealed my fate. It happened on a particularly busy day in the plant, when even the German supervisors were overburdened with work. One of them ordered me to move his car, which was blocking the entrance to a nearby storehouse. As a mechanic, I was presumed to know how to drive a car. In fact, I had never touched a steering wheel and had no inkling of the mysteries of driving a car. There was no time to think about how to extricate myself from this trap. I stepped out, and was dismayed to see that the car was a brightly polished black BMW. With trembling knees I climbed in and sat down behind the steering wheel, hoping salvation would come from somewhere. The keys were in the ignition. I started to play with the gearshift, when suddenly a familiar face appeared at the window. It was a middle-aged man, one of my hut mates, who had come to help me, an angel from heaven. He put the gearshift in neutral and released the handbrake. Together we pushed the car a few feet. I reported the mission completed to the supervisor, Meister Baecker, with the feeling of having received a new lease on life. From that day on I kept a safe distance from supervisors, to avoid being nabbed for a similar task.

Instead of tools for metalworking or mechanic's work, I was given a spray gun. During work hours I sprayed white paint on armored vehicles and overhauled tanks to camouflage them for the white of winter on the Russian front. Apart from one German slave driver, Meister Brunner, who harassed us at every opportunity, most of the overseers were reasonable. They were held to tight schedules, and accordingly demanded high productivity, but the *kapos* who policed the living quarters persisted in their customary abuse.

Lulek spent the days alone in the hut, warned not to let himself be seen outside, lest he be caught by one of the Germans or the Polish police. All day he waited impatiently for me. When I returned from work, his face would light up and he'd greet me with whatever scraps of food he had managed to hoard. As darkness fell, we had to maintain an absolute blackout inside the hut. Hungry and freezing from the fierce cold, we could only huddle together for warmth, trying to sleep despite the periodic bombing raids from the air and shelling from nearby artillery, which kept waking us.

Lulek, at seven, was the youngest child in this camp. During the seven weeks we were there, his life was endangered several times. The duty commandant, who wanted to eliminate the children, had to be bought off with a bribe. Mother had hidden a two-carat diamond from her ring in a seam of my coat. I had had it appraised by a reliable jeweler and goldsmith, Mendel Brandwein, a frequent visitor to our house, and knew it was worth much more than the thousand marks required for the bribe. Rosenzweig, the Jewish head of the camp, wanted it for his *SS* superior as Lulek's ransom. I also had a smaller diamond that had been sealed inside one of my back molars by the family dentist, Dr. Sigmund Rosenberg. Brandwein, who was now a fellow prisoner, tried to get it out, but it had been sealed so tightly that it seemed impossible. He finally succeeded in extracting it by breaking through the outer crown of the tooth, and that was the stone I gave to Rosenzweig as the first ransom.

Ten days later, a new *SS* officer, higher in rank, ordered a roll call and surveyed us at close quarters. Suddenly, he took a few steps back and announced: "Children, forward!" No one moved. The German began to shriek "*schnell, schnell*" (fast, fast), accompanied by a refrain of *SS* curses.

Rosenzweig and Izo Fragner, chief of Jewish police in the camp, passed along the ranks taking out the children. There were eleven, including Lulek, the shortest of all. Now the German ordered the parents to step forward. Ten men stepped forward and stood next to their children. Lulek stood alone, not turning toward me, furtively pushing the dirt to make a pile under his feet, in an attempt to stand taller. Kiessling, the *SS* officer, interrogated every one of the parents. When he reached Lulek I stepped forward and stood with the parents. This was my first roll call in this camp. I felt my knees knocking. The German surveyed me from head to toe, and asked Rosenzweig: "Is this a father or a child?" Pointing to Lulek, Rosenzweig answered that I was his brother.

Then two *SS* sergeants ordered the children to move forward. They took them to a little hut next to *SS* headquarters, with us parents following behind. After about a half hour, Rosenzweig came out and told us to return to our huts. He promised to come back right away to discuss the children's fate with us. We refused to believe him, but *SS* guards drove us away. After about an hour, Rosenzweig came with the news that the children would be returned to our huts. He whispered to me that this time we must find a lot of money. I don't know how much he succeeded in getting from the others. From me he got the remaining large diamond that I took out of my coat lining as my share in the redemption money. There was no way of knowing how many additional times I would need such resources. But I knew I still had one last treasure in case of need: A gold Schaffhausen pocket watch, which Father had left me, was hidden inside the wooden heel of my shoe. I would have to guard it for any future emergency.

In the latter half of December, toward Christmas, the production line for tank and armored car overhaul and painting was closed down. About two hundred of our group were transferred to other camps. One of the very few to remain in our camp, I was assigned to the *Stahlkerne Betrieb*, a plant producing steel-jacketed ammunition. The work conditions were far worse and we felt the heavy hand of our German and Polish overseers, tough and despotic. There was little change in the living conditions in the hut, except that it was no longer so crowded because of the frequent transfer of "unemployed" laborers to other camps. Elazar Sheinfeld, Arye Eizner, Shimshon Maimon, and Yitzhak Blumstein, all from Piotrkow, disappeared. They were sent to Buchenwald concentration camp at the beginning of January 1945. My Cracow friends from the Mandelbaum group went in the same transport. From there they were dispersed to subcamps attached to Buchenwald. It was very gloomy without these dear friends. The bitter cold and the hunger pangs became even more unbearable without the support and companionship of kindred souls.

Beginning on January 10, the artillery bombardments began coming steadily closer. Some of the men could identify the source of the firing, whether it was from the Russian or the German side. Apart from the heartening fact that the Russians were indeed approaching and might put an end to our ordeal, the ever closer shelling was disturbing. Being hit by an artillery shell, whether from Hitler or from Stalin, made little difference. Rumor had it that the Soviets had staged a successful offensive to straighten their lines, after having broken through the German fortifications in western Poland. We had no doubt that the Nazis would be retreating within days. There were even some who hoped that the Germans would abandon us here when they fled. Spirits rose and fell alternately. Finally, on January 14, our hope to stay on in Czestochowa was dashed.

That day we were ordered to stay in the huts. The arrival of Ukrainian reinforcements under *SS* command was bad news. Hut after hut was cleared and the inmates were herded onto the assembly ground. Our hut was vacated on January 15, just a few hours before the German withdrawal. According to the drill, with which we were all familiar, they organized us into blocks of one hundred, twenty rows of five abreast. To my right was David Feiner, in his thirties, scion of a well-known Piotrkow family. He had spent a year in the Hachmei Lublin Yeshiva and was considered a learned scholar. In the last stages of the ghetto, he had served in the sanitary service, which at some stage was put under the command of the Jewish police. As far as I remember, he carried out some very sensitive duties with great circumspection. While we stood waiting for orders, baskets of bread were carried past, two loaves tossed to every row of five men. We gave the loaf meant for David, Lulek, and me to the child to hold.

As we trudged through the deep snow on the roadside, heavy shellfire swooped down on us. We immediately dropped flat on our faces in the snow. The guards took cover in a ditch to the right of us. When the shelling stopped, they aimed their rifles at us and let loose a few bursts of deadly fire. I lay on top of Lulek, covering him with my body and my sack of belongings. I peeked to my right and saw David Feiner lying with his head toward the ditch, the snow around him slowly turning red.

Angered by the shellfire falling equally on all, the Ukrainians forced us to run, beating our heads with their rifle butts. Those who fell on the snow, dead or wounded, received an extra dose of lead from the guards. Nightfall found us on the freight platform of a railroad depot. The Germans rearranged us into five-by-twenty blocks, filled the missing ranks, and counted us anew. In front of us stood a cattle train with the familiar brown color. Each block of one hundred men was placed in front of a wagon. Ten wagons had already been loaded and sealed with evacuees from Warta, Rakow, and Pelcery camps, which had also supplied labor to the Hassag munitions plants.

Our group numbered nine blocks, headed by a group of about fifty women. When the blocks were arranged alongside the wagons, a senior *SS* officer, snugly wrapped in a fur coat, appeared. He walked down the ranks and counted off each of the blocks with a wave of his cane. Suddenly, he stopped at our block. Seeing Lulek clinging tightly to me, he jabbed his cane into Lulek's face. I broke out in a cold sweat as he pried Lulek loose from my grasp, grabbed him by the collar of his coat and tossed him in the direction of the women, shouting: "Children go with the mothers!" Within seconds came an order and the Ukrainians shoved us into the cattle cars. I just managed to see Lulek getting onto one of the leading cars with the women. The last thing I saw was the loaf of bread in his hand, held high above his head.

Aharon Bornstein and Leibel Boimgold were the last Piotrkow men remaining with me in the transport. The three of us shared a corner of the wagon into which we had been thrown. My friends tried to raise my spirits, dejected at the abrupt separation from Lulek. No matter what, I refused to give up hope of finding him. The train began to move after dark. I tried to reconstruct in my mind the order of the cattle wagons behind the locomotive. Finally, I remembered that the wagon with the women and Lulek was separated from the locomotive by only two sealed cars.

Exhausted to the point of paralysis, I could not sleep. Neither could Aharon, nor Leibel. At a train stop, one of them heard a woman calling for someone to come and take the child. It was already late evening and I was filled with hope that maybe I could snatch Lulek from the women's wagon. I confided my plan to Aharon and Leibel, asking them to wait by the wagon door. Having previously tried the door and found that it was not locked from the outside, I released the bolt with relatively little effort and opened it a narrow crack. At the next stop, I opened it a bit wider, slid through the opening and jumped down. The snow was thick enough to muffle the sound of my fall and I heard nothing. Crawling under the wagon, slipping between the tracks, I advanced on my belly toward the locomotive. Reaching the third wagon ahead of mine, I almost fainted from fright when I heard voices and footsteps. I pressed myself to the ground, as close to the wheels as I dared. The footsteps and voices receded into the distance. Afraid to move further forward, I crawled back to our wagon where the crack remained open, thanks to my two friends who pulled me up through the doorway.

I repeated the attempt three additional times, at every stop. Twice I returned empty-handed. The third time, feeling more confident and using the experience from previous attempts, I crawled faster and got farther. When I emerged from under the third wagon behind the locomotive and knocked on the door, a woman's voice answered. I pulled the sliding door back with all my strength and called, "Lulek!" Within seconds, he was in my arms, hugging and kissing me, his face wet with tears. I lowered him to the ground under the wagon and together we began to crawl back as fast as we could, like gophers in an underground burrow. We reached the seventh wagon, which I calculated to be ours. All was quiet. The door of the wagon was still open a narrow crack, as I had left it. Protests that cold wind was blowing through the cattle car had not deterred my friends from guarding the opening. I pulled Lulek from under the train and held him up to the waiting hands of Aharon and Leibel. Before being pulled up myself, I had even managed to gather some fresh snow into my cap for drinking. Once inside the wagon, I could discern the tearful eyes of my brother in the dark; only then did we break down. Enveloped in each other's arms, we burst into choked sobbing.

Lulek fell asleep, and slept like a baby on the floor of the rocking train, unperturbed by the screeching of wheels against the tracks every time the train stopped. I heard his teeth chattering and realized he was trembling with cold. I covered him with the feather quilt from my sack.

The pace of our journey was very slow. Those familiar with the region calculated that we must have traveled a mere one hundred miles during the night. At our first daylight stop, early in the morning, we could discern the characteristic German countryside. The signposts and the neatness of the well-kept village houses, in contrast to those in Poland, told us we were in Germany. By noon we saw signs with names like Leipzig and Halle. The train stood idle for many hours on a siding, then began to move again at dusk. We had hoped to receive some bread, or at least water. But this was not to be. There were more stops and starts during the night, but it seemed that we were just marking time and making no progress. In the early afternoon of the third day, we could tell by the sun that the train had turned to the southwest. The direction signs now read Weimar and Jena. Then somebody saw a sign pointing to Buchenwald.

The train turned into a siding and stopped. The locomotive was detached from the wagons, moved back past us to the rear, and began to push the wagons into a barbed-wire compound through an opening guarded by armed sentries. Along the length of the rail siding, prisoners in striped uniforms were clearing the snow. Questioned about our location, some of them gave the familiar gesture for slaughter, moving their hands across their throats.

Veterans of the death camps argue that Buchenwald was the worst of all the concentration camps, built in 1933 on the fringe of a forest north of Weimar. Its first inmates were political prisoners, communists (including the party leader Ernst Thahlmann), and also some Jews. Within a year a "small camp" had been erected inside Buchenwald, along with a tent compound for thousands of Jews. As time went on, the small camp became the Jews' camp, with wooden huts that served as a model for the blocks at Majdanek death camp. A quarter of a million prisoners passed through the Jews' camp, a reservoir of slave labor for the Nazi munitions plants. Many came for only a short transit stay. The peak occupancy at any one time was fifty thousand.

The better informed among us knew that there were no gas chambers in Buchenwald. But there were torture rooms and crematoria for the mass burning of bodies. Aharon and Leibel were worried that Lulek would not be allowed to enter the camp. He might be put to death right away, like children in other camps. It was difficult to believe that a seven-year-old child could survive under the harsh conditions and iron-fisted *SS* discipline of Buchenwald. The three of us wrapped him in my quilt. I emptied my sack of its contents and we slid Lulek in.

As the train halted, all the wagon doors opened simultaneously. The air was rent with the terrifying shouts of the *SS* guards, reinforced by the barking of their dogs. I had a sudden flashback to my reception at Auschwitz, three-and-one-half years earlier. But this time I was not alone. I had in my care a little boy, facing the threat of immediate execution. As a veteran of such scenes, I related to the shouts with equanimity. We advanced as ordered, in the direction of the main camp, our feet sinking into the mud and snow, with Lulek in the sack on my back. Bypassing the assembly ground, we turned down a path to the right into a pen enclosed by barbed wire. Luckily we were not taken through the main gate, where a *Rapportfuehrer* (chief registrar) recorded the number of people who came or left. We were not checked or counted as we entered the pen, but it was hard to shake off the foreboding that we were going down a road with no exit.

On the edge of the pen was a huge heap of suitcases, sacks, briefcases, clothes, shoes, books, blankets, and pillows. I carefully lowered my sack, placing it gently on the floor near the pile, untied the rope and pulled Lulek free. He was pale and frightened. On the other side of the fence stood a *Lagerschutz* (inmate guard) observing us closely. He was relatively well dressed, with the red triangle of a political prisoner over his breast. The absence of any letter in the center of the triangle testified that he was German. Below the triangle was his personal number – 1111.

He approached and asked why I had kept the child in a sack. I answered something, to which he smiled reassuringly and said there was nothing to fear, "If he gets to Block 8, he will be all right." I asked if he would be able to help us and he nodded assent. An identity number such as his could not be forgotten. I hoped to see him again. Noticing the fear in our eyes, he said, "There is no killing by gas here, here you must strive to preserve life. The *musselmen* (prisoners who have despaired and lost the will to live) have no chance. They die very quickly." He described the procedure: We would go into the building naked and come out in prisoners' garb: "You can take nothing with you. Sometimes they even check teeth to see if anything is hidden."

In the hope that he would help in the future, I took off my right shoe, peeled back the inner sole and extracted Father's gold watch from the hollow heel. The watch was carefully wrapped in silver paper. It was my last treasure, but there was no hope of keeping it. Casting my bread upon the waters, I hinted to No.1111 that I had something to give him. He pointed to the foot of the fence. I threw the watch down. He started to walk back and forth along his side of the fence, each time scuffing soil away from the spot where the packet had fallen. Finally the hole under the fence was large enough and the watch slipped through from my side to his side. He stopped pacing, bent down as if to tie a shoelace, picked up the watch, and put it in his pocket. I tried to catch his eye so he could acknowledge the present, but in vain. He went on walking about, ignoring my presence as if he had never seen me.

Disappointed and angry, Lulek and I got into the line of men waiting to enter the enormous building for classification and absorption, a procedure of which we knew very little. While waiting and roaming about the pen, my thoughts were concentrated on saving the manuscript of my father's book, *Kiddush Hashem,* which I was still carrying with me. My friends could not advise me. I pushed the package into an empty backpack lying on the pile, in the faint hope that maybe in the future I would have some opportunity to come back and retrieve it.

As the last light of day faded, we entered the first large hall where we would be registered. Along the walls sat veteran prisoners acting as clerks. We were to approach one of the clerks individually and give our personal data: name, age, occupation, land of origin, and country from which we had last come. Lulek knew that he should say he was thirteen, and that he had worked as a helper in the kitchen. The prisoner registering our details winked at me, " It doesn't matter much whether he's five or fifteen. Everyone here needs a lot of luck, whatever his age or situation," he said in French-accented German. I noticed the letter *F* on his red triangle.

In the second large hall we were told to take off all our clothes and shoes and throw them on a steadily growing pile. *Kapos* appeared with clubs in their hands and chased us into a nearby hall. On benches along both walls stood inmate barbers with hand-operated electric shavers.

They shaved every hair on our bodies, from head to toe. Then we were made to run into yet another hall. At the entrance stood two prisoners with paint brushes, which they dipped into pails of a stinging disinfectant and applied to the sensitive places on our bodies that had just been shaved. The excruciating stinging was merely a prelude to the agony of immersing ourselves in a chlorine tub.

The next station was at the end of a long, vaulted, tunnel-like corridor. This time there was no need to prod us. We ran into a large closed hall with scores of showerheads hanging from the ceiling, which brought to mind stories we had heard about the deceptive showers that turned out to be gas chambers. Samelson, a tailor from a town near Piotrkow, collapsed on the floor. Someone who knew him said that he had kept a vial of poison between his teeth. The sight of the shower-heads unnerved him and he swallowed the poison.

For quite a while we stood there naked, looking at one another and at the worrisome showerheads. I could not shake off the feeling that these were the last moments of our lives. At the same time, paradoxically, I did not lose faith that this was not the end. As we trembled from cold and fear, the doors slammed shut and a powerful stream of ice water descended upon us from overhead. Color returned to our blanched faces. Some even managed to smile with relief.

We were herded into yet another hall, this time with a battery of doctors and medical orderlies, all numbered prisoners, waiting to inject us for immunization. When our turn came, a Czech doctor asked Lulek's age. "Thirteen," said Lulek. Hearing thirteen, the doctor turned to me and demanded the truth. "He's too small for that age. If I give him a full dose, he'll die," he warned. I told him the truth. He squirted out half the contents into the air and injected Lulek with the rest of the antityphus vaccine.

While we waited for the next phase of "processing," the Czech doctor came over to us, accompanied by another veteran prisoner. After some whispering, the newcomer indicated that we were to follow him. He took us to a clothing warehouse. At each of a series of window hatches along the wall stood a long line of naked prisoners, waiting to receive a blue-gray striped shirt, a pair of pants, and wooden clogs like those I remembered only too well from Auschwitz. Dressed in our newly acquired garb, with a personal serial number in hand, we reported to clerks in the long corridor that led out of the building. Here we were stripped of our personal identity, transformed from prisoners with names into slaves with numbers. Once again I was reminded of Auschwitz and found little consolation in that experience, and no escape from the worry about what lay ahead. Thanks to the Czech doctor and his comrade, Lulek received civilian clothes and shoes that were an approximate fit. I got a tattered, worn uniform, still with the red triangle of its previous owner on the shirt. My number was 117029, Lulek's was 117030. The loudspeakers announced that all numbers in the 117000s were to line up on the assembly ground and follow the guards, who led us to Block 52.

11

WHITE HELL

At the entrance of Block 52 we met the *Blockaeltester* (head of block), who was virtually the absolute ruler of the two thousand inmates. His name was Wilhelm Lenz, of German origin, active in the Communist Party. Everyone called him Willy. He was the supreme authority for anything relating to internal relationships between us. He had a few helpers. One of them was Stephan, a young Pole, his clerk responsible for keeping a register of the living and the dead.

There was a violent snowstorm the evening we arrived, the bitter cold freezing our very bones. Willy arranged to bring us a few vats of what was meant to be hot black coffee. But except for the name, no coffee ever bore any resemblance to this turbid, foul-tasting liquid. But Willy was at least making a friendly gesture to the new prisoners, who had just gone through their absorption. He made this point in the short welcome speech he gave his new "subjects." Then, at his command, we raced for the two rows of rough boards that faced each other down the length of the block. These were similar to wooden storage shelves up to the ceiling, four tiers high. These boards, about eighty inches wide, were divided into four bunks – that is, sleeping spaces for four prisoners lying side by side, twenty inches for each. As new transports kept arriving, every bunk had to accommodate five, sometimes even six men, a thirteen-inch space apiece. When we raced to these shelf-bunks, we found that the "good" ones on the upper tiers had already been taken by the previous day's arrivals, evacuees from Auschwitz, mostly Hungarian Jews who had arrived from their "death march," so named because so many died en route to Buchenwald.

The underground communications system among the veterans worked fast. That same night, Willy called on his megaphone, "Where is the Polish boy?" No one responded. Finally, I descended from the third tier and reported to the *Blockaeltester*. I told him about Lulek, knowing full well that there had been no other child in our transport. He took me into the *Schreibstube* (block office) and thrust a torn old army blanket into my hand, promising that on the following day a better place would be found for Lulek. Feeling very relieved, I thanked him and made my way back to the bare rough planks of our bunks.

Just as I found my place on the boards between Lulek's bunk and that of the as yet unfamiliar neighbor on my other side, a blast of cold air penetrated the block as the main door opened. A voice instructed the new arrivals in German and Yiddish to listen carefully. The faint light from the bulb in the center of the block did not permit a clear view of the speaker, but I recognized the voice of Gershon Pytowski. He was from Piotrkow, had been in my work squad at Hortensja, and had been deported to Buchenwald a year earlier. Standing with three other inmates, he read out the names of four men who had served as ghetto policemen in Piotrkow. He walked down the aisle between the rows of bunks, shining a flashlight from side to side on the occupants of the bunks. He kept repeating the names. Two of the men he sought were among us, but no one volunteered any information. Gershon continued to call out the names, adding that two Piotrkow ghetto functionaries had been in his hands for some time. One of them was Solomon Gomberg. Cultured and personable, he had come as a refugee from Lodz to Piotrkow, where he had served as exemplary head of the sanitary service in the ghetto, and had been in charge of our camp at the two glass factories.

The second man was M. F., member of a well-known family in Piotrkow. His behavior was a matter of controversy. Unlike Gomberg, who was open and friendly, M. F. was arrogant and unapproachable. He was always dressed impeccably, including jackboots styled like those of the *SS*, which might have been the cause of the distrust he aroused. I personally knew of nothing he did to help the Germans or hurt the Jews.

As Gershon passed, I jumped down from my berth. He recognized me at once. I requested his help in moving Lulek to Block 8, as No.1111 had advised, and told him that no one from Piotrkow was going to speak against Gomberg. He said that Gomberg was dying. At this point another man, flicking a rubberized stick, joined the discussion. He was dressed in a green military coat, high boots, and a black beret, with a *Blockaeltester* armband on his left sleeve. This was "Red" Gustav, self-appointed head of a vigilante group that sought out collaborators with the Germans, tried them, and executed them, usually by strangling. Gustav was *Blockaeltester* of Block 66, which contained mostly youth, five of them under the age of fifteen. He had gathered a number of prisoners around him, Gershon Pytowski among them, to serve as a field court and as executioners. Pytowski had meanwhile found his two-man quarry, and removed them to Block 66. Two days later, they and M. F. were among the bodies brought out to morning roll call. Gomberg suffered great pain from his illness and died in agony shortly thereafter.

That first night in Buchenwald I did not sleep. With the torn blanket wrapped around Lulek, whom I held close to me, we managed to warm up a bit. A few of my neighbors were holding a whispered conversation in Hungarian. One looked like a *musselman*. I felt a steady drip on me from the tier above, and tried to decide whether it was melting snow from the roof or urine from a neighbor above, when the door burst open. A number of men entered, screaming, *"Raus! Raus! Los! Los!"* (Out! Out! Quickly! Quickly!) Lulek, close to me, was fast asleep. I had not yet succeeded in waking him when a strong jet of icy water washed all the boards and everyone on them. In minutes we were all outside, standing in front of the block, forming rows of five for morning roll call.

The roll calls were a significant part of our daily routine. Morning and evening, in rain and snow, frost and wind, we had to stand for roll call for hours at a time harassed by commands like, "Hats on! Hats off!"

The night's snowfall formed a white carpet about eight inches deep. No one was allowed to go to the latrines. We were cautioned to wait until the roll call was over. It was still pitch dark outside, the only light coming from the whiteness of the snow. I looked around and saw that nearly everyone was shivering. Some were trembling from the cold, standing with legs locked together in a supreme effort to avoid urinating. Everyone feared that a yellow trace on the white snow would constitute a severe infraction of discipline. We stood this way for nearly two hours, until daylight. During this time, some men were taken from the ranks to bring out the bodies of those who had not lasted the night. The average number of bodies per night was about forty from a block of two thousand. The corpses had to be laid alongside the block of prisoners waiting to be counted. The *Blockfuehre*r, with the rank of *SS* sergeant or sergeant-major, would later approve the count of living and dead.

At daybreak a German officer came to receive the count from the *Blockfuehrer*. He walked between the ranks, counting off prisoners by fives. Wherever he discerned a yellow stain on the snow, he flailed away with his stick until the victim dropped to the ground. After the complete count of living and dead, he again snapped, "Hats on! Hats off!" repeatedly, until even he tired of the game. About a half hour after he left, we were dismissed and burst like a whirlwind back into the relative warmth of the block. Our water-doused, striped uniforms had frozen to our bodies like tinplate armor, cutting our flesh and scraping our skin. Now, as we were lying on our bunks, the icy clothes quickly thawed, flooding the bare boards with cold water. Some sought refuge in the center of the block while we waited for the vats of "coffee" to be brought. Since it was late in coming, we milled around aimlessly in the narrow passageway between the rows of bunks, like a column of ants suddenly blocked by an insurmountable obstacle.

From time to time we were required to line up at the central assembly ground at the camp gate for additional roll calls by the camp commandant, *SS Standartenfuehrer* Hermann Pister. For these less formal lineups, we were not compelled to drag out the dead. They were left lying by the blocks where the clerks recorded and included them in the daily count.

At noon we were allowed to go out for a breath of air. This was the first time I saw the full extent of this hell. It was a complete city, spread over a vast area, with a population of thousands upon thousands of prisoners. The surrounding area glistened from the whiteness of the snow. Beyond the barbed wire and watchtowers spread a huge forest, the boughs of its trees bending and breaking under the weight of the snow. The camp area was divided by roadways, paths, and fences that separated subcamps from one another, each with its dormitory blocks and various service installations. I took Lulek by the hand and we set off to explore the area. At Block 66, I looked for Pytowski, but encountered Gustav. Looking at Lulek, he asked his age. I told him the truth. "He's too young for this block." He apologized for not offering to accept him under his protection. Then he inquired about our names and origin. Some instinct told me by way of answer to add that Father was from Lwow and Mother from Cracow. "I was also born in Lwow," he responded without expanding. Then he promised to see that Lulek would be transferred to Block 8.

The brilliant sun and sparkling snow blinded me. For a moment I felt as if I were floating over another world. I saw myself tobogganing down a mountainside in the Tatras, and hearing the squeals of delight from the other children in the race. This reverie vanished in the twinkling of an eye. Coming toward us was a wagonload of *musselman* corpses collected from the blocks on the way to the crematorium. The prisoners, some pulling like horses and others pushing from behind, looked not much different from those whose heads, arms, and legs protruded over the sides of the wagon.

Reaching Block 59, where scores of men from Piotrkow were housed, we compared notes and tried to speculate about the future. Leibel Pszygorski came out of the building with a wide smile. "Somebody here has *tefillin* for the head, though not for the arm," he said, and urged me to go inside and make the appropriate blessing. By now it was late afternoon and, apart from the cold snow that we swallowed in great quantity, we had tasted neither food nor drink. The veterans said that at about four o'clock we would be getting something to eat. We returned to our blocks. A few prisoners were roaming around outside, warming themselves in the sun and breathing clean air, but most were lying on their bunks inside.

Toward evening the *"bread kommando,"* as we called them, appeared with sacks of bread for distribution. We were all required to be lying in our bunks on the boards. The *"kommandos"* handed out a one-pound loaf for every five men. Having no knives, we improvised a saw from some steel wires. This enabled us to measure the width of each piece, allowing us to divide the loaf into five equal portions and to cut accordingly. We received nothing to drink in the evening. To quench our thirst, we drank the water that had drained from the snow on the roof into the barrel at the end of the block.

Lulek fell asleep right after our "meal," three-and-one-half ounces of dry bread apiece. I pulled a corner of the blanket away from him to get some cover for myself. During the day the blanket had served each of us by turns as a coat. Lulek was a little better off than I in terms of clothing. The jacket he had been given offered more protection than my striped shirt. His shoes too gave relatively good protection, though they were somewhat big on him. My clogs gave me no end of trouble during our walk around the camp. Frequently, one or the other would get stuck in the muddy snow, leaving me barefoot. To avoid this, I tied a string under the soles and onto my ankles.

As I tried to fall asleep on our second night in Buchenwald, I was not thinking about clothes or shoes, but rather of the following day. Worst of all was the fear of the approaching "morning" roll call, in the dark of night. I heard familiar voices in the middle of the block and was sure that the voice of Gershon Pytowski was among them. The block door was closed but the sound of blows and blood-curdling groans from outside could easily be heard inside. In the faint light of a ceiling lamp, I saw a giant mountain of a man staggering down the passageway like a drunk, looking for his bunk. It was Shia Biadra. Those who knew him from a camp near Kielce, where he had been a *kapo,* accused him of brutality against weaker prisoners and collaboration with the Germans. The men of the team had come to our block during the night, their time of reckoning, to take Biadra outside and give him a thorough beating. In the morning I saw that he had been beaten over his whole body, his swollen face showing all colors of the rainbow. The older residents of Buchenwald said he was lucky to be alive. But the bruises on his face were sufficient to mark him as a target for others, who would know how to deal with him.

The *musselman* who slept next to me the previous night was no more. All was quiet, but I kept waking and flinching at the thought of the stream of icy water soon to be aimed at us. When I heard the wake-up crew coming near, I grabbed Lulek, still wrapped in the blanket, and got him down from his berth. He was still asleep as I stood him upright and we quickly headed for the door, in hopes of escaping the freezing shower. We were among the first to appear on the parade ground. Willy noticed us and nodded, as if to say that everything would work out. I was careful not to stand in the front, but somewhere in the middle of the group, which still afforded eye contact with Willy. As before, it took a long time until the *SS Blockfuehrer* arrived to take the roll call. Meanwhile the daily quota of corpses was being dragged out and placed to our right, in straight rows. The clerk counted the bodies, then us. This time we were not dismissed after the count. A number of *kapos* came to choose the men they needed for the day's work details.

These were the "greens," so called because of the green triangles on their shirts. They represented a cross section of the peoples of Europe under the Nazi boot. The majority were Germans with criminal records. The non-German greens were also mostly criminals. The political prisoners were called reds, because of their red triangles. The reds ruled inside the blocks and the greens were in charge outside. The malevolence of the greens had free run in the work places, like the quarry, where they ruled. Now they came to the slave market to choose their victims for that day.

Before the *kapos* could reach my row, Willy appeared and called us to follow him. Lulek and I walked up a snowy incline toward the main camp. Close to a gap in the barbed-wire fence, Willy stopped and said he was taking Lulek to a block with better conditions. He promised that I would be able to visit and that the *Blockaeltester* of Block 8, a school teacher named Wilhelm Hammann, was a friend who would look after the boy. Parting was very hard for us, but I saw this as the lesser evil. Lulek hesitated to go alone. I had to promise that I would visit him that very same day. He went tearfully, and I returned to Block 52 with a troubled heart.

From a few hundred feet away, I saw two groups, both from my block, marching toward the main gate. Afterward, I found out that both groups, numbering about five hundred men, were being transferred to the Schlieben concentration camp, to work on the *Panzerfaust*. This was a primitive, hand antitank weapon similar to a Molotov cocktail, attached to a twenty-four-inch wooden rod. The Nazis were equipping their aging *Volksturm* troops with them, to attack enemy tanks and other vehicles.

I waited behind another block until the work detail had left, then returned to my bunk in Block 52 and wrapped myself in the blanket which, until a half hour ago, had belonged to Lulek. During the day I wore the blanket wrapped around me. At night I tied the ends around me, for fear of losing this valuable item. I was alone on the planks and fell asleep for quite a while. The noise of returning prisoners woke me and reminded me that the time for food distribution was nearing. So far, I had not felt hungry, though almost twenty-four hours had passed since I last tasted anything. This time I got a larger share of bread, since I took Lulek's slice as well. For three days I stayed alone on my bunk. During the day I avoided the *kapos* looking for laborers and at night I enjoyed my extra space and the luxury of a blanket. On the fourth night we were joined by a "new immigrant." Even though he spoke Hungarian, my Hungarian neighbors paid no attention to him since he came from a place they considered somewhat inferior. I found a common language – Yiddish – with him. He was in his fifties, very limited in his ability to communicate, but with a pleasant disposition. His name was Sandor, and he was an upholsterer by trade. He came from a village in the Carpathians and told me he had lost his wife and five children. I fell asleep while he talked, but not for long. He tapped me on the shoulder and announced in Yiddish: "Prayers."

It was Friday. I had completely forgotten. About thirty men were standing at the end of the block, praying. They found a place next to the water barrel, which served for drinking, washing, and drowning those among us found guilty of crimes against their fellows. I joined them in prayer. The only one I recognized was Leibel Boimgold from Piotrkow. When prayers were over, we agreed to an exchange. Leibel moved to my bunk and Sandor agreed to take Leibel's bunk on the fourth tier.

The Sabbath began with the usual daily routine: wake-up around five in the morning, in pitch-black darkness; icy cold water from fire hoses streaming down on us; roll call in the snow and wind; and the wait for the next order. But this time, after two hours on the assembly ground, we were left to do whatever we wanted. There were no *kapos* and we were not assigned to work groups. I sat with Leibel on a wooden support of the block and speculated about our future.

The sun warmed us a little. Here and there the snow was thawing. Prisoners walked between our block and Block 51, draping their striped shirts over their backs to dry in the warming sun. Just a bit earlier, I had seen several of them washing their shirts in the water of the melting snow. The water from the faucets had frozen in the exposed pipes.

For a few moments I imagined myself sitting on a bench in a zoo, watching the antics of the monkeys and chimpanzees. That was before I myself became captive in this jungle.

A *kapo* noticed the two of us sitting comfortably and recruited us for one of the periodic chores. We joined a team assigned to taking corpses from the blocks to the crematorium, where another group threw the bodies into the incinerator and removed the ashes. It was an assignment given every day to inmates who were not in work groups outside the camp. We followed the *kapo* up the path to Block 47, to a wagon with deep sloping sides, similar to the horse-drawn wagons used on the roads of eastern Europe for transporting coal or potatoes. On each side of the shaft stood two prisoners to replace the horses. We joined two others recruited from somewhere else, to load the corpses stacked by Block 47. This was the infirmary block, which daily supplied the greatest number of dead bodies. As I bent down, together with Leibel, to lift our first corpse and bring it to the wagon, somebody kicked me hard from behind and I went sprawling to the ground. Before I could grasp what my offense was, the *kapo* demonstrated how he dragged two corpses at a time, one in each hand, over the snow to the wagon. He demanded efficiency. The job of the other two prisoners was to lift them from the ground into the wagon. When the wagon was filled, all four of us pushed it from behind while the other quartet pulled from up front.

The bodies were of former *musselmen*, an expression for inmates who were starved and weakened, with no further will to live. Many had external symptoms: Their eyes had a vacant look, legs swollen above the ankles, tongues hanging from their mouths. They had difficulty balancing when standing or walking. Men of average height and a starting weight of about one hundred and sixty pounds had lost up to ninety pounds.

We lifted about fifty such seventy-pound corpses onto the wagon and trudged uphill to the crematorium six times that day alone. Among all the bodies we moved that day, I recognized the faces of two. One was Goldring, who had lived on our street in Piotrkow; the second was Asher Frankel, erstwhile owner of the bakery, whose delicious pastries we used to enjoy. It was ironic that he, who had made food for countless others, should die of starvation.

Upon our return to the block, we found the "Sabbath meal" already distributed. Every inmate received three potatoes, cooked in their jackets some time in the past. Working with corpses had driven away my appetite, even though I had had hunger pangs during the day. I stored my three potatoes in my trouser leg, and tied the bottom with a shoelace. In the middle of the night, when pangs of hunger woke me, I took out a potato and ate it with gusto, like a hearty meal after a hard day's work, keeping the other two potatoes in reserve. To my surprise I did not need them the next day. It was Sunday and we all stayed in camp. The Sunday meal was at noon and we each got a larger slice of bread, over five ounces, and a tiny ration of margarine. Other blocks, so we heard, got slices of horse-meat sausage.

A sentry stood guard at the gate between the main camp and our camp, the Jews' camp. He refused to let me pass, even when I explained that I had a little brother in the main camp in Block 8 whom I wanted to visit. When I added that he was under the protection of Hammann, the teacher, that name opened the gate for me. Within ten minutes I reached Block 8, surrounded by a barbed-wire fence that separated it from the rest of the main camp. I stood outside but close to the fence and called Lulek's name. After a few minutes he appeared, together with a boy perhaps three years older. Both were relatively well dressed. Lulek looked pale, but smiled broadly upon seeing me. He told me about his block, and added that he had tried to get me moved there. Then he told me about a German Jew from Block 22 named Margolis, who appeared from time to time to keep an eye on the Jewish youth. Since Margolis enjoyed relative freedom of movement, we decided to use him as our go-between. Lulek also mentioned that Block 8 contained a few hundred Russian officers of various ranks. One of them, Fyodor, had taken a liking to him and found a fur hat with ear-muffs to fit him.

I was relieved that Lulek seemed to be well cared for. Nevertheless, I wanted to keep in touch with him in case I should be moved out of the camp. With the help of Leibel, I got a message passed on to all the Piotrkow inmates, whatever block they were in, telling them that my little brother was in Block 8. I also looked for Margolis, but found him only at a later stage. He was indeed helpful in keeping me informed about Lulek in his distant block.

In the course of my inquiries in the Jews' camp, I found a number of acquaintances, among them friends from the Piotrkow ghetto. I met Yehoshua Zilber, who had been together with me in the Hortensja camp and later in Czestochowa. He was in Block 59. His younger brother, Beniek, was in Block 66 under Gustav the Red. I met Leibel Pszygorski, whose son, Moshe, was also in Block 66. Little by little, I made a mental map of the locations, by blocks, of acquaintances and friends from the past. In the course of time we developed friendly relationships that helped form a small circle that was to serve as a network between us.

The following day, Monday morning, after roll call, all the inmates of the block were assigned to work groups outside the camp. It was my fate to be sent to the stone quarry. The work at *Steinbruch Kommando* was back-breaking and totally without purpose, a mere pretext for harassment and incessant beatings. The heavy *SS* guard around us in the quarry had no precedent.

At the bottom of the open quarry, we had to lift heavy rocks and move them from one end of the pit to the other. Another team then carried them back again. The slippery rock floor and thick mud added to the difficulty of walking with a heavy load in our wooden Dutch clogs. Slipping into the swampy mud pools could often result in immediate death. At the end of the day, we had to carry the corpses back to camp to their own blocks.

I worked in the quarry for twenty-two days, one of the few to survive such a long period. One day a group of several dozen new prisoners was brought to the quarry. Some of us had seen them arrive at Buchenwald, impressive, well dressed, with fancy suitcases. Rumor had it that they were half-Jews from Holland. Until lately, the Germans had kept them in more humane camps, together with their families. Now the Germans decreed for them the fate shared by other Jews. These new prisoners had not yet grasped the full extent of their predicament and protested their treatment. One of them, a man in his forties, became my partner in carrying wooden beams from the bottom of the pit to the upper lip of the quarry. He spoke perfect German and was amazed that I was in this camp, despite my youth. I tried to explain to him that I was not the only young person here, and that all the Jews of Europe who fell into Nazi hands shared a similar fate.

"But I am not a Jew and my father and grandfather were not Jews. What am I doing here?" he protested. He asked me where I came from and how long I had been here. When he heard I was from Poland, he made a face, as if to say now he could understand why I was here. When I told him that I had arrived only recently, he was again astonished at how quickly I had acclimated, like a veteran long used to such adversity.

"Here you must learn to adjust very quickly," I said.

"But I am not a Jew, why should I adjust to this?" he continued stubbornly.

"Cruel fate befalls not only Jews," I tried to placate him.

"Yes," he said, adding, "But they are also human," pointing to the Germans.

"Are you sure of that?" I asked.

"I am not so sure anymore." Then, thinking aloud, he said, "No, no, I am not sure."

On that same day, we carried back to camp eight corpses from among the new prisoners, those who could not take the physical and mental stress, and jumped to their death from the lip of the quarry.

These were not former *musselmen*. Their normal weight meant that it required two of us to carry every corpse to the top of the pit and place it on the wagon. Eric, my partner, knew each and every one of them and told me the background of each one we carried up. "He, too, was not a Jew," said Eric, pointing to one of the corpses, a former bank manager from Utrecht. "He, too, was not a Jew," he repeated, very much traumatized by the experiences of his first day in the quarries of Buchenwald.

On our way back to the camp, we had to push the wagonload of corpses. Eric wanted to know how long it was possible to hold up under such circumstances. I tried to encourage him, and related some of the difficult experiences I had gone through in the preceding five years. "It cannot be! It cannot be!" he repeated to himself. After depositing the bodies in the crematorium yard, he disappeared, as if swallowed up in one of the swamps at the quarry.

12

ESCAPE AND RETURN
TO BUCHENWALD

In the second week of February 1945 we could see American bombers crossing the skies in broad daylight, flying to the northeast. At night we could hear the buzz of British planes. One night we heard a high-pitched siren followed immediately by a blast of explosions nearby. Our entire block shook from the explosions, and we reacted with shouts of joy. Our elation was short-lived. In the middle of the night cars with loudspeakers burst into the compound, and guards began to hustle us into trucks. Within the hour we arrived at the main square of the city of Weimar.

Sirens from ambulances and fire trucks blared, trying to push their way through the chaos. Here and there, fires raged in side streets. Entire families wandered about aimlessly, carrying their belongings. Local police and SS guards grouped us into teams and sent us into nearby streets to clear the rubble and rescue the wounded. Some buildings had collapsed and people were foraging in the rubble. My detachment was assigned to a tall building that had taken a direct hit, leaving only its outer walls standing. We had to go down a flight of steps into the bombed basement and extricate survivors, but found no one alive. Ironically, the sweet aroma of freshly baked pastries permeated the air. We had long ago stopped dreaming of such delicacies. One of our teammates, Dov Ziegler, traced the source of the aroma and came out with his face covered with a thick layer of whipped cream. I could not help laughing at the sight of him relishing a gooey pastry extracted from the ruins, the cream oozing from his chin in this macabre setting.

We returned to camp at daybreak, celebrating during the five-mile return to Buchenwald, and bearing the loot of war: eggs, apples, chocolate, cheese, and sausage. Yosef Rosenblum, a high school teacher, sat next to me on the floor of the truck and raved about the opportunity of visiting the city. "Weimar is the most important and most interesting city in Germany. It was the home of the intellectual and artistic giants: Goethe, Schiller, Bach, Liszt - the same city where Martin Luther died."

"Who was Martin Luther?" someone asked.

"A priest and Jew-hater," Rosenblum replied.

We returned after morning roll call, and thus avoided a day's work in the quarries. However, the *SS* were looking for laborers to replace the exhausted workers at Dora-Mittelbau camp, near Nordhausen, fifty miles north of Buchenwald. I did not even get to reach my block before I was nabbed, and in no time found myself among thirty prisoners on a truck, part of a convoy of six, all traveling north toward the new camp, a subcamp of Buchenwald. Dora-Mittelbau was one of the worst forced-labor camps. Workers there had a very short life expectancy, but I knew none of that until after we arrived.

My first glance told me I must find a way out as fast as possible. No sooner were we off the truck than the *kapos* and *SS* guards began rushing us to the entrance of a tunnel cut into the mountain, where prisoners were clearing rubble from the previous day's air raids. The tunnel itself was off limits to prisoners. Inside, Nazi scientists were working on the V-2 missile launchers. The *kapos* and the *SS* accelerated the pace of work with blows on our heads. From time to time we heard the command *"Ablegen!"* (Do away with him!). Anyone who could not maintain the pace or fell back was doomed.

We spent the night in a storehouse, exposed to the wind on all sides, with no roof overhead. When it was still dark, forgoing roll call, the *SS* and their dogs began driving the prisoners back toward the tunnel without the usual ration of bread and water. I remained on the ground exhausted, and did not join the other prisoners. No one noticed me. Even the dogs did not catch my scent. It was one of the few times when the will to live almost abandoned me. After they left, I looked around, and saw about two hundred living skeletons wrapped in blankets and rags, swaying like a grove of scorched conifer pine trees. I approached them. A closer look revealed them to be a group of *musselmen* whose hours were numbered. These were the exhausted prisoners we were brought to replace. Close to the end of their lives, they were to be returned to Buchenwald, since the Dora crematorium did not function at the time (see appendix B). I joined them and, by evening, returned with them to Buchenwald, which I had left just one day earlier. Since I was one of the few healthy enough to stand firmly on my feet, I was assigned to carry on my back the bodies of those who died. I made four trips from the truck to the entrance of the crematorium. As I was busily going back and forth, a *kapo* gestured to me to make myself scarce. I quickly returned to the camp but, afraid of going back to Block 52, I took refuge in Block 62, where I had some friends.

I succeeded in dodging work for four days. After each morning count, I sneaked back to the block and roamed about, trying to get closer to Block 8. When I did get there, Lulek was shocked by my altered appearance. His look of dismay served as a mirror wherein I could see my own dismal reflection. Wanting to be of help, he gave me a slice of bread with margarine, and tried to find me a pair of shoes - without success. Fyodor, the Russian officer who had adopted Lulek, also tried to find me some shoes, and finally concluded that the war would be over before he would find any.

Except for the bread from Lulek, I had not eaten a morsel of food for two days, not since the Germans had instituted a system of tokens for daily rations. At evening roll call, every prisoner would get a metal disc, like a thin coin, which he could exchange for his daily portion of bread or soup. Since I had been hiding in Block 62 for two days, I received no token and no bread.

The new system led to theft, even murder, among the prisoners. One night I heard a gasp of pain from a bunk near me. One of the inmates was trying to force open the clenched fist of a *musselman* to remove the token. The *musselman* tried to cry out, but the thief silenced him effortlessly, and permanently. Those who witnessed the murder stripped the perpetrator of his clothes, stood him in the center of the aisle, and sentenced him to death. His protestations that the *musselman* could be considered as already dead were of no avail.

The execution created tension between the Polish and Hungarian inmates. The Hungarians, who arrived at the end of 1944, were unable to acclimate to the inhuman conditions. Having come straight from their warm beds at home, they were ill equipped to cope with the brutal realities in the camp. The physical abuse – hunger, arduous labor, beatings, and disease – undermined their mental balance. The Poles, on the other hand, had had over three or four years to get accustomed to the prevailing bestiality and were already "conditioned" to life among beasts. Some even managed to preserve their human dignity. The tension between the two groups sometimes led to major conflicts.

A number of Jews in Block 62 were known as scholars. At least two had served as rabbis. One of them decided that Purim (celebrating the deliverance of the Jews from extermination in Persia twenty-five centuries ago), should be observed despite the bleak atmosphere. Someone found a copy of the Book of Esther. We formed a makeshift congregation of about twenty in a corner of the block, and listened to the reading of the story of Esther. This was the closest we could come to observing the joyous Purim celebration, manifestation of miraculous divine grace.

The following morning I experienced my own personal miracle, but of a different kind. An *SS* officer needed two workers. The block clerk, seeing me idly chipping ice off the entrance to our block, told me to join another young man standing nearby. The two of us were led to the camp gate, where a waiting senior *SS* officer took us under his protection. We followed him out of the camp, and after a fifteen-minute walk arrived at some well-tended houses. I found it difficult to get used to walking outside the camp grounds without a *kapo* or armed *SS* escort. The officer led us to a residential area belonging to the *SS* and their families, and stopped at one of the houses. Pointing to shovels and straw brooms standing behind the entrance, he ordered us to clear the path, to remove the snow and accumulated trash. It took me an hour to finish my half of the job. Yozek, my partner, advised me to slow down. "We have to make this last as long as possible," he said.

I continued to sweep away with my broom, when suddenly we heard: "You two, come here!" I couldn't believe what I saw. At the door of the house stood the officer holding out two cheese sandwiches, carefully wrapped in napkins. "When you finish eating, take some coffee too," he said, pointing to two china mugs on the threshold of the stairs.

We finished work by the afternoon and waited for further instructions. The officer came out, told us to scrape the mud off our shoes, and then come inside to clean and tidy the house.

Having experienced nothing but prison camps, freight trains, marches, and subhuman conditions for almost two years, I was filled with nervous curiosity about being inside a private home again. This home was furnished in good taste. In one corner of the living room stood a grand piano, topped with a family photo of a pretty wife, two girls, and a boy. According to the framed certificates on the wall, the officer was a building engineer named Hermann Krieger, or maybe Brieger, since the Gothic *K* and *B* are so similar. His rank was *Sturmbannfuehrer*, a rather high rank in the SS, equivalent to lieutenant colonel.

He didn't exchange a single word with us, except to explain our tasks. We cleaned the windows in every room, rolled up the rugs to polish the wooden floor, and finally polished several pairs of shoes and boots. Pleased with our work, he threw each of us an apple. At four in the afternoon, he led us back to the camp gate and told us to tell the block clerk that we were to report the following day at the gate at eight o'clock in the morning.

Yozek, a veteran of the death march from Auschwitz, was from Warsaw. Young and handsome, he was a few years older than I. He barely knew Yiddish and virtually no German. In communicating with the Nazi officer, I served as spokesman for both of us. Seeing a helpful partner in me, he moved to an adjacent bunk that same night. He spoke little of his family, but could not stop talking about Wanda, his Polish girlfriend, the girl he met in the non-Jewish area where he lived, the girl he grew to love and dream about. For a boy like me, with a strict religious upbringing and no such experiences, his stories were intriguing. I listened fascinated, consumed with curiosity, especially since he spared no details about his association with her. Because of my total inexperience in such matters, I had no way of knowing what was true and what was pure imagination. Perhaps Yozek's stories were enhanced by the influence of the family atmosphere in the officer's home. Only the intervention of an elderly Jew lying next to him finally put a stop to his romantic effusion. "Stop your nonsense! Lie down quietly and let the rest of us sleep!"

The following morning, getting up for the usually exasperating roll call seemed less intimidating to us. We knew that we would soon report to the gate for a relatively pleasant day of work in humane surroundings. Thirty minutes before the appointed time, we were already meandering in the central square, eyeing the gate. At precisely 8:00 A.M., a black sedan pulled up to the gate. Our officer emerged, and without a word motioned us into the car. We sat down in the back and he drove off.

Earlier that morning I had chanced upon a functioning faucet to wash up as best I could, using a torn and discarded striped shirt as a towel, which I kept tied around me under my shirt. Before it could dry from my body heat, it froze my bones. I had also scraped off the mud and grime from my clothes. Now, at least, I could feel at ease in Krieger's car. Yozek had not been that fussy. Sitting next to him with his accumulated layers of sweat and mud, I realized how much I had needed that morning's cleanup. Unlike the previous day, we took a detour through a neighborhood of neat little houses with flowers growing from boxes under the windows. One house particularly stood out. After liberation I identified it as the Koch villa, named for the former commandant, Karl, and his notorious wife, Ilse.

One of her famous hobbies was to look for healthy, attractive young men. When she found one who fitted her requirements, he was brought to her house and ordered to expose his chest. If he met her standards, she would tattoo a picture on his chest and, when the result pleased her, she would have the young man executed by injection, so that his tattooed skin could be removed by an expert, to be used for lampshades. The American liberators of Buchenwald found a storage place near this house with a large collection of such lampshades. They were later displayed by the Americans as one of the exhibits at the trial of Nazi war criminals in Nuremberg in 1946-47.

Krieger parked the car at the back door to his house. When we emerged, he looked us over and asked when we had last washed. Yozek looked at me. "This morning," I said.

"You too?" he asked Yozek. "Wasn't there any water in the latrine faucets?" Apparently Krieger was familiar with the setup of the camp. He turned to Yozek and told him that he should have taken the initiative to wash and clean up before reporting to work.

If not for the special work assignment at the officer's house, I too would have avoided going to the latrine building to wash up. It was a giant-sized, long building that served as the public outhouse for the inmates. On one side was a row of faucets for washing. They worked only during certain hours of the day. A series of latrines was placed on both sides, along the length of an open rectangular pit, ten meters long and two meters wide. To relieve themselves, the inmates sat back to back crouching above the pit, along its length. Frequently we had to stand and wait in line until a place became available, especially since there was an epidemic of dysentery and the lines for the latrines seemed endless. The stench and the nauseating sight were enough to keep anyone away unless absolutely urgent.

For the first half of that day we repaired the picket fence around the garden, not yet awake from its winter slumber. In addition to flower beds, plants, and some trees, there was a small vegetable patch with cucumbers and tomatoes, which we were to hoe. Neither of us knew anything about farming, but Krieger promised that by the end of the day we would be full-fledged professionals. We saw no one near the house aside from Krieger, who came out occasionally to see how the work was coming along. Only in the afternoon, when we were called inside to move a heavy dresser, did we encounter his wife and one of the children.

I felt strange to be working as a worthless slave in a Nazi officer's home, without feeling the slightest hostility toward him or his family. However, I realized that this was neither the time nor the place to dwell on that. I suddenly felt as if I were working in a display window, exposed to the searching eyes of Krieger's wife. She passed by a few times, ignoring my existence. Yozek was sent back outside to continue hoeing the garden, while I remained in the living room to spread the rugs on the floor and return the furniture to its place. From one of the other rooms, I could hear Frau Krieger saying to her husband, "They're so dirty and smelly, I can't stand it." Then she shrieked, "What? Jews?"

I felt like a leper, ostracized and shunned. It was Krieger who restored my almost forgotten human self-respect. Handing me a brown towel, he pointed to a room next to the storeroom with a water heater, where I could undress and wash. I never expected that here in this hell I would be treated like a human being. When I returned to thank him, he noticed my own "towel" peeking out from under my striped shirt, imprinted with my personal number.

"What's that," he asked. I told him the truth. "Throw it over there," he pointed to the garbage can by the storeroom and gave me a folded towel, which I was to guard well.

Before returning us to the camp, he invited both of us into the kitchen and offered us slices of bread with margarine and pieces of cheese on top. He also served us mugs of coffee with milk. For the first time, I was addressed as *Junge* (young man) instead of *Heftling* (prisoner). He did not relate to Yozek at all, probably because of communication problems.

As we sat in the kitchen, his wife came in and looked us over. I don't know how we appeared in her eyes or what she thought of us, but what I felt at our encounter so close to hell, was the novelty of seeing a woman again, a woman about forty, pretty, well dressed, reminding me of any typical woman one might meet in normal times. When she heard me answer her husband in German, she asked what German city I came from. I told her that I was from Poland and knew German from home. She inquired whether my parents were with me. At this point Krieger stood up and said it was time to return to the camp.

Both Yozek and I were genuinely sorry when our two good days were over. On the way back to the camp gate, I dared to ask Krieger whether we could continue to work for him, or his neighbors. He turned around and gave me a wink. "Yes, you will continue to work for me," he promised. When we returned to the gate, he told us to wait, just inside the camp. He entered the *Rapportfuehrer*'s office for a few minutes, then returned to tell us, "Tomorrow at eight, wait for me here."

We spent two more days at *"Pension Krieger,"* our nickname for this special work place. In the morning we cleared the sidewalk in front of the house. We were raking the leaves, when two passing SS officers stared at us in amazement. One of them asked who was overseeing us. I pointed to Krieger's house and they moved on. Only at noon did we see Krieger, coming home for lunch. He brought us out a few sandwiches and a jug of black coffee, then ordered us to rotate the tires on his car. We did not have the slightest idea what that meant. When he returned from the storeroom, he brought tools and showed us what to do. "Tomorrow you'll wash the car thoroughly and when it is clean we'll give it a cosmetic treatment." The promise of another day at the *"pension"* raised our spirits. The car was a four-door Auto Union, and Krieger looked after it like an expensive toy. During all the time we worked there, nobody came near us and we did not even know if anyone was home. We were surprised by the confidence the officer placed in us, leaving the car, his valuable possession, in our hands.

The following day the activities were more or less the same. After he brought us to his house, he showed us a faucet with a garden hose, two buckets, sponges, rags, and cleaning fluid, and told us to finish cleaning the inside and washing the outside of the car by the time he returned at noon. In the afternoon he supervised the waxing and polishing of the car until it shone. Satisfied with our work and as a token of thanks, he gave each of us a bag of sandwiches and two apples. We thanked him but were disappointed to hear that this was to be our last day of working for him.

It was hard to return to camp routine after having been pampered for four days. But my survival instincts remained alert and helped me avoid many of the traps for the unwary. I preferred to hide and wander from block to block, rather than be caught and assigned to outside work that often hid surprises. One day I happened to come to Block 63, where I found acquaintances from Piotrkow and from Czestochowa. I joined these youths who, like me, were looking for ways to dodge work outside the camp. The work with officer Krieger was most unusual and no one could expect a repetition of such a windfall.

I saw a familiar face on the adjacent bunk – a man in his fifties who had been with me in several camps and transports. His name was Malinarski and his physical build showed he had at one time been strong and muscular. Now he looked like the shadow of a person, so weakened that he could barely move his body. He sat and nibbled his portion of bread, crumb after crumb. This was one of the methods supposed to help overcome sharp hunger pangs. Others would eat their portion of bread all at once. The young men sitting with me on the bunk watched Malinarski nibbling his bread, and commented what a shame it was to waste the bread. In their eyes he was already dead, and the bread in his hand tempted them. However, Malinarski did not succumb; he survived, reached Israel, and there set up a new family.

The dysentery in the camp kept spreading and began to take on the dimension of a full-scale epidemic. The more experienced among us scrounged in all the camp garbage cans to find splinters of charred wood. Charcoal was supposed to have medicinal properties against dysentery. I joined with the other searchers, in the hope of finding relief for the afflicted. Luckily, I escaped the disease, but some of my acquaintances were taken to Block 47, *Scheisse Block* (diarrhea block), from which no one came out alive. On one of my trips between the blocks, I met Moshe Pszygorski, a fifteen year old from Block 66. His father, Leibel, had been taken that very morning to Block 47. Moshe asked me to visit his father with him. At the entrance, I could already see Leibel Pszygorski's body among those lying outside.

I had not seen Lulek for almost two weeks. I got as far as the outer fence of Block 8 a number of times, only to be told that he was not there. I could not find out where he was, but I did know that he was alive and well from his block mate, Fradek, an eleven year old. Then, four days before Passover, on March 25, I succeeded in finding him and talking to him. He looked well, smiling, his hair grown back and his clothes clean. He looked at me and noticed the shaved strip dividing my hair down the middle of my head. It had still not grown back, leaving me marked as a concentration camp prisoner. He stared at my hair with surprise, obviously forgetting that he too had had his head shaved when he arrived at Buchenwald. My impression was that he was living on a different planet from mine.

The approach of Passover aroused expectations. We had hoped that spring would bring increased pressure on both military fronts. Many firmly believed in the symbolism of Passover, the festival of freedom, and were sure that we would be liberated during the eight-day holiday. In the meantime, there were those who sought substitutes for bread for the festival, when eating bread is forbidden. A brisk trade began well before the holiday. A week earlier, a day's bread ration could buy three cooked potatoes. As demand for potatoes increased, the value of bread declined. By Passover, on March 29, I had more than four pounds of potatoes stuffed into my two pants legs. My only fear was that the strings tied around the bottom of my pants would not take the strain. Returning to Lulek's block, I deposited most of my potato treasure with him for the Passover holiday.

I spent the *seder* night (the recounting of the delivery of the Jews from slavery in Egypt) in Block 63, with a group of people who had planned to celebrate the *seder* together. Arieh Eizner, a Ger *hassid*, led the *seder* and helped others recite passages of the *Haggadah* (*seder* text) from memory. Some, lying on the bunks, contributed comments and interpretations, while others offered military and political analyses. In between, we sang the traditional songs of the *seder* and the festival. The most popular songs were "*Karev Yom*" (A day is coming that will be neither day nor night) and "Next Year in Jerusalem." We dispersed with the feeling that the day of deliverance was very close. In the middle of the night, there were loud explosions, which some believed to be artillery shells, rather than aerial bombs. We heard no sirens.

The following morning, we found that prisoners had been taken from other blocks to clear away rubble at a nearby military plant that had been heavily bombed. Hundreds of prisoners were killed in the bombing. Before long, it was our turn to clear the debris. The Gustloff Werke missile assembly plant had also been badly damaged. What had remained of the plant after a heavy bombing raid in August 1944 was now totally destroyed. There were many casualties in both plants, mostly prisoners. We dug around the destroyed buildings to extricate the injured and equipment from under the rubble. Fleets of American bombers flew overhead. The Germans ran for shelter while we stayed put, exposed to a possible bombing but enjoying the sight of our captors in panic. We continued clearing wreckage for two days. On the third day, Monday, April 2, 1945, we were returned to Buchenwald and dispersed to our bunks.

Early in the morning, *SS* cars appeared in the Small Camp with loudspeakers blaring, *"Saemtliche Juden sofort antreten"* ("All Jews to report for roll call immediately"). There was panic. Everyone tried to hide under floorboards of the blocks or between foundation pillars. Those with no place to hide milled around on the pathways as if drugged. Many remained lying on their bunks, too weak and apathetic to do anything, resigned to their fate. Somehow I found myself in a stream of men headed for the assembly area near the main gate, where we were to report for evacuation from the camp. I felt borne along against my will. I had not foreseen the dangerous trap lurking ahead. There was no way to turn back. *SS* guards were keeping a watchful eye on us. (See appendix C.)

At one of the turns toward the main camp, I broke free of the crowd and turned toward Block 8. When I got there, I saw several *SS* men at the entrance engaged in some tense conversation with the head of the block. I was afraid of getting too close, but did manage to call Lulek to come to the back fence. My hopes of getting into his block were illusory. There was nothing left to do but to say good-bye and instruct him about the future. In my heart I believed I would still see him again. To be on the safe side, I told him what was likely to happen in the next few days and made sure he knew all he needed to know about himself: his full name, the probable location of relatives in the Land of Israel, where he must go if left alone. Bursting into tears, he begged me to come back quickly. I promised and prayed that it would indeed turn out that way.

Forced to return to the main gate where the prisoners were still streaming toward the assembly area, I joined in without being noticed. Several thousand of us were herded into a railroad siding inside the camp to board a train. The train was overloaded and I was among those left behind. We were taken into a huge building that served as a wood store, munitions plant, and skilled carpentry shop, known as D.A.W. (*Deutsche Ausruestungs Werke*). It was to be our prison until another train arrived.

This was obviously the last flutter of a dying Nazi regime, and none of us was prepared for a last-minute evacuation to yet another unknown destination. For me, the prime consideration was staying close to Lulek. When I was inside the building, I felt that there surely must be a way to escape. *SS* officers pushed us into a central courtyard encircled by several floors of workshops with carpentry equipment. The ground-floor exits were locked. The gallery, only seven feet above ground, was blocked off. The third-floor windows were easy to open, but the jump to the ground was twenty feet.

Before dark, the main door opened and loaves of bread were thrown in, to be grabbed up immediately. I was too far away and remained empty-handed, my stomach growling. However, I still had a few potatoes in my right pants leg. I passed up the fight over the bread, ate two of my potatoes, and settled down on a pile of rough boards and fell asleep, intending to use the darkness for escape. A volley of gunfire into the building brought me to my feet. A few people were wounded, but none dead, as yet. The area where I was standing seemed too dangerous. I found a pillar and slithered down to the second floor. To my great amazement, I landed in the midst of a group of *hassidim* shielded from the stairway, reciting the *Hallel* in the Wizhnitz melody. I couldn't believe my eyes. These Jews had somehow succeeded in locating a prayer shawl, which was now wrapped around the man leading the worship. They all prayed with great fervor. At that particular moment I was hardly in the mood for prayer. But the fervid cry, "Please save us, O Lord, we beseech thee... Please give good fortune, O Lord, we beseech thee," convinced me that it might be advisable to invoke divine mercy. I knew no one there, but joined in the prayer. With an easier heart and more self-confidence, I broke a window and jumped out, back into the camp grounds, and walked toward Block 66, in the hope that the young inmates would not be evacuated. On the way, I met others at a loss for a hiding place, searching for some way to escape. Several of us teamed up and tried to clear a space under the floor of Block 67. The area between the floor supports was below ground level and out of sight. We thought we would be able to hide there for a day or two. There were six of us, all Yiddish-speaking, including one with a strong Hungarian accent. Our common cause quickly created a close-knit group with a bond of solidarity between us, even though we still didn't know each other's names. One of the men, exuding optimism, promised it would be just a matter of a day or two until we would be liberated. Another, an older man, with an attempt at gallows humor, asked us to bring him news of the liberation to the pile of ashes by the crematorium, "Don't forget me! Shout loud enough for me to hear the good tidings."

We spread out under Block 67 and lay on the frozen ground. The blanket I had taken from Lulek and guarded as an irreplaceable treasure was lost at the Dora camp at Nordhausen. Now I suffered from the freezing cold and dampness that penetrated my bones. That night I could not fall asleep. I pulled out the last potatoes from my pants leg and began to nibble on them, one after the other. There was no one lying close to me, but still I heard a disquieting sound in the dark. Straining my eyes, I could barely make out two giant-size rats, each the size of a grown cat, staring at me and my potatoes. Grabbing anything I could lay my hands on – stones, rags, pieces of metal and broken glass – I threw everything at them and chased them until they disappeared along with any sleep I might have anticipated.

In the morning I volunteered to go out and scout the area. I saw no movement in the immediate vicinity and thought of getting a closer look at Block 66, but dropped the idea. Somehow, on that morning I felt somewhat sluggish, with a lack of initiative. I returned to my friends under Block 67 and reported what I had seen. We decided to stay hidden until the situation was clearer. Somebody volunteered to bring water from the latrines. He took a broken bucket, and brought back enough water to rinse our faces and swallow a mouthful each. The liquid froze on our hands and faces. I didn't use Krieger's towel for wiping. It served a much more important role – keeping my body warm under my numbered, striped shirt.

Around noontime we heard cars approaching. Several vehicles took up positions in our vicinity and German shepherd dogs sprang out, barking wildly. Loudspeakers again blared: *"Alle Juden sofort antreten"*

("All Jews report immediately"). The loudspeakers and the threat of the scenting dogs quickly flushed us out of our hiding places, and one by one we went to stand at the entrance to Block 67, which appeared to be abandoned. The dogs surrounded us and all others who came out of their hiding places. Superbly trained, the dogs attacked only on command. They stood next to their masters, watching our movements. I knew that here I was not going to outsmart them. I had lost the instinct and resourcefulness that had helped me in the past. Now I found myself walking together with the herd under the scrutiny of German shepherd dogs and their masters.

It was Thursday, April 5, the last day of Passover. Approaching the camp gate, I was propelled by the ever-growing stream of prisoners. Walking with the wooden clogs was very difficult. The string holding them to my feet cut into my ankles until they bled. I had long wanted to be rid of them, but found no replacement. Walking with the others, I noticed a good pair of shoes on one of the bodies lying by the side of the path where we were marching. Looking around to make sure the coast was clear, out of sight of guards and dogs, I stepped off the path, lay down next to the body, and set to work to free one of the shoes. Feeling the foot move, I dropped it in alarm and revulsion. Before I had time to think, "the body" whispered in Yiddish, "Let go of my shoe and lie down next to me." It was Arieh Eizner, or Leibel as we called him. He was 25 years older than I, but in spite of the difference in age we were close friends. Years later, when I would visit him at his store on Ben Yehuda Street in Tel Aviv, we would joke about the shoes.

Eizner lay there with his shoes on. Neither the dogs nor the *SS* guards were interested in the bodies along the path, leaving it to the *kapos* to haul them to the crematorium. I left Arieh and his shoes and continued with the rest onto the waiting train.

At last light, I found myself in one of the wagons with dozens of others. Unlike me, they had not tried to evade deportation. The train proceeded slowly, stopping frequently. One of the longer stops was near the station of the city of Jena. I estimated that the train had about twenty cattle wagons, with two thousand Jewish prisoners en route to yet another unknown destination. Just behind the locomotive there was one passenger car of *SS* guards. Other than that, I saw no additional guards on the train. The icy wind blowing through cracks in the sliding door forced us to huddle in the corners of the wagon, far from the door. My previous successful experience in a similar train, in extricating Lulek from the women's wagon, encouraged me to try my luck again. While the others lay dejectedly on the floor, trying to sleep, I began playing with the door, pushing and pulling it in every possible direction and taking advantage of the jolting of the train. We were moving very slowly on long curves and I finally succeeded in freeing the outside bolt. Through the barred opening I could see a sign, Kahla, but didn't know whether it was a station behind us or still ahead.

Two boys about my age lay nearby watching me. I told them what I was doing but got no reaction. With great effort I managed to slide the door open sufficiently to stick my head out. The train was on an embankment twelve to fifteen feet high. A dimly-lit asphalt road ran alongside the tracks, about a hundred feet away. While I was studying the landscape, the train slowed to make a sharp left turn. At this moment my car was not visible to anyone in the other train wagons. I jumped out, rolled down the embankment, and lay still at the bottom until the train passed. I lost a shoe in the jump but gained two companions who jumped after me and joined me.

Two weeks later, on a siding near Namring, American soldiers discovered an abandoned train of twenty cattle cars, with hundreds of dead prisoners – eighteen miles along the track from which I had jumped.

I shared no common language with the two Hungarian boys who followed my lead and jumped off after me. From the conversation between them, I gathered that one was called Zsiga and the other Erno. I threw away my other clog and gestured to the boys to follow me, keeping a reasonable distance between us. We crossed the deserted road, entered the frozen fields, and headed for a forest visible from afar. With hand gestures they asked: "Where to?" I pointed in the direction we had just left, "Buchenwald!" At first they were alarmed, but finally followed me.

I had no real idea where we were or where we were heading. To the right was the railroad embankment, and to the left spread a dense forest. It was a dark, cloudy night. Fortunately there was no wind, but the forests on the hills made it difficult to walk. I fashioned substitute footwear from Krieger's towel, which had been wrapped around me. I tore it in half, wrapped it around my feet, and tied it with yarn torn from the towel. We walked westward on the edge of the forest. It was safe enough as a hiding place if necessary. Erno was beginning to limp and plodded on only with great difficulty.

We entered the forest and lay down to rest between the trees at its edge. They were pine trees, and the fallen needles made a comfortable mattress. Our plan was to take a short nap and continue, but fatigue won out and we slept till dawn. Erno felt better and we continued northwest, along the edge of the forest. Here and there we found isolated vegetables, spoiled and frozen beets or potatoes – our feast for the final day of the Passover festival.

Walking a long stretch by daylight, we eventually arrived at the northern edge of the forest, with a hilly area to our left and village houses scattered over a large area in the center. We stopped for a moment and looked at one another by way of consultation. My two friends accepted my decision to approach the nearest house, over a mile away. When we came near, we were greeted by the frightful barking of a fearsome dog. Luckily it was chained and we came closer, a few feet from the house. An elderly woman came out onto the entrance. She looked us over closely, while the dog continued to jump and bark furiously, straining on the leash. She seemed frightened.

"Who are you?"

I hesitated, but finally admitted, "Prisoners from Buchenwald." I pointed to our numbered, striped uniforms.

"What do you want?"

"Water," I begged.

The conversation calmed all of us, including the dog. She reentered the house, but not before looking us over again apprehensively, and reappeared with a jug of water and three mugs. She did not come near us, but left the jug and mugs on the stone wall of the porch, and backed off toward the door. While we drank, we heard the sound of a motor vehicle approaching. Within a minute a small van, covered with a brown tarpaulin, pulled up.

Two older men emerged from the driver's cabin, with rifles pointing at us. Without words, they gestured for us to climb into the back of the van. "Watch them," the driver told his companion. "Don't worry, they're weak and stupid," came the response.

Our journey took us past a little church in the middle of the village. On the steeple of the church was a large, black clock showing 3:15. Apart from a few grazing cows and two young women on bicycles, we saw no one. We left the village, and after a half hour we pulled up in front of a small police station at a nearby village. The sign read: MAGDALA and beneath that POLIZEI. An aging gray-uniformed policeman, hatless and unarmed, came out to talk to the two Germans in the van. After a short discussion, the policeman returned to his post and we drove on. According to the sun, we calculated we were traveling in a southeasterly direction. Zsiga and Erno conferred with each other in great trepidation. I tried to calm them in sign language, indicating that nothing would happen to us. They were not so sure. This trip was longer. At a crossroads, our captors stopped for a consultation.

They took the left fork, a narrow and neglected road. I estimated that we traveled for close to an hour. At one of the intersections, we saw a sign showing twelve kilometers to Gera. We turned right and soon saw a crowd of people in a field by the roadside. As we drew closer we could see the striped uniforms of the concentration camp prisoners. We drove past most of the prisoners, reaching the far end of the group, but saw no guards in charge. The van reversed and returned to the other end of the group. One of the old men got out of the cabin, came around to the back, and ordered us to jump off and join the other prisoners.

I saw this as a golden opportunity to lose myself in this large crowd. I jumped, with my Hungarian friends right behind me. We promptly blended into the group unnoticed. Two prisoners nearby brought me up to date. This group consisted of prisoners evacuated from several camps, who had been marching along the roads for the last six days. They lost eight hundred of the original two thousand. Some died on the way; others, too weak to walk, had been shot. We were near the village of Eisenberg and would stay there until the following morning. The group was fed only before beginning the daily march: one loaf of bread for five, and a large central container of water for those who had a utensil.

At night, the German guards found shelter for themselves, leaving night guard to the Ukrainians and Latvians, who preferred to stay in their sleeping bags, trusting that exhaustion would prevent prisoners from escaping. That was very encouraging. Despite hunger and thirst, I managed to nap a while. I awoke in panic, afraid I had missed my opportunity, but was reassured by the darkness that enabled me to crawl until I reached an open area, continuing to distance myself from the group. When I felt sure that I was sufficiently far away, I rose to my feet and ran like one possessed, until I came to the forest. There among the dense trees, I felt a certain sense of security, but continued walking. Eventually, totally exhausted, I lay down to rest, but for some reason I felt very tense and remained awake, my ears cocked for any suspicious sound. I began to imagine various scenarios on my way back to Buchenwald. I didn't know where I was or how far I had to go. But I did know that Lulek, still in Block 8, might be in trouble. During my last visit to him, I had seen *SS* men debating with the head of Block 8, Wilhelm Hammann. I had no idea what transpired there, but my heart told me that the fate of the Jewish boys hung in the balance, a fact that was confirmed forty years later by the testimony of Ludwig Wolf, a German veteran prisoner at Buchenwald. He came to Israel to attest to Hammann's role in saving the Jewish children of Buchenwald. He testified that four *SS* men had come to Block 8 in April 1945, shortly before liberation, to take away the Jewish boys. Hammann denied that there were any Jews in the block. He hid the boys and saved them from certain death. As evidence, Wolf listed the names of the Jewish youngsters in the block. Lulek appears under his own serial number but, afraid to reveal his age, he gave my name and my date of birth. As I lay in the Thuringer Forest I knew none of this, but the recollection of the SS officers at the entrance to Block 8 intensified my concern for the child.

A few hours' rest was sufficient to restore my strength and I resumed walking. Still under cover of total darkness, I came to the edge of the forest and headed in what I reckoned to be a westerly direction.

As sunrise approached, I saw I had not been mistaken. The path I had chosen, though I didn't know it then, led me clear of the town of Jena to the south, to an area of wooded hills. Eating abandoned green stuff scattered in the fields was enough to keep me going the following day. I was even able to increase my pace once I reached the open fields. Far to my right, I could see traffic on a parallel but distant road. I continued in the direction of a forest visible on the horizon. The rags on my feet, saturated with water and mud, made it harder and harder to walk. The ground was muddy and, toward evening, partly frozen with a very thin layer of ice on top. At nightfall I began to look for a place to sleep.

The forest I was hoping to reach was still some distance away. To my left I noticed an abandoned orchard lean-to. On closer inspection, it turned out to be a sheet-metal roof with no walls. At least it was a roof over my head and more than I really expected to find. Scavenging around, I found a few planks and some remains of sacking to make a relatively comfortable bed. By the last light of day, I lay back and took in the cloudy sky above. Here and there an isolated star twinkled. Suddenly I remembered that it was the Sabbath. The first three adjacent stars signal the end of the Sabbath and the beginning of the new week. But my immediate concern was that the clouds overhead should not bring on a downpour.

The silence around me, undisturbed even by the rustle of leaves or the chirping of birds, was soothing. Various scenes came to my mind, but I suppressed them and turned my thoughts to taking stock of my situation. My thoughts converged on Mother, from whom I had parted half a year earlier; on Father and Milek, who had perished together in the gas chambers, incinerated at Treblinka; then back on Mother. Perhaps she was in a camp somewhere, wondering and worrying about our fate. I continued to worry about Lulek, not yet eight years old, alone in Buchenwald. I took stock of my own situation, a boy of eighteen, wandering alone through the forests and fields of Germany like a hunted animal. I also thought of our future: If and when we should be liberated, where would we go? Would Lulek survive? Would I? Would we find Mother alive? Would there be any Jews left in the world?

That night, hour after hour, I kept turning these thoughts over in my mind, until I finally fell asleep.

I awoke at dawn. It was Sunday, April 8, 1945. The dull thunder of distant artillery reminded me that a war was going on not far away. Heartened by the possibility of approaching liberation, I gathered strength and again started walking.

It seems I was guided by an inexplicable instinct in the direction of my goal. The names of villages and towns on the signposts along the dirt paths told me nothing. Finally I turned to the right, toward the parallel road, the one with a flow of traffic. As I got closer, I looked for a junction, in the hope of finding signs that would guide me.

Some six hundred feet from a junction, I sat down and waited. I wanted to be sure that there would be no unforeseen hazard when I came to the road. As I sat there, I heard a hum like a swarm of mosquitoes. The sound kept coming closer and closer until I saw a large fleet of heavy aircraft flying rather low, coming from the southeast. The planes advanced, wave after wave, for three or four minutes. The racket they made was like a sedative to me. I decided to walk in the direction of the planes. In order to do so, I had to cross the road from southeast to northwest. There was a dirt path that led in the right direction. About ten feet away, I sat down to rest and saw two people on bicycles turning in from the main road to the dirt path near my hiding place. As they got closer I saw they were two young girls, one of them wearing a bright red coat that caught my eye.

I remained sitting on the ground. As they came alongside, I called out: "Water, please. Water." They stopped. Getting off their bikes, they looked visibly shocked to see the wretched figure I must have represented. I am not sure what frightened them most - my appearance, the clothes I wore, or the isolated place of our encounter. One of them raised a hand, as though to say; "We have no water." I asked how far we were from Weimar, and in which direction I was to go. One said "about twenty kilometers" (twelve miles); the other said, "a little more than thirty." Both pointed in the direction I had been following, in the path of the planes. I estimated that if the girls were right, I had another six to eight hours to walk to the outskirts of Weimar. Another five miles would get me to Buchenwald. I planned to bypass Weimar from the southeast, aiming north toward Buchenwald and continued on my path, postponing the crossing of the road and the parallel railway tracks until dark.

Just before dark, I saw a large village spread out in front of me. I decided to turn north to avoid it. This meant I would have to cross the main road. Along the way, I came to a post with two signs: Mellingen and Taubach, though I could not see which way they pointed. I ignored both and continued until I reached the edge of the main road, a rural, narrow asphalt road with unlit lampposts along its length. Night had settled by the time I reached the other side of the road. There I came upon another hurdle: a flowing stream that I had to cross. Fortunately I discovered a narrow, wooden pedestrian bridge. I knew my destination but not how to get there. Again, some hidden intuition guided me. I felt like a lost dog finding its way back home by sheer instinct.

I decided to spend the night in a densely wooded forest. Utterly spent, I dropped to the ground and slept. In the middle of the night I awoke, shaking uncontrollably, my teeth chattering and my head hot with fever. This was not exactly the time or the place to be ill, or to seek aid. Trying to ignore my condition, I attempted to sleep, but lay awake all night, afraid I would not be able to reach my destination.

With determined effort, I got up and took a few dozen steps but my legs failed me. Overcome with numbness, I again lay down to rest. The only way to overcome this condition was to rest as best I could, hoping the illness would pass quickly. I don't know whether it was the fever or my particular predicament that brought on the horrifying scenes that filled my mind; events I had managed to repress kept surfacing in my consciousness, particularly the fragmentary tale of Dudek Levkowitz of Piotrkow.

Dudek was the last person to see Father alive at the threshold of the gas chamber in Treblinka. They were in the same transport. Dudek, in his thirties, was assigned to the work group that sorted the clothes of the murdered. Two weeks after his arrival, he managed to escape and return to the Little Ghetto in Piotrkow. His story: On October 21, 1942, when the fourth and last transport from Piotrkow reached Treblinka, he was waiting with his work group for the clothes of the seven thousand men, women, and children huddled at the entrance of the gas chamber.

"I saw the people of Piotrkow, many friends and relatives. They all stood quietly, on the threshold of death. Suddenly we heard a strong voice, the familiar, powerful voice of Rabbi Lau. I couldn't hear everything he said to the last remnants of his community, but I heard many people crying, repeating after him, '*Shema Yisroel Adonoi Elohainu Adonoi Echod*' (Hear, O Israel, the Lord our God, the Lord is One). Even the waiting work group was affected."

What Dudek Levkowitz could not relate, my imagination filled in. I pictured Father and my young brother Milek standing naked in the gas chamber, together with the rest of the community. I remembered the shower room at Buchenwald, which we entered the day we arrived. I remembered how we all thought that these were the last moments of our lives, as indeed they were for my father and brother. I pictured to myself how they embraced each other, suffocating as the gas penetrated their lungs. In my delirium, I saw their bodies being dragged and thrown into the furnace, together with hundreds and thousands of others – a montage of horror scenes, from the time of the first ghetto in the fall of 1939 until spring 1945.

I became aware of something bright nearby among the trees. Thinking it might be something of value, I dragged myself along the ground and discovered the remains of a patch of snow. Gathering a handful, I swallowed some and rubbed some on my feverish forehead.

Again I closed my eyes and tried to sleep, despite attacks of terror, nightmares, hallucinations. I heard Mother calling me, urging me: "Look after the child! Look after the child!" The voice penetrated my sleep like a haunting echo of Father's exhortation at our last meeting on the staircase of our home on October 13, 1942.

I lay helpless until the sun rose. The warm rays refreshed me a little, but I still couldn't get up. I tried to think of what Mother would do to get me on my feet. I did not know then that she had perished two months earlier in Ravensbrueck concentration camp for women. All I knew was that Lulek had been entrusted to me by Father in October 1942, and by Mother in November 1944. I could not fail them.

Somehow I summoned the strength to get up and resume walking. I walked for hours without a break, through field and forest. Eventually I could make out Weimar on the horizon, and I knew that I was walking in the right direction.

In the late afternoon I allowed myself a short rest, leaning against a tree, surveying my surroundings. By dusk I reached familiar ground. Like an experienced tracker, I had sniffed out the correct path and had not erred. The huge flock of crows that always hovered over the camp told me that I was near Buchenwald. I could see the camp, sprawled over the wooded slopes of Mount Ettersberg. To reach it I would have to bypass the village of Ettersburg and cross the road to Buchenwald. There was no cover. The entire area had been denuded of foliage

I lay on the ground, a short distance from the road. When I was sure there was no approaching traffic, I ran across the road toward the railroad siding. The second obstacle was easier to cross. On the road to the quarry I arrived at the *SS* living quarters, an all too familiar area, with the low clump of shrubs facing the camp close to the gate.

By retreating to the rear of the covering shrubs, I avoided the few cars coming in my direction. The shrubs offered a convenient lookout position alongside the road leading to the camp. I still did not know how I would get to the gate and into the camp. Two small prisoner *kommandos* appeared from my left, passed me by, and entered through the gate.

I was gambling on the possibility of joining a group of prisoners. It would have to be a relatively large one, so that I could slip in without drawing attention. The *kapos* usually walked ahead but sometimes alongside the column, while the *SS* guard rode a motorcycle up front, or sometimes in back.

The gate was lit up by a few lampposts casting a weak light, and I could see a large company of prisoners approaching from my left toward the gate. This was an opportunity I could not pass up. My breathing became difficult as my excitement rose. Defying my physical condition, I shot like an arrow from my hiding place across the ten feet to the nearest marching file. No one noticed me. Exhausted from their day's work, desiring only to rest their weary bones, both prisoners and guards were absorbed in their own thoughts. I filled an empty place in one of the last ranks and anxiously anticipated entry into the gate. I was now breathing with great difficulty and didn't even notice the precise moment I entered. No glaring lights illuminated us and we were not counted. At the assembly ground the prisoners, numbering about one hundred, were dispersed as we arrived.

I dragged myself to the Small Camp. Some of the blocks I passed looked like ghostly ruins. I saw someone move in Block 62. Entering like a long-time resident, I lay down on a bunk, utterly depleted. Such a sweet sleep as this I could not recollect. The daytime aches and pains, the nightmares gave way to overwhelming fatigue. When I woke at dawn I realized, to my delight, that there was no roll call. I stayed where I was until the prisoners began taking out the day's quota of dead bodies. Everyone was drafted to help. When they came to me, they could not decide whether to place me among the carriers or the carried.

No one spoke of food or drink. The block authorities were nowhere to be seen. As a Jewish block, it was supposed to have been evacuated and shut down. Everyone who had managed to evade the transports was in hiding and officially did not exist. Toward noon I went outside to go to Block 8. It was a bright, pleasant day under a warm sun. Heavy artillery barrages were clearly audible. Some said the source was the vanguard of an advance unit of American tanks approaching from the west. As I reached Block 8, I heard a veteran German prisoner exclaiming joyfully: *Panzerspitzen!* (Tank vanguard).

I leaned on the barbed-wire fence, my head against the barbs, barely able to stand on my feet. Blood ran down my forehead from the gashes made by the wire. I was close to fainting when, in a blur, I saw Lulek standing on the other side facing me, holding hands with Fyodor, the Russian officer who had adopted him. This time the block senior let me enter the block yard. I washed my face. Fyodor brought me a mug of hot coffee. They were afraid to take me into the block itself, so I lay outside, nibbling on a slice of bread. The head of the block, Wilhelm Hammann, came over to see what was going on. When he heard my story from Fyodor, he allowed them to take me into the block until evening.

I was filthy and bruised all over. The soles of my feet were swollen and blood oozed from numerous open wounds. Lulek held my hand, crying with joy at my return. He told me of the fear among the Jewish boys during that last week. Fyodor said that liberation was near, "but the bastards are still capable of liquidating us at the last minute." Just the previous day they had again come to check whether there were any Jews in the block. Hammann lied to them. The boys pretended not to understand German and didn't answer the *SS* questions about their identity. For safety's sake, Fyodor said it would be best for me to return to the Small Camp for the night. I promised Lulek to be back in the morning. Supported by Fyodor and another Russian, I walked back to Block 62.

"I smell freedom," said Asher Weiss, who lay next to me. He too had been taken to the D.A.W. plant and escaped back into the camp, hiding there during the week I had been roaming the forests and fields on my way back to Buchenwald. "I was left alone," mourned Asher, "my three friends and my older brother, who had all been together with me on the way to Auschwitz and from there to here, all died, one by one. My last friend died yesterday and I have nowhere to go, even if I should be liberated." He was about twenty, the sole survivor of a large Hungarian family. Two days later, I saw his body being taken to the crematorium.

The explosions during the night were now close enough to jolt the blocks violently. For the first time I could feel imminent liberation. Unafraid of the *SS,* we went outside to watch the flashes on the distant horizon. Here and there the sky was red from fires on the ground. Slowly the paths and the assembly grounds filled with prisoners who came out of the blocks to feast their eyes on the sight. Some thought the guards had gone and that we were free. Others cautioned against a possible trap. We remained outside most of the night, waiting for whatever was coming.

My rest in Block 8 had refreshed me temporarily, but now I was again overcome by weakness and fell to the ground. Later I managed to return to my bunk and lay there until late morning. Awakened by the sound of prisoners running jubilantly from the block, I stumbled to my feet. Outside, I could see crowds running to the outer fence, pointing to the empty guard towers. All of the *SS* had abandoned their guard posts and disappeared.

On my way to Block 8, I met several dozen veteran prisoners marching in military formation with rifles on their shoulders. They were new rifles, still fresh from their packing. These were communists, sent to Buchenwald as early as 1938, who had hidden weapons – to be used when needed. Now, with their weapons retrieved, they were taking over control, lest the fleeing Germans decide to burn down the camp. According to the gate tower clock, it was 9:20 A.M., Wednesday, April 11, 1945. Two hours later, two American planes flew very low over the camp, and later in the afternoon two jeeps with American soldiers burst through the gate and stopped at the center of the assembly area.

13

LIBERATION

Six soldiers jumped out of their jeeps. One of them was black, the first black person any of us had ever seen. They took off their helmets and looked around in disbelief. An eerie silence reigned over the camp. We were all speechless and stared at the six soldiers, knowing that they were our saviors for whom we had waited so long. No one uttered a word. Suddenly, there was a shout: "Hurrah!" and we stormed the six embarrassed men. They still had no idea of the scenes they were about to see. For the moment, the crowd advancing on them and their vehicles was trauma enough. An old man in front of me fell on one of the jeeps and began kissing it. Others stood by quietly, wiping tears from their eyes. It had been months since I saw an adult cry.

One of the soldiers, speaking a German that sounded more like our Yiddish, asked, "What is this place?" "Buchenwald," someone replied. "Tens of thousands have been murdered here," someone else added. "There are thousands of bodies in the camp. Those of us still alive need urgent medical care." The soldier translated into English, and his comrades exchanged glances of disbelief.

As if on signal, they began to hand out chewing gum, candies, and cigarettes. The now liberated prisoners jostled to grab a share. The soldiers, sensing that the situation was more than they could deal with, got back into their jeeps and drove off. A half hour later, a convoy of ten vehicles led by two tanks came through the gate. An officer called out through a megaphone, in broken German, for us to come closer and pay attention. He introduced himself by name and rank and said that we were now free men and could return home as soon as our health and conditions permitted. In the meantime, we should maintain discipline and obey the orders given by the American troops taking charge of the camp.

Standing among my liberated comrades, I feared that I would not meet the health requirements. My legs failed me and a cold sweat covered my forehead. Shalom Tepper, a boy my age who, like me, had spent the night before the liberation in Block 62, was standing next to me when I collapsed to the ground. He pulled me to my feet and helped me back to the block. He laid me on a bunk, gave me water, and dampened my forehead. I missed the spontaneous celebration of liberation, but the noise reached me inside the block, and I could hear the gratifying sounds of the inmates landing blows on any SS sentries they could catch.

That same evening someone brought Lulek to me, apparently afraid this would be our final encounter. I was burning with fever, only partly conscious, and was barely able to speak to my brother, who stared at me in shock. The following morning, a Czech doctor from among the liberated inmates came to see me. He checked my pulse, heart, and lungs and ordered that I be moved immediately to the camp hospital.

Dov Landau and Shalom Tepper helped me down from my bunk, wrapped me in a blanket, and supported me on the way to the hospital. When my legs failed me again, they laid me on the blanket and carried me. The "hospital" was inside the camp. Its conditions were subhuman by any medical standards. The staff consisted of doctors and orderlies who, like the rest of the liberated prisoners, were mostly concerned with going home as quickly as possible. The French doctor who received me injected camphor into my chest. Assisted by two orderlies, I climbed up to the upper bunk. A single woolen army blanket served both as mattress and cover.

For almost twenty-four hours not a drop of water passed my lips. Thirsty and dehydrated, I begged for water, to no avail. Finally a doctor took the trouble to explain that I had typhus and, until they diagnosed the strain, I would receive nothing apart from drug injections. The room held sixteen patients under strict quarantine, in eight two-tiered bunks. The day I was hospitalized, five bodies were removed from our room. Six more died during the night. Of the sixteen patients that were there when I arrived, only five survived. I was sure that liberation had come too late for me.

My head was filled with nightmarish scenes. I kept hearing a strange voice calling: "Lau, come to the washroom window." Somehow, I managed to get to the washroom, where I heard Lulek's voice calling my name, saying: "Come to the window!" I climbed onto a toilet bowl by the window and tried to look out. Again my strength failed. I fainted and fell to the floor.

I woke in the morning to find myself on a lower bunk, which had been vacated. A German doctor who, judging by his number, had been in Buchenwald for a very long time, told me that the diagnosis was complete and that I was to be transferred to the SS hospital outside the camp. This time I was carried on a stretcher by medical orderlies to the *SS* "Revier," some distance away. This was a standard accredited hospital, which had served the guards and their families and now served the inmates.

In the shower room, I was stripped of my worn-out clothes. My original striped shirt and pants with my personal number had become rags and emitted a powerful stench. When they were thrown into the trash, I felt a strange twinge of regret. I had traveled so far and gone through so much wearing these striped tatters that they had almost become part of me. I was bathed with hot water and soap and, for the first time in years, I could see myself in the mirror – a shocking sight. Clean and naked, I was led into a room with twenty beds, in two facing rows of ten. I was placed in an empty bed next to an emaciated youngster who seemed to be hovering between life and death. Two orderlies wrapped him in a sheet soaked in iced water and put an ice pack on his forehead. As our eyes met, I sensed that he was Jewish and addressed him with the code used among Jewish prisoners, *"Amcha?"* to which he nodded, *"Amcha."* We were both fighting fever and suffering from hallucinations and nightmares. It was only later that we really got to know each other. Bunim Wrzonski, now a scholar and educator, eventually established his home and family in Israel. We have remained friends until this day.

At first we had difficulty communicating. When one of us was clearheaded and could speak lucidly, the other was feverish and hallucinating. Only after our fever went down were we able to talk. He asked me whether he was a *musselman*. I tried to reassure him, saying he looked good to me. He was more honest. Looking me over from top to toe when they changed my iced sheet, he said, "Yesterday, you were a *musselman* for sure. Today you look better, but still not good."

On the third night, my condition became critical. This was clear from the many doctors assembled around my bed, although I could not understand a word they were saying. They gave me injections one after the other in my rear and in a vein in my arm. I had no idea what they were injecting, or what it was supposed to do. It was only days later that a Dutch nurse, Margit, told me I had been lucky: A Norwegian inmate doctor making the rounds noticed my labored breathing and irregular pulse. He saw that I was perspiring profusely and shivering; he quickly summoned the team on duty, who succeeded in pulling me through.

I felt a pleasant warmth from the sun's rays coming through the window above my head. I expected Lulek or one of his friends to come to the window, but obviously no one was allowed into the quarantined hut. Brigitte, a Danish nurse, who together with Margit was volunteering through the Red Cross, gave me my first glass of orange juice. "You're allowed to drink now. In two or three days you'll get solid food." Meanwhile she gave me news of the outside world: President Roosevelt had died ten days earlier and, more significant to me, a large concentration camp at Bergen Belsen had been liberated. The camp apparently contained many women, and I began to hope that maybe Mother was among them.

Bunim was suffering from lung complications and a persistent cough. The doctors decided to isolate him and placed him in intensive care. I remained alone among non-Jews, all much older than I. In the bed across from me lay a man in his fifties with his right arm raised, who hallucinated, repeating, "I, Hans Laman, swear to serve the city and its residents." He had been in Buchenwald since 1937, imprisoned for anti-Nazi sympathies. A member of his city council, he remained loyal to his civic duties in the last hours of his life. On the day that Bunim returned to his bed next to me, the body of Hans Laman was carried out.

Margit, the blond Dutch nurse, came over to us, her beautiful face beaming. She wanted us to know that we would shortly be receiving an important visitor. I thought that maybe they had finally relented and let Lulek in. During the previous week I had seen him every day through the window, but it had been virtually impossible to talk. As Margit moved away, three soldiers in unfamiliar uniforms came up to us. The highest ranking of the three was of medium height, with a thin mustache and gold-rimmed glasses. He did not come too near, but I could see a gilt badge with the tablets of the Ten Commandments on his lapel. "Do you speak Yiddish?" he asked. Bunim smiled at me, signaling me to answer. The officer spoke tenderly and compassionately, asking us question after question, wanting to know more about us. When I told him my name, he asked whether I was a relative of the rabbi of Piotrkow. Then he informed me, as if I didn't know, that Rabbi Meir Shapira of the Lublin Yeshiva was also a relative of mine, whom he knew personally.

"My name is Hershel Shechter. I am the chaplain of the division that liberated Buchenwald."

"Where are you from in America?" asked Bunim.

"New York. I am the rabbi of a synagogue in the Bronx." Shechter already knew of my existence from Lulek, whom he met right after liberation, but he had not been allowed to approach the typhus ward until now. He gave us a few cans of orange juice and promised to look in on us. Meanwhile, he wished us "a complete recovery and *mazal tov* (congratulations) on emerging from slavery into freedom."

Forty years later Rabbi Shechter celebrated his seventieth birthday in New York. I was unable to attend, but my wife, Joan, represented me and expressed on my behalf and on behalf of all my family our gratitude and appreciation to the first person who, after liberation, offered me encouragement and helped restore my self-confidence and faith in mankind.

One morning a Polish medical orderly named Wladek jubilantly informed me that the war was over. The date was May 8, 1945. The Allies announced the defeat of Germany and accepted the surrender of the Third Reich. Wladek was waiting for the repatriation of prisoners, and was sorry he couldn't celebrate together with his family in Kalisz. Meanwhile he continued working as an orderly, but was now getting paid by the International Red Cross and the U.S. Army. "Soon you will be well enough to join me," he remarked. I explained that I no longer had a home in Poland, and that no one was waiting for me there. He generously offered to take me to his home, where his brother and sisters would gladly accept me into the family. Thanking him, I said I would be seeking a new home elsewhere.

"I understand," he said, "You will be going to America with that officer who was here."

"I will be going to the Land of Israel, Palestine, not America."

"But that's where the Germans wanted to send you," he said. "Why go of your own accord?"

The following day Wladek suggested that I join him for a walk. Although still very weak, I enjoyed our stroll. The warm sun felt good. On the way, he told me how he had come to end up in Buchenwald two years earlier. By mistake, he found himself in what the Germans took to be a hostile demonstration. They seized him, along with others, for work in an industrial plant in Germany, sending the weak and those singled out for punishment to concentration camps.

When we got back from our walk, Lulek and Fyodor were waiting at the entrance to the hut. Lulek looked well and was dressed in clean clothes. "Fyodor wants me to go with him to Rostov," he announced. "He is returning next week and I want to go with him." I told him that I would soon be back on my feet, and would take care of both of us. I thanked Fyodor for looking after Lulek, but told him that the boy would be going with me.

"To Poland?" he asked.

"No, to the Land of Israel," I answered. He looked at me as if I had lost my mind. Afraid that while I was still hospitalized he would entice Lulek and take him along, I called for five boys I had met through Shalom Tepper, Dov Landau, and Chaim Halberstam, and asked them to keep an eye on Lulek, never to let him out of their sight. The brothers Elazar and Chanina Schiff from Hungary, Yehuda Kleinhandler, Yaacov Pozner, and David Perlman (all from Poland) became his personal bodyguards. They reported daily on Lulek's welfare.

On May 16, two days after my release from the hospital, a convoy of Red Army trucks arrived at the camp. The liberated prisoners of war and civilian captives were waiting for the arrival of this convoy, which was to take them part of the way home. They stood with suitcases and backpacks full of loot taken from nearby cities and villages that they had raided. Among them I saw Lulek carrying a small suitcase in one hand, and holding on to Fyodor with the other. "I wanted to see him off," said my brother. The suitcase was indeed one of Fyodor's, which Lulek was carrying to the bus for him.

The liberated prisoners, waiting their turn for repatriation, had markings on their sleeves identifying their nationality. We Jews were the only "unmarked and unclaimed" group.

At the end of May the veteran prisoners, mostly Germans, Austrians, Czechs, and French communists, organized a memorial meeting for those who had perished in the camp. In the center of the assembly ground stood a monument of plywood bearing the number 61,000, the number of those murdered in Buchenwald during its eight years of existence. Beneath it was a list of the nations of the victims. There was no mention of Jews. Walter Bartel, a German communist leader who was head of the camp after liberation, gave a speech about the crimes of fascism and the victory of socialism under Stalin. We stood there, a few dozen Jewish youths, feeling a deep sense of hurt. Even now that we were free, we were being denied our identity.

Shalom Tepper, born in Bialobrzeg, Poland, on May 20, 1925, had just passed his twentieth birthday. We stood together during the ceremony until he slipped away during the singing of the "Internationale." The crowd was already starting to disperse, when I saw a group of men raining blows on Shalom's head as he lay on the ground by the monument. Next to him stood a can of red paint, which he had used to paint in bold red letters JUDEN (Jews) above the list of nations, embellished with a Star of David.

In the former *SS* quarters where Lulek and I, along with all the other youngsters, were now being housed, the boys began to amass spoils that they brought back from their forays on Weimar and nearby villages. From time to time they urged me to join in. Although I could understand their behavior now that they had an opportunity to pour out their wrath on the Germans, I myself felt no need for vengeance. I knew that on the first day after liberation, crowds of prisoners attacked some *SS* sentries and beat them mercilessly. The *SS*, who until liberation had been tormenting and killing us, were now at the receiving end, pleading for their lives. No matter how natural and understandable, I could not take part in these acts. When my friends went out on their daily raids, taking whatever loot came to hand, I remained apart. My friends, Dov Landau and Chaim Halberstam, concerned about my health, brought back eggs and butter to help me regain my strength.

Every morning I went out to canvass the organizations that had set up offices in the camp – the offices of the International Red Cross, the headquarters of the U.S. army, and the Polish delegation, which had compiled a list of Poles for return to Poland. At the Red Cross I searched for some trace of Mother, in the hope that she had perhaps survived in one of the camps. I gave them all the information I had about her, but they found no hint or sign of life. The Polish government office was also unable to help me and suggested that I return to Poland and look for her there.

At the American army headquarters, I met Rabbi Marcus, a chaplain, who told me that the Buchenwald camp would soon be turned over to the Russians, and that all the Jewish youngsters would be transferred to France and Switzerland, where the Jewish organizations would look after us.

While talking to Rabbi Marcus, we were joined by a few of my friends, including Zvi Rosenbaum and Elazar Schiff, who asked the chaplain to get them a *Sefer Torah*, required for the oncoming festival of Shavuoth. He didn't have one, but we held festival services anyway. The recreation room of the *SS*, which also served as a hall for lectures and movies, was now converted into a synagogue, where hundreds of young Jews gathered for the first communal service as free men. Because none of us had prayer books, the organizers asked for men who remembered the prayers to lead the services. Although I did remember the prayers, I told them that I did not. I was unable to pray, and felt I could not represent those who truly wanted to. However, in order not to separate myself from the others, I stayed at the service, holding Lulek's hand, explaining the service to him. He had just that morning got up from his sickbed after a week-long bout of measles. We attended services on the second day of the festival as well, and sat on the side, watching the others pray and listening to the leader reciting the prayers from memory, verse by verse. It was a strange scene. Here I was sitting in the room of *SS* murderers, observing hundreds of young Jews who had just been saved from death, praying with intense fervor and emotion, while I looked on with detachment, alternately angry and apathetic.

On Shavuoth we were still in the SS quarters. It was a good time to think about the future. I knew that in a matter of days we would be leaving this place to start life anew elsewhere. No one knew what lay ahead, not even what to ask for. I wanted to leave this accursed place, but I did not know where to go. I was aware that I was fully responsible for my small brother's life, as well as my own, and I was determined to carry out my responsibility. However, instead of concentrating on survival and remaining together, I would now have to direct my efforts for the two of us to rehabilitate ourselves as quickly as possible to our new life.

The uncertainty of Mother's fate was a source of deep concern. I thought that since many of the liberated prisoners would be passing through Buchenwald, I might be able to get some information by questioning them. Every convoy or vehicle that arrived at our camp with liberated prisoners from other camps kindled anew the hope that we might still find her. By the time we were to leave for France in June, I had almost despaired of finding her alive.

We left Buchenwald on June 2. A passenger train with second-class cars waited for us at the station. Rabbi Marcus, some American officers, and representatives of the International Red Cross escorted us through the main gate of the camp onto the train, so different from the cattle wagons we had come to know only too well. We were each given a bag with food and sweets. I noticed that while Lulek and I were carrying little more than these small bags, the others were loaded down with suitcases, backpacks, and parcels containing loot they had accumulated in the weeks following liberation. We were both wearing civilian clothing from the *SS* hospital, but neither of us had a change of clothes. Lulek was one of the smaller boys who had been given the military uniforms of the *Hitler Jugend* (Hitler youth), since nothing else was available in his size. When the others saw us devoid of all possessions, they tried to come up with a shirt and a suit for each of us. The only thing I consented to accept from one of my friends was a bolt of green-gray cloth, which four months later became my first suit – made by a Petach Tikva tailor. When I first wore the suit, it reminded my friends of the dress uniforms of the *SS* officers.

The merry shouting of the youths when the train pulled out of the station was like the beating of hammers on my head. I found a seat near a window. Lulek sat next to me, happy and carefree at the prospect of this new adventure. A deep gloom settled over me. Leaving this place, this country, its inhabitants and surroundings, brought to mind the harrowing experiences and scenes I had pushed aside; as in a horror film, I saw gallows, corpses, my family being torn from me. I knew we were traveling to an unknown country, but I had no idea how long this journey would take, how we would reach our destination, and how we would start to rebuild our lives without our parents, and without the knowledge of the language of our new country.

At one of the station stops, my thoughts were interrupted by a group of American soldiers standing on the platform. Noticing the placard on one of the train doors: "Children of Buchenwald Coming Home," written in English and French, some of them got on the train and started talking to us. Lulek was sitting next to me, nibbling on an apple. One of the soldiers asked him in Yiddish what he would most like right now. Lulek did not hesitate. Pointing to the soldier's rifle, he said he wanted the gun to kill German murderers. The soldier exchanged glances with his friends and got off the train. A few minutes later he returned, carrying a small rifle with the firing mechanism removed. "Kill as many as you can," he said, giving Lulek the gun. Lulek shouldered the rifle and wouldn't part with it until we reached Eretz Yisrael.

The journey was long and tiring. The train stopped frequently. At every stop our fellow passengers invaded the orchards along the track and came back laden with fruit, including whole branches of cherries and plums. Just before we got to the German-French border, Rabbi Marcus explained that we were about to enter a friendly country that had been captured by the Nazis, and that we should behave properly. From that point on, we sat quietly in our seats until the train reached Towenville, near Strasbourg. Some of the boys noticed German prisoners of war working near the train, supervised by French soldiers. The boys jumped out of the doors and windows, rushed toward the astonished Germans, grabbed their shovels, and began beating them. The French soldiers standing by smiled at the unanticipated entertainment.

14

RECUPERATION IN FRANCE

Two days' travel brought us to an enchanting village in Normandy, in northwest France. An impressive delegation was waiting for us at the station: the mayors of the nearby towns and villages; the leadership of O.S.E., the organization for the welfare of Jewish children, headed by Dr. Minkovski; and a man in a French military uniform, Captain Rosen. They took us in a convoy of buses to a convalescent home, consisting of a "chateau" used previously as the palatial home of one of the local gentry, surrounded by several small buildings. The location, near the village of Ecouis, was charming. The rooms were large and sunny. The bedrooms, equipped with pillows and sheets, were luxuries that we had long since forgotten.

Almost the entire staff spoke French exclusively. Only a few knew a little German or Yiddish, but their warmth made up for the lack of a common language. They quickly learned to understand our needs, and we learned to appreciate their devotion and goodwill.

The first two days in this delightful place were given over to medical tests. A radiologist discovered signs of damage to my right lung, which he attributed to the typhus in Buchenwald. He recommended that I be reexamined and maybe hospitalized for a few weeks in a special hospital. His proposal did not fit in with my plans to leave for Palestine at the earliest opportunity, so I took responsibility for my health into my own hands, hoping that the traces of the disease would vanish on their own, without need for lengthy hospitalization in France.

During the second week, we were visited by a delegation of O.S.E. who, with UNRRA, were our hosts in Ecouis. The eminent head of the delegation spoke to us with great warmth, choking back tears, extending the welcoming arms of French Jewry, hoping we would decide to stay in France. We sat round him in a circle on the lawn. Next to him stood a short woman, Rachel Mintz, who translated his words into fluent Yiddish. She was like the proverbial Jewish mother, looking after us day and night. She was a good listener, offering advice only when asked. She encouraged us to write our life stories and experiences, and organized a wall-newspaper where many exhibited their first literary attempts. One member of our group eventually achieved world fame as well as the Nobel Prize for his books on the Holocaust – Elie Wiesel.

Rachel made a list of those interested in settling and studying in France, with the help of scholarships from local Jewish organizations. Only a few responded. Most of us wanted to go to Eretz Yisrael, even though O.S.E. tried to influence us to remain in France.

"Life there is hard. Jews are fighting both the Arabs and the British. After what you've been through, you are better off staying here or emigrating to America, countries with better opportunities to develop your talents," Rachel Mintz advised us.

Such advice, plus our own ambivalence, led to mental anguish and arguments among us. Some spoke of emigrating to remote countries where there would be no Jews. "If it is decreed that European Jewry must vanish, then who am I to contest the decree?" argued Mark forcefully. He came from a traditional family but spoke harshly and insolently of anything that resembled religion or tradition. A few supported his rebellious attitude and discussed a list of acceptable and receptive countries. When it was pointed out that they were not likely to find a suitable country without any Jews, they extended the list to include remote islands in the Indian Ocean. Others considered the feasibility of going to established communities in Western Europe or North America.

Those who felt that they had a legitimate complaint against Heaven, considered assimilation and flight from the Jewish people. Here in the calmness of the Normandy landscape, we did not have to worry about shelter, food, clothes, studies, or employment, and vociferously debated the proposals and counterproposals. There were times when I thought that a large majority would be induced to assimilate, but as the moment of truth approached, when we had to make a choice, a very large majority turned to the camp of the Zionists, determined to find a way to Eretz Yisrael. Our slogan, "We will not help Hitler complete the job," caught on. It influenced many in their decision for *Aliyah Artza* (going up to The Land – emigration to Israel). For me it was also a reason not to abandon the framework of religious observances, which had all but vanished over these last years.

One day Rachel invited me to her room and tried to convince me to stay on in France with Lulek. She knew about my daily efforts to find traces of Mother. She had written letters for me in French to the International Red Cross, asking them for help. She argued that there was a greater chance of finding Mother in France than in a land cut off from Europe. I found out later that she already knew Mother was no longer among the living at the time she used this argument.

One sunlit morning I was strolling alone in the grounds of the castle, making changes on a draft of a Yiddish essay, "Between Life and Death," which I was writing at Rachel's request. It related more to my current speculations about the future than to the past. As I walked along the edge of an orchard, Lulek ran after me bearing an envelope with my name on it, in Hebrew. I had expected to learn of Mother's fate from official Red Cross or Polish government letters. I could not imagine what this Hebrew-written envelope contained. What I found was a brief note written in Hebrew: "You must say *Kaddish* because your Mother is not among the living. She died at Ravensbrueck." I could not identify the anonymous handwriting, but I felt that it was the bitter truth. Lulek looked at me anxiously.

"What happened?"

The pallor of my face was answer enough.

Again he asked, "What happened?"

I told him: "From now on we have no mother either."

He burst into tears and fell into my arms.

Lulek could not identify the boy who had given him the envelope. When we returned to the main building, a few friends who had already heard the news were waiting for us, offering to make up the necessary ten men of a *minyan*, so I could say *Kaddish* for our parents and our brother Milek. This was the first time that I had recited prayers in a public service. Lulek stood close by me, pressing his entire body to me, while continuing to cry ceaselessly. He did not know the Hebrew alphabet. As I taught him the first words of *Kaddish*, he learned the Hebrew letters.

Forty-five years later, at the wedding of one of Lulek's daughters in Tel Aviv, after the ceremony, Moshe Pszygorski – my friend from Piotrkow who shared my fate in Czestochowa, then Buchenwald, Ecouis, and finally Israel – told me that he had been the one who gave the envelope to Lulek, without knowing its contents. He received it from Arye Eizner who, after surviving Buchenwald, had gone in search of his wife and found that she and Mother had been on the same transport to Ravensbrueck, where they both perished about two months before liberation. In Paris, on his way to Eretz Yisrael, Arye heard about the "Buchenwald children" at Ecouis. He came and met some of our friends but avoided me, giving Moshe the envelope with the message about Mother. Moshe and I were on the same ship to Israel but he never mentioned his part in delivering the message, neither on-board ship nor during the thirty years of his life in Tel Aviv, a period during which we often met.

I still had not accepted the death of Father and my brother Milek, who perished in Treblinka in October 1942. Now the news about Mother's death, and the mandatory requirement to recite *Kaddish* three times a day for Mother, Father, and Milek encouraged me to accept this and other *mitzvoth* even though my faith was shaken.

Deep down my heart was torn by all I had experienced. It was hard to come to terms with all that happened to me. As an eighteen year old, with my religious and educational background and upbringing, there was only one "Address" to which I could turn with questions and complaints. My conflict with that Address first expressed itself in throwing off the daily religious observances, but only for a short time, a time of upheaval and trauma. I soon realized that my basic education from home had implanted in me the value of religious observances so deeply that I could not be without them. I felt the need for the daily rituals: putting on *tefillin*, keeping the Sabbath and festivals, avoiding nonkosher food, and the like. These had a stronger influence on me than any challenge to my faith.

Day and night at Ecouis, I tried to remove the obstacles to a Jewish way of life. At times I had visions of Father, particularly of our last conversation. I remembered his trenchant words about the destiny of the persecuted Jewish people, and the wrong we were doing to ourselves. I remembered his exhortation, though I did not understand it as such at the time, when we parted on that last night before the deportation on October 13, 1942. Now I saw his words as an obligation to follow the road that he and his forefathers had traveled for dozens of generations. Now I also remembered the verse he quoted from Jeremiah on that last night, "Thy children shall return to their own border." That was the message he had wanted to convey to me.

Now I was at a crossroads, facing the temptation of staying in an established community like France or settling in the U.S. It seemed a tempting opportunity to compensate for generations of suffering. Although he did not say so explicitly, I deduced from Father's words that he was referring to our reluctance to emigrate to Eretz Yisrael, choosing the comforts of the Diaspora instead.

My sense of obligation to preserve the family heritage, and the need to maintain a Jewish way of life, gradually strengthened my observance.

In our third week at Ecouis, the O.S.E. leaders continued to deluge us with promises, enticing us to choose our future in France. Among the leaders were Captain Rosen, Dr. Minkovski, and Mr. Gurevitz, who visited us frequently. One day we were told that Mr. Nachum Chanin, a leader of the Arbeiter Ring, the Socialist Movement in New York, was about to visit us. We were seated in a circle on the lawn; all was quiet as the distinguished visitor stood in our midst and, looking around him, burst into tears. Collecting himself, he began speaking in Yiddish, begging our forgiveness for the fact that the Jewish people in the Free World had failed their brothers in the hour of need. We sat withdrawn, unmoved by his emotional plea. He stretched out his arms to give us his blessing, inviting us to come to the great community of Jews of the United States, who wished to absorb us in their midst.

Apart from a few who wiped their eyes, we sat in silence, without reaction. Suddenly Aharon Feldberg, who at twenty-two was one of the oldest among us, stood up and, in quite good Hebrew, expressed the wish of the survivors to go to Eretz Yisrael. Switching to Yiddish, he thanked our visitor for his warm words, not sparing him a little dig by commenting that unfortunately the outstretched arms came too late.

The following day I went to Paris with two friends, to seek a link with Eretz Yisrael. Local Jews directed us to Ruth Kluger (Eliav), an emissary of the Jewish Agency for Palestine. She knew nothing of the five hundred youths, survivors of concentration camps, only fifty miles from Paris. We told her we wanted to emigrate to Eretz Yisrael as soon as possible. "How many?" she asked. "All of us," we answered. She promised to come to Ecouis as soon as possible to make the necessary arrangements. Meanwhile, she gave us sweets and money for the train fare back, so we would not have to hitchhike. Three days later, she came with Marc Yarbloom, a leader of the French Zionist Movement, to meet us. They received a cold and even hostile reception from the staff of O.S.E., who were unhappy at this trespass of the Zionists. But we already had our list of three hundred sixty-five candidates for aliyah, out of the total of four hundred eighty-six.. They took the list and promised to stay in touch. A week later we were told that the first one hundred and fifty youngsters could leave early in July, and the others a month later. The only condition was that we be under eighteen, to qualify within the framework of Youth Aliyah. The British were respecting the youth quotas, unused since 1939, under the White-Paper policy that restricted Jewish immigration. The older ones among us adjusted our dates of birth to 1928. The youngest of all was Lulek, born in 1937.

15

LEAVING EUROPE

Early in the morning on July 3, tourist buses arrived at the gates of Ecouis, each escorted by a representative from the Jewish Agency. Saying good-bye to our friends was painful; many of us cried our first tears in years. It was only after we had traveled quite some distance from Ecouis that we felt able to smile again.

We reached Paris at about noon and toured the city for several hours. Toward evening we arrived at the Lutezia Hotel, where a great many Jews, including some survivors, were waiting for us. The arrival of one hundred fifty survivors of Buchenwald, mostly from Poland and Hungary, created a stir in the Jewish community. Many came in the hope of hearing news of relatives and friends, and some just to see and even touch us. To those who had lost family at the hands of the Nazis we were a living miracle. The affection and concern showered upon us continued throughout the following day, when men and women brought us small gifts and food for the journey to Eretz Yisrael. Some admired our decision to start a new life in the Jewish homeland; others were worried about us, concerned that we were heading for new dangers.

At the Gare de Lyon station in Paris, over three hundred Jews came to see us off, the "Buchenwald orphans," as they called us. People hugged and kissed us, wishing us well in our new life. At dusk the train pulled out. One by one, we dropped into our seats and fell asleep, overcome by fatigue, which had been building up during the thirty hours since we left Ecouis.

Travel was slow in postwar France, so that it was only at about noon the following day that the train arrived in Lyon. We stepped onto the platform and found ourselves surrounded by a crowd of Jews asking for news of relatives and friends we may have encountered during our wanderings.

A German-speaking man in his thirties asked Lulek where he was from. Hearing that he was from Piotrkow, he mentioned that relatives of the chief rabbi of Piotrkow were living in Lyon. "Who?" I asked. "The Shapiras," he replied. I told him that the chief rabbi of Piotrkow had been our father, and that Rabbi Meir Shapira, his cousin, had preceded him. "I knew them both," said the man, who introduced himself as Marc Breuer. He drove us to the home of Rabbi Shapira's nephew, Dov Shapira, but no one was in. We could not wait, and returned to the station. I thanked Mr. Breuer, who promised to tell the Shapira family of our visit and that we were well and on our way to Eretz Yisrael. Twenty years later we met again, when I learned that he and my wife were first cousins. His mother and my mother-in-law were sisters; his father was Rabbi Yosef Breuer of Frankfurt, later of Washington Heights, New York.

After another night on the train we arrived in Marseilles. Here we were taken to a former army camp next to the port, where we waited for a ship to take us to Palestine. In the camp we found French and Belgian families, including liberated prisoners of war, waiting their turn to embark. We spent nearly a week in these improvised quarters, waiting for a ship. Meanwhile we had many visitors, including Hillel Seidman, the author and journalist, who circulated among us, asking our names. When he heard my name, he stepped back in surprise. "You're the son of Rabbi Lau from Piotrkow?" he asked. "You probably don't remember me, but we met before the war."

I did remember him. In 1938, when I was twelve, I accompanied Father on a trip to Warsaw, where he often traveled on congregational business. This trip was in order to attend a meeting of the national leadership of Agudat Yisrael, an ultrareligious political party, to discuss whether its supporters should play an active role in settling Eretz Yisrael. The anti-Zionists opposed settlement on Jewish National Fund land because it implied acceptance of Zionist funding. Father, one of the leaders of Poalei Agudat Yisrael, the counterpart of Agudat Yisrael, was in favor of settlement of Eretz Yisrael, one of the few rabbis who was. This meeting was likely to decide the fate of the program for or against settlement of Eretz Yisrael by Poalei Agudat

Yisrael, which would not openly oppose a decision of the senior Agudat Yisrael. Father came to lend his support in favor of settlement.

Our first stop in Warsaw was the Agudat Yisrael offices at 1 Zamenhoff Street. We were staying in a nearby Jewish guest house on Gesia Street, opposite the Jewish cemetery, which I could see from the window of my room. Even as a youngster I was interested in politics and I very much wanted to go along to the meeting. Father tried to convince me that the debate would bore me, and that I would be better off visiting friends who had children my own age, but I was adamant and he finally agreed. I listened to the first part of the debate with great interest. Among the speakers were Alexander Zusia Friedman from Warsaw; Yosef Moshe Haber from Kalisz; Leibl Mintzberg from Lodz, a member of the Sejm, the Polish parliament; Yaacov Trokenheim, a Jewish senator of Warsaw; and Dr. Hillel Seidman from Lwow, secretary of the executive. However, Father was right and I soon fell asleep. I awoke feeling a hand on my head. It was Dr. Seidman, who took me by the hand and led me into his office next door.

Now he was standing before me, in Marseilles, holding a small package, which he asked me to deliver to Yosef Heftman, editor of the Tel Aviv daily *Haboker.* "It's my diary of the Warsaw Ghetto," he said. "*Haboker*, which I represent here in France, will publish it in the original Hebrew, the language in which it was written in Warsaw and in Camp Vitell in France." Three weeks later the diary reached the editor of *Haboker*, in which it appeared a few months later as "Warsaw Ghetto Diary," the first published record of life in the Warsaw Ghetto before 1943. Dr. Seidman, who came to us as a reporter, wired Tel Aviv about the impending arrival of the "Buchenwald children," among them the Lau brothers, sons of the last rabbi of Piotrkow.

The Jewish Agency staff at the Marseilles camp took good care of us. One day one of the staff members with whom I had become friendly came over to me and ran his palm over my face. "I didn't know you were so observant that you don't shave during the Three Weeks," he joked, referring to the period of mourning before Tisha B'Av, which commemorates the destruction of the Temple, during which the strictly orthodox do not shave or cut their hair. I touched my face and found, to my surprise, that whiskers had started to grow. That day I managed to borrow a shaver and enjoyed the novelty of shaving for the first time.

The neighboring huts housed families from Alsace and Belgium, also awaiting their turn for *aliyah*. Among them were the Zilberstroms, who had several children, some around Lulek's age. I hoped that he would make friends, but while the other children played together, he stood by and did not join in.

Elsewhere in the camp Zionist youth movements, including the religious Bnei Akiva, the right-wing Betar, and the left-wing Hashomer Hatzair, were involved in their social activities. They sang and danced, encouraged by their Hebrew-speaking counselors. They tried to include the Buchenwald group, but most of us just watched from the sidelines. The Jewish Agency kept promising that the ship would come "tomorrow."

On July 7, "tomorrow" finally arrived. The ship was a scrapped French boat that had served as a troopship and supply vessel in the navy during World War II. It had now been fitted out to make short runs between France and North Africa, and was to take us as far as Genoa, Italy.

Our embarkation was chaotic. We ran down to appropriate for ourselves places close to friends in the long rooms in the lowest deck, then came back up on deck to watch the ship being readied for the voyage. It was the first time at sea for all of us, and we were fascinated by the noise and bustle of the sailors and porters. I found a spot next to the railing on the top deck, which afforded me an excellent view of all the action.

I stood there for some time, musing about the future and about Lulek. The waves broke against the bow and seagulls circled overhead, cawing shrilly. A queasy sensation I had never experienced before overcame me. Even before the ship weighed anchor, I discovered the meaning of seasickness. I found a water faucet on deck, rinsed my mouth, and wiped my face. I returned to my lookout by the railing, knowing that Lulek was being looked after by friends.

At twilight the ship weighed anchor and slowly began to slide through the waters of Marseilles Harbor. The rocky cliffs above the shore slipped back, the color of their shading changing from moment to moment as the rays of the setting sun gradually disappeared and the cliffs melted into a grayish haze. On the horizon I saw a rainbow, which seemed to rise up from the water, its bow vanishing among the clouds. I was reminded of the story of Noah, who came out of the ark after the flood receded. God promised him that He would never destroy the world again, and brought forth a rainbow as a sign of the covenant between them. I felt like Noah or one of his sons, having survived the modern deluge, with the rainbow appearing as a guarantee that there would be no repeat of the engulfing flood.

I was aware of the permanence of this departure, of the fact that I was leaving for good the continent in which I, along with countless generations of my family before me, was born. It was in Europe that I experienced the happiness of childhood, but now I saw it as a charred forest in which everything that had once been so dear to me had been destroyed.

Standing there alone in the growing darkness, leaning on the railing, the floodgates of memory opened. All that had accumulated in me during those years of torment and dehumanization now began to drain away as my tears flowed into the waters of Marseilles Harbor. Gazing at the foaming wake on both sides of the stern, I relived scenes that had taken place during the preceding five years. Even worse were the scenes I imagined.

I recalled the story of Dudek Levkowitz, who had escaped from Treblinka and told me of Father's last moments at the entrance to the gas chamber. I tried to imagine how his life ended. Was he with my brother Milek? What was he thinking? For years he had been writing about the test of a Jew facing martyrdom. How did he face his own test? Did he remain resolute in his faith? And what of Milek, aged only thirteen? Was he alone when he breathed his last, or was Father with him, holding him tight? And how did Mother's life end? She was such a beautiful and aesthetic woman, such a caring and devoted mother, so learned yet so gentle. I could not come to terms with the thought that she died of hunger, disease, and beatings, like so many others I had seen in Buchenwald. Was she also dragged out of her block and dumped on a pile of other bodies? Was her body thrown onto a cart and pushed to the crematorium?

Who was left? Only Lulek and I. Lulek, at the age of eight, had not yet tasted life and would already have to fend for himself. Would I be able to measure up to my responsibility for him? Of my own future I was not yet ready to think.

I hoped that other family members also survived. I knew that during the war my half brother, Shiko, had been living with his uncles,

Rabbi Eliezer, Rabbi Chaim Meir, and Rabbi Baruch Hager. I hoped that he had been saved, together with the Hager family.

Leaning on the railing of the ship, I parted from the continent of Europe in the name of my whole family. Our footprints were imprinted all over the continent – north, south, east, and west. On my mother's side, distinguished rabbis had led communities in Germany and France in the eleventh century. From there they migrated to Poland and Russia. On Father's side, eminent rabbis had served as spiritual leaders since the sixteenth century in the Ukraine, Russia, and Poland. All that remained of their descendants was ashes scattered around the crematoria. At that moment I was not thinking of the rich cultural heritage that they bequeathed to the Jewish people, a treasure for future generations. It was very late when I finally went down to my berth on the lowest deck, where Lulek was fast asleep.

We docked at Genoa the following afternoon, and disembarked for a two-hour tour of the town. By the time we returned to the port, the *Mataroa* was waiting to take us to Haifa. Our group was now augmented by other immigrant families, and by a few Jews from Palestine who had been stranded in Europe during the war. Among them was a pleasant man dressed in khaki, who introduced himself as Hillel Brokental, not mentioning that he was in fact the rabbi of Kibbutz Hafetz Haim. Many of us gathered around him to listen to his stories about life in Palestine.

A group of religious boys and girls from France, belonging to Brith Halutzim Datiyim, joined in Israeli-style group singing. Some of the Hungarian youngsters from Buchenwald protested strongly against mixed socializing and singing, and a real fight was just barely averted. Strife also broke out because the Hungarians would not eat the food, which, by their standards, was not kosher. Tension grew, and even Rabbi Brokental's authority was insufficient to reassure them. They dismissed him as a "Zionist pioneer" and sneered at his casual dress. On Shabbat we held a prayer service at which Rabbi Brokental gave a sermon. The Hungarians refused to join and organized their own service. This divisiveness, scarcely three months after liberation from our common hell, placed a pall over the atmosphere.

On the last night of the voyage we were told that by early morning we would be able to see the shores of Eretz Yisrael. That last night on board I did not close my eyes. I felt that a new chapter in my life was about to open. I tried to think about future plans for Lulek and myself in this new land, but the more I thought of the future, the heavier the cloud of the past hung over me. I clung to the hope that someone from my family might have survived. We were saying *Kaddish* every day for Mother, Father, and Milek, but there was still a corner in my heart that believed that at least one of them was still alive, and perhaps all three. I tossed and turned on my berth, with thoughts of the past and plans for the future. The eagerly anticipated arrival in this new Land aroused great excitement, tempered with anxiety.

All the years, like a puppet, I survived by subservience, following orders, reacting rather than initiating, never needing to plan ahead. I was daunted by the inevitable struggles and challenges in making my way in a new place, relying on my own initiative. I was keenly aware that these last years had robbed me of a proper education and of the natural passage from youth to adulthood. I doubted whether I could recharge my run-down batteries, drained by the daily struggle to stay alive.

Brokental described to us something of the new Jew growing up in Eretz Yisrael, the liberated Jew working his own land, master of his own destiny, confronting and overcoming all challenges. His enthusiastic description of the sabra, the Jew born in independence, aroused both curiosity and trepidation. I too wanted to escape from the image of the Jew that I had encountered over the last five years. Yet I was somewhat intimidated by this picture of boys and girls born in Eretz Yisrael, contemptuous of the Diaspora heritage, proud and confident of the model they were creating. Brokental's description of the hostile environment within which the new Jews were rebuilding their country made me wonder about the exaggerated self-assurance of these sabras. Apart from thoughts about my own personal future, I was worried about my ability to help Lulek through his first steps to a new life. That night my mind wandered in many directions, each one leading to a question mark.

At first light we heard joyous voices from the top deck, shouting the news that Mount Carmel was coming into view on the eastern horizon. Within minutes all the passengers were on deck, staring in that direction. The rising sun soon blinded us, but it was still possible to make out the majestic shape of the Carmel Mountain ridge, growing ever larger as we approached.

In the morning hours of July 15, the *Mataroa* glided through the waters at the entrance to Haifa Harbor. Hundreds of seagulls escorted us on the last stage of the voyage, their raucous cries lending a festive mood to the occasion. By eight o'clock the ship docked in the quay, where a huge sign, "WELCOME TO THE GATES OF THE LAND," greeted us in Hebrew. Beneath the sign stood some Jewish Agency officials, journalists, policemen, British soldiers, and throngs of curious Jews.

I stood, glued to the deck rail, watching the turmoil on the quay. Arab porters wearing baggy pants with a sack hanging down their front aroused my curiosity. A Jewish official who came on board was promptly besieged with questions about this phenomenon. He explained: "They are devout Moslems who believe that the Messiah will be born to a man. To be ready for the occasion, every self-respecting Moslem male wears a sack to provide room for him."

From my lookout point on deck, I could see the nearest street in the lower city. Above each of the various stores were signs written in Hebrew. Those with sharp eyesight could make out the word "Egged," spelled in Hebrew, on the front of the buses.

Before disembarking, we were told that we were not yet free to go our own way. We were led to a fenced-in area guarded by British troops, surrounded by officials and journalists.

Two Jewish reporters circulated among us, asking questions. Answering in Yiddish, one of the boys said, "I am the only survivor of my family."

"What happened to them?" asked one of the reporters.

"They were all murdered," came the reply.

"He must be exaggerating," said the reporter to his colleague, in Polish.

"Yes, I think they make up these horror stories," agreed the colleague.

Overhearing this exchange, I said to them in Polish, "It's your luck that you were here and not there." They were embarrassed and suddenly began to show an interest in what had actually happened. I was reserved and in no mood to enlighten them. In later years I often met both reporters, one of whom was a colleague in the same city room of the paper where I worked. They remembered the quayside incident in Haifa, and always seemed embarrassed to see me.

Lulek stood next to me, his small rifle on his shoulder. Someone had attached a flag with the word BUCHENWALD to it. His picture was taken by three or four photographers and appeared in several newspapers the following day.

The sight of the many guards and British soldiers violated our sense of freedom. Then someone noticed the cattle wagons on the train siding and remarked how similar they were to the Nazi cattle wagons we knew so well. It never entered my mind that they were waiting there for us, until the police and British soldiers escorted us to them and ordered us to get on. My heart sank. We were not yet free.

Some of the welcoming committee climbed onto the cattle wagons, joining us as a sign of solidarity. These included Yaacov Katz, deputy mayor of Haifa and later a member of the Knesset, and Hans Beit, head of Youth Aliyah.

We set off and, after about a half hour, arrived at the British detention camp in Atlit, south of Haifa, after about half an hour. Once again we were imprisoned in a camp surrounded by barbed wire. The British kept their distance, perhaps out of consideration for our feelings. Our contacts were with the Jewish staff recruited from nearby towns, kibbutzim, and moshavim, who ran the camp and looked after our needs.

As Lulek and I walked toward the hut assigned to us, a voice called out: "Lau, Lau. Where are the Lau brothers?" I walked over and introduced myself to the man, who was wearing a chef's apron. "My name is Kisman," he said. "I'm a friend of your brother Shiko. He's standing on the other side of the fence and wants to see you." He said that he had met Shiko on a ship about a year earlier. My head spinning, I went into our hut, put down my small backpack on a free bed and, taking Lulek by the hand, followed Kisman to the fence.

I told Lulek that we may have found a brother. Until that moment he knew nothing about Shiko's existence. The last time I had seen Shiko was twelve years earlier, when he left with Father to celebrate his bar mitzvah at the home of his grandfather, Rabbi Yisrael Hager, rabbi of Wizhnitz. Now I was about to see him again, though I knew that the news I had for him would not bring him joy.

Hundreds of people were standing on the other side of the fence, looking for relatives. People were shouting back and forth across the barbed wire. While still about a hundred feet away, I heard someone call "Tulek." Only Shiko could have known my childhood nickname. I turned and saw him, waving a gray cap. I went over to the fence and looked at him closely. I would never have recognized him. Lulek and Shiko merely stared at each other, while Shiko and I shook hands heartily through the fence. Lulek refused to stick his arm through the barbed wire. Shiko said that he recognized me immediately. As far as I remember, this was the only reunion between long-separated brothers on opposite sides of that fence, and even the British guards were moved. A British officer, accompanied by a Jewish policeman, guided us to the gate and invited Shiko into the camp. We hugged each other, under the curious eyes of the British guards. Shiko's only questions to me were about our journey. It was as if, for the moment, a thick line had been drawn across our past. It was only when we parted, after the few minutes together that we had been allowed, that I saw the tears streaming down Shiko's face.

We returned to our places on opposite sides of the fence and continued to talk. Shiko told us about his life in Kibbutz Kfar Etzion, in the Jerusalem hills, which he had joined a few months after arriving in Palestine the previous year. He described the social life of the kibbutz, and his work in clearing rocks and preparing new ground for grapevines and fruit trees. He hoped that I would join him there, and urged Kisman and another religious kibbutznik to help convince me. They did their best, but I was not ready to make any decisions about either my future or Lulek's.

16

DETAINED IN ATLIT

We returned to our hut, drained from the oppressive mid-July heat. Some of the lads were standing by the faucets, splashing themselves with the water from the exposed pipes. There was no shade to be found, no tree, no shrub. Inside the huts it was suffocating. Only the dining hall, synagogue, and clubhouse had a few noisy fans slowly circulating the hot air.

The exhilaration that I had felt on April 11, the day of liberation, vanished the moment I set foot in Haifa and saw the cattle train, so familiar from "over there," that was to take us to the British detention camp in Atlit. The conditions within the camp did nothing to allay my growing dejection.

In contrast to the personal care from the Ecouis staff at the O.S.E convalescent home in France, here we encountered a matter-of-fact, no-nonsense approach, without any trace of tenderness or empathy. We slept on field cots, meals were served impersonally, instructions given in crisp, almost military style, and our questions answered in terse responses – all reminiscent of the life we had been trying to blot out from our memory.

The dominant language around us was Hebrew. The staff was polite, but the austerity and bleakness around us underscored the reality of our new world. Somehow I felt none of the joy of the "homecoming" I had so long anticipated. I sometimes thought how different things would have been had I come under different circumstances, with my parents, family, and friends. I remembered how we had talked about going to Eretz Yisrael as if it were just another neighborhood.

The day after our arrival in Atlit, I was called to the camp office. At the door stood a middle-aged man, wearing a white straw hat. He looked familiar, but I could not quite place him. He ran toward me, hugged me, and with tears in his eyes kept saying again and again, "They didn't believe me. They didn't believe me . . . Some still don't." It was Yaacov Kurtz, who had lived in Tel Aviv before the war, came to Europe, and then got stranded in the Piotrkow ghetto at the outbreak of war. I had last seen him in October 1942, in a courtyard in the Little Ghetto. One of the lucky few to be traded for Germans held by the British, he left for Vienna and went on to Palestine. He spoke about what he had witnessed, and published *The Book of Evidence*, the earliest report of its kind. No one believed him. Now, he was coming to me for corroboration of his story.

Adding to our sense of gloom was the timing of Tisha B'Av (Ninth of Av), the saddest day in the Jewish calendar, commemorating the destruction of the First and Second Temples. No one suggested that we observe it in the traditional way – by fasting, praying, and reciting the book of *Lamentations*. Nevertheless, as evening fell most of the immigrants and the Jewish staff spontaneously headed for the overcrowded camp synagogue. As is customary on that day, we sat on the floor of the synagogue or on the ground outside, and listened to the mournful chanting of *Lamentations*. At the end of the service we returned directly to our huts. Even those who did not intend to fast passed the dining hall without a glance.

I felt the need for some sort of religious observance, some salve for the scars from a more recent destruction, the one in our own generation. I found nothing in mourning for a Temple that was no more. I could only mourn for a humanity that was no more. Before Auschwitz, Buchenwald, Treblinka, I too could grieve over the ruins of the past, two thousand years ago. Now my past was too recent, too raw. I could not grieve over a Temple destroyed; I could only grieve over a people dismembered – my people.

The next day we were lined up by the hut that housed the Jewish Agency offices to be interviewed by representatives of the settlement organizations. Every organization was affiliated with a political party that wanted its share of the new immigrant youth. Staff members with whom I had become friendly explained the procedure, but I still could not understand the political rivalry generated by our presence. Party

The historic meeting of Israeli Prime Minister Menachem Begin
and the President of Egypt, Anwar Sadat in Jerusalem, 1977

The first Israeli-Egyptian-American round table negotiation
for peace. The author participated in the Israeli delegation

Chairing a meeting of the Conference of Presidents of Major Jewish Organizations in America with Prime Minister Shimon Peres, 1984

With Secretary of State, Cyrus Vance, and Executive Editor of the New York Times, Max Frankel

At the White House with President Jimmy Carter. From right;
National Security Advisor, Prof. Zbigniew Brzezinski,
Secretary of State, Cyrus Vance, The President, Moshe Dayan,
the author Naphtali Lau-Lavie and Ambassador Simcha Dinitz

Joan and Naphtali Lau-Lavie at a reception in New York
with Vice-President, George Bush, 1984

With the late Yitzhak Rabin at the author's home, 1983

With Shimon Peres, 1986

Hanukkah candle lighting
with actress Elizabeth Taylor
at her suite in New York, 1982

Hanukkah candle lighting with mayor of New York,
Edward I. Koch, at city Hall

Reunion with Rabbi Hershl Schaechter, chaplain of the U.S.
armed forces who liberated Buchenwald, at a ceremony
of Yeshiva University in New York, where the author was honored
with a doctoral degree, 1985

Being honored with a Doctor Honoris Causa degree by Bar Ilan
University at a ceremony in the Pierre Hotel in New York, 1984

At the Israel Parade on Fifth Avenue in New York, 1985

Fixing the first "mezuza" at the gate of the
newly opened Israeli Embassy in Cairo, 1979

With Prime Minister Menachem Begin and Foreign Minister
Moshe Dayan during the peace negotiations with Egypt, 1978

With Prof. Henry Kisinger, Prime Minister Rabin
and Mayor of Tel Aviv, Shlomo Lahat, 1974

representatives circulated among us on the camp grounds, seeking recruits. I was reminded of the advice of Hillel Brokental, whom we had met on the ship, not to let others make decisions for us.

In the Agency office, we were faced by a group of officious individuals sitting behind a long table. Hans Beit, head of the Jewish Agency's Youth Aliyah Department, spoke German rather than the Yiddish used by most of the staff. He questioned us extensively about our background, family, education, and asked if we had any relatives or friends in Palestine who would be willing and able to help us.

On either side of him sat the representatives of the different political parties and settlement organizations. They included kibbutzniks whose deeply lined faces and khaki clothes suggested that they were down-to-earth, hard-working people. Two of the representatives stood out from the rest: Rabbi Shimshon Rosenthal, with a bushy beard and large *kippa*, represented the Mizrahi Workers Party and the Religious Kibbutz Movement; David Bernholc (later Bar Nahor), with a dapper mustache and small *kippa*, represented Poalei Agudat Yisrael. Judging from his appearance alone, Rosenthal seemed closer to my parents' religious affiliation. Bernholc gave me the feeling, especially after hearing him tell the others that our father was Rabbi Moshe Chaim Lau of Piotrkow, a leader of Poalei Agudat Yisrael, that he was ready to appropriate for himself the role of mentor for Lulek and me.

While Hans Beit was questioning me about family and background, Bernholc kept interrupting, in an obvious attempt to sidestep the issue of religious affiliation. "For these two brothers," he declared, "suitable arrangements have already been made." I glared at him. How dare he decide our future before even getting to know us? There was an embarrassed silence. Now I understood what the camp staff had been trying to tell us. Right in front of our eyes sat officials haggling over our souls, not as would-be benefactors for newly arrived young orphans but as political hucksters recruiting members for their parties.

Bernholc noted my anger. Taking me aside, he tried to explain the system: Our group would be apportioned among the different political parties according to predetermined percentages, regardless of our personal preferences.

"No one will be forced to go anywhere, but all the parties have ways of attracting members."

"I'm not in the hands of any decision maker. I will decide where I go," I said.

"And your little brother?"

"He, too, will go where I decide."

I did not yet have a feel for the social and political realities of our new country, and found the bickering disenchanting.

The camp staff, which represented various political parties, explained: The British issued the quota of immigration certificates permitting entry into Palestine. These were then allocated to the parties according to their political strength, thus allotting a mere fifteen percent to the religious parties. Bernholc was simply trying to ensure that Lulek and I would get in as part of that fifteen percent. Our shipload was the first to arrive after World War II, and it upset the system: Eighty-five percent of the Buchenwald youth wanted to go to religious institutions, with half (mostly the Hungarians) insisting on being sent to yeshivas. The nonreligious parties were concerned that the quota system would break down, and that acquiescing to such a distribution would set a precedent that could eventually diminish their power.

This explanation and gesture from Bernholc restored good relations between us, and I was now able to talk to him about some of the younger boys I had taken under my wing. They all came from religious homes, but some of them had not had any education whatsoever. I asked that they be sent to the type of school their parents might have chosen. Bernholc was glad to help and arranged for a few dozen to be sent to religious schools, but these constituted only a fraction of the eighty-five percent who wanted to attend religious institutions.

Our brother Shiko came that evening, smiling broadly, bearing candy for Lulek and a Hebrew grammar book for me. Again we had to talk through the fence. As we were talking, an impressive-looking man with a trim beard and a black hat came up to us. I stared at him for a second, then my heart leaped with joy. It was our uncle Mordechai Vogelman, the last rabbi of Katowitz. Shiko had thought to surprise us, but I recognized him immediately from my ten-day visit to his home in Katowitz, when I was nine. Apart from a little gray in his beard, he had not changed at all. He was delighted to see us, and apologized that

Aunt Bella, Father's younger sister, did not come; she could not bear to see us behind barbed wire.

Uncle's status as rabbi of Kiryat Motzkin, just outside Haifa, gained him entrance to the camp so that we could talk face to face. Shiko managed to slip in with him. Uncle Mordechai came with strict instructions from his wife to bring us back to their home, at least for the time being. I promised that as soon as we were released from the camp, we would come to Kiryat Motzkin for a visit. However, our release was postponed from day to day – whether because of bureaucratic complications or because the British were deliberately delaying the process, we didn't know. Finally at the end of July, after two weeks in detention, we were allowed to leave.

We did not go straight to our family. In accordance with the allocation among the political parties, Lulek and I were put on an Egged bus taking some of our group to a religious children's home in Kfar Saba, a small farming community near Tel Aviv.

A young man my age in hassidic garb sat next to us on the bus. He introduced himself as Nachman Elbaum, from a well-known Warsaw family. He had arrived in Palestine two years earlier with the "Teheran children." After staying in a religious children's home, he went on to the Ponivezh Yeshiva in Bnei Brak. He was a volunteer assisting in the absorption of the Buchenwald youngsters, and became our helpful friend and guide.

On the way from Atlit to Kfar Saba, Nachman pointed out all the places we passed. He also gave us a rundown of the current political situation, including the relations between the Jews and the Arabs and between the Jews and the British. He explained the differences between the various Jewish underground organizations. We were captivated by his extensive knowledge and outgoing personality.

It was beginning to get dark by the time we got to the village of Kfar Saba. The bus turned off onto a dirt road and stopped in a neglected yard, near a large building surrounded by huts. We were warmly welcomed by the staff, and taken to the dining room for a meal, which we ate by the light of kerosene lamps.

Our counselor, Avner Shaki, spent many hours teaching us the history and geography of our new country. He was a seventh-generation native of Eretz Yisrael, from a highly respected family of

Spanish origin, later going on to become a member of the Knesset, eventually serving as minister of religious affairs.

Soon after our arrival in Kfar Saba, the leaders of Poalei Agudat Yisrael gave a reception for us. The delegation was led by their spiritual mentor, Rabbi Meir Karelitz, and included Binyamin Mintz, Rabbi Dr. Kalman Kahana, and Yaacov Landau. Although I did not follow all the speeches given either in Hebrew or Yiddish, I was impressed by their sincerity. I was especially moved by the words of Zalman Yankelevitch (Ben Yaacov), a Tel Aviv school principal, who later became a member of the Knesset. At one point he was so overcome by emotion that he broke down weeping.

The following day, a Friday, we were taken on a tour of Tel Aviv. In those days it was a drab and lackluster town. All the buildings looked the same. We went to the Gordon Street beach, and those who wanted to swim were provided with swimming trunks. Unfortunately we were not yet used to the Middle Eastern sun and got severely sunburned. Our first immersion in the Mediterranean became a blistering initiation. The walk to synagogue for Sabbath services was agony. We could barely sit through the service. However, our physical indisposition was offset by the warm welcome we received from Rabbi Rinnik and his congregation.

17

PILGRIMAGE TO JERUSALEM

On Saturday night our friend Nachman offered to take us on our first trip to Jerusalem. Accordingly I told Avner that we would be in Jerusalem from Sunday until Tuesday. He seemed none too pleased at this show of independence, but raised no objection.

I was very excited about going to the Holy City, of which I had read and dreamed even as a child. That night I hardly slept, kept awake by anticipation and by the howling of jackals in the nearby orange groves.

The following morning at the Tel Aviv bus station we saw a long line of people waiting for the bus to Jerusalem. Nachman reckoned that we'd have to wait at least an hour for a bus, and suggested we travel via Jaffa. In Jaffa we boarded an Arab bus headed for Jerusalem, and were on our way. The bus moved so slowly that we soon realized why people preferred waiting an hour in Tel Aviv. At Abu Kabir, joining the main road to Jerusalem, the bus was already sputtering, even before we reached the incline. Two stops later, in Ramle, the bus chugged down the main street at a snail's pace. Brightly clad people walked alongside sheep, goats, donkeys, dogs, and cats in a marvelous display of coexistence. The bus had barely stopped when hordes of street urchins besieged us, huckstering candies and sesame-coated bagels. A woman with a basket of fruit on her head thrust bunches of grapes through the windows, getting a few coins in return. Lulek was hungry and begged me to buy him a bagel, but I had no money. Nachman assured us that we would soon be in Jerusalem, where there would be a better selection. I suspect he assumed that the bagels were not kosher.

A raven-haired girl in a red blouse, black skirt, and high-heeled shoes got on the bus, reminding me of my stay in France. All eyes were on her as she made her way down the aisle. Unable to find an empty seat, she sat down on the step by the rear door, facing the three of us. I was sitting by the window, Nachman by the aisle, with Lulek between us. Even before the bus began to move she started to sing, first in Arabic, then Hebrew. Some passengers complained, demanding that the driver tell her to be quiet. Yielding to pressure, he turned on the radio, and the loud Arab music drowned her out.

She then turned provocatively to Nachman, commenting on his good looks and suggesting that he shed his hassidic garb and shave his beard. Embarrassed, he turned his back to her and began talking to me about the places we were passing, along the winding road into the Valley of Ayalon. He pointed out dozens of tents dotted across the parched land next to the Latrun police station. This was the Latrun detention camp, where most of the leaders of the Jewish community in Palestine were to be imprisoned by the British the following year.

There were hardly any trees or bushes alongside the road leading up to Jerusalem, only an occasional yellowing patch of grass. Only when we left the coastal plains behind and wound our way through Sha'ar Hagai (known as the gateway to Jerusalem) could we see woods of newly planted trees by the roadside. Nestled in the wooded hills, on the curving slopes, was the Arab village of Abu Ghosh. On the hilltop overlooking the village, perched on top of a church, stood a statue of the Madonna. At the stop of Abu Ghosh, some of the passengers got off to buy drinks. An old Arab, with a big tank of yellow liquid on his back, stood by the bus, selling tamarind, which he served in dirty glasses. Courtesy of Nachman, I had my first and last taste of the cloying liquid.

Nachman pointed out the sites we passed, shouting to be heard over the noise of the radio. At Motza he told us about the massacre of Jews there at the hands of the Arabs in 1929. Among the victims was the entire Makleff family. Its sole survivor, nine-year-old Mordechai (Motke), later became chief of staff of the IDF in 1952.

After the bus wheezed around the last bend of the serpentine climb, red roofs suddenly came into view. "Jerusalem!" announced Nachman.

I felt a jumble of emotions – excitement, awe, apprehension, disbelief and achievement – Jerusalem! At long last! I finally reached my destination, after the longest, most arduous ascent imaginable.

Nachman pointed out a large building to our right. The sign said, "Diskin Orphans' Home." Lulek, who was beginning to understand a few words and even an occasional sentence in Hebrew, wanted to know who lived in the building. Nachman said that it was for other children, not us.

We got off the bus at the Arab bus station on Jaffa Road and headed straight for the Western Wall. This time we did not have to wait long for a bus, a small, shabby vehicle, making frequent stops. We got off and walked through the narrow alleyways of the Arab market, amid a stream of people and animals. Nachman knew his way around and led us through a maze of cobblestone alleys and narrow plazas, to the Western Wall, which in those days was also in a narrow cobblestone alley. A number of elderly Jews stood praying, some by heart and some from a book, their heads leaning against the stones. Nachman handed me a prayer book, while I stood there, gazing up at the Wall, filled with disappointment. Other than the old men and pigeons around the huge stones, I saw no sign of life. Even Nachman had vanished. I opened the prayer book looking for an appropriate psalm and chose Psalm 130, "Out of the depths, I cried unto Thee..." This psalm had often given me comfort throughout my long journey. I believed in its power to raise my spirits in times of distress.

Lulek, standing next to me, was unsure what to do. I tried to convey to him the significance of the place, but he merely gazed at the Wall waiting for me to finish. Hearing footsteps, I turned and saw Nachman, out of breath, leading a group of men of various ages all in hassidic garb. He had recruited them from a nearby synagogue in the Jewish Quarter to enable us to recite *Kaddish* at the Wall. He wanted me to lead the *mincha* (afternoon service) prayers. Seeing that I was suddenly too overcome with emotion, he took over. Lulek and I recited *Kaddish* haltingly.

We left the Wall and headed for the New City. My heart was heavy. I had finally set foot in Jerusalem, and was certain that I had made the right decision in coming to Eretz Yisrael, but I was far from certain where my life was heading now. Nachman must have sensed my mood and tried to distract me, pointing out the different Arab types we passed – Bedouins in their black caftans and white kaffiyehs, and city dwellers in red tarbooshes. When we reached King George Street, he led us into a cafe and ordered drinks and watermelon. We sat there for a while under the ceiling fan, refreshed by the generous portions of watermelon.

With great tact and delicacy, Nachman asked whether I would be prepared to visit the Gerer Rebbe, Avraham Mordechai Alter, spiritual leader of the Polish *hassidim*. As a child I had heard of crowds of *hassidim* coming from all over Poland to be close to the Gerer Rebbe, particularly on Shavuoth and Rosh Hashanah. His influence extended far beyond his own court, near Warsaw. Father had been one of his ardent admirers, and I was sure that the Gerer Rebbe would remember him. Yes, I would feel privileged to receive a blessing from him.

We left the cafe and headed for Tel Arza, a suburb of Jerusalem, to the apartment where Nachman had arranged for us to stay. Our hostess, Mrs. Werdiger, received us warmly and went out of her way to make us feel at home. Her husband was related to the Gerer Rebbe. She showed us to our room and offered us fruit and drinks. Lulek was exhausted and fell asleep. Nachman and I left to visit the Gerer Rebbe, who lived on Sefat Emet Street.

Only ten people a day were admitted to his august presence. They would write their brief request on a slip of paper, hand it to an aide, and wait their turn. In my khaki pants and light short-sleeved shirt, I felt out of place among these black-garbed *hassidim* who were ahead of me. Nachman whispered something to the aide, who went straight to the Rebbe's room and came out in less than a minute to usher me in.

Except for the barest essentials, the room was devoid of furniture. The Rebbe sat in a high armchair, his white-stockinged feet resting on a footstool. With his flowing white beard, wide, wavy earlocks, and big hat, he made an awesome figure. However, I could not accept the belt-like sash Nachman held out to me, the kind worn by *hassidim* when praying, learning Torah, or appearing before the Rebbe. The aide took the note, on which I had written my name and that of my parents and brother Milek, and handed it to the Rebbe. Holding it up close to his eyes, he read it and immediately called me over. Following the example of the aide, I walked on tiptoe. The Rebbe held out his hand and grasped mine warmly, gazing at me. He whispered a few words, which I could not quite grasp. Without letting go of my hand, he stared at me for another minute, then released his hold. The aide signaled the end of the visit. Again following his example, I walked backward to the door while facing the Rebbe.

Outside, the *hassidim* crowded around me, wanting to know what he said. The aide repeated the Rebbe's words: "Brands saved from the fire by the mercy of Almighty and by the merit of your ancestors, the blessed God will stand by them, watching over them wherever their paths may lead."

I was very moved by the meeting, and was still excited when we sat down to dinner at the Werdigers. As a child I had been so affected by stories about the Gerer Rebbe, that I came to visualize him as somehow beyond this world. That afternoon I had actually been in his presence, my hand in his.

At half past five the following morning, Nachman knocked on my door to wake me for morning prayers. It was a cool, pleasant day as we walked to the Rebbe's *Beth Midrash* off David Yellin Street. Prayers began at 6:15 A.M. upon the arrival of Rabbi Yisrael, son and designated heir of the Gerer Rebbe. Walking toward his seat by the east wall of the room, Rabbi Yisrael saw me and shook hands. "You are Naphtali, son of Rabbi Moshe Chaim from Piotrkow," he said. "Where's your little brother?" He was dressed in the traditional manner of the Ger *hassidim*, his pants tucked into high socks. He had sparkling eyes and a sharply expressive face

It was Monday, a day when the Torah scroll is read. The rabbi signaled that I should be given the honor of reading the portion. I was about to say the final blessing when the rabbi handed me a prayer book and told me to recite the *Gommel* blessing, a prayer of thanks for being saved from danger. At the end of the service, when all the mourners were about to say *Kaddish*, Rabbi Yisrael tapped for silence, and announced that I alone was to say the *Kaddish*.

He invited Nachman and me to his home for breakfast. His apartment had three interconnecting rooms. The first, leading to the street, contained a table, a few chairs, and several bookcases. The second held two beds along the walls, opposite each other. The third and farthest was Rabbi Yisrael's room. He had been living alone ever since reaching Palestine, not knowing what had become of his wife and children, who had remained in Poland.

Breakfast consisted of bread, margarine, olives, cucumbers, yogurt, and tea. Rabbi Yisrael ate very little, but kept offering me more food. Following grace after meals, he suggested that I tour the city. He whispered to Nachman that he wished to invite me for supper, so that we could talk. Then, without another word, he left the room.

On the way back to the Werdigers, I told Nachman that I had relatives in Jerusalem. Father's uncle, Rabbi Avraham Zvi Shor, had emigrated from Galicia before World War I, and became the head of the *Ashkenazi Beth Din* in Jerusalem. As far as I knew he lived in the Old City, but I did not know exactly where. Nachman suggested we go to Geula, where he was sure that one of his "sources" would know my uncle's address. There, we learned that Rabbi Shor had died two months earlier, and that his family were living in Mea Shearim.

Nachman wasted no time. Turning east into Mea Shearim Street, he led the way down a narrow lane and stopped outside a building bearing a Hebrew sign: *"Chevrat Machazikei Hadat"* (Society of Preservers of the Faith), and a smaller sign identifying it as the offices of *Sabbath Candles Weekly.*

"This is the place," said Nachman.

We climbed the worn stone stairs to the offices of the newspaper. Sure enough, the editor was Rabbi Mordechai Hacohen, my uncle's son-in-law. His family lived upstairs, and although they knew that Lulek and I had made it to Palestine, were pleasantly surprised to see me. My cousin Rivka burst into tears. Within minutes we were surrounded by the whole family, including my aunt, Rabbi Shor's widow.

Nachman, feeling that his mission had been accomplished, wanted to leave. But I insisted that he stay a while and enjoy some of the cakes that were pressed upon us. After the excitement had somewhat subsided, I told my newly found family that I had to get back to Lulek. Three of my young cousins, Shmuel, Pinchas, and Menachem, insisted on accompanying me. Shmuel was around my age, while the youngest, Menachem, had just celebrated his bar mitzvah. They were all in yeshiva garb, complete with long earlocks. Though they were studying in *haredi* yeshivas, all three held strong Zionist convictions. Their father, Rabbi Mordechai Hacohen, was a product of the old Jewish community in Eretz Yisrael; a scholar and modern intellectual, who had imbued his sons with a love of Zion along with their yeshiva studies.

All three brothers grew up to become rabbis and were active in public life. Shmuel became known as Rabbi Shmuel Avidor Hacohen; Pinchas (who changed his surname to Peli) became a professor of Bible studies at Ben-Gurion University; and Menachem became the rabbi of the Histadrut and a member of the Knesset.

On the way to the Werdigers, the Hacohen brothers offered to take us to see Shiko in Kfar Etzion, but I knew that Nachman had other plans for us. Consequently, Shmuel promised to contact Shiko and arrange for him to come to Jerusalem the following day. I agreed to be their guest the following Sabbath.

In the afternoon, Nachman, Lulek, and I walked through the older neighborhoods of Jerusalem. He showed us Mea Shearim, the Hungarian Houses and the Bokharian Quarter. None of this impressed me nearly as much as the sight of so many children running around, the little boys with earlocks bobbing up and down. It reminded me of similar scenes in Warsaw, Cracow, Lublin, or Piotrkow before the war. All the neglect, dirt, and noise could not detract from the vitality of these neighborhoods.

That evening Lulek went to bed early and I went back to Rabbi Yisrael Alter's home. A young yeshiva student served us soup, roast chicken, and vegetables. Again Rabbi Yisrael ate very little, but kept urging me to take more. While we ate he said not a word. Following the grace after meals, he stood up and gestured for me to follow him. We went out on the street, turned right, and then right again on to Yosef Matityahu Street, which was deserted. We walked in silence toward the British military base known as Schneller. From time to time he stopped, took a deep breath, gave me a long, hard look and, without a word, continued walking.

We walked up and down that same street about a dozen times. Finally he stopped, looked at me, and burst out:

"Did you see the smoke rising from the chimneys?"
I did not know what to say. We continued walking.
He took hold of my shirt collar and shook me gently.
"Did you see the fire with your own eyes?"
Again, I had no answer.
"And the Holy One, Blessed be He?" he asked.
"Did you see Him at your side?"

I was stunned by this outburst of anguish. Exhausted, I followed him back to his apartment. "You're tired," he said. "Go to sleep." My roommate, the student who had served us the meal, was already asleep.

I went to bed, but could not sleep. I could hear the rabbi pacing up and down in his room. When I was finally about to fall asleep, I heard a noise by my bed. Without lifting my head, I saw the rabbi place a bowl of water and a glass by my bed, for me to wash my hands in the morning, in keeping with tradition.

After the rabbi left the room, I lifted my head and saw a pair of phosphorescent eyes. A cat was sitting on the open window ledge. I got up to chase it away, but it refused to budge. I had no choice but to try to sleep under the watchful eyes of my uninvited visitor.

By 5:00 A.M. full daylight poured through the open window. I got up, rinsed my hands in the bowl, and got dressed. Rabbi Yisrael came into my room with a white towel draped around his neck. "The *mikve* is not far from here. If you want, you'll find me there." I realized that he expected me to follow him, but instead I headed to the *Beth Midrash*. It was empty. I sat down at a table piled high with books and opened the nearest volume, *Betza* (egg), one of the tractates of the Talmud. Five years had gone by since I last opened a Talmud – the text in the middle of the page, Rashi's explanations on the inner column, *Tosefoth* on the outer column. It all rushed back to me. It was as though I had just stepped out of the classroom in which I had learned the first chapter, which deals with the legalities of an egg laid on a festival day.

When Rabbi Yisrael returned and saw me sitting in front of the open Talmud, he joined me and asked whether I wanted to learn in a yeshiva. I replied that sooner or later I would want to resume my studies. "Good," he said. "But not here. A hassidic yeshiva is not for you." He was right. I had no intention of attending such a place. Although I had not spoken to Rabbi Yisrael about my religious uncertainties, I felt sure he sensed them. We talked for a long time but he was careful to avoid the subject.

Nachman took me to the Hebron Yeshiva, next to the Tnuva dairy in Kerem Avraham, saying that he thought it would suit me. I noted his recommendation, but never went back there.

That afternoon Shiko came to Jerusalem to see me. Although he himself had been educated in the yeshivas of his uncles, Rabbi Eliezer Hager and Rabbi Chaim Meir Hager, leaders of the Wizhnitz hassidic dynasty, I knew that, with his Zionist pioneering views, he would negate my learning in a yeshiva. He was convinced that I should settle in one of the new kibbutzim, a suggestion that I rejected at once. Lulek, he said, should go to live with our aunt and uncle, Rabbi and Mrs Vogelman. To this I agreed.

Leaving Jerusalem, we boarded the express bus to Tel Aviv, where Lulek and I got to meet Nachman's family. Later, he escorted us all the way back to Kfar Saba.

Nachman's unforgettable solicitude helped smooth our way during our first days in the country. To this day, whenever our paths cross, whether in Israel, the United States, or anywhere else, I associate him with the experiences of my first pilgrimage to Jerusalem.

18

ABSORPTION IN HOMELAND

Upon our return to Kfar Saba, both Lulek and I came down with high fever. The doctor diagnosed jaundice. Lulek had a mild case and recovered quickly, but mine was more serious. I was ordered onto a strict diet and put into quarantine in the steaming heat of my wooden hut. After ten days I felt much better and began to think about our future. Lulek needed a home. The only realistic possibility was with our uncle and aunt, the Vogelmans, in Kiriat Motzkin. They were urging us to come, but it was suitable only for Lulek, and he refused to part from me.

The Kfar Saba children's institution was beginning to irk me. The staff did its best to make our stay pleasant. The counselors and teachers tried to impart a wide knowledge of the country and its problems, teaching us Hebrew and modern history. I knew that this place was not for me, but I had no idea where to go. I considered turning to a yeshiva for a while, since I felt that my religious commitment needed reinforcing. I also wished to pursue my secular education, and needed to acquire some profession that would make me self-supportive. I had many ideas, with the common denominator that they take me as far as possible from the trauma of the past and open a way to the future.

Many of our friends who had come with us to Kfar Saba began to disperse. Some turned to relatives, who arranged for their studies or employment. Others left to study in *haredi* yeshivas in Jerusalem. A small number went to kibbutzim.

By the last Sabbath in August, we were also ready to leave. Lulek agreed to go to our family in Kiryat Motzkin, provided I would stay with him for a while. I decided to attend a yeshiva in Petach Tikva for the High Holidays. My announcement at Friday night dinner that we were leaving Kfar Saba put something of a damper on the Sabbath atmosphere, but an unpleasant incident the following morning completely overshadowed our imminent departure.

I was walking with some friends toward a neighboring orange grove, when an open truck with about a dozen boys and girls from a Hashomer Hatzair (far-left, non-religious) kibbutz drove up and stopped alongside us. Some were wearing swimsuits, and invited us to join them for a ride to the beach. I took it as a friendly gesture, an offer of a pleasant outing on a hot day. Most of my friends felt otherwise. They saw it as a provocation, a taunt against our religious feelings. One of my friends vocally criticized their impudence in suggesting that we violate the Sabbath. In the midst of the ensuing argument, some of the boys jumped from the truck with sticks in their hands and began beating us. The physical pain was negligible, but the disillusionment and mounting anger were exceedingly painful. This was the first and, fortunately, the only time I heard sabras jeering at us, "Soapbars, get out of here! Who needs you?" Only later did we learn the meaning of that epithet.

This incident generated a furor in many newspapers. The distorted versions in several newspapers drove home to me even then the political polarization and the divisiveness among Jews in the country. I was too preoccupied to deal with the problem at the time, but my heart was heavy with disenchantment over the underlying discord.

The single-story Vogelman house in Kiriat Motzkin was surrounded by thick foliage and flowers. My uncle and aunt outdid themselves in making us welcome, spoiling us. I hoped it would allow Lulek to recover some of the joy of childhood that had been stolen from him. We spent a week in the Haifa Bay area, visiting Haifa and its surroundings. The Vogelmans bought Lulek his first schoolbag, complete with textbooks and notebooks. Though he still did not know Hebrew, he was placed in second grade and two days later moved up to third grade, where some of the younger children were his age.

When the time came for parting, Lulek held on to me and would not let go. I promised to return the following Sabbath. He walked with me to the bus stop at the Great Synagogue on Hashoftim Boulevard. When he saw the number 52 bus to Haifa approaching, he clung to me, crying bitterly. I reasoned with him, until he finally agreed to let me board the bus. But my heart was torn as I saw him standing at the bus stop, crying bitterly.

At the Lomza Yeshiva in Petach Tikva, under the leadership of Rabbi Reuven Katz, rabbi of Petach Tikva, I was received with warmth and friendliness. Most of the students were in their late twenties or thirties, refugees from Lithuania who had escaped the Nazis by crossing Russia to Shanghai and, after the war, went on to Eretz Yisrael. I was one of the youngest students and, as such, was privileged to receive additional attention from the senior students and some of the senior rabbis, including Rabbi Eliezer Menachem Shach and Rabbi Moshe Leib Ozer. The Lomza Yeshiva became my home for the next three years, except for the times I stayed with the Vogelmans to be with Lulek on the festivals.

I tried to immerse myself in my studies and enjoyed returning to certain Talmudic issues that I had dealt with six or seven years earlier. However, a total and absolute devotion to Talmud studies did not last for long. I found it difficult to regain that very special mode of exclusive Talmud study under the existing political conditions. About five weeks after coming to Petach Tikva, I was recruited to join the Hagana. I took part in a series of surreptitious military exercises with batons and light weapons in one of the orchards east of the city.

One winter night at the beginning of 1946, I caught a severe cold. Dr. Auerbach, our elderly physician, confined me to bed, but my condition did not improve. A second physician, Dr. Bachrach, suspected pneumonia and referred me to the Maavarim Lung and TB Clinic in Magdiel. Two house physicians, Dr. Huppert and Dr. Loewenstein, diagnosed my illness as pleurisy and decided on immediate hospitalization. They assumed, correctly, that I had been carrying this disease with me for many months. In their view, it could be cured by proper treatment, which would avert the danger of tuberculosis. I was kept at Maavarim, a small hospital, for about five weeks.

After recovery I resumed my studies, this time including some secular education. Particularly interested in the history of the Jewish people and international relations, I took every opportunity to go to the Hebrew University in Jerusalem, then the only functioning university in Palestine, to sit in on the lectures as an unregistered student.

During the Passover vacation, I brought Lulek to Petach Tikva. He stayed in my room and we toured the Tel Aviv area and visited relatives. On one tour, we were invited to stay in Tel Aviv at the Rothschild Boulevard home of a friend from the yeshiva, Yisrael Mintzer. This eventually became my regular home when in Tel Aviv. By coincidence, Yisrael's eldest sister, Tzipora, met my brother Shiko when she spent a holiday at his kibbutz, Kfar Etzion – a chance meeting that eventually led to their wedding.

Lulek was doing well in his studies, adapting quickly to his new environment. I kept close ties with him. He wanted to know how long he would have to stay with the Vogelman family and I promised him that after his bar mitzvah, in another four years, he could transfer to study in a Jerusalem yeshiva. Father's former student, Rabbi Yosef Reiner, was one of the leading rabbis at the Kol Torah Yeshiva in Jerusalem and was prepared to look after Lulek. I chose this yeshiva because of its *Torah im derech eretz* (Torah studies combined with secular studies) curriculum, and I hoped that there he would receive a general as well as religious education. Lulek's quick grasp and excellent memory promised him a bright future. Deep in my heart I was hopeful that perhaps he would extend the unbroken chain of rabbis in our family to the thirty-eighth generation.

In June 1946, at the height of the struggle of the Jewish underground against the British, I took part in Hagana squad-training exercises near Kibbutz Ramat Hakovesh in the Sharon coastal plains. Without warning, we suddenly found ourselves surrounded by a large net of British paratroopers, combing the area. In what would become known as "the Black Sabbath," the British searched for all the leaders of the Jewish Settlement movement in Eretz Yisrael, primarily the Jewish Agency executive members. Their search led them to many kibbutzim, looking for caches of hidden weapons and ammunition, as well as Hagana activists. We split up and, individually, managed to slip through the cordon of paratroopers, called *callaniot* (red anemones), because of their red berets. The Black Sabbath operation became a turning point in the struggle of the Jews to liberate Eretz Yisrael.

My frequent absences from the yeshiva did not attract special attention. I was not the only one. At least four other students were active in the Irgun Zvai Leumi (known as the Etzel or simply the Irgun); Another one was in Lechi, known as the Stern Group. The heads of the yeshiva were aware of these activities but turned a blind eye. It was only at the end of the year, after the absence of an entire week when I was engaged in bringing illegal immigrants ashore near Herzliya and helping them find accommodation in the nearby settlements, that I was called for a heart-to-heart talk with the spiritual counselor of the yeshiva, Rabbi Dov Zhukovsky. A wise man, he understood what I was doing and why, but nevertheless advised me to take better care of my health, as the yeshiva physician, Dr. Bachrach, had counseled me in the light of his periodic examinations subsequent to my illness.

During the winter and spring of 1947, tension rose to a new high. The execution of Etzel and Lechi prisoners by the British fueled a rebellion, and at certain stages even brought about a degree of cooperation between all three organizations (Hagana, Etzel, and Lechi).

One night in March 1947, our yeshiva dormitories on Montefiore Street in Petach Tikva were surrounded by British soldiers. Dozens of paratroopers, with their red berets, broke into the dormitory, hauling us from our beds and turning over our mattresses. Here and there, fists and rifle butts descended on our heads, as they chased us out and lined us up in the rear courtyard. They searched our pockets and every inch of our bodies for any suspicious objects. Not finding anything, they let us return to our rooms.

My friend Sholem Ozer was the son of one of our teachers, Rabbi Moshe Leib Ozer. His older brother, Simcha, had been active in Etzel and was killed while assembling a bomb, which detonated in his hand. The Etzel command distributed mourning notices on the death of "Ezra," his underground nickname. Hundreds of Petach Tikva residents, including all the students of the yeshiva, attended the funeral. British undercover agents noted suspects among the mourners, while Etzel recruiters sought prospective members among the youth who marched in the funeral.

On the following Sabbath, I was resting in the dormitory when a young man I did not recognize tapped on the door and asked to speak to me. He had red hair and a black beret, and introduced himself as Chanania Winitzki. He was referred to me by a mutual acquaintance and suggested that we go for a Sabbath afternoon stroll. We went out in the direction of the monkey zoo, walking down Rothschild Street. "This is no place to be seen together. Too many people know both of us," he said. I was surprised at his secrecy but said nothing. We walked on toward Givat Hashlosha. On the way, he began to preach to me about the indifference of some of the young men who refused to enlist in the national struggle against the British, ignoring the fact that I was already enlisted with the Hagana.

After some time, he explained the purpose of his visit. "Our commander wants to meet you, to explain the importance of the Irgun." I was curious to meet the commander, thinking, in my naivete, that he meant the commander of the Etzel. We agreed on a rendezvous for the following evening, next to the ritual bathhouse on Chaim Ozer Street. From there he would take me to the commander. At the appointed hour, Chanania approached and gestured for me to follow. We entered an empty lot, which later became the city commercial center, with Chanania leading the way. He bent almost double between the low bushes, indicating that I should do likewise. Finally we arrived at a small clearing where a man sat on the ground, with a cloth cap pulled low over his eyes and a handkerchief tied over his nose, mouth, and chin. Chanania saluted and mumbled something to him, which I did not catch. Then it was my turn to stand in front of the commander, who told me to sit down on the ground, facing him. He launched into a long speech, lecturing me that active Zionism demands deeds, and that people with my Holocaust experiences were obligated to show the way to others. I patiently listened to his long discourse and then told him that I was doing my national duty in the ranks of the Hagana. He acceded to my request to leave, stating that his comrades would be in touch. I returned to nearby Mohilever Street and have never seen him since.

Rabbi Shach, one of the three heads of the yeshiva, paid particular and affectionate attention to me. Though he taught the younger grades, his scholarship and astuteness made him an accepted authority among the older staff. One day as I was coming down the stairs of the yeshiva building at 7 Herzl Street, I saw the rabbi waiting for me on the sidewalk. He joined me as I was about to walk over to the newspaper kiosk, where I customarily scanned the front pages of the dailies. From his comments I realized that he knew of my underground involvement. "You were snatched from the inferno, and act as father to a boy with a promising future. It is forbidden for you to endanger yourself too much," he said in his hoarse voice and Ashkenazi (European) accent.

He went on to criticize the Jewish leaders severely, pouring out his anger particularly at the underground organizations for provoking the authorities and thus risking retaliation against the entire community. He quoted a famous passage in the Talmud, *Ketuboth* 111A, in which God tells the Children of Israel not to rebel against their fate in the Exile. This point of view was and still is the classic approach of the ultra-religious who were, and still are, opposed to Zionism. I did not see myself qualified to argue the point with a head of the yeshiva, so we moved on to politics, in which he had considerable interest. Even now, 50 years later, in his late nineties, the rabbi remains the acknowledged leader of the *haredim*. The heads of all the large secular parties in Israel court him, seeking political support. He has not changed his views during all the years and is not above trying to dictate his philosophy to others.

That year of national tension and defense activities frequently took me away from my studies. The peak came in October 1947, as the date approached for the United Nations General Assembly debate on the recommendation of the UN Special Commission on Palestine (UNSCOP) for partition of the country into two states, Jewish and Arab. There were many indications that violent clashes would erupt between Jews and Arabs. The critical question was: What would be the stand of the British government? Whom would they support? There was no doubt the Arabs were going to oppose vigorously the UN decision for partition. Accordingly, the Hagana prepared for the possibility of war and mobilized its forces clandestinely.

I was mobilized one week before the fateful session of the General Assembly at Lake Success, set for the twenty-ninth of November. Armed gangs of Arabs from the village of Fejah, on the outskirts of Petach Tikva in the direction of Lod Airport, had been attacking and harassing international air traffic. Along with fifteen others, I had been assigned to set up ambushes. I spent several nights concealed there, with the smell of gunpowder in the air, but nothing happened. Shortly after we pulled out, another Hagana unit did get into a shooting battle with one of the gangs. The unit's commander, Shlomo Miller from Kibbutz Givat Hashlosha, lost his life in that encounter.

On the Sabbath prior to the UN vote, I was on leave in Tel Aviv. On November 29, 1947, I was among the tens of thousands of Tel Avivians packed into Magen David Adom Square, in the middle of Allenby Street, listening to the vote at the UN. We stood there, tensely waiting as the radio announcer counted the votes for and against partition. Finally, we heard the results announced (33 for, 13 against, 10 abstentions) – a state for the Jews would be established. Yosef Heftman, editor of the daily newspaper *Haboker*, took the microphone and proclaimed, "Hear O Israel, on this day you have become a nation." A wave of euphoria set the masses singing and dancing, transforming the square into a mass of jubilant humanity.

All too quickly the ecstasy subsided and gave way to anxiety. The local Arabs were organizing for war in various parts of the country, concentrating their efforts in Jerusalem, but especially in the north. The forces in the north were grouping under the command of a veteran gang leader, Fawzi el Kaoukji. He came from Syria via Lebanon and organized his units for aggressive activities against the kibbutzim and the traffic arteries in the north. In the center of the country, the Arab forces were functioning under the command of two leaders: Abdul Kader el Husseini in the Jerusalem hills, and Hassan Salameh on the coastal plain between Tel Aviv, Ramle, and Lod. All of these local forces acted with the unofficial assistance of the regular armed forces of Egypt, Jordan, Syria, and Iraq. However, it was only when David Ben-Gurion officially declared the establishment of a Jewish country, the State of Israel, on May 14, 1948, that the regular armed forces of the neighboring Arab countries openly declared war and invaded the newly established Jewish state, to make sure it would be stillborn.

One of the hardest blows was the attack of the Jordanian Arab Legion against the Old City of Jerusalem. The Jewish Quarter of the Old City was completely besieged. Hundreds of civilians and dozens of fighters were wounded and many were killed. All were starving and exhausted. Finally, on May 28, the Jewish Quarter raised a white flag and its defenders were taken prisoner to Jordan. Its synagogues and public buildings were razed to the ground by the Jordanians, and the Jewish homes and shops were looted by the neighboring Old City Arabs.

On May 13 local Arab forces in the Hebron Mountains, assisted by the Jordanian Arab Legion, attacked the four kibbutzim of the

Etzion Bloc, south of Jerusalem. The women and children had been evacuated. In Kfar Etzion, the oldest of the four settlements in the Bloc, about one hundred and fifty defenders fell. Many of the fighters had been close friends, some of them survivors of the Holocaust. The Arabs looted everything they could lay their hands on, then burned the homes and property of Kfar Etzion. A similar fate was visited on the other three kibbutzim in the Bloc: Massuot Yitzhak, Ein Tzurim, and Revadim. Their inhabitants were taken into captivity in Jordan.

Between November 1947 and May 1948, the Hagana succeeded in forming an almost regular army force. Recruits were mobilized according to health and fitness criteria: Red identity cards were given to the Field Corps combat units, and green or blue ones to the Guard Corps. In January 1948, while stationed with the Field Corps in the North Sharon Plain, I came down with a high fever and was sent back to Petach Tikva for treatment and convalescence. Six weeks later I returned to duty, this time with the blue card that identified me as belonging to a rear intelligence unit.

Arab gangs were running wild on the roads, firing on Jewish vehicles, and almost paralyzing all transport. Their attacks on remote settlements in the Negev and Galilee were extremely well planned and caused heavy losses in life and property. Jerusalem was under siege and completely cut off from the rest of the country. A growing sense of hopelessness pervaded the community. Young men my age enlisted in fighting units while I, in my new assignment, commuted every day from Petach Tikva to Tel Aviv. Occasionally I managed to visit friends in forward units and get a feel for the real emergency around us. We still had to hide our personal weapons to avoid confiscation by the British, who patrolled the city streets and the interurban roads.

In the four months following the UN decision, the Arabs sowed death and destruction at will. There was a feeling that almost all was lost. Haj Amin el-Husseini, the Grand Mufti of Jerusalem, who had collaborated with Hitler in planning the extermination of the Jews in the Middle East, wildly incited vast numbers of Arabs against the Jews, inflaming their passions to new extremes. With every successful strike against the Jews, they broke into cries of *jihad* (holy war). The killing of Jews spread everywhere, even to the major Jewish cities of Jerusalem, Safad, Tiberias, and Haifa. Jewish morale fell to such depths that some were predicting a destruction that would overshadow the devastation we had experienced in Europe.

In my work, I could glimpse a ray of hope. Early in March I learned of the help that was to come from Czechoslovakia. My hopes rose from day to day as I checked the quantities of weapons and equipment due to arrive by sea and air under the very noses of the British.

During this month, the Hagana was busily preparing our first offensive action, aimed at breaking the siege of Jerusalem. Meanwhile we were sustaining heavy blows and painful losses. The Arabs carried out terror attacks, with British assistance. In the heart of Jerusalem a car bomb exploded on Ben Yehuda Street, causing heavy casualties. Another explosive-laden car was detonated after being driven into the courtyard of the Jewish Agency, which was leading the struggle. The Arab war effort was also getting diplomatic assistance from the United States. The U.S. ambassador to the UN, Hershel Johnson, proposed a repeal of the partition decision and imposition of a United Nations trusteeship in place of the British Mandate rule.

At the end of March, the Hagana was ready for the first offensive, which was to take place on the Jerusalem highway in an attempt to break the siege of the city. For the first time in its history, the Jewish defense force was mustering three battalions for one operation. On April 3, thanks to the arrival of weapons from Czechoslovakia, "Operation Nachshon" succeeded in breaking through to Jerusalem, bringing water, food, medical supplies, and reinforcements. The Arabs responded in force, while pinning down other Hagana units across the country. Once again the Jerusalem road was blocked under heavy gunfire from the Arab Legion. Local forces dug in along the canyon of Sha'ar Hagai, on the climb into the hills. Only later was the siege on the beleaguered city of Jerusalem permanently broken, by a new bypass road paved in the mountains of Jerusalem, known as the "Burma Road."

The momentum of Operation Nachshon encouraged the Hagana, Palmach, Etzel, and Lechi to increase their pressure on Arab weak points and to initiate local actions. In less than a month, Jewish forces gained control of Haifa, Safad, Tiberias, the eastern Galilee, and the Jordan Valley, including the city of Beit Shean. Special effort went into consolidating the Jewish hold over West Jerusalem. In the course of several battles, control was established over the Arab neighborhoods in Katamon, the German Colony, the Greek Colony, Baka, and the southern villages. Jaffa had become a serious threat to nearby Tel Aviv over the preceding four months, with Arab snipers firing from the minaret of the Hassan Bek Mosque in Manshieh onto Allenby Street, the business center of Tel Aviv. Residents crossing Hayarkon Street to reach the seashore took their lives in their hands. The snipers from Jaffa inflicted a heavy toll in human life until, on the eve of Passover, Etzel and Hagana forces took Jaffa. Tens of thousands of Arab inhabitants fled by land and sea.

The transfer of initiative to Jewish hands had a heartening effect on the morale of the frontline soldiers and the population. But the ranks were steadily thinning and the stocks of arms and ammunition were diminishing. On the afternoon of May 14, a Friday, the Provisional State Council was scheduled to meet in the Tel Aviv Museum, 20 Rothschild Boulevard, to declare the establishment of the Jewish state at midnight, when the British Mandate would end. Despite the heavy losses, the atmosphere was festive. I was attached to the security units assigned to close off a section of the boulevard between Allenby and Herzl streets. Next door to the museum was the Mintzer house, on 18 Rothschild Boulevard, where I was a regular visitor. From the upper floor, I could see into the main hall of the Tel Aviv Museum.

19

A NATION IS BORN

On Friday, May 14,1948, a few minutes before 4:00 P.M., David Ben-Gurion arrived, accompanied by his wife Paula and his military aide-de-camp, at the entrance to the Tel Aviv Museum. He ran up the steps and entered the building, leaving Paula trailing behind. No loudspeakers had been installed, and the days of ubiquitous portable radios had not yet arrived. The Hagana Broadcasting Service, still underground, had provided a technician and only rudimentary equipment. Neighbors turned on the underground broadcast at full volume so that we could all hear Ben-Gurion proclaim the establishment of the State and read the Declaration of Independence. The proclamation electrified the crowd. Men and women who had never seen one another before were hugging, kissing, and crying, overwhelmed by the momentous event.

In contrast to the jubilation on Saturday night, November 29, 1947, when we learned of the partition of Palestine into two states, the public now was restrained. After the broadcast of "Hatikva," the national anthem, there was no singing, no dancing in the streets. The euphoria was muted by grief over the losses of the many who had fallen, and anxiety about Arab reaction. Would they stand by their threat to invade with all the forces at their command? The people all across Israel kept their exhilaration subdued, with little outward display.

Close to the onset of the Sabbath, at sundown, the radio announced the creation of the Israel Defense Forces (IDF), which would absorb all the underground units of the Hagana, Palmach, Etzel, and Lechi. For the first time we heard the voice of Etzel's leader, Menachem Begin, on the wavelength of his organization's radio. He announced the dissolution of Etzel and the enlistment of its members to the IDF. Even before there was time to analyze the implications of this announcement, we pulled our weapons out of their hiding places and carried them openly to demonstrate, at least symbolically, the establishment of a Jewish army that would defend the newly established state. Only a few days later did units begin to hold swearing-in ceremonies and award rank badges to officers. Officially the IDF came into being only on May 31.

The following day, on Saturday morning, the regular Arab armies launched a concentrated countrywide offensive. The Egyptians activated their navy and air force, in addition to moving their infantry and armor from Sinai toward Tel Aviv. The Jordanian Arab Legion attacked in the Jerusalem area and forced the surrender of the Etzion Bloc. The Syrian army invaded the Jordan Valley, almost capturing Degania, the "mother of the kibbutzim." The Iraqi army reached Samaria and took a position facing Netanya on the Mediterranean coast. Additional Iraqi forces moved against Jerusalem from the north and forces of the Egyptian army reached Bethlehem on the city's southern approaches. The Lebanese army also joined the invasion, but before they had a chance to move the IDF captured several Lebanese villages. At the end of the war these villages were returned, even prior to the signing of the cease-fire agreement with Lebanon.

Fierce fighting broke out all over the country. The Arab forces appeared to be weakened and the IDF, fresh out of the underground, needed breathing space and time to get organized. The equipment and manpower at their disposal were inadequate. When the Arab armies invaded on May 15, the IDF could muster only forty thousand members from different organizations, some of them veterans of the World War II British army. To the last day Britain did what it could to hamper the organization of the Jewish forces. The United States had imposed an arms embargo on Israel and forbade Americans to volunteer for the IDF. Of the western countries, only France quietly permitted the flow of equipment and reinforcements. Czechoslovakia was the only country that allowed almost overt activity, including arms supply and training facilities. Little by little, volunteers from abroad called Machal began to arrive, followed by recruits from the Displaced Persons camps of Germany and Austria, the remnant of Jews who had survived the Holocaust. A babel of different languages became common among the fighting forces, hampering command and coordination in the fighting units. In the first two weeks after the Arab invasion, thirty thousand additional men were recruited and assigned to their appropriate ranks.

The IDF forces, which had started organizing upon the establishment of the State, were beginning to function at the brigade level. Arriving from all parts of the world were units of armored vehicles, artillery, and fighter aircraft, surplus from World War II, crated in the bellies of B-17 "Flying Fortresses." These German, British, and American fighter planes were the nucleus of the Israel Air Force. On their way from Czechoslovakia, the B-17 bombers made a slight detour to drop bombs on Cairo before landing in Israel. The Egyptian army continued its advance on Tel Aviv, reaching the outskirts of Ashdod and cutting off twenty-seven Negev and southern settlements in their rear. Suddenly, on May 24, they were surprised by the first sortie of the newly born Israel Air Force.

On June 10, 1948, a UN-sponsored truce was declared. The IDF had built up momentum in the preceding week, but the political leadership welcomed a cease-fire that would allow a reorganization after six months of bloodletting. During the truce, I was summoned by one of the commanders and cross-examined about my knowledge of Slavic languages. I had a good command of Polish and Slovak and a lesser familiarity with Czech. The commander, Benzi, gave me a note to take to the Red House on Hayarkon Street in Tel Aviv.

The Red House, now the site of the Sheraton Hotel, was the headquarters of the Hagana and the Mossad L'Aliyah Beth. All the illegal activities that had brought Holocaust survivors to Palestine during the British Mandate had been directed from there. The same organization was now coordinating arms procurement and recruitment primarily from eastern Europe. A sentry asked for identification. My ID card and draft card were insufficient, so I showed him the crumpled note from Benzi, which said, "To Danny, the bearer has been examined and found suitable for a mission." The signature was "Hillel." This was the mobilization paper that would move me into a fascinating world as part of my military service.

Like a ping-pong ball, I was bounced from floor to floor, room to room, and person to person. Finally I ended up facing a man in his late thirties with faded red hair – Ze'ev Shind. This was the "Danny" to whom I had been directed by "Hillel," Yisrael Galili, a senior commander of the Hagana and the Palmach. "Danny" was one of heads of the Mossad L'Aliyah Beth; later he served as the director general of the Ministry of Defense. He looked at me in wonder, and tossed off his first question, "Are you a yeshiva boy?" He grilled me with more questions without knowing anything of my past or qualifications, then concluded with: "Come, it's OK." He led me to another room and told someone called Ivri, "This is the boy. Make all the arrangements!" His tone was one of command.

I spent the next two weeks in relative isolation in a one-story stone building in Sharona, the German Templar quarter of Tel Aviv called the Kirya, destined to become a center of government offices, particularly the ministry of defense and IDF General Staff Headquarters. Here I began to learn some of the most closely guarded secrets of the day, including certain connections with the Czechoslovak security establishment and the means by which volunteers and essential equipment were being transferred via that country.

One day, a man with thinning black wavy hair approached me. Shaul Meirov, a very senior Hagana official, looked at me with his dark, sad eyes and asked me to accompany him. He gestured for me to sit down and asked my full name. He spoke almost in a whisper, keeping his penetrating gaze on me and radiating unchallenged authority. A confidant of Ben-Gurion, he was in the classic mold of one of the outstanding leaders of the underground, carrying all the topmost plans and secrets in his head.

Shaul Meirov was the brother-in-law of both Moshe Sharett, first foreign minister, and Eliahu Golomb, the admired head of the Hagana who died in 1944. The pocket notebook of Meirov and his desk drawer contained many of the most sensitive secrets of this new country and of the struggle that had preceded its establishment. He had also borne the responsibility for the organization of illegal immigration, and now was in charge of the procurement of combat equipment and the recruitment of Jewish soldiers from Europe and America.

After asking me a few questions, Meirov told me I would be flying to Prague on Monday on a Czech Airline (C.S.A.) plane. I was to report to Ehud Avriel, the Israeli minister to Czechoslovakia. "Ehud will tell you where to stay, and Michael Hoterer will tell you what to do." Flying to Europe, even during a lull in the fighting, bothered me very much. Although I was not serving as a fighting soldier at the frontlines, just being in the country, especially in such a sensitive position, gave me a sense of partnership with the combat soldiers. I had lost four friends in battle, friends who had shared my fate during the Holocaust years up to liberation day in April 1945. The first was Mordechai Steinberg (Motek), from my home city Piotrkow. He had joined Kvutzat Degania, where he met his future wife, a daughter of Yosef Baratz, one of the founders of the kibbutz. Motek met his death in the Battle of Zemach against the Syrians, who were trying to capture Degania, his new home. The second was Shalom Tepper, my age, from a town in central Poland. We had been released from Buchenwald and came to Eretz Yisrael together in July 1945. Unable to concentrate on studies, he looked for work. I found him a job with my cousin, Shmuel Lau, in Tel Aviv. Shalom became an expert in making handbags and suitcases and was adopted as a Lau family member. Both friends, Shalom and Motek, the only members of their families to survive the Holocaust, fell in our war for the independence of Israel.

The other two, David Zwebner and David Singer, were friends I met in Israel. They were about four years older than I, instructors during different periods in the Hagana. Zwebner, from a well-known Jerusalem family, was one of the famous thirty-five soldiers who set out from the Hartuv area near Beth Shemesh, aiming to reinforce the Etzion Bloc. Spotted on their way through the mountain valleys they were wiped out to the last man by Arab villagers from the Mount Hebron area. Singer, who had immigrated to Eretz Yisrael from Romania at the beginning of World War II, joined Kibbutz Kfar Etzion, served in the unit that broke into the Old City. He was wounded in the fighting in the Sheikh Jarrakh Quarter of East Jerusalem and died of his wounds.

The death of my comrades and the critical situation in Israel made it hard to leave for an indefinite period. At least I was reassured that Lulek was in good hands. Visiting the Vogelmans briefly before my departure, I was gratified to see how well and happy he looked, practically a sabra now. No tears this time, just a request that I return in time to spend Rosh Hashanah with him.

As I sat in the garden with Lulek, glancing at a newspaper, I caught the announcement of the death in a recent battle of Gur Meirov, son of Shaul Meirov, the man who had just briefed me for my mission to Prague. Later, Shaul Meirov decided to change his family name to Avigur, father of Gur (a young lion).

20

MISSION TO PRAGUE

The fighting resumed on July 9 and lasted ten days. During that brief period, the IDF took the offensive on all fronts, achieving considerable success. It gained control of the center of the country, taking the towns of Ramle and Lod. At least fifty thousand Arab inhabitants of these cities and the surrounding villages fled east. In the north, the army captured many villages and gained control of Nazareth, the largest Arab city in the Galilee. On July 19, the tenth day of fighting, the United Nations called for a second cease-fire. This second truce held until October 10, the day on which the last and most decisive battle of the War of Independence began.

During the second truce, the IDF successfully reorganized in larger formations at the brigade level. In addition, it began fortifying with more modern weapons, armored vehicles, tanks, and artillery. Large quantities of crated, disassembled aircraft were flown in from abroad, which, when assembled, considerably broadened the capability of the IDF. By the end of December, the Arabs were decisively defeated on all fronts. In January 1948, the UN called for a third cease-fire, and within three months, cease-fire agreements were signed with Egypt, Jordan, and Lebanon, with Syria signing three months later.

The IDF came out of the war well organized and well equipped but sadly licking its wounds. Roughly six thousand had fallen in battle, about one percent of the entire population. In addition to this bloodletting, the wounds had not yet healed from two clashes between Prime Minister David Ben-Gurion, also serving as minister of defense, and two underground organizations, the Etzel and the Palmach. When the State was established in May 1948, the Etzel announced its own dissolution and the enlistment of all its members in the newly formed IDF. Nevertheless, a few days later a dispute arose regarding the ship *Altalena*, which had arrived from France, bringing much-needed ammunition, weapons, and manpower. The Etzel leadership refused to let the arms it had purchased be distributed exclusively by the IDF. Ben-Gurion would not consider even the slightest compromise on this issue, which he saw as an attempt to organize a separate army, independent of national leadership. The confrontation ended tragically when the ship, full of explosives, which had anchored off the Tel Aviv beach, was shelled by IDF artillery. Etzel commander Menachem Begin and the men aboard had to jump for their lives from the burning ship. Begin escaped unhurt, but many of his men were killed or wounded in this divisive incident.

The second confrontation was with the Palmach high command. Ben-Gurion demanded the dismantling of the Palmach headquarters and its total integration into the IDF, as had been done voluntarily by the other underground organizations. The Palmach commanders, who were members of the left-wing opposition parties (mainly Mapam and Achdut Ha'Avoda), refused. They viewed it as a political action against their movement. Ben-Gurion persisted and dismantled this independent politicized military force, fortunately without bloodshed.

The killing of Jews by Jews and the intrusion of petty politics into matters of life and death was most distressing. I could not accept it and it was with a heavy heart that I reached the improvised airport near Shemen Beach in Haifa, to embark on my mission to Prague. A Dakota plane belonging to the Czech airline was due to take off for Prague from the military landing strip. Among the passengers at the hangar, which housed customs and passport control, I met some Mapam functionaries, as well as Eliezer Preminger, leader of the Jewish Communist Party in Israel. They were all flying on a political pilgrimage to Prague, which had become a popular meeting point for leftists and communists from all over the world.

Among the Mapam members was Menachem Bader, a senior functionary, who later held high governmental positions. He was very bitter at the mention of Ben-Gurion. Bader and his colleagues believed that the dismemberment of the Palmach was an attempt to eliminate the influence of the Israeli left.

Preminger was competing with Shmuel Mikunis, the head of Maki (the General Communist Party), who had been very active in creating the arms-deal link with Czechoslovakia. Bader was engrossed in his vendetta against Ben-Gurion, and Preminger kept badmouthing Mikunis.

While I listened to the backbiting of these two, Rabbi Alter, leader of the Ger dynasty, and his entourage entered the hangar. He was the son of the late Rabbi Avraham Mordechai Alter, recently departed leader of the Ger dynasty, whom I had visited on arrival in Palestine. Rabbi Bunem Alter, a businessman, was on his way to Belgium with his family. According to a member of the entourage, this trip was to be a temporary self-imposed exile in reaction to being overlooked as successor to his father's leadership role. The distinction went to his older brother, who was childless. Rabbi Bunem felt that the mantle of the Gerer Rebbe should have fallen on an heir who could pass on the heritage to his own offspring.

Rabbi Bunem was pleased to see me among the passengers and greeted me enthusiastically. "Now I don't need to worry about a *minyan.*" In this year of mourning for his father, he needed to say *Kaddish*, and for that he needed a *minyan*. When the plane stopped in Athens, en route to Prague, he asked me to find eight additional male Jews to make up the required quorum. I asked Bader and Preminger, who reluctantly agreed. In Athens, I was able to recruit another six Israelis who had been fellow passengers on the plane, to come to the rabbi's room for evening prayers.

Arriving in Prague, I had only the faintest childhood memories of this beautiful city. Following instructions I had received in Israel, I located the Central Hotel and checked in. To my surprise, a number of people in the lobby were speaking Hebrew, apparently quite common in Prague at the time. Registering was a long and complex procedure, requiring me to answer questions that I could never have anticipated, such as the date and birthplace of each of my parents.

At the Israeli embassy, I was received by the head of the delegation, Minister Ehud Avriel, a key figure in recruitment and arms procurement abroad. His part in the arms deal with Czechoslovakia had been decisive. In his incisive way he explained the purpose of my mission, briefed me on my role, and discussed the different exigencies I might have to face. Ehud was not yet forty, a friendly, engaging man.

His wife and daughters were still in his Huleh Valley kibbutz, Neot Mordechai.

He invited me to have dinner with him in his hotel suite and went out of his way to arrange a kosher meal for me. The following morning he summoned Michael Hoterer, also a kibbutznik, who was responsible for recruitment activities, and introduced him as the man who would be giving me assignments and to whom I would report.

Prague was full of Holocaust survivors and refugees returning from the Soviet Union, seeking a country that would accept them. Many had chosen Israel and were waiting for transit arrangements through Austria and Italy, countries where the agents of Aliyah Beth were active. Among the thousands of Jews seeking a home were professional officers, some still serving in the Red Army or the armies of its satellites, and others who had been demobilized and had no idea which way to turn.

Little by little, I penetrated the concentration of Jews in Prague, the Sudetenland spas, and the Slovakian towns such as Bratislava and Kosice. The Czech authorities had placed an air force base at Zatec, Bohemia, at our disposal for the training of Israeli pilots and volunteers, mostly from the United States, Canada, and South Africa. To avoid detection by espionage agents, our men wore the uniforms of the Czech air force. However, that ruse did not prevent the American agents, determined to enforce the embargo on weapons and manpower imposed on Israel, from tracking us down. The training and processing of recruits from the East European armies was easier. They departed for Israel after relatively little training and made an important contribution to the professional consolidation of IDF units.

As a cover for my activities, I was given an assignment as teacher and counselor to young people emigrating to Israel. To complete my cover, I was listed as a part-time employee of the "Joint."

In August 1948, there was a lull in the fighting. During the third week of that month, Yigael Yadin, IDF head of operations, arrived in Prague to take a close look at the recruitment of professional soldiers and the procurement of weapons and ammunition from European army surplus, especially from Czechoslovakia. Yadin was a personable young man of thirty-one, and looked particularly impressive in the new IDF uniform that had not yet been seen, not even in Israel. He was received at an official ceremony at the Tomb of the Unknown Soldier, where he laid a wreath in the presence of a military guard of honor. It was the first time that we heard a foreign army band playing our national anthem. The crowd, mostly Jews who had gathered in the square, was visibly moved. Upon our return to the hotel, Yadin asked me to guide him on a walking tour of the synagogues and cemetery of the ancient Jewish Quarter.

By the summer of 1949 there was a decided change in Czechoslovakia's attitude toward Israel and we had to keep a low profile. At some point I realized that the local authorities had begun to shadow me. To shake them off, I detached myself from the embassy and acted as a lone wolf. I tried to elude my shadows by going to Poland on a mission initiated by Dr. Joseph Schwartz, director-general of the "Joint." I was to locate Jewish children who had been hidden with non-Jews during the war and who were still being held in monasteries, convents, and orphanages. I later learned that it was Mintz who had first suggested my name to Galili and Meirov (Avigur) for the mission to Prague.

Through the Israeli minister in Warsaw, Yisrael Barzilai, I was put in touch with local contacts, including Leibel Zamosz from Lodz and Dov Eigel from Wroclaw, who helped me in my assignment. Apart from one hitch that resulted in the arrest of a housemother in one of the communist institutions (the Yevsekzia) who had been cooperating with us in smuggling out Jewish children, all the operations were successfully executed. Hundreds of children and youths were returned to the Jewish people and brought to Israel via Czechoslovakia, Austria, and Italy.

My first visit to Poland, four years after my concentration camp internment, evoked strange feelings. In spite of the complexities of my mission and the protective measures to which I had to resort, I was keenly aware of the familiar environment. It beckoned to me, as if I had come back to seek some trace of my lost childhood, to touch some stone, some spot that would evoke another age, another life. But I found no rapport with anyone or anything around me.

One night in March 1949, I boarded a midnight train in Warsaw en route to Cracow. I was sitting alone in my cabin when the train made its first stop, and I noticed the sign PIOTRKOW. I grabbed my bag, stepped down onto the platform, and walked toward the dimly lit waiting room. Hesitantly, I approached the cashier's booth and saw a familiar face. The man looked at me with astonishment and fear in his eyes, asking what I was doing there at that unearthly hour, 2:40 A.M. It was Jagiello, who had been a foreman at the glass plant Hortensja where I had been employed at hard labor. Jagiello had been a decent foreman, but that night I felt he was afraid I came to settle an old account with him. He nervously explained that he too had been a forced laborer, just like the Jews. I reassured him and turned toward the city.

The square in front of the station, usually full of people and vehicles, was empty and quiet. I recoiled from the thought of going out alone to roam the streets so familiar to me. The last time I had been at this station was in August 1941, when I was smuggled out of Auschwitz. From this square I had sneaked my way back to our home in the ghetto. This time I had nowhere to go. I retraced my steps and returned to Jagiello. Joining him in a glass of tea during the three-hour wait for the next train to Cracow, I told him about my life in Israel.

In Cracow I received a coded warning transmitted by Dr. Yisrael Carmel, the Israeli consul in Warsaw. It pertained to my new activities in Poland. Not wanting to speak about it on the telephone, I took the night train back to Warsaw. There he told me that the security police, the U.B., was taking an interest in my activities, and advised me to leave as soon as possible.

Two days after my return to Prague, I went to evening prayers in the famous Altneu Synagogue of the great medieval rabbi, the Maharal. There I met an old friend, Azriel Brock, from Kibbutz Nir Etzion, an emissary from Israel to Bratislava. He had come to Prague for a brief visit. I invited him to share my hotel room at the Palace Hotel, next to the central post office. In the early hours of the morning, the reception clerk phoned and whispered to me that two men had inquired about me and were on their way up to my room. From his tone I gathered that these were security police.

At great speed I threw a few important belongings into my overnight bag. I told Azriel that I was leaving town, and that he should tell the security police that he had not seen me since the previous evening in the synagogue, where I gave him my key and invited him to use the room. I had already familiarized myself with the emergency exits from the hotel, and had no problem getting out unseen.

Once in the street, I walked to the Wilson railway station. Luckily a train was due to leave for Bratislava within a half hour. Six hours later I was in Bratislava, the town that was the checkpoint to the neighboring city of Vienna, across the Czech-Austrian border. Following instructions from my supervisor in Prague, I joined a group of Hungarian refugees on their way to Austria the following day. At the Rothschild Hospital in Vienna, which served as a transit camp for refugees, Bruce Teicholtz, the camp director, booked me a room in a nearby hotel and arranged a rendezvous with my new supervisor, Mordechai Ben Ari, later president of El Al.

My first assignment from Ben Ari was to screen the three thousand Hungarian refugees in the Rothschild transit camp and determine which ones were likely candidates for *aliyah* to Israel. Only a few seemed interested. Most wanted visas for the United States or Canada, and were understandably afraid of getting caught in a war zone. As part of my activities, I located a few youngsters committed to *aliyah* and arranged for them to act as counselors, keeping the younger children occupied. Eventually, they were to influence their parents to consider *aliyah*. During the three months I was there, some two thousand five hundred refugees from the Rothschild camp left for Israel.

At that time Vienna was controlled by the four allied powers, and the streets were patrolled by jeeps with military police from each power. Espionage and counterespionage nets covered Austria, particularly Vienna. As the flow of refugees from the East kept increasing, we had to organize a way to move them quickly from the temporary facilities in Vienna to Italy and on to Israel. The procedure entailed moving convoys of refugees from the eastern border of Austria to the southern border and crossing the occupation zones of all four armies – the Soviets, the British, the Americans, and sometimes the French – depending on the particular route. The job of coordinating the mission was assigned to me. This often entailed mediating between representatives of the four allied powers, who maintained headquarters in large hotels in the city center. To my surprise, three of them were Jews. This Jewish presence was most helpful in cases where payments and gifts to lower ranks were insufficient.

While in Vienna, I received a message from Ehud Avriel, who had been appointed Israeli ambassador to Czechoslovakia and Hungary. (At that time, one person served as ambassador to both countries.) He was on his way to Budapest to submit his credentials, and asked me to join him to help make contact with the local Jews. In Budapest I met

Shmuel Peterfy (later Ben-Tzur), a Hungarian Zionist leader who later became deputy director-general of the Israeli foreign ministry.

The orthodox Jewish community in Hungary had no contact with the Zionist movements or with the embassy. At Ehud's request, I met with the heads of the community and invited them to a meeting with Israel's first ambassador to their country. The Hungarians (Eliezer Zusman-Sofer, Dr. Laszlo Hausner, Zigmund Braun, and Simcha Stein) were impressed, and promised to place their educational and organizational resources at the disposal of the embassy. Within a year, all four settled in Israel.

My brief visit to Hungary enabled me to establish contacts with local Jews who had access to the authorities, particularly the ministry of the interior and the AVO, the security police. Following up on these contacts, I made a number of short trips to Budapest and returned with a large quantity of new Hungarian passports. These were a vital commodity for the foreign volunteers for the IDF – known as Machal (volunteers from the West) and Gachal (volunteers from Eastern Europe) – who needed to be flown to Israel on commercial planes via European transit stations. Many of the Machal members, particularly the Americans, could not use their own passports because of the U.S. embargo on Israel. A number of Gachal volunteers did not have a passport at all.

Early in 1950 I requested to be recalled from Europe. At a Paris meeting of the Mossad, I said that I would like to be in Israel by the coming Passover. Lulek's bar mitzvah was coming up in June, just after Shavuoth.

Yosef Barpal, one of the directors of the Mossad, received a request from MK (Member of the Knesset) Binyamin Mintz, that I remain in France for three months to help close down the Hennonville transit camp of Poalei Agudat Yisrael, where orphan children from Eastern Europe and North Africa had been housed prior to leaving for Israel. Mordechai Ben Ari, my supervisor in Austria, requested that I return with him to Vienna to wind up our work there.

At the approach of Israel's second Independence Day, a few weeks before Lulek's bar mitzvah, I returned to Israel to join in the celebration. Lulek was overjoyed at my arrival, and my aunt was overwhelmed by the windfall of delicacies I brought. At a time when the austerity in Israel was so severe that modest treats were scarce even for special occasions, I came with an ample supply of smoked meats and a variety of specialty foods. The celebration was held in the home of the Vogelmans, and all our relatives and friends attended.

This was the first bar mitzvah celebration I attended since my own, eleven years earlier, just before the outbreak of World War II. I do not count the gloomy bar mitzvah of Milek as a celebration. It was held under the murderous conditions of August 1942, just two months before he was deported with Father to Treblinka.

Lulek, the bar mitzvah boy, gave an impressive speech, attesting to his considerable scholastic achievements. Immediately after his bar mitzvah, he asked me to make good on my promise made shortly after he came to live with the Vogelmans – to let him study in Jerusalem when he reached the age of thirteen. He was happy at the Vogelmans, but felt that it was time for a change. We went to Jerusalem to see about enrollment at Kol Torah Yeshiva, headed by Rabbi Kunstadt and Rabbi Schlesinger, both of whom were born in Germany and believed in the philosophy of *"Torah im derech eretz"* which emphasized the importance of a secular education as well as religious studies. Rabbi Yosef Yehuda Reiner, a former student of my father, was in charge of the lower grades, and took Lulek under his wing.

To stay near him, I looked for work in Jerusalem. Binyamin Mintz, head of Poalei Agudat Yisrael and a family friend, was looking for a young reporter to write on Knesset debates for the daily party newspaper *Shearim,* and offered me the job. Thus began my career in journalism. I found that not only could I make a living through journalism, but that I also had time to pursue some academic studies.

It was a five-minute walk from the Knesset, in its temporary home in Beth Frumin on King George Street, to the Kol Torah Yeshiva. This allowed me to be close to my brother, now known as Yisrael, "Lulek" having been all but abandoned. I worked and studied in Jerusalem, returning to Tel Aviv for weekends.

The Knesset was a new feature in the life of the country, and journalistic coverage was challenging. After eighteen months as a parliamentary correspondent, I transferred to the Tel Aviv editorial offices as news editor, and began writing my own weekly column. *Shearim* gave me first-rate training as a journalist. There was no area in which I was not involved at one time or another.

After years of shuttling from country to country, from one uninviting hotel room to another, I found a pleasant room in the home of a Tel Aviv family. Here I felt I had my own niche. For the first time, I began to feel independent, free from the scrutiny of hotel reception clerks and fellow guests who were total strangers. It was an essential step on the way to having my own home and family.

21

JOURNALISM

The four-page newspaper, *Shearim*, turned out to be an excellent school of journalism for me. Its founder and first editor, Binyamin Mintz, was a superb teacher who knew how to guide, criticize, praise, and encourage a beginner. Both as a writer and journalist, he wielded a very sharp pen. It seemed to me that he enjoyed writing and editing more than his political activities as party leader and, later, as minister of communications in the Israel government.

In this small newspaper I learned to be a political and military correspondent and served as editor of international news for the front page, and domestic news for the back page. I enjoyed the work, especially the hectic pace before the 1:00 A.M. deadline, the final chance to include some last-minute item before the paper was closed and sent to press. It generated creativity within me. I found myself rising to the challenge of scooping the large afternoon dailies, especially with something important. The paper's relatively limited circulation and small size allowed me to hold the final layout until the very last moment, when the larger papers had already gone to press.

My first assignment as a field reporter was on January 7, 1952, when the Herut (right-wing party) leader, Menachem Begin, led thousands of demonstrators in Jerusalem against Israel's acceptance of reparation payments from Germany. I waited with my fellow Knesset correspondents in the crowded press box for the anticipated, heated debate on this sensitive issue. I could understand the attitude of the opponents to the reparations agreement. On the other hand, I could not come to terms with the idea that the Germans would then evade their responsibility for murder without even this minimum compensation to their victims. My own natural response to the Germans was to ask, "Hast thou killed and also taken possession?" (1 Kings 21:19). The debate went on in every home in Israel, often dividing husband and wife, parents and children.

Journalistic curiosity took me to Zion Square in the center of Jerusalem. Crowds, which the police estimated at fifty thousand, were streaming into the square. Menachem Begin stood at an iron railing on a small balcony and raised his voice in response to the stormy cheers of the crowd, "It shall never come to pass and it shall never be. . . . This will turn into a terrible war between us," he shouted.

When he finished, an aging historian, Professor Yosef Klausner, began to speak. I didn't want to hear him, and raced back to the Knesset, where Begin was scheduled to speak next. Even before I reached the Froumine Building, temporary home of Israel's Knesset, I heard the increasingly angry shouts of demonstrators marching up Ben Yehuda Street toward the Knesset. Begin had not yet reached the podium when the mob outside began to storm the building, throwing stones as they advanced. A number of Knesset members and newspapermen were injured by glass from the shattered windows. The uproar outside was matched by the clash inside between Begin, on the podium, and Ben-Gurion, seated at the head of the government table.

For the ten parliamentary correspondents in the narrow press box, the dreadful scene on the Knesset floor made for a dramatic story. We represented the entire political spectrum in Israel, from the extreme right to the revolutionary left, but all of us would have willingly forgone this news story. Yaacov James Rosenthal, the senior among us, a reporter who could remember sessions of the Reichstag before Hitler's rise to power and who represented the liberal newspaper *Ha'aretz,* was white as a sheet, mumbling to himself: "This is the end, this is the end. . . ." Even Shalom Rosenfeld, a right-wing revisionist from the afternoon paper *Ma'ariv,* was appalled by the scene we were witnessing. In our hearts we prayed that it would be just a passing uproar, soon to be forgotten. This emotional outburst was my first plunge into the riptide of journalism.

On July 23, 1952, a group of Egyptian army officers staged a coup and dethroned Farouk, king of Egypt. It was headed by General Muhamad Neguib, but its prime architect and the power of the uprising was Lt.Col. Gamal Abdul Nasser. Ten months after the coup, U.S.

Secretary of State John Foster Dulles arrived in the region, intent on strengthening American influence in the Middle East. He came as the emissary of U.S. President Eisenhower and stopped over in Egypt, where he met the new revolutionary head, General Neguib. As a token of the United States' recognition of the new regime in Cairo, and at the prospect of opening a new chapter in relations with Egypt, Dulles presented him with a gift of a silver pistol – a symbolism that aroused astonishment and concern in Israel.

Dulles' schedule included visits to Jordan, Saudi Arabia, Iraq, Turkey, and Israel. On May 14-15, 1953, he visited Israel. In a long conversation with Ben-Gurion, they discussed far-reaching proposals for new relationships between the nations of the region. According to a joint communiqué, nothing concrete was proposed by Dulles except for the mutual hope for peace in the area. Dulles' entourage maintained a total blackout on the content of the discussion. The spokesmen of the prime minister's office and the Israeli foreign ministry were no more forthcoming, either because they would not say or did not know. The absence of hard news inevitably gave rise to rumors, some of which later proved to be true.

Like all the other correspondents, I was running around trying to find something newsworthy regarding the contents of the talks. Here and there we gathered some crumbs of information, but found very little that was new. By pure chance I picked up an item from a member of the secretary's entourage, which was likely to jolt many people out of their complacency. On rechecking, I discovered there was more than just a kernel of truth in my information, that Dulles had told Foreign Minister Moshe Sharett of America's desire to reshape regional Middle East relations in the wake of new developments in Egypt. In his opinion, there was now an opportunity for Israel to reach an understanding with Egypt on a state of nonbelligerency. To motivate Egypt to such an agreement, Dulles proposed that Israel absorb from seventy-five thousand to one hundred thousand Arab refugees, and withdraw from virtually the entire Negev south of Beersheba, to allow for territorial contiguity between Egypt and Jordan. He spoke of the need to redraw the signed 1949 armistice lines agreed upon at the end of the 1948 War of Independence.

Foreign Minister Sharett responded with an outright rejection of the proposal, but committed himself to keep the conversation secret.

Undeterred by Israel's refusal, Dulles appointed a two-man diplomatic team, consisting of one U.S. representative and one British foreign office member, to prepare a detailed plan in the spirit of his proposal. The Anglo-American team labored for close to two years and then submitted "Project Alpha" to Dulles and the British prime minister. The two teammates were the minister at the U.S. Embassy in Israel, Francis H. Russell, and Charles Arthur Evelyn Shuckburgh, assistant to the foreign secretary in London. Essentially, the prerequisite for an understanding remained the double concession by Israel: withdrawal from the Negev and absorption of Arab refugees.

Details of Alpha were not made public until the end of 1954. In August 1955 Dulles announced the general principles to the council on foreign relations in New York, but without the slightest mention of the demand for Israel to give up the Negev and take in tens of thousands of 1948 refugees. It was an attempt by Dulles to calm the American Jewish community, which was up in arms at the administration's proposal, only a year away from a presidential election.

I prepared the story with all the appropriate caution required by the delicate situation, taking great care not to compromise my source. I laid the handwritten article on the desk of the editor, MK Avraham Goldrat. Until that moment he knew absolutely nothing about it. When he read my copy, he paled. Feeling the full impact and pressure of responsibility, he went straight to Jerusalem to consult with editor-in-chief Binyamin Mintz. The two decided to shelve the story until further notice. They both praised the journalistic scoop but, as they took pains to explain, they could not take responsibility for the damage that would result from its publication.

Twenty years after Dulles made his demands on Israel, I was traveling with Defense Minister Moshe Dayan to the United States. This was the era of U.S. Secretary of State Rogers' initiative and Kissinger's mediation, pressuring Israel to withdraw to the 1949 cease-fire lines; in other words, to the pre-June 1967 Six-Day War frontiers. I reminded Dayan of Dulles' demand from Sharett and he smiled, adding: "Dulles' proposal to Sharett in May 1953, his obstinacy about Alpha and the pressure on Israel to accept it, in late 1954 and 1955, were what caused the Old Man [Ben-Gurion] to decide on the Sinai Campaign."

According to Dayan, Ben-Gurion was disappointed by U.S. efforts to placate the Arabs at the expense of Israel's vital interests. He could see an opening for talks with Egypt after the 1952 coup, believing that the new rulers would prefer to deal with internal Egyptian problems and would want some sort of understanding with Israel. He felt that the Americans were wrong to court the Egyptians without calling for unequivocal recognition of Israel's existence. This was the stage at which Ben-Gurion decided to join in the Franco-British plan to counter Egypt's blocking of the Suez Canal. Ben-Gurion viewed France and England as more likely to advance common interests in the region, and preferred to rely on them, rather than to go along with American moves that promised only danger to Israel. With this in mind, he accepted Dayan's 1955 strategy for a strike against Egypt, which was blockading the Gulf of Eilat and the Suez Canal against Israel-bound cargo ships and organizing *fedayeen* (terrorist infiltrator) teams to wreak death and destruction throughout the country. This led to the 1956 Sinai Campaign and Israel's subsequent withdrawal from the Sinai Peninsula, under joint pressure from President Eisenhower and the Kremlin.

The summer of 1956 was a hot period on Israel's frontiers. Arab *fedayeen* terrorists were penetrating villages, robbing and murdering indiscriminately. The IDF retaliated, thus arousing angry reactions in world opinion. By the end of October, the atmosphere heated to explosion point. In coordination with Britain and France, Israel initiated "Operation Kadesh" and, for the first time, captured the entire Sinai Peninsula and Gaza Strip, breaking the Egyptian blockade of the port of Eilat on the Red Sea and removing the terrorist threat emanating from Egypt and Gaza.

One hot August evening, on my way home from a friend's wedding in north Tel Aviv, I dropped in on some very close friends, Yisrael and Sara Minzer. Sitting on the balcony were a few couples, friends in common, but what caught my eye was a beautiful girl I had never met before. I was struck by her charm and personality. Joan was a girl I definitely wanted to get to know better. It took only a week or two for me to decide that she was the girl I wanted to marry. To my good fortune, the feeling became mutual. Her Hebrew betrayed her English origin. She was born in London and was evacuated to Switzerland to stay with her sister during World War II. After the war she returned to

London to complete high school. Later she volunteered as a youth counselor with Youth Aliyah children in France. In 1951 she came to Israel and studied in the School of Social Work at the Hebrew University in Jerusalem. I was already thirty and ready to think in terms of settling down in a home of my own, now that I found the right partner.

We decided to marry, but things were not so simple. Joan came from a very conservative English home with an orthodox Western European background. Her parents expected me to ask their permission for such an important step. They wanted to know more about the man who was asking for the hand in marriage of their eighth and youngest child. A phone call to London from Tel Aviv was not enough to convince Hugo and Celine Lunzer. I had to draft a polite letter to introduce myself more formally.

On the eve of Rosh Hashanah, the positive reply arrived, and to this day our paths have never separated. She has been my wife and partner, bringing up our four children, supportive in my demanding career, first as a journalist and later in government service. After our children were grown and had gone their own ways, Joan returned to her profession as a medical social worker.

One week before our wedding day, set for November 5, 1956, the army began to mobilize its reserves. My function was that of military correspondent. I was assigned to the Ninth Brigade. Nobody yet knew why we were mobilizing. Major Danny Gov, the senior officer in the IDF spokesman's bureau, ordered me to remain close at hand and wait for the call to report. I told him that we had already sent out invitations to our wedding just one week hence. He promised that all would be over in time for me to attend my own wedding ceremony.

I flew in a Dakota from Sde Dov Airport in Tel Aviv to Eilat, on my unknown mission. On the morning of Monday, October 29, I reported to the Ninth Brigade commander, Colonel Avraham Yaffe, at his headquarters south of Eilat. He was involved in pushing the brigade southward across the desert, to Sharm-el-Sheikh at the gateway to the Red Sea. Still, he found time to listen to my personal problem and told me not to worry. On Friday morning, November 2, I received an order from Colonel Yaffe to board a plane in Eilat and return to Tel Aviv for my wedding.

The wedding ceremony took place in the Commerce and Industry Club in Tel Aviv. Most of the guests were beyond mobilization age. Only a few of my friends could make it, including Danny Gov and some of the correspondents who had already returned from the conquest of Gaza. As the victory became known and the occupation of Sinai and Gaza was completed, our rejoicing took on an added dimension. The blackout curtains were removed; the lights seemed all the more dazzling for our wedding – symbolic indeed.

The guests reflected the spectrum of diverse lifestyles of Jews worldwide, ranging from East European rabbis, *hassidim*, and community leaders, to Jews of Western European elegance, including my unshaved friends still in their sweaty uniforms, just returned from the front for a few hours' leave. Absent were some of the most important people in my life, my dear parents and brother Milek. I tried to concentrate on this special occasion, signifying the opening of a new page in my life, as I was being escorted to the ceremony by my uncle, Rabbi Dr. Vogelman, and Joan's father, Mr. Hugo Lunzer. Watching my brother Lulek, now a handsome young man of nineteen, gave me some consolation, filling me with pride. Then, of course, the headlines of the military victory on the day of my wedding added to my happiness.

Two weeks after our wedding, we traveled to London to meet my new family. It was a unique experience for me to encounter a whole Jewish community that had not been directly affected by the horrors of the Holocaust. Although Joan's nuclear family remained intact, her mother's family had not escaped unscathed. Her maternal grandmother had been deported from the Hague to Westerbork and on to Bergen-Belsen, where she died. Many of my mother-in-law's immediate family perished in Nazi concentration camps. I was received with open arms by my new family, and very soon felt at home despite the differences in cultural background.

When we returned from a three-month honeymoon in Europe, I began to write for *Ha'aretz* on public and political issues, and to edit the news pages. For the ensuing fourteen years this newspaper was my second home. I started as an area reporter alternately covering the south, down to Dimona and Yerucham, and the north up to Zichron Yaacov. From this start, I climbed the journalistic ladder, writing and editing, commenting in editorials, and writing byline articles on public affairs, until I terminated my work at *Ha'aretz* in June 1970.

During the subsequent five years, three of our children were born. The fourth was born in April 1969. The four of them complete our family mosaic, each in her/his own unique way. Our daughter, Chaya-Naomi, Chen (charming), as her friends call her for short, is married to Itamar Ben Aris, an agriculturist. They have two children and live in Kibbutz Erez, near the Gaza Strip. By any definition, political or military, this is a border settlement whose members may correctly view themselves as the pioneers of Israeli society. Chaya holds an American degree as a professional medical assistant. Our son Shai, a horticulturist, lives with his wife, Varda Steinberg, a speech therapist, and their five children on Mitzpeh Hoshaya, in the Galil. In addition to working on the kibbutz, they are both continuing their academic studies. Benyamin and his wife, Noa, are members of Kibbutz Sa'ad in the Negev, where they live with their five children. Both have completed their academic studies and are active in education. Benny (Benyamin) is an ordained rabbi and serves as the kibbutz rabbi in addition to his work as an educator. Our youngest, Amichai-Yehuda, completed his regular army service and is now a counselor for local as well as foreign visiting groups, while pursuing his academic studies in education and psychology.

I get gratification from the fact that all my children are living in Israel, deepening their roots in this country. Joan and I endeavored to imbue in our children the love of the Land, and are content to see them establishing and building their lives and the lives of the next generation in the tradition of our people, in Israel.

22

GERMAN ENCOUNTERS

In 1958, Gershom Schocken, the editor of *Ha'aretz*, gave me a difficult and sensitive assignment. I was to prepare a series of articles on nuclear research in Israel. I had to maneuver cautiously between published papers on nuclear physics and the possible application of these research results, kept under the strictest secrecy, under veritable blackout. Thanks to this assignment, I became acquainted with the senior scientists in the field: Julio Racah at the Hebrew University; Amos de Shalit, Yigal Talmi, Yisrael Pelach, and Yisrael Dostrovsky, all at the Weizmann Institute; and, especially, Ernst David Bergman, founder of the IDF's Scientific Corps and director of the Scientific Research and Planning Division of the Ministry of Defense.

Knowing of my contacts in this field, Schocken suggested in early December 1959 that I visit the Weizmann Institute to interview two prominent nuclear scientists from Germany. He was aware of my reservations about meeting Germans. Perhaps for that reason, he told me about Professor Hahn's role in preventing the manufacture of an atomic bomb for Hitler. That was sufficiently enticing and tempting to send me to the Institute to meet eighty-one-year-old Otto Hahn and his younger colleague, Wolfgang Goentner.

I met them in Professor Amos de Shalit's laboratory. The silver-haired Hahn answered my questions courteously. Subjects he did not wish to discuss he referred to Professor Goentner. Even before I got to ask a single question, he made a point of saying:

"Don't believe all the published books and newspapers that claim Hitler almost had an atomic bomb. True, we worked on the theoretical aspects of nuclear explosions, but we were very far from producing a bomb. Anyway, even if we could have made the bomb, we wouldn't have given that madman the means to destroy the world."

Other nuclear physicists differed. They claimed that Professor Hahn's team had made far-reaching progress and that he indeed did seek to produce the bomb. Hahn vehemently denied any such assessment. He described in detail his scientific work as head of the Kaiser Wilhelm Institute and later as director of the Max Planck Research Institute in Goettingen.

For a period of thirty-five years Otto Hahn had been trying to penetrate the mysteries of the atom, ever since 1904, when his mentor, Sir William Ramsey, discovered the radioactive isotope known as radiothorium. In December 1938 and early 1939, Hahn discovered that the atomic nucleus of uranium could be split, a breakthrough that garnered him the Nobel Prize for Chemistry in 1944. Six years after the revolutionary 1938-1939 discovery, the principle was applied to make the atomic bombs dropped on Hiroshima and Nagasaki. Hahn stated emphatically:

"I didn't believe that anyone could have succeeded in developing the infernal bomb based on my discovery."

"Did you try to slow down the tempo of research and development, to prevent such a device from falling into Hitler's hands?" I asked.

"Up to 1938, I worked with Lisa Meitner. That summer, she was forced to flee to Sweden because she was Jewish. Her place in the team was taken by another scientist, a pure Aryan, Dr. Fritz Strassmann, who lacked her imagination."

At that stage the research was accelerated. In September 1939, two weeks after the outbreak of World War II, the senior German physicists were summoned to the Reich War Ministry and required to put their knowledge and technology at the disposal of the war machine. That meeting created the "uranium team," which was supposed to use nuclear science to develop an atomic bomb for Hitler. Its new center was established in the Kaiser Wilhelm Institute in Berlin, headed for a while by Professor Otto Hahn himself.

"What truth is there in the rumors prevalent in postwar Germany that your partner, Lisa Meitner, sabotaged your effort to produce the bomb?" I asked.

Hahn exchanged glances with his colleague, Professor Goentner, and frowned.

"None of us wanted to give him the bomb. But, if the truth be told, I didn't yet see it as a reality. I thought we would need many more years to develop it. We were surprised by the pace of research in the United States, which overtook the Germans by a few years," said Hahn, with an odd expression on his face, registering neither satisfaction nor regret.

Goentner was less circumspect in his reply. He was director of the Nuclear Physics Institute at Heidelberg University and vice president of CERN (European Council for Nuclear Research). In his view, German research had come close to producing an atomic bomb. When World War II broke out, Goentner was at Berkeley University in California, and it was there that he learned of Hahn's discovery and heard a talk by Niels Bohr, the famous Danish physicist, evaluating Hahn's work as truly revolutionary. Goentner found it very encouraging. He was aware of the urgency among his American colleagues in nuclear physics to advance in this field. The motivating force behind this project in the U.S. was Professor Robert Oppenheimer, who later headed the American effort to develop an atomic bomb.

At the end of 1939, Professor Goentner returned to Germany with mixed feelings. Following the conquest of France, he was sent to Paris to direct the Joliot-Curie Research Institute. According to him, he reached an understanding with the two leading French scientists there not to make military use of research results, should there be any.

Many years after this interview, in a biography of Lisa Meitner, it came to light that she did not sabotage the work, though Hahn's evasive answer did not say so. In fact, after she escaped from Germany to Sweden, Hahn carried on an extensive correspondence with her, and she effectively directed the research from abroad. They even met in Denmark just a few weeks before the crucial (experimental) discovery. In a letter dated December 11, 1938, Hahn asked her help in finding a reasonable interpretation of the results of the experiment, which later brought him the Nobel Prize. She responded on New Year's Day, 1939, with the full explanation of the experiment resulting from the fission of the uranium nucleus. It was a remarkable insight, going against the firmly held view that it was impossible to split the nucleus of an element of nature, such as uranium.

During the war, Hahn at first denied any connection with Meitner, a Jewess, for reasons of personal safety. However, he persisted in this denial and thus received the Nobel Prize individually, a great injustice to his colleague and close friend of over thirty years. She never publicly criticized him, though in private conversations she was very bitter about his behavior.

Continuing our interview, Hahn switched to what sounded like an admission that, despite their best efforts, they did not succeed in producing the atomic bomb, as Hitler had demanded.

"There was no truth in the accusations that the scientists acted treasonably in depriving Hitler of victory over Germany's enemies," he contradicted his earlier statement – substantiated by later developments. The British occupying authorities arrested the senior nuclear physicists in Germany who, they suspected, had done their best to serve Hitler's war machine. It was only chance, if not a miracle, that sent them down the wrong track and kept them from providing Hitler with the ultimate weapon. After the war, Britain placed these German nuclear physicists in detention in a sumptuous English country manor called Farm Hall. They were not allowed to communicate with anyone, but otherwise were well treated.

When the U.S. dropped atomic bombs on Hiroshima and Nagasaki, a British officer called together all of these German nuclear scientists and told them of the U.S. atomic bomb. Hahn, one of the interned scientists, turned to his colleagues and said:

"If the Americans have a uranium bomb, then we are all second-raters. Poor old Heisenberg." This statement was secretly recorded by the British.

The German scientists were devastated by the news. Walter Gerlach suffered a nervous breakdown. Heisenberg and Weizsaecker kept looking in on him several times at night, fearing he might commit suicide. The following morning, Max von Laue said, "The main question is naturally, why we in Germany did not achieve our mission in producing the bomb."

These secretly recorded comments indicate their true attitude. They had tried their utmost to produce an atomic bomb and were deeply disappointed by having been outdone by the Allies. It was a terrible blow to their German pride.

The real irony of the story is that, had Germany not forced its Jewish nuclear scientists to flee and join the allies, it is very likely that the Germans would have won the race to make the (atomic) bomb.

While I was writing the story of the interview with the two German scientists, and shuddering at the thought of what might have happened had Hitler obtained the bomb first, I got an urgent call from Joan. Labor pains had started. I rushed home to drive her to the maternity ward of Rabin (Beilinson) Hospital, where she gave birth to our firstborn, a daughter, named Chaya after my mother.

It was a most exciting event in our life, the forerunner of what was to follow within a few years – the birth of our three sons: Shai, Benny, and Amichai.

Another highlight was the wedding of Lulek, now a twenty-three-year-old ordained rabbi. He married Chaya Itta, daughter of Rabbi Yitzchak Yedidya Frenkel, who became chief rabbi of Tel Aviv. The wedding guests represented a Who's Who in Israeli society. For me, this happy family occasion signified an additional milestone: the discharging of my mission in the role of caretaker and mentor of Lulek, who, as an accomplished young adult, could now take his rightful place in carrying on the family heritage, as envisioned by our father.

The Eichmann Trial

The second encounter with my German past came in the spring of 1961. In April of that year, the trial of Adolf Eichmann opened in the Beth Ha'am courtroom in Jerusalem. Eichmann had been kidnapped from his hiding place in Argentina and brought to Israel for trial, accused of crimes against the Jewish people. This gray-haired bureaucrat, who had served the Nazi murder machine with efficiency and devotion, became an abhorrent symbol of Nazi crimes. He could neither bask in the glory of a military past nor claim a major ideological contribution to the Nazi racist philosophy. He had advanced from his position as a low-level bureaucrat, rising in responsibility, performing his duties with precision and enthusiasm, and progressing through the SS ranks to become the top figure responsible for implementing the planned, methodical murder of millions of human beings.

For the survivors, bringing Adolf Eichmann to trial in Jerusalem was an act of justice and a condemnation of the crime, but also a painful reexposure. The psychological and emotional wounds had not yet healed. All too many had not returned, and perhaps never would return, to "life as usual."

Two days before the trial, Yisrael Finkelstein, secretary of the editorial board, assigned me to cover the proceedings. I was to start from the second week of the trial. I knew that three other journalists, one from Tel Aviv and two from Jerusalem, had been assigned to the case, and wondered what was behind my assignment. Yisrael said that he wanted a daily column with my impressions. Though he did not say so explicitly, I realized that he sought my personal reactions and feelings. I hesitated and discussed the matter with Joan, who left the decision to me.

Until then I had not listened to the radio broadcasts covering the trial. It was enough to read State Prosecutor Gideon Hausner's well-organized opening address. Later, the standard repeated question, "Why didn't you rebel?" began to grate on my nerves. The first evidence was given by a Polish-born historian, Professor Salo Wittmayer Baron of Columbia University, in New York. He described the living conditions and demography of the different Jewish communities in Europe before World War II: their suffering from anti-Semitism and poor economic conditions; their customs and spiritual life; as well as their cultural contributions to the host nations. He spoke of Jews fleeing their bitter fate through conversion and assimilation, while others obstinately clung to their Jewish identity throughout. He also mentioned the 1937 testament of Henry Bergson, who admitted that Catholicism had greatly attracted him but, upon witnessing the wave of anti-Semitism that threatened to engulf the world, stated, "I decided to remain among those destined for persecution."

Following the account of Professor Baron, I wrote impressions of the testimonies of author Abba Kovner and of Zindel Shmuel Greenspan, father of Hershel Greenspan. Hershel had been studying in Paris. Upon learning that, on October 27, 1938, the Nazis had deported twelve thousand Jews of Polish origin, including his parents, he went to the German embassy in Paris and killed a German diplomat, vom Raat. In retaliation, the Nazis staged a massive pogrom against the Jews of Germany and Austria on November 8 and 9; it was to become known as "Kristallnacht" because of the shattered glass from Jewish homes, shops, and synagogues all across Germany and Austria.

One of the witnesses at the trial was Rivka Yoslavska, a forty-year-old woman who related how she had emerged from a mass grave filled with the bodies of dozens of her relatives and friends in White Russia. My own memories of that nether world began to explode within me as I listened to her story. Next to me sat Mordechai Namir, mayor of Tel Aviv, formerly minister of labor and ambassador to the Soviet Union. Next to him was Benny Marshak, a Palmach veteran who had seen his own share of battles, tragedies, and bloodshed. Both were crying as Rivka, straining for control, in an emotional voice broken by occasional sobs, spoke, in snatches, about her brush with death.

Together with dozens of Jews of her town, she had been forced to run two miles to a hill where four *SS* murderers were stationed, waiting with pistols drawn. The Jews stood at the foot of the hill, near a deep pit that already contained a pile of a dozen bodies. When Rivka arrived, holding the hand of her little daughter, she saw naked men and women standing there by the pit, awaiting their fate. Up to that point she had still hoped that the purpose was only torture. Her daughter, wearing Sabbath clothes donned in preparation for deportation to an unknown destination, asked, "Mamme, why did I have to wear my best clothes? After all, they're going to shoot us and kill us." Directed to a pile of clothes, Rivka and her child had to strip and add their clothes to the pile. Standing naked on the brink of the pit, the girl asked again, "Mamme, why are we just standing and waiting? Let's run away." Rivka paused, then resumed, "A few youngsters did try to run, but they didn't get more than a few feet away before they were shot and killed on the spot."

In answer to the judges' questions, she described the process by which all her relatives, who had been forced to run with her, were killed:

After my sister and her girlfriend, my father and mother were shot and thrown in the pit ... it was my turn and my child's. We walked forward together toward the pit. I closed my eyes ... I turned my head away. An SS man asked who should be shot first, my daughter or I. I did not answer ... felt her being torn from my grasp – heard her last cry ... the sound of a shot. Then he turned to me ... I turned away again ... he grabbed my hair ... shot at me. I heard the shot ... but I was still standing. I opened my eyes – he swung me around – began to reload his pistol ... fired a shot. I fell into the pit ... felt nothing at first. Then ... a heaviness, a weight on me, getting heavier. I thought I was dead ... still, I could feel something. I was suffocating, bodies were falling on top of me. I felt I was drowning ... I thrashed around ... realized I could move ... must be alive. I was choking ... hearing shots ... corpses piling up on me. I struggled ... no more strength ... suddenly I became aware that I was somehow crawling out from beneath the bodies... I felt people shoving, biting, scratching, pulling me down, pushing me down. . . . Frantic, with the last of my strength I rose to the top, lying there, just lying there. When I finally had the strength to get up, I could not relate to anything, so many people ... death sprawled all around me. Terrible voices. Awful voices. Children screaming 'Tatte, Mamme!' I crawled away ... couldn't stand on my feet. By then the Germans were gone. No one was left ... just the dead.

I sat through her testimony, stunned, detached from everything around me. I took notes mechanically. When she finished, I looked at my "notes" and could not find a single legible sentence. I left Beth Ha'am and, like a sleepwalker from another planet, began to roam the narrow lanes of the ancient Jerusalem quarter around the courtroom, one of the first built outside the old city walls. Parched to the point of suffocation I could not bring myself to ask for water at a nearby kiosk. After two hours of wandering, I returned to the courtroom to get a copy of the transcript from the stenographers.

I drove back from Jerusalem to Tel Aviv alone, not wanting to see anyone. I needed to be alone. Descending the Sha'ar Hagai canyon, I saw workers putting Israeli flags on the wrecked armored vehicles, relics of the 1948 convoys to Jerusalem. It was just before Israel's thirteenth Independence Day. The nation was about to celebrate its bar mitzvah. I wondered whether all this would have happened at all if only Israel had been born ten, or even seven years earlier.

I did not go to the editorial offices to write my column that evening, but went straight home and stayed there for two days. Joan sensed my mood and took pains not to intrude. On the third day, Finkelstein phoned to find out what happened to me – what about the column I was supposed to write for the paper? After the midday editorial meeting, I went to his office and told him that I could not cover the trial any more. He understood and suggested I take a week's vacation.

Months later, as the trial drew to a close, the editor in chief, Gershom Schocken, called me to his office. For the first time since I had known him, he asked in a straightforward way about the Holocaust. I was sparing with descriptions and he wanted only dry facts. Finally, at the end of our conversation, it evolved that he wanted to publish a series of articles on the stand taken by the Jewish leadership in Eretz Yisrael regarding the Holocaust, to examine their decisions and actions to save the Jews. He got the idea from comments made by Moshe Sharett, director of the Jewish Agency's political department (subsequently Israel's first foreign minister). Sharett spoke about information that had reached Israel regarding the fate of the European Jews under Hitler and the efforts made, or not made, to save them. He brought to the fore the weakness and helplessness of the Jewish leadership in the face of the decimation of European Jewry. Schocken wanted me to research in depth, since I had been on the "other side," in the bowels of the inferno.

I explained to him that in my opinion there had been serious errors of omission, but this did not seem to be the right time to deal with our "sins," while we were judging one of the main perpetrators of the genocide of our people. He promised to hold off publication until after the Eichmann trial, but asked me to prepare the series.

He allotted three months for collecting data and writing. I again mentioned my opinion that now was not the time to get involved in this sensitive subject. I also tried to withdraw for personal reasons. I was not willing to have Hausner, or any other Israeli who had not been "there," point an accusing finger at us for not rebelling. By the same logic, I could not allow myself to judge the Jews of Eretz Yisrael or the United States or the entire world and their leaders for what they could have done, but did not do. Schocken was unmoved, merely telling me that he trusted my fair judgment in dealing with the subject.

When I took on the assignment, it never entered my mind to what extent the leadership in Eretz Yisrael had been stricken with blindness and helplessness, even years after the ongoing murder of European Jewry was no longer in dispute. I interviewed more than sixty people. The list included leaders, activists in the underground movements, emissaries from Europe who came to alert the world, parachutists sent to be dropped "over there," and survivors of ghetto uprisings. Because of the sensitivity of the subject, I kept extremely accurate records of my interviews. This was the first and only time in my journalistic career that I submitted to the editor the names of all those I interviewed, including even those whose material I did not use, so that he could check all information that might have influenced me.

The interviews that made the strongest impression on me were those of Moshe Sharett; Yitzchak Greenbaum, one of the Polish Jewish leaders who served as chairman of the rescue committee established in 1942 and later the first minister of the interior in the government of Israel; Joel Brandt, who came from Budapest on a mission for Eichmann, and was arrested by the British en route from Turkey to Eretz Yisrael; Yaacov Griffel, who ran the rescue activities of Agudat Yisrael in Turkey; and the written testimony of Rabbi Michael Weissmandel from Slovakia, who wrote in his book *From out of the Depths* about how he had alerted the world of the possibilities to save Jews, but received no response.

In his modest apartment, I found Moshe Sharett a bundle of nerves. For weeks I had been pleading with his secretary at the Am Oved publishing house, which he headed as chairman of the board, to schedule a meeting with him. She kept giving me the runaround, until I finally told her to tell Sharett that I was about to print remarks attributed to him and was offering him a chance to respond before I published. Then, and only then, did I get an appointment.

Even before I could get past the entrance to the guest room of his house in Jerusalem, he showed signs of nervousness. When I told him what I wanted to talk about, he advised me to speak to Ben-Gurion.

"Not me. Him! He was in charge at the Jewish Agency!"

I pointed out that as director of the political department in the Jewish Agency (the prestate "government"), he had been in contact with the outside world and must have known about events in Europe. It followed that he could have advised his colleagues on ways to act.

"There was nothing we could do and, anyway, why are you approaching me?" he erupted again.

For forty minutes I tried to get something relevant from him. He skirted the subject and resorted to administrative and formalistic obstacles. At some point I must have stretched his nerves too far and something snapped. He banged on the coffee table between us and announced that the discussion was over. His wife, Zipora, who was standing behind me holding a tray with glasses of tea, was so shocked at her husband's outburst that she dropped the entire tray on the floor.

Sharett was pale and angry when he saw me to the door. A few hours later, while sitting in the editorial office in Tel Aviv, I received a phone call. It was Sharett, calling to apologize. He tried to explain that my questions had no relevance to his functions in the past and that was why he lost his temper. He invited me to continue the discussion in a more relaxed atmosphere. I thanked him for the gesture, but declined the invitation.

Sharett laid the blame for negligence in rescue efforts on Ben-Gurion, chairman of the Jewish Agency executive and leader of the Jewish community. I investigated the position taken by Ben-Gurion on this subject and asked for an interview. The Old Man was not prepared to discuss the issue at that time, but his assistants referred me to statements he made about saving Jews way back when the news about extermination first reached Israel.

On November 30, 1942, during an assembly of the National Committee, an elected body that served as the parliament of the future state, Ben-Gurion pleaded: "We, the representatives of the Jewish people in our homeland, are gathered here to urge you, the prime minister of England, the president of the U.S., and the rulers of the great nations fighting Hitler, to do whatever you can. . . . There are German nationals in America, Britain, Russia, and other countries of the world. We urge you to insist that they be exchanged for Jews from Poland, Lithuania, and the other countries under the Nazi gallows! Let all the Jews that can leave the Nazi inferno come out; do not close your doors in their faces! Bring them out, first and foremost the children, to wherever possible, but save them!

"The Jewish community in Eretz Yisrael will absorb any Jew for whom the free world will not find room, any Jew who succeeds in escaping the valley of death," Ben-Gurion cried out to the nations of the world, but it was a voice in the wilderness.

England, in control of Palestine, was unwilling to open its gates to Jews, just as the U.S. adamantly blocked entry for survivors. One week later, on December 8, 1942, Ben-Gurion asked Dr. Nahum Goldmann in America to expedite "the fast pullout of Jews, and particularly women and children, from enemy countries." That same day he sent a message to Justice Felix Frankfurter, saying: "Hitler's decision to exterminate all the Jews in Poland is apparently the first step to purge all the conquered lands of Jews." The information was there, the will was there, but the action was missing.

I interviewed Yitzchak Greenbaum in his room at Kibbutz Gan Shmuel. He was old and a little forlorn, but completely lucid. In our conversation, in June 1961, he repeated what he had said 18 years earlier at the Zionist executive session that received reports on the genocide: "The duty of the movement is to bring more Jews here, to create more settlements, and to build more farms." He related that at that time he had been suspicious of the offer brought by the Hungarian messenger, Joel Brandt: a hundred thousand Jews in return for ten thousand trucks supplied to the Germans. Even now, he still believed that Brandt's mission was a German ruse, aimed at creating a rift between the Zionist movement and the Allies.

In a little cafe in the Yad Eliahu district of Tel Aviv near the home of Joel Brandt, I heard his version of the mission, for which the Nazis had sent him to Turkey. He did not speak Hebrew, so we spoke German. "The Jewish Agency people didn't believe me. They thought I was a Nazi agent come to trap them. From the moment I arrived in Turkey they had me followed, and finally betrayed me to the British secret service, just to put obstacles in my way." Though he spoke in a confused fashion and appeared paranoid, convinced he was being pursued by the Israeli establishment, he leveled very serious charges against the Jewish Agency and the Histadrut (the General Federation of Labor, the most powerful political organization in Israel), headed by leaders of the community – accusations that I was able to corroborate from other sources.

Brandt mentioned names of leaders who were completely deaf to the proposals he brought from Hungary. Some said the Germans were not to be trusted, others argued that the British would not permit an exchange that would indirectly help the Nazi war machine. One leader argued that the Hungarian Jews should help themselves by revolting against the Nazis instead of relying on outside help. At the end of the Zionist executive meeting, that same leader called Brandt aside and asked whether the people of Budapest had any contact with Auschwitz and whether it was possible to get someone out of there. It turned out that he was worried about his son, who was a prisoner in that camp.

At the end of three months of work, including off-the-record conversations and not-for-attribution interviews, I concluded that the same cloud that had befuddled the judgment of those trapped "over there," had dulled the senses of those here. They had lost or lacked the ability to evaluate what was going on around them. They could not look beyond the limits of their horizon. Even after the terrible reality had been revealed, they were still unresponsive, devoid of courage. The initiative and understanding that so successfully served these same leaders in 1946 to 1948 was nonexistent from 1942 to 1945, when catastrophe was decimating the Jews of Europe.

With a very heavy heart, I summed up the gist of all the interviews, but hesitated to put it down on paper. I confided my hesitations to a senior member of the editorial staff, Dr. Shlomo Gross, whose judgment I especially valued. He urged me to write and then look at it again before deciding whether or not to publish. I did as Dr. Gross wisely suggested and began to write. At least four times I stopped writing, feeling convinced that this was not the appropriate time to dig into our collective conscience. Finally I submitted a series of three articles to Schocken under the heading, "Why Didn't You Act?" and again suggested that publication of the articles be postponed or perhaps permanently shelved.

A few days later, Schocken summoned me to his office. Dr. Gross was sitting next to him, reading one of the articles. "This is very serious. I cannot possibly publish it," he said. Schocken agreed that the articles comprised too harsh an accusation against the Jewish leadership in Eretz Yisrael, which failed to make a concerted effort to save the Jews of Europe in order to avoid a clash with the British regime.

He hardly spoke a word. Now he understood why I had objected to publishing this material. Perhaps he regretted having ignored my comment that this was not the time to deal with the subject. At my request, he returned the articles. On the way back to my room, I decided to show them to Meidad Schiff, our style editor, one of the greatest experts on the Hebrew language and an absolute straight shooter. I wanted to get his honest opinion as an editor and expert Hebrew stylist. Later that same day he phoned me, insisting I give them to him for publication. "This has to be published. You cannot silence this!" he shouted into the telephone. Knowing his impetuous nature, I raced to his home to retrieve the articles before he might succumb to the temptation of publishing them himself.

Two years later I had my third confrontation with Germany. Israeli intelligence was picking up information about West German cooperation with Egypt in science and technology for military purposes. According to these reports, Egypt was employing several senior German scientists in the missile industry in developing unconventional weapons: biological, chemical, and perhaps even nuclear.

In a meeting with the editors of Israel's newspapers, Isser Harel, head of Security and Intelligence Services, warned about Egypt's war effort and her employment of German scientists. Influenced by that meeting, the editor of *Ha'aretz* assigned me to go to Germany and investigate the scientific and industrial research institutes, scientists, industrial supply companies, shipping firms, and politicians, to find out the extent of Egypto-German cooperation. This time I had no reservations about a confrontation with Germany.

In the light of reports in the European press, I gave first preference to investigating the involvement of a company called Intra. On March 23, 1963, I arrived in Munich, checked in at the Metropole

Hotel in the city center, and went straight to Intra's offices on Schiller Street. I asked to speak to the managing director and was ushered in to Herr Erasmus, who introduced himself as acting director in the absence of the general director, Dr. Heinz Krug, who had vanished. Herr Erasmus did not quite understand who I was and what I wanted from him. He invited me in, and it was only after he helped me off with my wet raincoat and offered me a seat that I handed him my business card. He blanched and quickly ran his hand under the desk-top. A secretary immediately materialized and stood waiting for instructions. He wrote something on a piece of paper and handed it to her. She left, and he began to talk with growing nervousness. I asked him if I was disturbing him at that particular moment. He responded politely that he would tell me whatever I wanted to know, but I should be aware that everybody in the office was tense since the kidnapping of Herr Krug and his vanishing without a trace. He seemed to imply that I must be among the suspects, possibly having some connection with Krug's disappearance.

After about ten minutes I could hear noises in the neighboring rooms that had previously been quiet. I now heard people coming and going, doors opening and closing, as though the whole establishment had come to life. It was obvious that all the activity was related to my visit, but I chose to ignore it.

I asked Herr Erasmus a series of questions concerning the character of the shipments of his company to Egypt, the types of products supplied, consignees, freight agents, and the shipping companies involved. At first he answered readily enough, but then, as the conversation continued, he started evading the issues. Finally, he began to show a stubborn resistance, claiming that he was not prepared to initiate any unauthorized person into Intra's commercial secrets. I had been there about two hours and apologized for taking up his time, but not before he had given me some addresses of companies and research institutes with connections to Egypt. At my request he agreed to another session the following day for any further questions. As we parted at the door, two unmistakably plainclothes policemen withdrew and slipped downstairs. Waiting for the elevator, I was sure that I would see these two, and perhaps a few more, waiting at the entrance.

A light rain was falling as I came out onto the street. No one was in sight. It had been my intention to head for the nearby Olympia kosher restaurant on Goethe Street, to eat and prepare my first dispatch, which seemed very thin on detail. As I crossed the street, two plainclothes policemen arrested me, showing me their ID cards. They very politely invited me into a car, driven by a third man. Officers Baumann and Hermann, as the two policemen introduced themselves, apologized for detaining me at this late hour, nine in the evening, and promised to return me to my hotel after a short session at police headquarters.

My personal pride said I should refuse to accompany them to the police station. I had a powerful urge to confront German policemen, even though I knew it would not begin to balance my past accounts with Germany. However, it struck me that I might just learn something relevant from them that could be useful in my investigation. For about an hour, the two of them interrogated me: Why had I come to Munich? What was my connection with Intra? Was I acquainted with Dr. Krug, who had mysteriously vanished, and so on. My passport and press credentials were thoroughly inspected. After several telephone calls made from a nearby room, they were finally convinced of the veracity of my claimed identity and profession. Once they were satisfied, they started to show a willingness to help in my investigation. It was with their guidance that I arrived the following day at the plant of Messerschmidt-Blohm-Boelkow, where one of the directors confirmed all the information that I had already acquired about German scientists in Egypt.

Meanwhile, as the two policemen debated with their superiors about what to do with me, I was writing the cable that I intended to send that night to Tel Aviv. At 10:30 P.M. they offered me a ride back to my hotel. Instead, I asked to be dropped off at the general post office, where I handed in the first story on activities of German scientists working to advance the military plans of Egypt against Israel. The banner headline on page one of the Israeli paper the following day read, "*Ha'aretz* correspondent interrogated by Munich Police." That created an uproar but did not hamper my journalistic mission.

Exhausted and tired, I arrived at the Olympia kosher restaurant at about eleven o'clock. At first the restaurant seemed completely empty, but then I noticed a familiar face hidden in a corner. It was my friend, the Swiss film producer Arthur Cohn. In his spare time he also sent short pieces to *Ha'aretz*, which I sometimes edited. He lived in Basel, Switzerland, and was here on a visit. He was surprised to see me and astonished to hear where I had just come from. As the local reporter for *Ha'aretz*, he wanted to report to the paper that I had been arrested, investigated, and released, but I explained that the story was already on the desk of the night editor of the paper.

The cooperation of German experts in the Egyptian war machine proved to be much more extensive than had previously been known. Following my investigation of scientists and their liaison with Egyptian agencies, I took a look at shipping companies in Hamburg that handled the shipment of sensitive equipment to Egypt, including strategic materiel that West Germany had committed itself to refrain from producing or selling. On October 3, 1954, the German chancellor, Dr. Konrad Adenauer, had given a pledge to the Council of European States in Brussels that Germany would neither produce nor export offensive weapons or material for making such weapons.

I arrived in Bonn equipped with the information gleaned in arms plants and weapons-development research institutes in Munich, and information on the shipping companies and their cargoes in Hamburg. In Bonn, the West German capital, I held a series of meetings with politicians, members of the government and parliament, and senior officials in the chancellor's office; and at the foreign ministry, including Finance Minister Erhardt and Foreign Minister von Brentano. I did not hear any denials of the cooperation with Egypt in any of my meetings. Some politicians in Bonn contended that the United States had pushed Germany into accelerating scientific and technological cooperation with Egypt in order to prevent the Soviet Union from filling the vacuum; that the United States did not want to be involved directly, so the Germans were encouraged to do the job.

On Brentano dropped broad hints about the U.S. president's special emissary, Averell Harriman, who had recently visited Bonn and recommended that the Germans create a controlled, scientific-technological presence in Egypt. The U.S. embassy confirmed that Harriman had visited Germany, but no one there would discuss the content of his talks in Bonn.

I published my findings while still in Germany, then returned home to a political storm raging around my stories. Prime Minister Ben-Gurion objected to the publication of the Egypto-German cooperation, a project based on the warning of Isser Harel, his intelligence-and-security chief, who acted on the authorization and with the approval of Foreign Minister Golda Meir. But supreme authority over the security services was vested in the prime minister's office, and Harel had clearly not received a green light for publication. Ben-Gurion perceived damage to Israel's relations with Germany as a consequence of the publication and forced Harel to resign. It was the first time that the head of such a sensitive agency was brought to resign by a newspaper story. Following this incident, the secret service was reorganized. It was split into two separate agencies: the Mossad (foreign secret service) and the Sherut Bitachon Clali (internal secret service, also known as *Shin Bet* or *Shabak*). Both were placed under the jurisdiction of the prime minister's office.

23

POLITICS AND WAR

During my years at the *Ha'aretz* newspaper, and particularly while covering the major political parties, I was an eyewitness to the inner struggles that finally erupted into a storm. I closely followed the growing rift within Mapai (Labor – Ben-Gurion's ruling party) from the onset of the first cracks in the apparent harmony. While still in power in 1962, Ben-Gurion granted me an interview in which he hinted at the extreme action he was contemplating. He spoke bitterly of a group of veteran leaders in his party that was uniting around Levi Eshkol and Golda Meir, who eventually became party leader and prime minister of Israel, respectively. He called these veterans a "Bolshevik Group," putting narrow party interests above the national interest.

His anger derived from the support they were giving to Pinchas Lavon, the defense minister whom Ben-Gurion had deposed following a security blunder in Egypt in July 1954. Ben-Gurion repudiated the authority of a government-appointed committee of seven cabinet ministers who investigated the charge against Lavon and concluded that he had not given the direct order to carry out that ill-advised operation in Egypt, and thereby cleared him of any guilt. Ben-Gurion considered this committee a political body, whose conclusions were not binding. In his opinion, the matter could be equitably settled only by appointing an independent national commission of inquiry with judicial authority.

Pinchas Lavon was secretary general of the Histadrut, and thus wielded great personal power, a fact that deterred Mapai veterans from attacking him. But Ben-Gurion had no such qualms. He stubbornly insisted on what he called true justice. He asserted that, "for the sake of peace and quiet in the party they are twisting the facts, perverting the truth, and poisoning the soul of the people."

As part of my job, I was supposed to be *au courant* regarding the political struggles within the party. From my talks with the accused leaders, including Levi Eshkol, Golda Meir, Pinchas Sapir, Mordechai Namir, Zalman Aranne, and party secretary general Reuven Barkat, I got the clear impression that the Old Man, as Ben-Gurion was called, was irksome and had become a burden rather than an asset to the party. The veterans were opposed by the younger generation, including Moshe Dayan, Shimon Peres, Teddy Kollek, Yosef Almogi, and Giora Joseftal, who saw themselves as Ben-Gurion's disciples.

It appeared to me that the veteran leaders were secretly aiming to replace Ben-Gurion. In the past, on several occasions he had submitted his resignation as a means of getting support for his programs. The cabinet had always responded by convincing him to retract his resignation and letting him have his way. It seemed to me that the next time Ben-Gurion would threaten to resign, they planned to agree.

My analysis of the Mapai leadership was published in *Ha'aretz* in January 1963 under the headline, "A New Alignment Takes Shape in Mapai." I described the mood of the veteran leaders in the face of Ben-Gurion's anger. I felt they were preparing for a sharp and quick strike, appointing a new prime minister the moment Ben-Gurion would resign, whatever the issue.

On the Friday that this article appeared in *Ha'aretz*, tempers flared at party headquarters, 110 Hayarkon Street in Tel Aviv. The secretariat, which served as the politburo, guiding the party, usually met on Fridays behind closed doors. On rare occasions the spokesman would issue a communique to the press on some unimportant detail in the discussions. This time the party spokesman departed from his usual practice and published a long statement, sharply condemning *Ha'aretz*, and me personally, for "the evil lies" published that morning.

That afternoon Ya'acov Orenstein, the Mapai spokesman, phoned me to describe the stormy debate led by Zalman Aranne, minister of education and culture, one of Ben-Gurion's strongest opponents. The sharp words in the communiqué issued by the spokesman had been dictated by Aranne, who feared that my article might forestall the veterans' planned revolution against Ben-Gurion.

Their coup did indeed succeed. A half year later, on the first Saturday night of June 1963, Ben-Gurion informed the cabinet secretary that, at the weekly meeting the following morning, he intended to tender his resignation. The move stunned his supporters and admirers, but not the veterans who were ready and waiting for this moment, for the opportunity to name his successor. Much to their gratification, not only was Levi Eshkol entrusted with forming a new government, but it was at the recommendation of Ben-Gurion himself. The younger generation, Ben-Gurion's supporters, felt like abandoned orphans. Now they would have to rely on their own power to attain party leadership, without the aura of Ben-Gurion to help them along. Moshe Dayan, minister of agriculture; Yosef Almogi, minister of labor; and Shimon Peres, deputy minister of defense, continued in Eshkol's government.

The Mapai veterans wasted no time. An alliance took shape quickly, though secretly at first, between them and Achdut Ha'avoda (a more activist version of Mapai) leaders: Galili, Ben Aharon, Allon, Carmel, and others, sworn enemies of Ben-Gurion ever since he disbanded the Palmach when the State was proclaimed and the non-partisan IDF was established. Within a short time, differences between Mapai veterans and Achdut Ha'avoda leaders were overcome, permitting the alignment of the two parties that soon merged into one, named Ma'arach (Alignment). Ben-Gurion's young and loyal supporters in Mapai were shunted aside.

The first to quit Eshkol's government was Moshe Dayan, followed by Almogi and Peres. On November 3, 1964, I was sitting as usual at my desk in *Ha'aretz*, at Maazeh Street in Tel Aviv, preparing my article for Friday's paper, when the phone rang. It was Moshe Dayan calling to say that he was waiting for me at the nearby Lilit Cafe, a five-minute walk from *Ha'aretz*. Golda Meir and Zalman Aranne were sitting at a table on the terrace. Dayan was sitting by himself at another table, sipping tea. "I once promised you a scoop for your paper. Now you'll have it," he said with a smile. Before I had a chance to speculate what his scoop might be, he told me that a half hour earlier, he had tendered his letter of resignation as minister of agriculture in Eshkol's government.

"That's no scoop any more," I responded.

"It will be until tomorrow morning. Eshkol will be in no hurry to publish it, and I have told no one but you."

When I published the story on the front page the following day, it caused an uproar in the Labor Party building. After Dayan's resignation, Peres and Almogi followed suit, leading to a split in the Mapai party.

In June 1965, Ben-Gurion instructed his supporters to set up a new political party named Rafi, by which he hoped to wrest control back from Ma'arach. In the 1965 Knesset elections, Rafi won only ten seats. Its role was limited to functioning as an aggressive opposition to Eshkol's Ma'arach. On the eve of the Six-Day War, in June 1967, public pressure brought Moshe Dayan of Rafi and Menachem Begin and Yosef Sapir of Gachal (merger of Herut and the Liberal parties) into the government. After the war, Rafi returned to its original party, Mapai, but now found a stepsister, Achdut Ha'avoda, wielding disproportionate power.

I followed this political drama for seven years, as a correspondent. Some of the events, causing considerable ferment and leading to other stormy developments, kept me busy day and night. Throughout this period I followed with concern the political decline of the Old Man, who had created the Mapai Party, led it through the most critical moments in the life of the nation, and finally abandoned it. He never rejoined Mapai, as did his disciples, who left him in isolation for the remaining eight years of his life. With Ben-Gurion's departure, Mapai declined and became bogged down in personal conflicts. It finally abandoned the arena to its rival, Herut, in its later incarnation called the Likud.

The internal conflicts, storms, and crises within Israel did not exempt her from external threats. Several factors may have combined to make the time propitious for Gamal Abdul Nasser of Egypt to move against Israel. After he brought his army home from its indecisive ten-year adventure in Yemen, he had to demobilize them or find another use for them. It was ten years after Israel had returned Sinai and the Gaza Strip to Egypt. However, the strategic emplacements under the command of UN forces stationed there were a humiliation for Nasser. On the economic side, the recession and its concomitant lowering of national morale may have induced him to strike at this time. He began to sharpen his knives, threatening Israel.

On May 15, 1967, Israel celebrated Independence Day with a modest military parade in Jerusalem. During the parade, Levi Eshkol, who served as both prime minister and defense minister, was informed that a state of alert had been called in the Egyptian army. Military units had already crossed the Nile bridges and the Suez Canal and had entered Sinai. In the following days, the Sinai Peninsula became an armed camp, deployed for attack. Egyptian airfields in the desert were placed at the highest state of readiness. Egypt demanded that UN detachments in Sinai, emplaced in fortified positions at Sharm-el-Sheikh at the entrance to the Red Sea and in the Gaza Strip, evacuate their positions or place themselves under Egyptian command. At the same time there were indications of Syrian army movements on the Golan Heights.

Events developed at a dizzying pace. On May 19, the UN flag was hauled down from its flagpole at Gaza headquarters. A day later the Egyptians dropped a paratroop force at Sharm-el-Sheikh, followed two days later by an announcement from Nasser that he was closing the Straits of Tiran, thereby imposing a naval blockade of Red Sea traffic to Israel's southern port of Eilat. This Egyptian threat, an act of war by naval blockade, and the growing troop concentrations on the Egyptian, Jordanian, and Syrian borders, created a state of urgency in Israel.

In Israeli public opinion, the government appeared inept, lacking resolve and ability to deal with the escalating crisis. The reserve forces of the IDF had been positioned in their fortified emplacements for three weeks, waiting for some signal. The IDF could not permit itself to be caught in a simultaneous surprise attack from three different fronts. According to a treaty signed between Egypt, Jordan, and Syria, Jordan's army would act under the command of Egypt, in coordination with Syria. This treaty sent warning signs to Israel that time was running out. Israel would have to take the initiative.

The Eshkol government, even though bolstered by the security-minded ministers from the ranks of *Achdut Ha'avoda*, was having difficulty deciding on the appropriate initiative. The public sensed the indecisiveness of the government. With each passing day, there was a growing outcry from writers, intellectuals, retired IDF officers, reservists, housewives, and people everywhere to strengthen the government by appointing Moshe Dayan as minister of defense. Those who defended Eshkol compared this situation to the revolt of the

"Wives of Windsor," trying to minimize the significance of the insistent popular demand, which spread even to the party ranks. On June 1, the government yielded and invited Moshe Dayan, Menachem Begin, and Yosef Sapir to join its ranks. This was the first unity government in Israel, established because of critical external conditions and unrelenting internal pressure.

As a war correspondent, I roamed among the various army units during the prewar waiting period. I felt that the men were tense and gloomy, especially in units far behind the front lines. However, among the troops in the front line there seemed to be a feeling of alertness and the expectation of an order to move. Together with other war correspondents I toured several units and arrived in time to see the exercises of a reserve paratroop brigade under the command of a bearded fighter, Danny Matt, one of the most admired paratroop commanders.

He sat under a tree in a grove at Kibbutz Na'an and told us about the high turnout of reservists reporting for duty and the upbeat morale of the mobilized units. On the home front these were fearful days, clouded by threats from Nasser, who led the newly forged war coalition with King Hussein of Jordan and the president of Syria. Meanwhile the Palestinian leader, Ahmed Shoukeiri, was whipping up the masses in the refugee camps of Gaza to get ready for "the day of revenge on the Jews," a day close at hand. Public morale plunged. Fearing its effect on the army, I asked Danny Matt how his soldiers were reacting to the saber-rattling of the Arab leaders. "We'll fight hard, if we have to, but I'll promise you one thing: There will be no Auschwitz here!" That sentence gripped me and remained engraved in my memory for a long time. Years later, reminiscing about this conversation, he admitted that there were moments when he did fear a repetition of Auschwitz.

My personal mood was grim. Again I saw us alone, abandoned to the wolves. It was almost twenty years since we had attained political independence in a war that threatened our very existence. Now, once again, our nationhood was in jeopardy. Behind the leaders of neighboring states inciting the masses to "throw the Jews into the sea," stood the nations of the world, aloof and unresponsive. General de Gaulle, leader of a friendly nation, issued a warning, not to the aggressors poised for attack, but to Israel, not to fire the first shot, lest the entire world sever its relations with her, blaming her for aggression.

In the White House, President Lyndon Johnson could not find a copy of Eisenhower's 1957 document guaranteeing Israel's freedom of Red Sea shipping – a promise made to compensate Israel for agreeing to withdraw from Sinai and the Tiran Straits, whence she could have controlled her own shipping lines. Now, instead of honoring its solemn commitment, American officials seemed unable to carry out their obligation without the help of an international naval flotilla to assure Israeli access to its sea-lanes, a flotilla that never got off the ground. In the face of such disregard for a signed agreement with Israel, it was not surprising that no country was prepared to take a stand on our side against Egypt's aggression.

Amid the prevailing gloom, some Israelis pinned their hopes, however feeble, on help from Jewish people in the Diaspora. All over the world Jews worried about Israel, but no one did much to avoid disaster. Data reaching our intelligence sources indicated the possible Arab use of bombs with poison gas. When rumors of this leaked to the public, panic broke out. The country had no antigas defense. At one policy session in the ministry of defense, Deputy Minister Zvi Dinstein mentioned that large quantities of gas masks could be obtained from Germany. Prime Minister Eshkol was appalled to learn the identity of our new standby. Another European country was offering masks at a very high price, but wanted payment in cash, apparently concerned that Israel, with its existence in question, was not a good risk. The finance ministry had no such cash reserves.

Late in May 1967, at a consultation in the Dan Hotel in Tel Aviv attended by a few cabinet ministers and members of the Jewish Agency executive, it was decided to appeal to world Jewry for emergency funds, without mentioning the exact nature of the needs. The British Jews responded immediately with a promise to raise five million British pounds within three days. Rabbi Herbert Friedman, executive vice president of the United Jewish Appeal, arrived from the United States on May 22, promising to activate emergency fund raising. The UJA president, Max Fisher, was cruising on a yacht near Greece with his friend, Henry Ford. He agreed, at Friedman's urging, to come for one day to discuss the situation. Finance Minister Pinchas Sapir and Jewish Agency chairman Louis Pincus begged him to join in organizing an immediate emergency appeal, and were shocked at the insensitivity of this Jewish leader, who regretted that he could not join in their efforts since right now he had to return to his friends on the yacht. However, he did offer to convene an emergency conference two weeks later in New York, on June 13, to launch such a campaign, on condition that Golda Meir come to rouse the donors.

On the evening following the conversation with Matt, prior to the Six-Day War, I was sitting in the Engel Cafe on Arlosoroff Street in Tel Aviv with Liberal Party leaders Yosef Sapir and Elimelech Rimalt. They were telling me about their meeting with Eshkol and the possibility that he would reshuffle his government and transfer the ministry of defense to Yigal Allon. As we spoke, a military jeep drove up and Moshe Dayan, in dusty khaki uniform with a long-visored baseball cap on his head, jumped out. He had just returned from a visit to the troops on the Sinai border and came to meet my two companions, leaders of the Liberal Party wing of Gachal, the party under Menachem Begin. As Dayan approached, I vacated my seat. He turned to me and said, "Listen, there's no avoiding war! Matters are out of control. I've spent three days visiting a lot of units and I found the reservists determined and steady. Don't let the tears and anxieties of the home front weaken the army's resolve!"

I listened to the message he obviously wanted me to relay to the public and asked him whether he would join the government. "I'm ready to serve in any military role that the minister of defense will give me. I'm not seeking power," said Dayan. Nevertheless power was handed to him when, two days later, he was appointed minister of defense, eliciting an audible sigh of relief from the Israeli populace.

As the army prepared for war, so did the home front. The civil defense ordered all windows and car lights blacked out and shelters prepared in case of air raids. The country was in total darkness except for the Soviet embassy, perched on a hilltop, overlooking Ramat Gan and Tel Aviv. From the windows of our bedroom the building loomed like a lighthouse bearing on an ocean of darkness.

The house we lived in had no shelter. We improvised one under the sturdily built staircase, where Joan and the children took shelter following the warning of the sirens. However, I was able to phone her even before the "all clear" to tell her that the threat of the Egyptian air force was over and that the family could return to the house.

Four days later, on the morning of June 5, Israel Air Force (IAF) planes attacked Egyptian air force bases. Within three hours the IAF had virtually destroyed the Egyptian air force and thereby determined the outcome of the Six-Day War against Egypt, Syria, and Jordan.

The Israel Defense Forces (IDF) completed their victory over the armies of Egypt, Jordan, and Syria on the day that the UJA president had scheduled the opening conference of his emergency campaign in New York. With resourcefulness and an attitude of *ain brairah* (do-or-die), the IDF smashed the Arab noose around our necks, beating back their attempt to invade the country and demolish Israel. The IDF prevailed, but in all too many homes bereaved parents, wives, and children were mourning the hundreds that had fallen in defense of their land. At the same time, Jewish tourists from all over the world poured into Israel to share in the joy of victory. Some could now walk taller with Jewish pride. Others deemed themselves full partners in the victory. They had shared with Israel her prewar anxiety, if nothing more.

During the six days of fighting on three fronts, I was riveted to the *Ha'aretz* desk as news editor, military commentator, and political correspondent. The enforced confinement prevented me from going along with the combat troops, but it did give me the chance to obtain the first reports on the course of the battles, since I was close to the general staff, and the briefing rooms of the minister of defense, the chief of staff and all the various area commanders participating in the war.

On June 7, I returned to my office with an article I had just completed after a briefing by Chief of Staff Yitzhak Rabin, relating the completion of the conquest of Sinai and the repulsion of Jordanian forces from the West Bank and the Old City of Jerusalem. I had not yet finished marking the text for press when there was another summons to the journalists' club on Kaplan Street to hear Defense Minister Dayan report on the campaign. He spoke in more general terms but could not conceal his emotion as he described the arrival of Israeli soldiers at the Temple Mount and the Western Wall, the holiest site for Jews, the last remnant of the ancient Temple, in the heart of the Old City of Jerusalem.

Again I returned to *Ha'aretz* and again started to edit the front page. Such a flood of momentous news in a single issue had never yet been offered to an Israeli newspaper editor. The decisive victory that came with the capture of all of Sinai called for front-page headlines; so did the removal of the sea blockade of Eilat, which had triggered the war. However, the banner headline had to go to the liberation of the Western Wall and the Old City of Jerusalem. As the only editor on the night desk, since all my colleagues were with army units in the field, I had to decide on my own how to give this historic edition the correct balance. This would be a front page destined, as everybody knew even before printing, to become a collectors' item, a keepsake for regular readers as well as avid collectors. On that dramatic night the manual typesetters, the linotype operators, and all the other employees of the press were crowded around my desk, eager to read the lead-cast headlines before the paper could roll off the presses.

24

FOLLOWING THE SIX-DAY WAR

The Six-Day War ended in a brilliant victory for the IDF, one that has been studied in military academies, both east and west, ever since. Not surprisingly, a feeling of euphoria prevailed in Israel and in Jewish communities abroad. Israel's prestige soared in the aftermath of victory, a welcome respite following two years of economic recession and social crises, and the weeks of anxiety that preceded the war.

Israel's victory was all the more gratifying in view of the horror of the widely anticipated alternative. There was no secret as to the intentions of the Arab leaders, repeatedly proclaimed in the world press during the period before the war. On May 27, 1967, for example, the *Beirut Star* quoted President Nasser of Egypt, "If war breaks out with Israel, it will be all-embracing, and its objective will be the annihilation of Israel."

The reservists returned home to a country flooded with books and picture albums commemorating the victory. Foreign publishers joined this vast literary enterprise. Two days after the cease-fire on all three fronts, a London publisher cabled me to commission an eighty-thousand-word biography of Moshe Dayan, which he wanted by August 15, 1967, later acceding to my request to move the deadline to the beginning of September. I could have made life easy for myself by collecting raw data from libraries and newspaper archives for most of the material. Dayan was a famous person, widely publicized. But I decided to approach him directly.

Since Dayan was well aware of his value on the book market, I was afraid he might not want to cooperate, saving for himself the as yet untold juicy morsels in his life story. He was a gifted, facile, and original writer and I was sure that, when the time came, he would write an autobiography. Nevertheless, when I phoned on Friday, June 16, to tell him about my assignment and to ask for his assistance, to my great surprise, he agreed immediately and invited me to come to his house the following evening, Saturday night.

Yoske Hadar, one of Dayan's regular bodyguards at the time, knew me well and led me straight to the garden. Moshe was sitting alone in a bamboo chair, absorbed in thought. After shaking my hand, he walked over to a plum tree sagging under the weight of its fruit and shook a branch, bringing down a cascade of ripe plums. We sat facing each other, savoring the luscious fruit. Dayan's first question was, "How much are they paying you?" He advised me not to compromise on the price. "Now's the ideal time to sell me," he said, "by next month I won't be quite so marketable." With direct and earthy sabra humor, he asked how I intended to deal with certain controversial public issues connected with his name. He showed no concern about how I would deal with his womanizing or his archaeological pursuits, both subjects that frequently provided provocative newspaper stories. However, he was concerned about the evaluation of his performance in two national roles: as IDF chief of staff, particularly in the political storm over the Lavon affair, and as minister of agriculture.

My main interest was his role in Israel's recent victory over the armies of Egypt, Syria, and Jordan. In the first days after the war, gossip had it that Dayan hesitated to move the army close to the Suez Canal; that he opposed the IDF breakthrough into East Jerusalem; and resisted the assault on the Golan Heights. This hesitancy generated comment not only from his political adversaries but also from senior officers who served under him. No one questioned his personal courage and daring as commander and warrior. But most of them did not recognize his caution in the face of diplomatic and poltical considerations that sometimes outweighed those of the battlefield.

On the day he took over as minister of defense, he ordered the transfer of two brigades from the general staff reserve to the southern command, which was responsible for the Egyptian front. Dayan explained, "The main effort would be against the Egyptian army. We sought no war with Jordan or Syria." When I asked about his proposal to encircle the Old City of Jerusalem, rather than to break in, he responded that the walled city was densely populated with Christian and Moslem holy places. If these were damaged in the fighting, world reaction would be extremely harsh. The same caution guided his thinking about storming the Golan Heights, urging caution because Syria was a Soviet protegé. Dayan viewed Egypt as the prime mover in the Arab world. He believed that with the neutralization of the Egyptian factor, Jordan and Syria would find it easier to accept the results and seek a dialogue with Israel. Many Israelis thought otherwise, believing that success in Sinai should be exploited to correct the injustice of 1948, when Israel had lost the Jewish Quarter of the Old City and access to the Western Wall. There were many others who felt that the time had come to square accounts with Syria for the twenty years of shooting and harassment from the Golan Heights over the settlements in the Galilee.

We sat for over three hours under the plum tree talking about events ranging from his service under Orde Wingate in the special night squads in the distant pre-World-War-II period, to his recent stint as a journalist in Vietnam for *The Washington Post* and *Paris Match*. He concealed nothing, and replied candidly on matters that had been cloaked in mystery for years. He talked openly about comradeship and competition with Yigal Allon and about his attitude toward Etzel and the Stern Group, against whom he had been ordered to take action by the Hagana; about his relationship with Ben-Gurion and the discord in relations with Prime Minister Eshkol, when Dayan, as minister of agriculture, was kept at arms length from security affairs, which were closer to his heart and the area of his greatest expertise.

"Everything that we've talked about is pertinent for your book," he said. "Now let's talk, off-the-record, about what's going to happen tomorrow, next week, next month, and in years to come." I had a feeling that he was continuing the chain of thought I had broken when I arrived and found him sitting in the garden.

A few days before our meeting, Dayan had been widely quoted as saying that he was waiting for a phone call from King Hussein. I asked him if there had been any response from across the Jordan River. "There are many means of communication besides telephones, but reporters hungry for a gimmick have latched on to the piquant phrase 'waiting for a phone call.' Neither Hussein nor I are call girls and we don't wait for phone calls," Dayan replied.

Two matters were of particular concern to me that evening in Dayan's garden. One was the fear of a Soviet response to the defeat of the Syrian and Egyptian armies, which had been armed and trained by the Soviet Union and its satellites. The second was the need for coexistence with more than a million Palestinian Arabs in the West Bank and the Gaza Strip, who did not want us and to whom we had nothing to offer.

Dayan felt powerless regarding the Soviet attitude toward Israel. "We're going to need the United States' help. In a context of superpower discussions, we might be able to reach some sort of understanding with Moscow," he said. On the other hand, he felt that with the Arabs we had better prospects of rapport, that he could initiate ideas and offer solutions. "War can be waged and won by stratagems. Creating coexistence and relationships between peoples demands wisdom, courage, and patience," he said. Surveying the Arab populations in the territories now controlled by the IDF, he insisted that there were fundamental conflicts of interest among them and that it was not possible to offer one solution acceptable to all the regions and leaders in the territories. He did believe, however, that a liberal and humane IDF attitude would prevent, or at least delay, united organized resistance. Knowing their way of life, he would be very careful to preserve Arab self-respect and facilitate economic development which, he hoped, would ward off violent confrontations between the Arabs and the Jews until an acceptable formula for coexistence between the parties could be found.

He was already putting out feelers to prominent Arab leaders in Nablus, Ramallah, Hebron, and the Gaza Strip, with the intent of establishing a framework for local self-government. He quickly learned the differences of opinion, personal conflicts, and various nuances among Arab leaders. Because the residents of the territories held Jordanian passports, and because their leaders continued to declare loyalty to the Hashemite crown, Dayan was convinced that any solution would have to be based on an understanding and dialogue with King Hussein.

In the field, local IDF commanders reported a strong affinity with Jordan. Hundreds of trucks laden with agricultural produce, which used to go via Jordan to the Arab markets of the Persian Gulf, were forming long lines, waiting to cross the two inadequate temporary bridges thrown across the Jordan River to replace the destroyed Allenby and Damia Bridges. The drivers did not know what to do. Some, with heavy vehicles, drove straight across the riverbed, which was almost dry at this time of year. The astonished officers, witnessing the scene, asked their superiors for instructions. Dayan ordered the troops to let the farmers take their produce directly across the river. Notice of the move was sent to the Jordanian authorities, who promptly acquiesced, setting up transfer points on the Jordanian side. This was the informal beginning of the "Open-Bridges" policy and the free movement of goods between Israel and Jordan across the Jordan River. "If I would have waited for King Hussein's written and signed agreement, we could never have done it," explained Dayan. He hoped to apply the same pragmatic approach to all aspects of life common to Jews and Arabs, believing that establishing practices to serve both sides was preferable to negotiating written agreements.

He was already speaking that evening of "a new map and new relationships" that he would offer Israel and the Arabs. Annexation of territory was out of the question. He could not accept the declaration of a united Jerusalem that meant annexing surrounding Arab villages to Israel. To stimulate dialogue with the Arabs, he believed in keeping all options open and rejected the establishment of unilateral policies unacceptable to the other side.

Dayan's foresight was unusual in those days of reliance on Israel's overwhelming strength against the Arabs. Dayan regretted the fact that the IDF had reached the Suez Canal and was sitting, as he phrased it, on the "Elephant Trail" of the Great Powers. Sooner or later Israel would be pressured into withdrawal. Egypt had no motivation to rehabilitate the cities and industries along the Suez Canal as long as we sat on the opposite bank, observing all ships sailing down the waterway.

On that evening of June 17, 1967, Dayan was already drawing the future map of Sinai. In the event of Egyptian willingness for an official end to belligerency between the two countries, Dayan would propose to divide Sinai from north to south, all the western part going to Egypt, while Israel would retain only a narrow land strip between Eilat and Sharm-el-Sheikh, to ensure freedom of the shipping lanes to Israel. He would suggest the demilitarization of the Sinai approaches to Israel, which had twice served as an Egyptian springboard into the Negev. He had nothing to say about the price that Israel might pay for full peace with Egypt, a subject he never referred to for ten years, until Sadat's visit to Jerusalem in November 1977. As for a comprehensive settlement of the Israel-Arab conflict, Dayan emphasized Syria's extremist role. "Without her we cannot achieve agreement with the Arabs in the territories, and without our agreeing to return the Golan, Syria will not sit at the negotiating table," he asserted. Regarding the Golan, he would be willing to compromise as long as Israel was guaranteed the water sources and measures to assure security in the north.

Two months later Dayan, as minister of defense, was invited to brief a small group of *Ha'aretz* staff. In Gershom Schocken's room, he reiterated the philosophy he had expounded on June 17 when I sat with him in his garden. My impression was that he had used me as a sounding board for testing his ideas. I escorted him down the steps from our editorial offices to his car, commenting that nothing appeared to have happened since our last conversation. "True, and don't expect new things every morning! We're not dealing with a newspaper that appears every day," he said with a cynical smile. As we parted he told me that there was something he wished to discuss with me and asked me to come to his office. Chaim Yisraeli, who had served as confidential assistant to all ministers of defense since Ben-Gurion's day, phoned the following morning and asked to see me as soon as possible.

Chaim, who was my age, was an institution in his own right. Every secret and tidbit of interesting information was channeled through him. He possessed unparalleled influence in Israeli government circles. I found him in an office just about big enough for four people, sitting behind a desk stacked with papers and files, holding a phone in one hand, jotting down notes with the other. Dayan's office was just across the hall, ten steps away. As I sat there sipping black coffee, the standard drink in that office, the door behind me swung open. Dayan entered, pulled up a chair, and sat down next to me. "All right, let's decide right now what I want to offer you," he said. Chaim moved his unlit cigar to a corner of his mouth and winked at me. I could not guess what offer I was about to receive. Dayan, in his direct manner and without introduction or formalities, offered me a job as his spokesman and media adviser, a position held at that time by Mickey Bar-Zohar

(Dr. Michael Bar-Zohar, later to become a member of the Knesset). To my question, what about the current spokesman, Dayan replied, "Mickey is leaving. He's had enough of it and wants to write. The job is open as of now." He promised to talk Schocken into giving me a two-year unpaid leave of absence "You will not resent the opportunity to be at the center of events in the country", Dayan said to me.

The offer was tempting and I was highly flattered, but I had to refuse, explaining that I had just about completed my biography for the British publisher. I was concerned that publication of a book on a public figure with whom I was to start work as spokesman and adviser, would be inviting justified criticism. I also told Dayan that a few of my critical sentences about his colleagues in government, most particularly the prime minister, would damage his relations with them. He did not refute my reasoning, but asked that, over the weekend, I let him examine the problematic chapter dealing with the criticism of members of the government.

A few days later, "Chera" (former chief of staff, General Zvi Zur), assistant to the minister of defense and number-two man in the defense establishment, called me to the ministry and returned the chapter. "Moshe asks you to moderate your criticism of Eshkol and the other cabinet members," he said. I agreed to moderate the criticism, while repeating that the appearance of the book itself, even without any criticism, would damage Dayan. Therefore it would be best if I turned down his offer. Chera agreed and asked me to recommend someone else for the job. I was not prepared to take that on myself and that ended our conversation.

During the following two and a half years I was asked to write by-line articles on public issues and the editorial once or twice a week. During that period, the papers were full of reports and commentary on the "War of Attrition" that Egypt was waging along the Suez Canal and on events in the Jordan Rift Valley, where terror squads were penetrating into Israel from Jordan and from the territories administered by the IDF.

In May 1970, when I had reached my peak status at *Ha'aretz*, Chera again invited me in for a chat. With a mischievous glint in his eye, looking at me from a corner of the thick frame of his glasses, he said, "You've already made the money from the book. Now come and work for Moshe." This time I did not hesitate and agreed on the spot.

Chera took me to Chaim Yisraeli, and the three of us went into Dayan's office for a short conversation. We agreed on a starting date, work conditions, the areas of my activity, and reporting relationships. Over the following two months I wrapped up my journalistic assignments at *Ha'aretz* and, on July 1, 1970, reported to the Defense Ministry to start a new chapter in my life, sometimes stormy but always fascinating. For me personally, this was to be the most exciting part of my life, in which I was to play an active part in two central events in the history of Israel: the 1973 Yom Kippur War; and the peace process with Egypt, which began in November 1977 and came to a successful conclusion in March 1979.

There had been many opportunities to meet Dayan as IDF chief of staff, member of the Knesset, minister of agriculture, opposition leader, and minister of defense, but this time, on my first day as his spokesman and adviser, I felt very excited just to be sitting with him in his room. That morning *Ha'aretz* had published an article with my byline, in which I discussed administrative methods proposed to the government by ministry of defense director general Yeshayahu Lavi, a long time friend.

The article had been on the editor's desk for a few weeks. For whatever reason, someone decided to run the article on the first day of my new job, the day after I left the paper. Dayan pointed to the article and said with a smile that he believed I would not be writing any more articles while I was spokesman for the defense establishment. He briefed me on the nature of our work together, and suggested that I bring myself up to date by checking with several people in the office on various sensitive subjects that were likely to attract public interest. "I have complete trust in you, and I'll give you a lot of latitude to speak in my name without checking with me," he said. That expression of confidence from the man responsible for Israel's security, and my sudden inclusion in the deepest of Israel's secrets, so overwhelmed me that I was unable to hide it. "No matter, you'll become used to your new status very quickly, and you won't regret the job you do here," he assured me.

It was difficult to make the abrupt transition from journalism, which involved gathering material and writing, sometimes without knowing the secret sources, to participation in the process of actually molding and shaping this material, as part of very small intimate groups, privy to all the secret and highly sensitive information. At the beginning, my satisfaction and excitement in the job was somewhat marred by my exaggerated fear that I might fail to maintain the required secrecy. I began to exercise extreme caution in conversations, even with old friends. I found myself censoring the jokes heard in the ministry even when they lacked any shade of political content. It was only in the regular discussions in Dayan's room, with the participation of the old warhorses of his staff, that I felt completely comfortable, all of us feeling free to exchange tidbits of gossip or jokes, sometimes even at the expense of absent colleagues.

The physical distance from the *Ha'aretz* offices in Tel Aviv to the defense ministry in the Kirya neighborhood was only about a fifteen-minute walk, but even on my first day at the new job it seemed light-years away from my work as a journalist.

That first workday in the ministry of defense, I returned home very late. Joan and three of our four children were sitting in our small garden, under a poinsettia tree covered with red blossoms. Our one year old was fast asleep in his crib. During the long summer-school holiday, we were in the habit of eating dinner together in the evening. This time they had to wait for quite a while. Joan was curious to know how I had done on my first day in the new post. There was little I could tell her, but she was happy to sense my excitement over my new responsibilities. "I've traveled a long road in my life up to this point," I said. Even though I myself had told them little about my Holocaust experiences, they knew enough to appreciate my feelings now. "To come from Auschwitz and Buchenwald to the center of responsibility for the security of the Jewish State is more than the realization of a dream," Joan commented. I myself had never dreamed such a dream, but she was verbalizing what I was feeling and thinking.

In July 1970, the escalation of the War of Attrition on the Egyptian front reached a peak. For the first time the IDF had lost a number of Phantom aircraft, shot down by Egyptian surface-to-air missiles (SAMs). The Russians had supplied Egypt with the newest rockets, which were deployed deep inside Egypt, parallel to the Suez Canal, hampering the IAF's freedom of movement.

The Soviets did not stop with merely supplying equipment and know-how to the Egyptians; they provided actual participation. In one IAF sortie against the missile batteries, Egypt sent up three quartets of

MiG 21s, the latest aircraft in the Soviet arsenal. In the ensuing dogfight, IAF pilots shot down five MiGs, whose pilots parachuted to safety. The air-to-air radio conversations revealed that these planes had been flown by Soviet pilots. We classified this information as top secret until it was revealed by Hassanein Heikal, the editor of the Egyptian daily *Al-Ahram* and confidant of President Gamal Abdel Nasser. The Egyptian leadership could not conceal their frastration and anger following the publication in *Al-Ahram*.

Even before the news was leaked by Egyptian sources, I had asked Dayan's permission to pass the item to one of the Western communications media. Much as he would have liked to publish this information, Dayan feared a further escalation of Soviet intervention if their participation in Egyptian operational squadrons became generally known. "As long as they want to hide their active involvement, we won't publish it," he ruled. This turning point in the war with Egypt aroused anxiety in the Israeli defense establishment. The U.S. had experience in combating missile batteries like these during the war in Vietnam, but President Nixon's administration was reluctant to give Israel this sophisticated equipment. It was only at the crux of the War of Attrition that Israel finally received electronic warfare systems and other means against surface-to-air missile weaponry from the United States.

On Air Force Day, traditionally held every year in July, I rode in Dayan's car to the airfield from which we were to fly to the base hosting the air show. Dayan jotted down on a slip of paper the points he would make in his speech at the air show. He was sparing in the use of language, usually choosing razor-sharp words, straight to the point. He passed the paper to me for comment. Seeing my astonishment that he was issuing a very clear threat to Egypt, mentioning two air bases, at Kutmiya and Tzalahiya, west of the Canal, as targets for Israeli retaliation by air, he asked whether I really thought he intended to do it. Without waiting for a response, he continued, "Rubbish. There's no point in escalating the situation and losing more pilots. We have to reach some understanding with them. I'm mentioning the two air bases only in order to raise the morale of the air crews and families at the show."

When we returned to the office in Tel Aviv, Dr. Yaacov Herzog, director general of the prime minister's office, met us on the steps of the building. Herzog was a scholar, wise in the ways of the world, with long experience as advisor to several prime ministers, including Ben-Gurion, Levi Eshkol, and Golda Meir. He had brought Dayan news of an American initiative for a cease-fire on the Egyptian front. In addition to the initiative of Secretary of State William Rogers, there was the mission of the Swedish UN mediator Gunnar Jarring, who was to have opened a political dialogue in the region, centering on the controversial UN Security Council Resolution 242 of November 1967. Most of the Arabs had rejected it, as had Israel. When the government of Israel decided to proceed in discussions with Jarring on the resolution that called for Israeli withdrawal to the pre-June 1967 lines, the Gachal representatives, Menachem Begin and Ezer Weizman (of the Herut-Liberal Block), left the government in protest.

The American pressure to initiate the Jarring talks, the gloomy atmosphere prevailing in Israel over the loss of life in the air force and at the Suez Canal strongholds, accelerated our agreement to a cease-fire and the commencement of peace talks.

The cease-fire date was set for August 7. That same day I had to prepare the foreign correspondents for Dayan's live appearance on Israeli Television. Our phones were flooded with requests for exclusive interviews from foreign television and radio. To give maximal coverage to Dayan's statement without injuring the prestige of correspondents who wanted exclusives, I prepared, in advance, a simultaneous English translation of the Hebrew broadcast in Israel. Dayan's words, reaching the whole world simultaneously, were effective in explaining Israel's position at the outset of the peace talks.

In a session with him before the broadcast, I discussed with Dayan the need to display goodwill and conciliation. He was very moderate in his broadcast, creating the impression that Israel was interested in furthering the peace process. However, he stipulated that that willingness had to be based on Egypt's sincere intention to advance toward peace and to abstain from using the cease-fire to improve its military position.

Just four hours after the cease-fire took effect on the Suez Canal line, Israeli intelligence was receiving information about Egyptian SAM missile batteries being moved up to the Canal in a deployment that would cut off IAF ability to fly near our side of the Suez Canal area. This violation of the status quo at the outset of the cease-fire aroused fury in the government and public. Prime Minister Golda Meir insisted on the return of the batteries to their previous positions. She received operational support from southern command Major General Ariel Sharon, who proposed to force back the batteries by military action. The inner cabinet, known as "Golda's kitchen," endorsed the idea of immediate military moves. Dayan first hesitated and then decided to oppose the idea, explaining that, "As an army officer, I would not pass up an opportunity to improve my position." Besides, he felt that we could gain political advantages from their violation, provided that we made no military move.

Two days before the full cabinet session scheduled to discuss the issue, Dayan indicated to me that he would oppose any action that could make Israel appear to be torpedoing the Jarring mission. He even went so far as to suggest that he might resign from the government over this issue. I had already been working with him for six weeks, long enough to understand his comments. I knew that he was interested in creating pressure by means of the rumored resignation. That same Friday noon, I invited the *New York Times* correspondent in Israel for coffee at a small cafe near the offices of the ministry of defense. Next day his paper published a report that Dayan was likely to resign. No reason was given but the prime minister and her other cabinet colleagues were well aware of the issue in question. The report was picked up by a number of local papers, after I drew the attention of a few reporters in Tel Aviv and Jerusalem to the story in the prestigious *New York Times*.

In the afternoon, after the cabinet meeting, Dayan asked me with a grin if I knew the source of the rumor about the possibility of his resignation. I had no need to answer his question since he immediately changed the subject. "The talks must not be stopped but they cannot be on Jarring's ideas based on Rogers' plan because that means withdrawal from all the territories," said Dayan. For the first time, I heard his concept of how to proceed – by a partial settlement with Egypt. According to him, it was possible to arrive at a settlement that would permit, or commit, the Egyptians to open the Suez Canal and rehabilitate the cities on the West Bank. For her part, Israel would withdraw from the Canal and redeploy some distance from the Canal. At first Dayan spoke of withdrawal to the western approaches of the Mitle and Jiddi Passes, about twenty miles east of the Canal. After some opposition from military circles, he agreed that the redeployment could be about six miles from the Suez Canal. Based on that conception, Major General Sharon and Major General Tal suggested construction of a chain of posts along that line to replace the Bar-Lev-Line (named after the former chief of staff) strongholds, which were on the water's edge of the Canal.

He kept the idea of partial settlement to himself for two weeks. Then he called me to his office one day and expressed his wish to test the idea on Israeli public opinion. Refusing to talk on the record to reporters, he nonetheless wanted the idea to be given a sounding board. In the initial stage, it seemed best for me to try it on the English-language readers of *The Jerusalem Post*, which included the foreign correspondents and diplomatic representatives. Characteristically, he left that entirely to my judgment. Accordingly I invited the editors of *The Jerusalem Post* - Ted Lurie, Leah Ben Dor, Ari Rath, Erwin Frankel, and Mark Segal - to his office. They caught on immediately and when the conversation with Dayan was over, they came up to my second-floor office and said in so many words that they were apparently to be used to float a trial balloon for Dayan's new idea. I did not try to deny it.

The following day an editorial appeared in *The Jerusalem Post* with an original idea of dealing with the situation, clearly hinting that there were important people with ideas on how to thaw the frozen Jarring talks. One concept deserving of support was that of partial settlement. Other newspapers picked up the theme leading to a debate among the leadership of the country, with some people attributing the idea to Dayan. Foreign Minister Abba Eban opposed the idea, viewing it as a "nonstarter."

Gamal Abdul Nasser, ruler of Egypt, died on September 28, 1970. His death, and an attempted coup d'état in Jordan by Palestine Liberation Organization (PLO) terrorists on September 16 and 17, upset the atmosphere of the talks. At the same time, Syria took the opportunity to threaten Jordanian territorial integrity. Two hundred Syrian tanks invaded from the north while the PLO tried to dislodge Hussein from his throne. The king used his loyal Bedouin army to carry out a massacre of the Palestinians who had taken part in the uprising against him, but he was helpless in the face of the Syrian threat from the north. At this point the United States turned to Israel for help.

Within the government there were those in favor of a positive response to President Nixon's request for rapid intervention to aid Jordan against the Syrian invaders. However, Dayan opposed active military intervention in a dispute between Arabs. Instead, to deter the Syrians, he ordered the IDF to move forces northward along the Jordan Rift Valley from the center of Israel, in order to signal possible intervention to Syria. The Israeli tactic apparently helped; the following morning the Syrian tanks withdrew from Ramta, a town in northern Jordan, and crossed back to their own side of the Syrian frontier.

There was an attempt to keep the request of the U.S. for a deterrent move against Syria secret, but despite the military censorship imposed, the knowledge spread among newspapermen. In keeping with my decision to maintain maximum credibility among journalists, I made no comment. My refusal to deny or confirm the facts in no way removed the story from the headlines. In fact, it may have given rise to the spread of stubborn rumors to the effect that there had been sharp disagreement within the government regarding the response to the American request. On the issue of the crises in the Jarring talks and the Rogers' plan, there was considerable media improvement for Israel, since America had approached Israel for help with Jordan and Syria. Media pressure on Israel, because of the deadlock in the Jarring talks, now eased. The Syrian invasion of Jordan, and the massacre of Palestinians that became known as "Black September," removed Israel from the headlines. Dayan, at least, recognized the achievement, part of which he attributed to my ability to steer the journalists. "It was well done," he said.

When the news of Nasser's death broke, PLO disturbances in Jordan spread to several population centers in the West Bank, and particularly to East Jerusalem. The rioters viewed his demise as the end of their hopes "to push Israel into the sea," as he had promised on various occasions. The mayors and other public leaders lost control of the streets. Dayan immediately went to Jerusalem and set up a personal command post in the building of one of the security services in East Jerusalem. Instead of using force on the rioters to break up the violent demonstrations, which had already caused considerable damage to property in the city, he ordered the arrest of all those suspected of incitement and their immediate deportation across the River Jordan that same night. The following morning, on Sunday, the BBC correspondent in Israel phoned me for confirmation of the deportations. I was prepared with my answer. I explained that Israel was not Jordan. We would not massacre thousands, but merely deport a handful and, if necessary, a few dozen of the ringleaders who were responsible for organizing the disturbances. That response satisfied most of the reporters. The prompt deportations took effect and the riots quickly stopped.

The Jarring mission died a natural death, and Jerusalem and Washington began to whisper about partial settlement. In Israel there were politicians willing to take credit for the idea, particularly when American teams began to arrive to assess the possibilities of its realization. Dayan refrained from claiming parenthood of the idea. At the same time, he gave me a free hand to brief editors and political reporters in order to advance it.

Early in 1971, the State Department in Washington was trying to promote the idea. The producer of *60 Minutes* of CBS cabled me a request for interviews with the prime minister and minister of defense. I passed the cable on to Golda Meir, and she agreed to be interviewed at her Tel Aviv office. I suggested that the interview with Dayan should be at Sharm-el-Sheikh in order to give a dramatic backdrop to the program.

The CBS bureau chief in Israel was my good friend Dan Blum, a veteran television reporter from Los Angeles. The interviewer from the United States was Mike Wallace, who had a reputation for being unsympathetic to Israel. On January 7, we flew in an IAF Dakota to Sharm-el-Sheikh, where the crew from the American network was already waiting. Joe Wershba, a long-time friend who was the producer, suggested that the interview should be taped with Dayan sitting in the passenger seat of a command car, alongside the interviewer in the driver's seat. Both Dayan and Wallace liked the idea. Wallace questioned Dayan on the future of Sinai, the navigation of the Tiran Straits, and the shape of coming relations with Egypt. It was the first time that Dayan spoke extensively about his idea for partial settlement with Egypt. In response to a question, he agreed to the stationing of Egyptian police units on the east bank of the Suez Canal within the framework of such a settlement.

Since the cease-fire with Egypt on August 7, 1970, the Canal front and Sinai had been quiet. The IDF was dug in on the fortified

Bar-Lev Line and was constructing a parallel line of strongholds five to six miles back from the Canal, on the line that Dayan and the general staff wanted in case of a partial settlement. "Even in the event of war, better these strong-points than the strongholds on the water line," commented Dayan during a tour of the Suez Canal area.

The quiet on the Egyptian front disquieted Dayan. He believed that sooner or later the Egyptians would violate the cease-fire. They would not reconcile themselves forever to the idea of the IDF sitting on the east bank, preventing them from reactivating the Canal and restoring the cities along its west bank. "We have nothing to gain from sitting on the banks of the Canal, as long as they do not interfere with our shipping to Eilat. We must reach an agreement with them," Dayan repeated to anyone who would listen.

Egypt had a new leader, Anwar Sadat, who was free of his predecessor's commitment to "restore by force what was taken by force." Sadat gave the impression of being pragmatic and interested in an honorable settlement. Dayan decided that he must periodically cast a "fishhook" baited with a partial settlement in order to create a movement toward talks between the countries, which he hoped would gather momentum.

In May 1971, Secretary of State William Rogers came to the area with his entourage. They had come to test the chance of achieving a partial settlement in the spirit of Dayan's suggestion. The prime minister took a tough position. She held to President Nixon's promise that without direct talks between Egypt and Israel, we need not withdraw from any area of Sinai. Dayan was willing to talk about "nonbelligerency" between Egypt and Israel within the framework of a partial settlement. In a conversation that took place in Dayan's Tel Aviv office, Rogers heard the suggestion that Dayan would be willing to withdraw about twenty miles from the Canal and redeploy on the western slopes of the Mitle and Jiddi Passes, passageways for crossing over the Sinai Mountains between east and west. Golda Meir consulted her close associates in the cabinet, Galili, Allon, and others, as well as Chief of Staff, Lieutenant General Chaim Bar-Lev. Relying on the advice of her military experts, she rejected Dayan's plan. Rogers and his assistants, Joseph Sisco and Alfred Atherton, left Israel empty-handed.

Dayan's opponents in the cabinet and in the party exploited his proposal in order to discredit him, and presented the idea of partial settlement as a defeatist view. A few days after the American delegation left Israel, an old colleague from *Ha'aretz* arrived at the defense ministry without prior notice. To me, this visit seemed suspiciously like an alibi for a leaked story he intended to publish. My efforts to verify the suspicion quickly bore fruit. He admitted possession of a startling bit of news that would appear in the paper the following day: Dayan's generous proposal to give up the Suez Canal and the greater part of Sinai in return for a partial settlement, without peace. To cover the traces of the leak, he had taken the trouble to visit the defense ministry on the day before publication. A quick clarification confirmed my guess that the leak originated in Deputy Prime Minister Yigal Allon's office. The publication did not harm Dayan, but it did upset the chance for later maneuvers that might have led to agreement with Egypt and might, perhaps, have prevented the Yom Kippur War of October 1973.

A three-way conversation about some kind of arrangement continued between Washington, Jerusalem, and Cairo.

Terror in the air

Meanwhile, the terror organizations continued to attack Israel on land, sea, and air. Terrorists succeeded in infiltrating from bases in Lebanon, where they had set up camp after their expulsion from Jordan. Here and there they did succeed in hitting targets in Israel, mostly civilian. In the air they began employing the tactic of hijacking aircraft, with limited success. An El Al plane was hijacked and forced to land in Algeria; another was attacked on the ground in Munich. There were more attacks in Athens, Zurich, and Rome. Luckily we emerged from them with relatively light casualties, except for the lives lost in a Swissair plane that exploded in midair over Switzerland caused by a bomb in the luggage compartment. The terrorists then succeeded in hijacking a Sabena plane, and landing at Lod Airport. The hijackers demanded release of the Arab terrorists who were detained in Israel, threatening to blow up the plane with all the hostages. They transmitted their demands through the captain of the plane, Reginald Levy, who followed their orders.

I sat with Dayan in the control tower of the airport trying to follow developments around the plane. Dayan was adamant about releasing the hostages by force and instructed Chief of Staff David Elazar to prepare the necessary operation. To gain time and obtain maximum information, Dayan briefed the officer of the security services handling the talks with the terrorists, who sent Captain Reginald Levy to the control tower to negotiate with them. It was an excellent opportunity to learn from him all the essential data about the condition of the passengers, the location of the hijackers, and the equipment at their disposal.

Hundreds of journalists from all over the world were assembled at the Ben Gurion terminal, waiting for action. Among them were old friends who gave me the latest news they picked up from the various wire services. Most of the commentators predicted an Israeli assault on the hijackers holding on to the hostages in the aircraft.

At 2:00 A.M., the special unit assigned to the operation was ready. The information in our possession allowed the detailed planning and preparation. I went down to brief the press, attempting to create the impression of a dialogue with the hijackers, assuming that they would be listening to news broadcasts. I saw Dayan and the rest of our party rushing off in the direction of the fields near the runway. I returned just in time to join the unit as it set out on its mission. Dayan wanted to assess the spirit of the soldiers and to encourage them. In the group I saw the commander of the assault, Ehud Barak, who nineteen years later would become IDF chief of staff; Muki Betzer, married to Dayan's niece, later one of the commanders of the elite units; and Moshe's nephew Uzi Dayan, now a general, son of Moshe's brother Zorik, who died in the 1948 war.

The assault took only minutes. There was one fatality and two injuries among the passengers. Two hijackers were killed and two young women terrorists were taken prisoner, one of them wounded. I went with Dayan the following day to visit the two women. Teresa Chalsa was born in Acre and now came full circle back to Israel, under military police guard in a hospital. Zena Tannous was from the Bethlehem area. She was placed in a Security Service installation for interrogation. Dayan met with both young women in an attempt to understand their motives, family, and social background. I took photos and made notes. They were both obsessed fanatics, their eyes spitting fire, though they answered Dayan politely enough. "These are not mercenaries, nor adventurers," was his only comment as we left.

25

COEXISTENCE

The relationship between Israel and the inhabitants of the territories became more complex and problematic as time passed. From my private conversations with Arab leaders in the territories, undertaken sometimes at Dayan's suggestion but mostly at my own initiative, I got the impression that we were in deadlock. I had frequent meetings with four Arab mayors, one from the Gaza Strip and three from the Jerusalem area. They all expressed concern that Israel's policy toward the inhabitants of the territories centered on one man only – Dayan. They all admired Dayan for according them personal and national dignity and for his efforts to improve their economic conditions, including the opening of the Jordan River bridges and Israel's employment of Arab workers. Dayan gave the Arabs some sort of hope for a political solution. However, Arab leaders were worried that if Dayan were to suddenly vanish from the scene, the whole delicate system of relations created and maintained since June 1967 would collapse.

Dayan, for his part, looked for every possible chink to break through the wall of hostility between the two peoples. He hoped for a prolonged dialogue that would result in coexistence between Israelis and Arabs, and scheduled frequent visits to Arab towns. I accompanied him on most of these visits, recording his conversations with dignitaries as well as with the ordinary man in the street. Individuals were invariably amazed to see him face-to-face and felt privileged to enjoy a personal encounter with the man they called *Abu-Ayin* (One Eye).

In May 1971 a terrorist bomb exploded at the Tel Aviv central bus station. When he heard the news, Dayan ran to his car and ordered his driver to head straight to the scene of the explosion. Assessing the growing rage among Jews, he wanted to be on the spot to ensure that there would be no attacks on innocent Arab bystanders. Ignoring the demands of his bodyguards that he return to his car, he remained in the bus station until he was sure that the police had the situation completely under control, and that they were looking for the perpetrators while preventing acts of revenge by Jews against Arabs.

Shortly after this incident, Dayan told me that Israel could not base its relations with the Palestinians only on the mayors and other dignitaries. Not that they were not legitimate leaders, but the very fact that they served under Israeli rule ruined their credibility with the Arab public. The masses rallied behind Arafat and the other leaders of terrorist organizations. "We have to consider talking to them," said Dayan. I asked him if he had ever tried to meet Arafat. He said that he had tried to meet him in 1967, but at that time the security forces were in hot pursuit of Arafat, who was forced to flee to Jordan disguised as a woman.

Dayan also told me about an attempt to make contact with Arafat through the fiery nationalistic poet Fadua Toukan, who had written a vitriolic poem declaring that her dearest wish was to eat the liver of an Israeli soldier. The daughter of a distinguished Nablus family, she held a privileged and honored position among the Palestinians. Dayan, curious to meet her, had invited her to his Zahala home. He was impressed by her forcefulness and honesty but was shocked by the intensity of her hatred for Israel. She spoke of the Jews as an alien presence that had invaded the region, seized all the natural resources, dispossessed the locals, and was now trying, in stages, to drive them out of their own country. She spoke with self-conviction and inordinate envy of Jewish achievements in culture, art, science, industry, agriculture, and the military, referring disparagingly to the despicable "successful Jews."

At that meeting in the summer of 1970, Toukan asked why Dayan refused to meet Arafat. Dayan replied that, on the contrary, he was willing to meet with him any time, and that two years earlier he had invited Arafat to a meeting, but that Arafat had refused. Fadua Toukan said that she found this difficult to believe; whereupon Dayan requested that she attempt to set up a meeting. She agreed, only to inform him a few days later that her attempt failed.

Moshe Dayan being presented with a newly developed assault rifle
upon leaving the Defense Ministry in June 1974. From right;
Director-General of the Ministry, Yitzhak Ironi, Minister of Defense,
Shimon Peres and the author

Being decorated by Defense Minister Peres
following the Yom Kippur war, 1974

Watching terrorist movements in the Lebanese valley from the top
of a military stronghold on the Golan Hights, 1972

Dayan seeking shelter from Syrian mortar shells on
mount Hermon, as photographed by the author 1974

With Dayan at the Huleh valley after emergency landing
with a helicopter, 1972

Dayan with commanders and elite unit on top of mount Hermon,
after re-capturing the area from the Syrians, as photographed
by the author, 1974

Dayan greeting the author's children at a bar mitzva
celebration of his son Shai, 1972

Peres with the author's family at the same occasion, 1972

With his youngest son Amichai before bar mitzva
in New York, 1982

With Moshe and Rachel Dayan at their home, 1973

With Secretary of State, Cyrus Vance, during peace talks with Egypt

With Prime Minister
Yitzhak Shamir, 1983

With Prime Minister Benjamin Netanyahu and Ambassador Meir Rosenne

With Dayan at Camp David in February 1979, before signing of the Peace Treaty between Israel and Egypt.

Secretary of State, Cyrus Vance, and Foreign Minister, Moshe Dayan, sign a memorandum of agreement between the United States and Israel, following the signing of the peace treaty with Egypt, as photographed by the author, 1979

With the Mayor of New York, Edward I. Koch,
Senator Frank Lautenberg and other dignitaries
on the reviewing stand of the Israel Parade 1985

With the Mayor of Jerusalem Teddy Kollek, 1986

I told Dayan that the military governor of Nablus, Colonel Shaul Givoli, suggested that I meet with Fadua Toukan. Givoli was one of the most successful governors in the occupied territories. A kibbutznik by origin, he was devoted to his job and treated the inhabitants of Nablus with all the respect due to fellow human beings. The locals trusted and respected him, even though he was a representative of the government they hated.

"Meet with her," said Dayan. "Find out whether she can set up a meeting with Arafat." His suggestion surprised me. I asked him who was permitted to know about this plan. "Just the two of you. But don't worry, it won't be a secret for long."

One evening in summer 1971, Shaul came to my home to take my wife and me to visit Fadua Toukan at her home on the slopes of Mount Gerizim, overlooking the town of Nablus. Another woman was also there. She introduced herself as "Raimonda Tawil from Acre." Her daughter Suha later married Yasser Arafat, after working as his personal secretary.

Both women demonstrated great hospitality toward us. They showed a familiarity with many aspects of life in Israel, including culture and the arts. Raimonda mentioned that she often went to concerts of the Israel Philharmonic, while our hostess made a point of saying that she did not visit public places in Israel. Raimonda spoke about the possibility of Jewish-Arab coexistence. Fadua was less conciliatory: "As long as you Jews rule, and we Palestinians are ruled by you, there can be no talk of coexistence," she said.

"Are you suggesting that the country be partitioned?" I asked her. Raimonda answered for her: "Haifa, Acre, Jaffa, Lod, and Ramle all belong to us, the Arabs." "Jerusalem and Tiberias too," added Fadua.

We stayed for over five hours, drinking endless cups of bitter black coffee. Although the atmosphere was congenial, we were quite unable to reach any kind of agreement. Both women were totally single-minded. Here before me were two members of the elite of Palestinian society who had not the least understanding of Israel's position. A couple of times Fadua asked where I was born but paid no attention to my answer. It was only when Joan mentioned that she was born in London that they both began to question our rights as Europeans to come to Israel and dispossess the locals. Again and again I asked whether there had ever been a Palestinian or Arab state in this land.

They did not answer. Eventually both women suggested that all the Israelis who had come before World War I could stay, and that all the rest should pack their bags and return where they came from.

It was two o'clock in the morning when we finally got up to leave. Our hostesses were not bothered by the hour and would have been happy to continue our pointless discussion. Before leaving, I invited them both to visit us at our home in Ramat Gan. I also whispered to Fadua the suggestion that she set up a meeting between Dayan and Arafat. She replied that the subject had already been broached once before and that she doubted whether any Palestinian leader would agree to meet with an Israeli official, not even in secret.

Shaul returned to his base to grab a few hours' sleep in his office, and his driver took us back to Ramat Gan. Joan fell asleep in the car while I mulled over the conversation of that evening. The two women, I was sure, truly represented the mainstream thinking of Arab society. Although they were educated and intelligent, they were quite incapable of overcoming their unbridled animosity toward us. Not for a moment did I ignore the reality of two national entities fighting over the same piece of land, but I had hoped that during the course of an honest, face-to-face discussion we might have reached at least one point of agreement. I consoled myself with the fact that we sat for hours, talking in a civilized manner. Not once did either side raise the voice or utter a threat. But I knew that despite the conviviality of this salon dialogue, we had not succeeded in breaking any ground, and that it would be difficult to achieve meaningful discussions on a practical solution acceptable to both sides. This was not my last attempt at discourse with official or unofficial Palestinians. However, it brought home to me the depth of the chasm and the distance the two sides would have to travel to reach an agreement. Mutual understanding seemed utterly beyond our grasp.

At about three in the morning we crossed the Green Line, the pre-June 1967 frontier between Kalkilia and Kfar Saba. All the way from Nablus we hadn't seen a single car, neither military nor civilian. The villages were cloaked in darkness and there wasn't a soul on the streets. The only signs of life were dogs who ran after our car, barking. At the entrance to Kfar Saba, we entered a different world. Streets, shop-windows, and homes were all lit up and, despite the hour, there were still a few cars on the road. The two worlds were separated by misunderstanding at best, hatred at worst.

The following morning I reported to Dayan the contents of the meeting. He smiled. "I heard such talk thirty years ago, but I have never despaired of the possibility of living with the Arabs. You can't ignore the complexity of the conflict between these two national entities; however, neither of us has any alternative but to find a way. It'll take a long time, but it will come."

The unofficial Israeli position vis-à-vis Judea and Samaria was Yigal Allon's proposal of territorial compromise, by which Israel would retain strategic belts of territory on the west bank of the Jordan River and along the Judea-Samaria north-south mountain ridge. The Palestinians would have a semi-independent state in the remaining enclaves, in confederation with Jordan.

Dayan rejected territorial compromise. He believed it would eventually lead to the creation of an independent state that would, in his view, endanger Israel's security. Instead, he proposed a functional settlement, by which Israel and Jordan would share the responsibility for security in the area, while the locals would enjoy complete control over their domestic affairs. Considering that for nineteen years, between 1948 and 1967, Jordan had had complete jurisdiction over the West Bank and had not given the locals any measure of self-rule, Dayan was convinced that his proposal would be acceptable to both Jordan and the Palestinians.

I was encouraged by the receptiveness of the Arab leaders in Judea, Samaria, and Gaza to Dayan's pragmatic suggestions. At a meeting in his summer home in Hebron, the charismatic Arab leader, Sheikh Muhamad Ali Jaabari, voiced support for Dayan's approach and quipped, "This Arafat is a Jew whom you planted among us in order to prevent dialogue and good neighborliness." Dayan, along with the Israeli officers and Arab notables who were present, laughed. It was obvious that these sheikhs and Bedouins had serious reservations about the terror organizations that used threats and violence to impose their will on both the leaders and the masses, many of whom would have preferred an honorable coexistence instead of a hopeless, bloody struggle.

Jaabari sat next to Dayan on a small, red velvet couch, and offered us freshly cut bunches of juicy red grapes from his vines. Suddenly,

Jaabari noticed that I was staring at a faded portrait on the green wall above his head. He explained that on June 6, 1967, following the withdrawal of the Jordanian Arab Legion from Hebron, he had removed King Hussein's portrait from the wall, promising, "It will never return here." Jaabari continued: " I served King Hussein and his grandfather, King Abdullah, before him. I was a member of his government and swore allegiance to the royal family. When the Israelis overcame his army, Hussein ordered the retreat from Hebron without warning me, even though he knew that the Jews would want to square accounts with me for the massacre of their settlers in the Etzion Bloc in 1948. We are finished with the Hashemites, even though we lived well under them, as we had lived well under the British, and before them under the Turks. With you Israelis, for the time being, we live well, but only Allah knows how long it will continue and how it will end." Jaabari talked for a long time, sharing the perspective gained throughout long years under foreign rulers, some of whom were viewed as enemies and others as friends with whom a modus vivendi could be found. "With you, Mr. Minister, we want to live together and in dignity," said Jaabari.

At that time, Jaabari was the only Palestinian leader of real stature. When the Israeli government decided to hold the first ever democratic municipal elections in the territories, it was clear that the outcome would result in a shift of power to more extreme elements. Recognizing the futility of fighting this trend, Jaabari retired from the political arena even prior to the elections. His retirement left a vacuum that was strongly felt in the Hebron area..

Despite the criticism of King Hussein voiced by Jaabari as well as by other Palestinians, Jordan continued to play an important role in the West Bank. Commercial, social, and cultural ties between both banks of the river strengthened the links between residents of the territories and Palestinian Arabs dispersed throughout the Arab world. The Open-Bridges policy moderated some of the resentment felt by families that had been divided as a result of Israel's occupation of the West Bank, as well as the frustration of Palestinians seeking a national identity. Dayan, who as minister of defense was responsible for the territories, developed extensive contacts among Bedouins, urban dignitaries, businessmen, farmers, and intellectuals. He made every effort to improve the standard of living, economic conditions, and educational opportunities. Several universities were established, the first in the region. Dayan was accused by Israeli politicians of the "Palestinization" of the territories, but he remained convinced that a responsible regime had to address inhabitants' needs irrespective of their political affiliations.

Even during periods of costly terrorist attacks, Dayan continued to visit the territories and talk to the inhabitants and their leaders. When three leaders of the Popular Front terror group hid in the home of the mayor of Gaza, Rashid a-Shawa, Dayan refused to take action against the mayor for harboring the terrorists (they were killed in a confrontation with the IDF). Dayan knew that while we were sitting with a-Shawa in his home, the terrorists were hiding in the cellar beneath us and could easily have attacked him. Dayan preferred to continue the dialogue with him in spite of his collaboration, hoping this policy would help foster coexistence.

Dayan was aware of the dilemma of the moderate Arab leaders in the territories. On the one hand, they wanted to cooperate with the Israeli authorities for the sake of the economic and social advantages this would bring. On the other hand, they could not alienate themselves from the nationalist, anti-Israel aspirations of their constituents, and found it hard to stand up to the constant threats against their lives from extremists in the Arab camp.

Dayan once gave me an example of the schizophrenia of the Arab leadership. Rashid a-Shawa, mayor of Gaza, was a rich landowner and respected leader of the Arab community. All the same, he once went to Brigadier General Yitzchak Segev, the IDF commander in the Gaza Strip, to ask for a rifle with which to protect himself against terrorists who threatened to kill him. Segev was astounded by the request but, late that night, brought him a Kalashnikov rifle. A-Shawa thanked the brigadier and asked him for instructions how to use the gun. The following nights, the Israeli commander and the Arab mayor went out to one of a-Shawa's orange groves for target practice. (The death sentence was never carried out, and Rashid a-Shawa lived to a ripe old age.)

In addition to his dealings with the Palestinians, Dayan was very involved in military affairs, including procurement of arms and equipment, as well as strategic planning. As minister of defense, he toured military installations all over the country, including forward positions on the Suez Canal and the Golan Heights. He always showed special concern for the morale of the troops, stopping to talk to soldiers stationed in the positions he was visiting. Whenever he noticed either me or his military adjutant scribbling notes during such conversations, he would say, "Write down their answers, not my questions."

Dayan had an uncanny ability to detect the slightest departure from the norm or the expected. He reminded me of a creature of the wild, alert to the slightest irregularity or danger signal. When it was necessary, he could pounce like a tiger on an unsuspecting adversary. When some new piece of information came his way, he didn't relax his concentration until he had assembled all the details needed to piece together the full picture.

26

KING HUSSEIN WARNS
OF YOM KIPPUR ATTACK

Early in 1973, Dayan tried to interest Kissinger in a partial settlement on the Egyptian front, similar to the one he had proposed in 1971, which was rejected by Golda Meir and cabinet colleagues. He proceeded on his hunch that the Egyptians would not sit idly by, in the absence of any political progress. He therefore viewed the intelligence reports of Egyptian preparations for war with gravity. In April 1973, when the Washington talks with Egyptian envoy Hafez Ismail failed, the stalemate sent a clear danger signal to Dayan. He promptly initiated several large-scale conferences with the officers of the IDF's three regional commands, in which he spoke about the political situation and his evaluation that the Arab states had abandoned diplomacy, and that we must now prepare for war. When we returned in his car from one of these conferences at the ten-thousand-seat Sport Palace at Yad-Eliyahu in Tel Aviv, I expressed surprise at his blunt words. "I pray that I will not be right," he replied.

Intelligence reports continued to pour in, with indications of Egyptian activities seeming to confirm Dayan's intuition. However, IDF Intelligence was not worried. Their interpretation of the intelligence data led to the evaluation that there was little probability of war. Chief of Staff David Elazar agreed with this assessment. Dayan interpreted the very same data differently. On his instructions, wide-ranging steps were taken to prepare for war. New units were established, fortifications built, sophisticated equipment procured, and operational plans updated. The expense of these preparations was enormous.

In contrast to Dayan's predictions of imminent war, IDF Intelligence predicted a low probability that war would break out. The most likely date anticipated for the outbreak of war, if any, was May 19. The day passed quietly. Nevertheless, Dayan persisted. He continued to appear before IDF officers and other military forums to alert them. He informed the cabinet and the Knesset Security and Foreign Affairs Committee that Egypt was on the warpath; Israel must prepare for war. He repeated his warnings to the IDF general staff and, indeed, to the entire IDF. On May 21, he admonished the general staff, "Gentlemen, please prepare for war in the second half of this year. The participants will be Egypt and Syria, without Jordan." However, during the summer war preparations subsided.

At the end of September, a new flood of warnings from IDF Intelligence again indicated Egyptian preparations for attack. They were a repeat of the warnings in late spring of that year. Once again IDF Intelligence believed that the probability of war was minimal, in spite of the clear Egyptian indications to the contrary. Dayan's warnings were disregarded and the intelligence estimates widely accepted. The chief of staff later said that, until the first shells dropped on the afternoon of Yom Kippur, he had not believed there would be a war. It seems that at the top level only Dayan had correctly anticipated the imminent eruption of hostilities.

During the interim period between the early portents and the actual outbreak of hostilities on October 6 (Yom Kippur day), Dayan decided to formalize his relationship with Rachel and marry her. This was almost two years after he had called me to his office, in the winter of 1971, to tell me of his impending divorce from his wife Ruth. The estranged status of his marriage to Ruth was public knowledge. Nevertheless, I was greatly saddened to hear his decision. I had great respect for Ruth Dayan and felt her pain over the divorce from Moshe, the husband of her youth who, together with her, had raised their three children. I could see that Moshe was also sad, particularly when he told me that the divorce was not his choice but her demand, which he felt he could not refuse. For a moment he considered asking me to accompany him, but finally decided to go alone to the formal ceremony of giving the *get* (the traditional bill of divorce).

On June 25, 1973, almost two years later, he again called me to his office for a personal chat, this time to say that he would marry Rachel

the following evening, in a ceremony to be conducted at the home of
the IDF chief chaplain, Major General Mordechai Piron. Dayan asked
three friends - Chaim Yisraeli, Yosef Ciechanover, and me - to help
form the *minyan*. I volunteered to act as photographer on this intimate
family occasion. At the appointed hour, we all assembled in Rabbi
Piron's modest apartment. While we were enjoying light refreshments,
the happy couple sat on a couch, radiating happiness, holding hands
and exchanging smiles. During the ceremony, I held up one corner of
the *huppa* (wedding canopy) with one hand while taking pictures with
the other. Only those who were there to observe it could appreciate the
deep bond of affection between the newlyweds. Indeed, this was a facet
of Moshe Dayan that I had never seen before. A few days after the
wedding, when I paid my regular Friday afternoon visit to his home in
Zahala, the feminine touch of Rachel was clearly visible: the two silver
Sabbath candlesticks ready for candle lighting, a white embroidered
cloth on the table tastefully set for two – evidence of an exquisitely
happy Dayan that I had not previously observed.

Rachel had an immense influence on his behavior and way of life.
For the first time since I knew him, he began to spend long hours at
home and to entertain guests. From time to time, he left the ministry at
noon or early in the afternoon, to "drop in" on Rachel, as he put it.
Previously, he used to drop in at all kinds of archaeological digs, to
roam about looking for antique finds. After the Yom Kippur War, some
of his friends commented that since his marriage to Rachel, who had
managed to "domesticate" him, his sharp instincts had dulled to the
point where he did not sense the threat of imminent war. However, his
clear-sighted evaluation of intelligence and his unremitting efforts to
rouse the military establishment, clearly contradicted that slur.

For Moshe Dayan, the imminence of war crystallized on
September 13, when the Israel Air Force shot down thirteen Syrian
fighter planes that had penetrated Israeli air space over the Sea of
Galilee and the Golan. The reaction of Syria was restrained. They
massed large forces on the Golan Heights. Dayan was worried by this
Syrian move, seeing it as the initial deployment prior to a large-scale
confrontation with Israel. At a cabinet meeting on September 16, he
warned against a vigorous Syrian reaction. A week later, on September
24, he participated in a general staff session where for the first time he
heard OC Northern Command Major General Yitzchak Hofi state that

his Golan force did not have enough advance warning of Syrian intentions. Dayan pressed the IDF general staff to debate fully this insufficiency in the north and to submit practical suggestions, even though the chief of staff tried to minimize the danger of armed confrontation with Syria. In the ensuing debate, a high-ranking senior member of the general staff expressed his view that there was nothing to fear from the Syrians, despite the fact that they had concentrated a force of eight hundred tanks on the Golan, facing less than one hundred IDF tanks.

Brigadier General Yisrael Lior, military secretary of Prime Minister Golda Meir, immediately brought Dayan's warning to her attention. Due to attend a Council of Europe session in Strasbourg and meet with Chancellor Bruno Kreisky of Austria in Vienna, she phoned Dayan to ask whether she could risk leaving Israel for a trip to Europe on September 29, the day after Rosh Hashanah. Dayan gave her his assessment of the likelihood of war and advised her to ask King Hussein of Jordan, scheduled to meet with her in Israel the following day, how he evaluated the seriousness of the portents of war.

Golda Meir met with the king, who had come for just a few hours on a brief and highly secret visit, accompanied by his prime minister and two aides. During that conversation in a VIP guesthouse near Tel Aviv, the king stated that the Syrian army was deployed for war. He mentioned the vast concentrations of tanks on the Golan, adding that in his appraisal they were deployed in offensive positions from which they could spring forward to attack. Asked whether Syria would go to war alone, without Egypt, he answered that in his opinion they would not. Golda immediately communicated all this to Dayan, to Chief of Staff David Elazar, and to the chief of IDF Intelligence, Eli Zeira. They did not concur with the king's assessment; they saw no new information in his message.

On September 26, the eve of Rosh Hashanah, Dayan convened a meeting of the chief of staff, the chief of IDF Intelligence, the deputy chief of staff, and a few senior officers, to discuss King Hussein's message, which Golda Meir had transmitted to them the previous day. Dayan understood King Hussein's remarks to mean that Syria and Egypt were ready for a war coordinated between them, in the very near future. The chief of staff differed: "I don't think this is a serious matter. It seems to me that the Syrians would have to be idiots to attack us alone, and all the signs are that Egypt is not preparing for a war against us," adding, "I suggest we do not make any preparations which could provoke hostilities on the Golan, since I think the whole matter has a very low probability." Elazar and Zeira were relying on a source who had established his reliability in the past, especially in May 1973, when he correctly predicted that the chance of war was very low.

The meeting closed, and Dayan remained sitting in his chair, staring out of the window, deep in thought. Sitting across from him by the coffee table, I caught his look. As if talking to himself, he remarked, "We'll go up to the Golan and see what's happening there." I left to inform Lieutenant Colonel Arye Braun, his military adjutant, of Dayan's plan, to arrange for a helicopter and invite Dado (nickname for Chief of Staff David Elazar) and OC Northern Command Major General Hofi to accompany him on a tour of the Golan. He asked me to include a few local and foreign correspondents, through whom he would pass a message to the Syrians that Israel was ready to meet any warlike challenge. I suggested that the meeting with the media should be in a civilian, rather than military environment. We chose Kibbutz Ein Zivan on the Golan as the place to toast the Jewish New Year with representatives of the settlements and, coincidentally, voice Dayan's message to the Syrians.

The chief of staff persisted in his view, and did not join us in the helicopter that took off at 11:00 A.M. from the Sde Dov airfield in Tel Aviv and flew directly to Golan headquarters at Nafach. We drove off in a convoy of cars along the IDF front line facing the Syrians. At one of our fortified positions, we set up field glasses to follow the movement of Syrian forces on the facing ridges. After the tour and an analysis of the situation, Dayan instructed Hofi to reinforce the Golan with an additional armored brigade, disregarding the contrary recommendation of the chief of staff earlier that day. Dayan viewed the Syrian concentrations with gravity and feared that they would use the days of Rosh Hashanah to launch a surprise attack, when thousands of holiday-picnicking Israelis would be choking the roads.

At 2:00 P.M. we arrived in Ein Zivan to meet the representatives of the civilian settlements and the media. To our surprise, we found the chief of staff there. He had arrived a few minutes earlier to participate in the meeting. Dayan voiced his warning via the media, in the hope that his message would reach the Syrians and serve as a deterrent.

Walking back to the helicopter, Hofi (later head of the Mossad) asked me for a lift from Sde Dov to his home in Ramat Gan. Dayan overheard, turned to Hofi, and said, "You stay here to make sure the armor reinforcements arrive by tomorrow." Hofi was disappointed. He tried to explain that the situation was presently quiet and he would return that night to check immediately after ushering in the festival eve with his family. "If the situation were not quiet, I would be staying here too," retorted Dayan. Hofi stayed on the Golan Heights to assure the deployment of an additional one hundred tanks to reinforce the seventy already deployed along the Golan defense border. It was these one hundred and seventy tanks that ten days later just barely held back the Syrian onslaught of thousands of tanks, poised to trample the Israeli population centers in the Hula and Jordan valleys.

On October 2, in the absence of Golda Meir, who was abroad, Dayan called Minister Yisrael Galili, a confidant of the prime minister, and apprised him that war was imminent. Dayan asked Galili to convene an urgent cabinet meeting immediately upon Golda's return, to share his grave concern about impending war in the north. Meanwhile he held meetings with members of the general staff and IDF Intelligence. The flow of intelligence across his desk was irrefutable evidence of preparations for war. He asked the intelligence officers on what they based their contrary interpretation. On the following day, October 3, Elazar submitted a document designed to explain his understanding of intelligence reports that war was unlikely. This was just three days before the actual attack on two fronts.

That same day, Golda Meir convened the cabinet meeting that Dayan had requested. Among the participants were Yigal Allon, Yisrael Galili, the chief of staff, the OC Air Force, and the deputy chief of IDF Intelligence. One of the participants, a friend of mine, coming out of the cabinet meeting in the prime minister's office, smiled at me and said, "Your boss is in a despondent mood. Something must have happened to him. He's frightening everyone with war scares." His deprecation of Dayan's worries calmed me, and I began to think that perhaps Dayan was really in a gloomy mood leading to groundless alarm. There were others among my colleagues at the Ministry of Defense who complained about Dayan's dire forecasts, viewing them as false alarms. During this cabinet meeting, the chief of staff and the deputy chief of IDF Intelligence repeated their appraisals, and Golda thanked the military for allaying her fears. Dayan was not reassured, but was pleased that his cabinet colleagues, including the prime minister, were cognizant of his anxieties, sharing in the responsibility for possible further developments.

In the early morning of the eve of Yom Kippur, October 5, we were informed of the hurried evacuation of the families of the Soviet advisers in the Syrian and Egyptian armies. At the same time, Israel Air Force planes brought back photographs of an unprecedented deployment of the Egyptian army along the Suez Canal, which could only be explained as actions preliminary to war. At that morning's session with Elazar and Zeira, Dayan said, "You are not taking the Egyptians and Syrians seriously. I take them very seriously, and do not *a priori* judge them incapable of war." Elazar and Zeira tried to minimize the significance of the Soviet evacuation. They persisted in relying on their source, despite the clear and indisputable facts to the contrary.

Dayan came to Golda Meir's office, taking Elazar and Zeira with him. He presented his fears and asked her to turn to Washington to convince the Russians, and through them the Arabs, that Israel had no warlike intentions, and that if the Arabs took offensive action, they would have reason to regret it. He attached considerable importance to the message, in order to impress on the Egyptians and Syrians that if they attacked, they would not have the advantage of surprise. Golda accepted Dayan's suggestion and summoned U.S. Ambassador Kenneth Keating to forward the message to Washington. Dayan also suggested that she immediately convene those members of the cabinet residing in the Tel Aviv area, to update them on impending events.

At 11.30 A.M., as staff in the Tel Aviv government-center offices went home to prepare for the fast, some cabinet members met in the prime minister's office to hear briefings from Dayan and the two senior officers. Zeira, twenty-six hours before the actual outbreak of war, repeated his assessment of a very low probability of an Egyptian and Syrian attack against Israel. The chief of staff reiterated his confidence in the evaluation of IDF Intelligence.

The limited mobilization that had already begun was not yet noticeable. The streets were almost deserted by that early afternoon when I drove home to Ramat Gan for Yom Kippur. Somehow, I did not share Dayan's anxiety and alarm that war was on our doorstep. I was inclined to accept the majority view in the government and the general staff, toying with the hope that it was only Dayan's natural pessimism that had led him to his exaggerated, gloomy forecast. After the traditional meal before the fast, I went to the nearby synagogue. People dressed in their festive best were streaming to the *Kol Nidrei* service. None of them suspected or foresaw the events just hours away. At four in the morning, the special phone at my bedside linking me to the office of the minister of defense startled me out of my slumber and thrust me into the reality of a terrible war that would begin on that very day, Yom Kippur 1973.

27

IN PRAYER SHAWLS TO BATTLEFIELD

In the early light of dawn on October 6, as I drove from my Ramat Gan home to the Ministry of Defense in Tel Aviv, there was not a soul in the streets, indicating that mobilization had not yet begun. Only later in the day did full mobilization begin, as more and more men were called out of the synagogues, still in prayer shawls, to report to their military units on this day of judgment, the holiest day of the year. Some of the military and civilian staff were already in the minister's office when I arrived, although it took another hour before all the others, including the secretaries, came on duty.

In Dayan's room I found Deputy Chief of Staff Major General Yisrael Tal, and Major General Shlomo Gazit, coordinator of activities in the administered territories. Also present were Chaim Yisraeli, head of the minister's office; Yosef Ciechanover, legal adviser; and Lieutenant Colonel Arye Braun, Dayan's military adjutant. The atmosphere in the room was tense. One could practically smell the gunpowder. Yesterday's assessments and wrong guesses about the probability of war were now history and gave way to a debate over procedure in a conflict predicted to start at six that evening.

This latest information came from the Mossad and not from the source that the IDF Intelligence had previously considered so reliable that it dismissed the probability of war on the two fronts until the very last minute. Chief of Staff Lieutenant General David (Dado) Elazar arrived at 6:00 A.M., and a debate began on the scope of mobilization needed to contain the Syrians and the Egyptians. Elazar contended that a single armored division would suffice for the north, and a second for the south; but to allow for a rapid shift to the offensive he would need four armored divisions and a preemptive air strike on airfields and missile sites in Syria. Dayan argued that an initial mobilization of that size and a preemptive air strike would be interpreted by the world as a war started by Israel. He recommended mobilization of only two divisions to contain the attack until the reserves were mobilized, and opposed the preemptive air strike. Elazar stood his ground. Dayan suggested that the issue be decided by the prime minister. Elazar did not immediately mobilize the two divisions Dayan had approved, and valuable time was lost. It was only at 8:30 A.M., two-and-a-half hours after Dayan had authorized mobilization of two armored divisions, that the wider call-up of four reserve divisions was activated, on the sanction of Golda Meir. She approved the wider mobilization, but opposed the preemptive air strike on Syrian missile batteries and airfields for the same reason that Dayan did.

At Dayan's urging, Golda Meir had the previous day summoned the U.S. ambassador to inform Washington of the gravity of the situation, in a last attempt to influence the Egyptian and Syrian presidents to avert the outbreak of war. But the State Department was unconvinced. Indeed, even after fighting began, Washington failed to go on record as identifying the Arabs as the aggressors.

The hands of the clock moved on toward zero hour. The debate in the defense minister's office thoroughly explored all possibilities, including the need to guard against local violence from within the territories. At 11:00 A.M. Dayan convened a meeting of the general staff. He asked about the deployment of forces in the south, and wanted to know what instructions had been given to the commanders in the field. The chief of staff responded that by five in the afternoon the IDF would be deployed to contain any attack, with one brigade along the Suez Canal and two more concentrated as mailed fists at a reasonable distance from the forward perimeter. The entire general staff agreed that three hundred tanks in the south and one hundred seventy-eight on the Golan Heights would suffice to contain the Syrian and Egyptian offensives until the reserves could be mobilized and brought to the front lines.

Unexpectedly, the war started at two in the afternoon, four hours before the predicted zero hour. At 2:00 P.M. the brigade of tanks assigned to the forward line had just begun to move toward the positions at the Suez Canal. The other two brigades were in central

Sinai, a distance of about fifty miles from the Canal. The surprise timetable change enabled the Egyptian army to assemble many bridges across the Canal, cross over a substantial force of armor and infantry, and consolidate a bridgehead on the east bank of the Canal.

About an hour before the firing started on both fronts, I went down to a hut in the general staff quarters, where a Yom Kippur prayer service was being led by the chief chaplain of the IDF. Soldiers and officers congregated with cabinet ministers who had come to the Kirya to keep in touch with events. During the services, an old acquaintance, a reserve colonel just mobilized, tapped me on the back. I followed him outside and heard the air-raid siren that signaled the outbreak of war. Returning to Dayan's office, I saw the utter dismay on everyone's face. Dayan sat hunched in his chair, deep in thought. He turned to me and asked, "Did you pray on my behalf as well?" His question was not glibly spoken. From his manner and expression, I understood the extreme seriousness of our situation. At this hour we were truly in need of God's mercy and help.

At 4:00 P.M., I invited the newspaper editors to a meeting with Dayan, where they heard the first information released about the opening moves of the war.

The fog of battle on both fronts prevented analysis of the course of war, but we realized very quickly that the line along the Canal had been broken, and that the few troops that were trapped in their own strongholds, were unable to repel the Egyptian assault. The situation of our forces on the Golan was even worse. Civilians had been evacuated from the Golan Heights, but now Syrian tanks had stormed across the plateau and threatened to descend into the populated valleys at the foot of the Golan Heights. Even before sundown, news came in of heavy IDF losses on both fronts. In this gloomy atmosphere, a few colleagues gathered in Chaim Yisraeli's office. One of us recited the *Havdalah* blessing (to separate the Sabbath and festivals from the weekdays that follow). With that, we ended the twenty-six-hour fast, during which we had tasted neither food nor water. This year the fast was hardly noticed, overshadowed by the emergency.

At 7:00 P.M. the defense minister reported on television and radio about the war that had erupted. Two hours later, he appeared before the foreign correspondents, who had begun streaming to Israel. At 10:00 P.M. members of the government convened in Golda Meir's office for the first cabinet meeting since the outbreak of war. The chief of staff gave a report that sounded optimistic. He predicted that the IDF would be ready to counterattack within twenty-four hours, basing his predictions on information given him by OC Southern Command Major General Shmuel Gonen (Gorodish). Both Elazar and Gonen believed in the capability of the IDF to drive the Egyptians out of Sinai within a few days. Dayan was skeptical. "They have crossed the Canal and poured a large force into Sinai. It will not be possible to just wave them away. It will take a lot of time and it will be at a high cost," he told me upon his return from the cabinet session, close to midnight. The situation in the north worried him even more.

One of the cabinet ministers came to my room at midnight, for a cup of coffee. "I didn't believe this would happen to us," he said, genuinely distressed. He told me about the cabinet's optimism on hearing Elazar's report, with its implication that within two or three days the Egyptians would be driven back from their positions in Sinai, and the Syrians would be soundly beaten, "hip and thigh." The prime minister gave instructions that reports in this vein be sent to all our representatives abroad. Dayan didn't share in this complacency. He raised doubts about the IDF's ability to carry out Elazar's plan. "Is there any basis for his pessimism, or is it his depression that drives him to such assessments?" asked my visitor. I gathered that Dayan must have put a damper on the upbeat report from Elazar. Already at this point he spoke about deploying a second line in Sinai, since the Canal line had collapsed and was no longer under our control. The IDF could deploy along that second line in preparation for a counterattack.

The ministers were astounded by Dayan's words. Some of them attributed it to defeatism and viewed it as a sign of weakness. Others, like my visitor in the Kirya office, saw in Dayan's words the cruel reality of this war. "It's very possible that he is right in his assessment, but it should not be voiced in public, to avoid lowering the morale of the people," he said, with the obvious intention that this message be passed on to Dayan as quickly as possible.

While I was sitting with the cabinet minister, talking about the anticipated military developments, Dayan was visiting the air force command and the war room of the general staff, known as the "pit," discussing IAF plans for the following day with OC Air Force Major General Benny Peled. Peled had presented a plan to attack the Egyptian missile batteries to gain freedom of action for the air force, while Dean insisted that the main thrust should be against the Egyptian forces crossing the Canal in order to block their advance. The decision remained in the hands of the OC Air Force Peled, and the chief of staff, who had given priority to attack the missiles. In the general staff "pit," Dayan received a disheartening report on the situation in the north, where the Syrians had broken through and were advancing to the western slopes of the Golan.

At 5:00 A.M. on October 7, the second day of the war, I walked down the steps with Dayan to his car, waiting to take him to Sde Dov Airport on his way to northern command. He had called on me to lay out guidelines for the information to be released. "Don't flex your muscles and don't plant any illusions of a quick victory, but promise stabilization of the lines on both fronts in preparation for a favorable outcome on both," was his suggestion. Before getting into the car, he told me that the situation in the north was particularly crucial. The battle could spill over into Israel proper, unlike the battles in the south on the sand dunes of Sinai, far from population centers.

Three hours later, at 8:00 A.M., he returned by helicopter. He informed Elazar that he had urged Benny Peled to allocate several quartets of aircraft to attack the advancing columns of Syrian armor on the Golan to retard their advance – a recommendation he made on the advice of Major General (reserve) Moti Hod, ex-commander of the IAF, now mobilized to serve as air liaison for northern command. The IAF planes had stopped the Syrian advance, thus allowing our two armored brigades to reorganize and hold out in their defense lines until the reserve forces could reach the Golan Heights.

In his brief conversation with Elazar after returning from northern command, Dayan advised against stubbornly holding the Canal strongholds which, in his opinion, had lost their military value, and to begin evacuating our forces immediately. At the same time, he demanded redeployment on a second line from which the counterattack could be launched. Within the hour, at 9:00 A.M., Dayan was on his way to the command bunker at Um Hashiba, to get a close look at the course of the battle in Sinai. He returned more depressed than before, realizing that the situation regarding the deployment of forces at the Canal was vastly different from that reported by the OC southern command and the chief of staff in the early hours of the war. The force of which they had spoken was very far from the Canal and had made no meaningful contribution at the beginning of the war. By the end of the first twenty-four hours, only one hundred tanks were still serviceable out of the three hundred that were supposed to have participated in the opening battle maneuvers.

Upon returning to the Kirya, Dayan summoned Elazar to his office and told him what he intended to propose to the prime minister at a meeting of the three of them, scheduled for 3:00 P.M. The chief of staff listened without comment. Finally, he agreed with Dayan's assessment on the need for a second line, but added that in his opinion it would be possible to open a counteroffensive near the Canal by the following day without the second line, if the divisions commanded by Reserve Generals Ariel Sharon and Avraham Adan would be deployed. Dayan suggested he check with the commanders in the field about the feasibility of the planned counterattack, and empowered Elazar to decide on his own if he was convinced of the feasibility of the plan and of the ability of our forces to carry it out successfully.

At 3:00 P.M. Dayan and Elazar walked toward Golda Meir's office on a path that crosses the garden of the Defense Ministry. I walked right behind them, together with two of their aides. Elazar listened as Dayan somberly related his impressions of the visit to the southern command bunker. He described as utterly inadequate the performance of OC Southern Command Shmuel Gonen, in spite of his earlier record as a war hero. He proposed to return the command to Ariel Sharon, who had transferred command to Gonen a few months earlier. Elazar reacted negatively, saying, "Shmulik (Gonen) will recover and function well. He's a first-rate soldier." Dayan did not concede and continued trying to convince Elazar to put Sharon back in command of the southern front.

At the meeting with Golda Meir, in which Ministers Galili and Allon participated, Dayan's report was greeted with astonishment. Only that morning in a cabinet session, they had been heartened by the assessment of the chief of staff that in a matter of days the Egyptians would be thrown back across the Canal. Now the defense minister was again spreading confusion and despair. Only Elazar supported Dayan's conclusion that a second line must be consolidated before making a counterattack. He was also confident that the divisions commanded by Sharon and Adan, together with Major General Albert Mendler's Sinai

Division, would be able to launch an attack in a day or two that would drive the Egyptians back across the Canal. As defense minister, Dayan could do no more than urge that Elazar personally meet with the commanders in the field before deciding.

Even before the end of the cabinet meeting that evening, and before Elazar's departure to southern command, I received a phone call from Arie Dissenchik, editor in chief of the newspaper *Ma'ariv*. "What's happened to Moshe? Has he really broken down?" he asked in alarm. Meanwhile, the rumor factory was apparently working overtime. All the politicians who had scores to settle with Dayan had decided that the time was ripe to do so. There were quite a few of them, and they were ready to talk to any of the media willing to listen. The prevailing buzzword was that Dayan's pessimistic predictions were based on his loss of nerve, in contrast to the cool courage of the army commanders who had not lost their heads and promised a quick and decisive victory.

That night when the chief of staff returned from the south, he reported to Dayan on his joint agreement with the field commanders to open a counteroffensive in the morning, retaining the option of exploiting the course of the battle and, if successful, to cross the Suez Canal westward. Elazar convened the general staff to present the planned counterattack. He exuded confidence in the success of the planned operation, in which three leading IDF divisions would participate. Dayan knew all the commanders intimately and respected their capabilities, but nevertheless doubted the chances of success. His spirits alternated between hope and apprehension. After his discussion with Elazar and the general staff meeting on the operational plan, Dayan returned to his office and phoned Golda Meir. It was after midnight, and the prime minister was resting at home. He told her what was to happen in the next few hours and asked her to convene the cabinet in the morning to hear the briefing of the chief of staff on the offensive.

On October 8, the third day of the war, at the 10:00 A.M. cabinet session, Dado Elazar radiated confidence and optimism about the offensive that had already begun. He even hinted at a crossing of the Canal on the bridges of the Egyptians. While the cabinet was meeting in Golda Meir's office to hear about the battle developments from the chief of staff, I was in the general staff "pit," tensely following the course of the battle outlined on the map. Senior staff officers, retired chiefs of staff, and reserve generals all followed the progress and interpreted the moves. After briefing the cabinet, the chief of staff joined the assembly, his face glowing with satisfaction at the change in the course of the war. Among the dispatches that came in was a report from the OC Southern Command about the success of Adan's division in crossing the Canal at the Firdan Bridge.

The atmosphere was suddenly charged with exhilaration. The house steward with his tray of sandwiches was besieged by rediscovered appetites. When the steward offered a sandwich to Elazar, he signaled a victory V and called out joyfully, "I'll have two, in honor of the victory." The visitors began to scatter, to pass on the good news of the turn in the battle.

I went up to Dayan's office and found him sitting alone, absorbed in thought, indifferent to the verbiage emanating from the operational radio on his desk. I told him what was going on in the "pit" and about the report just in from OC southern command. He looked at me, his solitary eye shining, either from emotion or fatigue, and voiced his doubts. He said, "To my mind, it doesn't fit with the situation I saw down there." He called his military secretary and asked to be connected to southern command. Within a few minutes he had an updated report from the general in command that the offensive had been a serious failure, with heavy losses.

Dayan requested another cabinet meeting that evening to apprise the cabinet of the actual situation on the Egyptian front, which was in sharp contrast to the earlier encouraging report. The chief of staff was very restrained and left no doubt in the ministers' minds that the offensive was a failure. At the end of the session, around midnight, Dayan left for the southern command bunker for a debriefing with the generals to determine what had gone wrong during the day and what needed to be done urgently in order to stabilize the front and extricate the soldiers trapped in the Canal strongholds. When he returned, at four in the morning of the fourth day, his face reflected the scope of the defeat and his utter fatigue. Not pausing to drink the cup of tea offered him, he went down to the "pit" to talk to Elazar. Dayan viewed OC Southern Command as inappropriate to conduct this war. He again demanded that Elazar replace him with either General Ariel Sharon or General Chaim Bar-Lev. But Elazar remained loyal to Shmuel Gonen and refused to remove him from command. Dayan was adamant and decided, with the prime minister's approval, to appoint Bar-Lev commander southern front. Sharon remained commander of the division, which later successfully crossed the Canal westward.

I had not changed clothes for three days and nights. There had been no time to go home. One of my secretaries, a woman soldier doing her national service, brought me a pair of uniforms and a blanket, which served as both sheet and cover on the army cot provided for me when I had a chance to catch a nap. The media kept our phone lines busy nonstop. Those reporters who somehow got into the Kirya besieged my small office in the hope of gleaning a few crumbs of hard information. My military knowledge was sparse. My last stint as a soldier, twenty years back, had earned me the exalted rank of corporal. However, my presence at the dramatic deliberations and decisions on the moves of the war and the various plans innovated to restore the IDF initiative on the battlefield afforded me a grasp of the events at the front lines and of the performance of some of the commanding officers directing the course of the war.

In the upper echelons, the officers noted for their levelheadedness in a crisis, boldness in innovation, decisiveness, and adherence to mission were Elazar, Bar-Lev, and OC Air Force Benny Peled. In the debates at the command bunkers and in the IDF general staff, I heard compliments about a number of the senior field commanders, among them Major Generals Ariel Sharon, Abraham Adan, Albert Mendler, Kalman Magen, Yitzchak Hofi, Dan Laner, Rafael Eitan, and Musa Peled. After the Seventh Brigade repelled the second Syrian assault on the north Golan Heights, its commander, Colonel Avigdor (Yanosh) Bengal, won acclaim for that "Battle of the Vale of Tears," as it was named, which became a graveyard for the Syrian armor.

I observed the behavior and self-control of Moshe Dayan from a very close vantage point during the most critical hours of this war. What particularly impressed me was his conduct during the early days of the battles, when the IDF was still reeling from the heavy impact of the first surprise blows. He returned pensive and brooding from debates with the chief of staff, with the generals in the "pit," with commanders in the field whom he sometimes consulted as often as twice daily. He had lengthy sessions with the prime minister and his other colleagues. Those who did not know him well might have formed the impression that his mood reflected excessive melancholy. But those who worked closely with him were witness to the new ideas that he put forward after each sortie or debate. He tested their merit on us, his staff, whom he used as a sounding board. Everything I heard and saw confirmed his correct, in fact almost perfect, reading of the moves on the war map, from the start of the outbreak on both fronts until its end, nineteen days later. He used his in-depth understanding to influence and move the entire establishment in many vital aspects:

He urged instructions to speed up the evacuation of the Canal strongholds that had become, in his view, militarily useless and a trap for their garrisons;

He urged redeployment along a second line, at which the forces could reorganize for a counterattack;

He insisted on the appointment of a suitable general as OC Southern Command;

He directed the OC Air Force to use air power to contain the Syrian advance on the Golan;

He questioned the wisdom of the counteroffensive of October 8, before establishing a second line for regrouping the troops;

He encouraged the IDF general staff to regain the initiative in the south and in the north by threatening Cairo and Damascus.

On the evening of the third day of war, four senior assistants to Dayan were sitting in the tiny office of Chaim Yisraeli, head of the defense ministry's office. It was October 8, the day of the abortive counteroffensive at the Canal. The door opened and an exhausted Dayan joined the group. He said, almost as if to himself, "The situation is even more serious than I thought, and I'm the professional pessimist around here. If there isn't a turning point in the next two days, one that returns the initiative to us, we'll have to use a very painful response."

The four of us in the room understood him completely and were stunned. Dayan walked out but came back a moment later, this time a bit more hopeful, "Let's wait and see what happens tomorrow in the battle up north," he said. In fact, the next day, October 9, there was a tough battle against the Syrians in the Golan, and we finally halted their advance. I followed him out on the way to my office on the floor above. He turned to me and said, "You've been through worse times and come out of them. I've also tasted tough times in my life. Don't worry. It's not the end. We'll get out of this too."

I returned to my room in a troubled mood. I had been through several wars in my life, losing many who were dear to me in every one of them: my immediate family, close friends, and companions – times of torment that had left their scars to this day. The hardest of all had been World War II, when I was still a youth and had not yet really tasted life. That was a war between various nations but we Jews, its ultimate victims, were viewed by all sides as the common enemy. We had no weapons to defend our lives, apart from the will to live and determination not to surrender, a determination nurtured by a steadfast faith in the Eternal of Israel. I came out of that war permanently scarred in body, and apparently in soul too, deprived of parents, home, and country.

The second war of my life was in 1948, Israel's War of Independence. At first I joined the Jewish underground, shouldering a weapon to defend my life and the life of my newborn country. I served as a soldier in the Israel Defense Forces, removed from fateful decisions and unaware of the perilous situation we faced. I lost four close friends in that war; two of them had been with me through the Nazi inferno. We came together to Eretz Yisrael.

My third war took place just when I was about to marry and set up a home. Eight days before the wedding, scheduled for November 5, 1956, I was called up for reserve duty as a military correspondent. This was the Sinai Campaign, in which the IDF took the Sinai Peninsula for the first time in just one hundred hours, with relatively few casualties. Three days before my wedding date, the commander of my brigade, the late Colonel Abraham Yaffe, released me from duty to return to Tel Aviv to attend my own wedding ceremony. Our personal joy was paralleled by the national joy over the victory. Dayan was brilliantly successful as the chief of staff in this war, which brought him to fame.

In the Six-Day War, in 1967, the difficult period was the three weeks preceding the war, during which our Arab neighbors threatened to annihilate our nation and people. As in previous wars, I felt that we were in a stranglehold. We didn't have a single ally. Though our Arab neighbors were the aggressors, they were the ones who benefited from outside intervention. As soon as it became clear that we might overpower them, they received political support and military assistance from Russia. Dayan had been appointed defense minister by overwhelming popular demand. The stunning success of this war confirmed his reputation in the eyes of the public. I functioned as military correspondent, in the role of observer. My involvement was far from the battlefield, but like all those on the home front I was caught up with the exuberance of snatching victory from defeat, the restoration of Jerusalem to our people, with its Western Wall of the ancient Temple, and the restoration of Hebron with its even more ancient, authentic double-cave burial site of our Patriarchs: Abraham, Isaac, and Jacob, and their wives Sarah, Rebecca, and Leah.

In the 1973 Yom Kippur War, my personal position and involvement were totally different. I was now in a position to see the battlefield reports and observe firsthand how fateful decisions were taken. I accompanied Dayan almost everywhere, whether in his office, in the cramped seat of a small aircraft or a noisy helicopter, at the sand table of a forward command position, or in the general staff "pit." I felt the pulse of the nation in this war. Every time a new casualty list was brought to my desk, my hands shook. I was always afraid to come across the name of a friend or his son. The lists continued to grow, even after the turning point, when we regained the initiative. At least two of the fallen had been the only sons of Holocaust survivors whom I knew, who had rehabilitated themselves and started new lives and families in our national homeland. With the death of their only sons, they had irreplaceably lost their hope for a living posterity.

When the Arab aggressors began to falter, they received help: expeditionary forces, equipment, economic resources, and political support from the Arab world and from Russia. Again I felt the familiar stranglehold on us, with the noose tightening around us. No one rushed to our side, neither the Jewish people across the globe, nor any foreign power – with one notable exception. The one person who did stand by us was President Richard Nixon of the United States who, for reasons of his own, decided to assist us. For a critical four days the U.S. administration delayed carrying out the president's directive. Efforts of the Jewish lobby to recruit aid for Israel moved neither the White House nor any other world power. The feeling of isolation in those grim days was pervasive.

Alone in my office, and in a mood to draw up the balance sheet of my life, I found it hard to believe that I had experienced five bloody wars in my lifetime thus far. I silently prayed that my sons should not have to face such ordeals. Unfortunately, my prayer was not granted.

Nine years later, when I was consul general of Israel in New York and physically separated from Israel, two of my sons were fighting in the war in Lebanon, where they served as commanders of advance combat units. In my frequent appearances on American radio and television, trying to explain the motivation and the strategy of this war, I attempted to detach myself from personal concerns and worries, not always successfully. Christopher Jones, senior political writer for New York's Channel 5 television station, noticed my distraction and asked, "What is bothering you at this moment?" I answered that two of my sons were soldiers fighting somewhere in Lebanon and I was a worried father. He asked, "Were you personally involved in other wars in your lifetime and is this time more difficult?" Only then did I realize that this war in Lebanon, in which my sons were fighting, was much more difficult for me than all the other wars in which I had been personally involved.

On the morning of October 9, at the nadir of our position in the Yom Kippur War, Dayan summoned me to his office. It was the day after our abortive counteroffensive in the south. "The nation must be informed of the true picture at the fronts. We have to be honest with them, not feed them heroic stories and false expectations of a quick, brilliant victory," he said, and launched into a long monologue about our obligation to keep the public informed. "We owe the people true and reliable reporting within the limitations of field security. I intend to appear this evening in a television and radio interview, in which I will tell them the truth, while emphasizing that it is not the end of the story. Within a reasonable time, we will reverse course and take the offensive, keeping the casualties down." I suggested that before going out to arrange for the public interviews, he first brief the newspaper editors in private and reveal to them a few added details that would not be mentioned in the public interview. He agreed, and was glad to have a live rehearsal with the editors, for off-the-record comments behind closed doors.

We convened the Newspaper Editors' Committee and the electronic media at 7:00 P.M. in our conference room. Some of the thirty invited journalists were milling around the corridor, with no idea whatsoever about what had transpired the day before on the southern front. They exchanged assessments of Elazar's press conference the previous evening, when he stated, "we will break the Egyptian and Syrian bones." Dayan was still conferring in a separate room with a few senior officers, among them, Chief of Staff David Elazar and OC Air Force Benny Peled, who were submitting reports about recent events. Peled's son, an IAF combat pilot, had been reported missing over Sinai that morning and searches of the area had not turned up any news. Peled, known as a brave man of integrity, now sat with sad restraint. Dayan offered a few words of encouragement and reminded him how he, Peeled himself, had been rescued by fellow pilots when his plane was downed in the 1956 war. Ben smiled as Dean placed a hand on his shoulder and said, in his earthy saber humor, "Ben, the Third Temple rests on your shoulders." One of the journalists in the corridor outside apparently caught the words "Third Temple," and immediately added his own interpretation, according to which Dean was predicting the downfall of the Third Temple. The first two Temples related to biblical times, while the third was taken to mean modern Israel.

Inside the conference room were some of the most prominent journalists in Israel: editors Gershom Schocken of *Ha'aretz*, Dr. Herzl Rosenblum of *Yediot Aharonot*, Arie Dissenchik of *Ma'ariv,* and Chana Zemer of *Davar*. At the head table sat Dayan; Elazar; chief of intelligence branch; and the OC Air Force General Peled. I had taken my seat next to Benny Peled. Dayan's secretary gave me a note to pass to him. Benny showed me the contents: "Your son has been found and is safe and sound."

During Dayan's presentation of the actual situation to the editors, Schocken had commented that divulging this information would cause a public furor. Dayan explained his motives: "The nation has a right and indeed must know what is happening to its sons at the fronts and what we can expect." At that point Benny Peled handed the note to Dayan, who could not restrain himself and told the editors that Major General Peled's son had been missing for twenty hours, and that word of his rescue had just been received. The story brought tears to some eyes in the room. In newspaper circles, the rumor spread that amongst the editors who heard Dayan's report on the true status of the battlefronts, there were even some who wept.

Shortly after the briefing, Dayan met with Golda Meir, who asked him to cancel his planned appearance on the media. One of the editors had told her about the briefing and expressed his fear that the facts would demoralize the public. So far, the public still believed the comforting reports from official IDF sources that the Egyptian forces in Sinai and the Syrians on the Golan had been rapidly and successfully repulsed. Dayan was not prepared to appear in public with another glib account that glossed over the true picture. He told me to cancel his appearance, and suggested Major General Aharon Yariv, spokesman for the IDF, as a replacement. Yariv appeared and presented a cautious and balanced report. Nevertheless, a credibility gap was created by the contrasting communiqués about the true situation on both fronts, details of which were now filtering back day by day to an ever-widening circle in Israel.

Dayan was extremely sensitive to the need to preserve the credibility of security-establishment spokesmen. He instructed me to strictly enforce his policy that all official communiquées be truthful, even if painful. He told me to brief the IDF spokesman on the information line, to pursue and to insist that all communiqués be approved by me before release. "I don't want our communiques treated like those from Cairo and Damascus," he said.

After the battle of October 9 on the Golan, in which the Syrians were thrown back, Dayan strongly recommended that OC Northern Command Yitzhak Hofi continue the momentum with an offensive toward Damascus. This would speed the attainment of a cease-fire on our terms. Hofi did not believe that his utterly exhausted forces would be capable, at this moment, of launching such an offensive, but Dayan convinced him to try. He pressed the cabinet to give top priority to the northern front, because of the vulnerable state of the Jewish settlements there. He wanted the Syrians out of the picture as soon as possible, and only afterwards to concentrate all forces on the southern front. He relentlessly and unceasingly advocated raising the threat against the Syrian capital. This aim was accomplished by the advance of IDF forces along all roads to the Syrian capital and the bombing of military and strategic targets in the city and environs.

The wear and tear of our forces was evident on both fronts. Our stocks of arms and ammunition were dwindling. Meanwhile, supplies were flowing into Damascus from the Soviet Union, via an airlift of giant Antonov cargo planes landing in Syria around the clock. The Syrians were also getting help from other Arab countries. A Jordanian armored contingent together with an Iraqi expeditionary force had already joined Syria in its fight against us. Both of these units sustained heavy losses. This led to growing concern that the Jordanians might open a direct front on the west bank of the Jordan River. The prime minister and minister of defense decided on a two-pronged political effort in Washington: first, to deter Jordan from attacking, and second to resupply Israel with the combat materiel expended in the war. Golda wanted to go to Washington for a face-to-face talk with President Nixon to convince him that the situation was indeed crucial.

On October 9, even before receiving Golda Meir's request for a meeting, President Nixon announced that the United States would resupply Israel with combat materiel expended in the course of the war. American intelligence services were already aware of the accelerated Soviet airlift to Syria, which was now running at the rate of twenty Antonov transport planes a day. Nixon feared that the Soviets, by means of the massive resupply effort, would guarantee a significant advantage for themselves in negotiations following this war, and decided to restore the balance by an accelerated flow of war materiel to Israel. His decision was not implemented. It was lost somewhere between the bureaucratic corridors of the State Department and the Pentagon. Secretary of State Kissinger hinted that the delay should be attributed to Defense Secretary James Schlesinger. But reliable sources in Washington pointed to Kissinger as the source of the red tape, claiming that he had decided to delay the airlift to Israel. Supposedly his aim was to assure that Israel would be more vulnerable and therefore more flexible during the cease-fire discussions that had already begun between Washington and Moscow.

On October 13, when Nixon learned of the delay in supplying arms and ammunition, he immediately ordered Schlesinger to put into service every available transport plane to resupply Israel with the needed materiel. On the following day, the American airlift began to arrive with essential supplies, sufficient not only for defense but even for massive counterattacks on both fronts.

Dayan pressed for priority on the Syrian front. He demanded a speedy offensive attack on the Syrian forces on the Golan. Opponents of this idea in the general staff argued that the Golan Heights could be "put on ice," since the Syrian forces were exhausted and no longer presented a threat to Israel. On Thursday evening, October 11, the cabinet approved the defense minister's proposal to open an all-out attack on the Syrians on the Golan the following morning. Dayan's strategy was first to create a threat to Damascus, though with no intention of capturing the city, and then to push back the Syrian army behind its prewar lines.

The offensive began at eleven on the morning of October 12, and within two days the IDF advanced until they were firmly in control on a new front line twenty-six miles west of Damascus and nine miles beyond the 1967 cease-fire line.

After the Syrian collapse on the Golan Heights, the Kremlin outlook changed drastically. As long as Israel was losing, there was calm acceptance of the fierce battles by both great powers. Now, suddenly there was an urgent demand for a cease-fire. Washington countered the Soviet demand for convening the Security Council to impose an immediate cease-fire, with an announcement that Kissinger was being dispatched to Moscow for a meeting with Soviet leaders. Dayan wanted, at all costs, to avoid a cease-fire under existing conditions, with Egyptians on the east bank of the Suez Canal, and the Syrians still posing a threat from their strongholds on Mount Hermon.

Influenced by the threat of a cease-fire that might all too soon be imposed by the two superpowers under the authority of the UN Security Council, Dayan pressed the general staff to prepare a large-scale offensive in the south, in order to carry the war to the west bank of the Suez Canal and pose a threat to Cairo. Following the consolidation of a new front line on the Golan threatening Damascus, the major effort now shifted to the southern front.

On Friday afternoon, the second day of Succoth, Dayan initiated a cabinet meeting to decide on the next objectives of the war. During this meeting, Lieutenant General Chaim Bar-Lev, now commander southern front, suggested a Canal crossing to establish an IDF presence on the Canal's west bank, threatening to encircle Egyptian forces on both banks of the Suez Canal. Deputy Chief of Staff Major General Yisrael Tal spoke against it, but Dayan urged the acceptance of Bar-Lev's plan. There was another consideration. The Israeli command expected an imminent full-scale Egyptian offensive eastward to advance farther into Sinai. But such an advance was blocked by the Sinai Mountains, and the only way to penetrate these mountains was via two passes, the Mitle and Jiddi. Any attempt to penetrate via these passes would bring the Egyptian forces into the jaws of a trap. Therefore the cabinet decided to postpone the Canal crossing until after the enemy attack. On October 13 and 14, Saturday and Sunday, large Egyptian armored forces did indeed attack and sustained heavy losses at the passes guarded by the waiting Israeli forces. Unfortunately, Major General Albert Mendler, the OC Sinai Division, was among the casualties in this battle.

At noon on Friday after the government debate on plans for the south, I sat facing Dayan in his office. He questioned me about the public mood. I had spent the previous day with my family and had gone to the local synagogue for the Succoth service. The harsh war atmosphere and the losses already known put a damper on the holiday festivities, which I described to Dayan. Because of our heavy losses from the surprise attack, he was not taken aback to hear about public criticism of him.

"From your words, I understand that they are blaming me. Should I resign?" he asked.

"It won't help the war, but for you personally it would help bolster your public image and prestige," I responded.

"Do you know anyone else who could direct this war better than I?" he asked. I had no answer.

He stood up and went home for a "refreshing shower," as he put it. I crossed the corridor to Chaim Yisraeli's office and told him of my conversation with Dayan. Chaim had sharp insight and knew Dayan better than anyone else did. He guessed that Dayan was likely to resign right now. With the help of Dayan's security detail, he located Moshe, who was closeted with the prime minister in her office in the adjacent building.

Chaim and our two other associates in the team of close assistants were concerned about the possibility that Dayan might at that very moment have already submitted his resignation to Golda. They all looked at me as the guilty party who had encouraged him to take this step. A few hours later, Dayan returned to the office and reported on his conversation with the prime minister. He had indeed offered his resignation, but Golda would not hear of it.

The crossing of the Suez Canal was scheduled for 7:00 P.M. on October 15. Ariel Sharon was in command of that force. His task was to forge a way through to the waterline, assemble a bridge for crossing heavy armor, and put sufficient forces onto the west bank to form a secure bridgehead.

We sat on a sand dune next to a forward command post and waited for reports from the battlefield. As in any organized military operation, there were mishaps of all sorts, the first of which was the blockage of the access route for moving the bridge to the Canal. A fierce battle was raging against the Egyptians, dug in at the "Chinese Farm", which controlled the access road. After the road was finally cleared, the transport and assembly of the monstrous and unwieldy bridge proved to be a technical nightmare.

Somehow, a temporary solution was improvised, and at 2:00 A.M. a paratroop force commanded by Danny Matt established a foothold on the opposite bank. However, it was inadequate and would be dangerously exposed if the Egyptians were to learn of their presence, and attack. At dawn a number of tanks were ferried across on rafts. Only after a pontoon bridge had been set up did a substantial number of tanks get across. Finally three sturdy bridges were assembled, which allowed a smooth and adequate flow of forces and supplies, enabling us to heave a sign of relief at our neighboring command post. During all this time, the fierce fighting at the Canal continued. The Egyptians, underestimating the size of the force that had already crossed, failed to bring in a large enough force until it was too late, but they poured down an inferno of artillery fire on the crossing troops, and our losses mounted.

During the next four days we spent more time with combat units than we did at the Ministry of Defense in Tel Aviv. Much of the time was in "Africa," the nickname given to the west side of the Canal. The command posts of the divisional commanders were in high spirits in spite of the artillery bombardment, which did not let up, and the growing casualty lists.

On October 19, while visiting with General Adan in "Africa," we heard that Soviet Prime Minister Alexei Kosygin was meeting with President Sadat in Cairo. The Soviets, alarmed by the Israeli crossing and the approach of the IDF toward the Egyptian capital, threatened direct intervention. American broadcasts received in Jerusalem expressed fears of Soviet intervention in favor of the Egyptians and Syrians unless there was an immediate decision on a cease-fire and a withdrawal by Israel to the pre-1967 armistice lines, i.e., the borders prior to the Six-Day War. Dayan was very cautious in assessing the Soviet threats. He took them seriously but still decided to take the risk in order to gain time, since every additional day of fighting gained us a better position for the negotiations that were sure to follow the cease-fire. That same day we also received news from Washington of U.S. consent to convene the Security Council and declare a cease-fire. The disagreement between Washington and Moscow over the cease-fire conditions was still unresolved. But time was running out and Dayan pushed the northern command to complete its objective to retake the Hermon positions, and the southern command to establish control from just south of Ismailia down to the Gulf of Suez.

U.S. Secretary of State Henry Kissinger was on his way from Moscow to Israel to persuade Golda Meir and Moshe Dayan to accept the proposed cease-fire worked out between the U.S. and the USSR, in which there was no mention of Moscow's demand for withdrawal to the pre-June 1967 lines. Dayan explained to Kissinger that the terms outlined were unsuitable for an effective cease-fire. Kissinger understood perfectly that Dayan intended to expand the territorial holdings west of the Suez Canal in order to encircle the Egyptian Third Army and pose a threat to Damascus in the north. Kissinger argued with him, but finally relented and allotted Israel another seventy-two hours, on the assumption that this would suffice for the IDF to achieve all its objectives.

The Security Council resolution set the cease-fire for October 22, at 6:00 P.M. Israel time. Israel accepted the decision, setting the precise time at 6:52 P.M., on condition that the Egyptians also comply. The Egyptians responded by setting the cease-fire at 6:58, but their forces in the field, as well as their air force, continued fighting after 6:58 in an attempt to seize terrain and improve their positions.

Only one day later did Syria announce its willingness to cease hostilities, on condition that Israel would withdraw to the pre-June 1967 lines. As a result, the IDF renewed the battle. At the northern end of the Canal, a further advance northward encircled the Egyptian Third Army and isolated it on the east bank of Suez. At the southern end of the Canal, one force took Jebel Ataka, a hill overlooking the town of

Suez, while another continued to mop up surface-to-air missile batteries that had been restricting the IAF's freedom of movement. By the evening of October 23, Adan's division was entrenched around the city of Port Suez. The fighting persisted in full force into the following day, when a combined operations force entered the city of Suez. At first the town seemed abandoned, but when the column reached the main street, heavy and precise fire poured down from windows and rooftops. The Israeli force took heavy losses. Israel withdrew to the outlying suburbs of Suez City, which remained encircled. The city itself remained in Egyptian hands. The price paid by the IDF was high: over one hundred dead and one hundred fifty wounded.

At the approach of midnight, October 24, the guns fell silent in the south, apart from sporadic exchanges of small-arms fire. The Third Army was cut off from Egypt. Throughout the day there had been urgent but confused messages from Washington insisting on an immediate cease-fire, otherwise President Nixon would cut off his support from Israel. This threat was followed by another if Israel persisted in the siege of the Egyptian Third Army. American spokesmen later explained that the Soviets had threatened to send troops to the aid of the Third Army, inducing the United States to put pressure on Israel.

Before the cease-fire took effect, I accompanied Dayan on a tour of the southern front, where he explained the government's acceptance of the Security Council resolution to the local commanders. We visited Adan's command caravan near the Egyptian air base of Fayid, and Jebel Ataka, the headquarters of Major General Kalman Magen. On our way back to Tel Aviv we landed at Arik Sharon's command post, south of Ismailia. Sharon was the only one who responded to the cease-fire with anger. In his opinion, it had been forced upon us too early. In another two days, he could have encircled the Egyptian Second Army, which was defending Ismailia. Dayan understood Sharon's feelings. He respected his military capabilities and resourcefulness as a commander, but differed with his political judgment. Dayan, with his sharp intuition, viewed the cease-fire as an opening to a new era. In the plane on the way back to Tel Aviv, I heard him say for the first time that this had been the last war in our time between Israel and Egypt.

The Yom Kippur War ended at midnight on October 24, after nineteen days of bitter battles that had cost Israel two thousand five hundred dead and seven thousand wounded. The cease-fire took effect on lines that cut off a ten-mile strip of Syria, placing Damascus under the threat of Israeli artillery fire. In the south, the Egyptian Third Army was cut off from all supplies and the IDF had advanced west of the Canal, threatening Cairo.

28

THE DAY AFTER

On the twentieth day after the outbreak of war, relative quiet prevailed on the battlefronts. Both armies licked their wounds. At Kilometer 101 on the road from Suez to Cairo, tents were erected on both sides of the cease-fire line to accommodate talks on separation of forces, prisoner exchanges, and border demarcation. Still, sporadic exchanges of fire continued until January 1974.

The fury of the battle and the thousands of lives it had claimed on both sides, gave way to repercussions at home and abroad. Knesset elections scheduled for the end of October 1973 were postponed to December 31. The campaign took place against a background of serious accusations of the political leadership and the military establishment. Bereaved families and soldiers on leave from extended reserve duty were beginning to demonstrate against the government for having been taken by surprise and caught unprepared. The families of prisoners of war in the hands of Egypt and Syria, literally besieged the Ministry of Defense in Tel Aviv. They demanded the return of the captives prior to any negotiation between the parties. Outside the prime minister's office in Jerusalem, there was a night-and-day demonstration by antigovernment protesters, initiated by a reserve officer named Motti Ashkenazi, who had fought at one of the Suez Canal fortresses in Sinai. Opposition leaders exploited the mood of protest and supported the demonstrators, using them as ammunition in the election campaign.

The prime target of the demonstrations was Minister of Defense Moshe Dayan and, to a lesser degree, Prime Minister Golda Meir. Dayan's enemies found the time ripe for revenge, making him the main target. My function as his spokesman and adviser sometimes placed me in sharp confrontation with the media serving the politicians who backed the demonstrations. Since I was not very concerned with answering provoking questions based on coffee-shop gossip, I generally ignored the issue. Of greater concern to me were the relations and discussions between Jerusalem and Washington, and the progressively closer ties between Washington and Cairo that were developing in the aftermath of the war. Cooperation with the U.S. administration had now become vital for Israel, in anticipation of forging a new reality with its Arab neighbors. The U.S. moved from its traditional role of advocate for Israel, faithfully supporting Israel's interests, to a new role as broker for both sides and as an accepted authority. This new role granted Washington greater credibility and decisiveness in situations of conflict. However, it also aroused anxiety in Israel, lest America stray from a position of neutrality, and lean toward the Arab side in an attempt to convince them of "even-handedness."

In order to allay these misgivings, the prime minister met with President Nixon and his aides. Upon her return to Israel, she sent the minister of defense to Washington with the objective of coordinating a position on prerequisites for the separation of forces: mainly the exchange of prisoners and laying the foundation for discussions preparatory to an interim agreement consistent with proposals Dayan had been making for three years. Leaving details regarding supply of military equipment and defense aid to his assistants, Dayan concentrated on establishing principles and obtaining American agreement on other pertinent matters.

On the day we arrived in Washington, December 7, 1973, we visited the State Department twice and found Henry Kissinger in good spirits, telling jokes. However, in our entourage, which included Ambassador Simcha Dinitz and Military Attaché Major General Mordechai (Motta) Gur, the mood was somber and uncertain. In a private conversation with Dayan, Kissinger referred to the probability of reaching a final agreement with all the Arab states on a treaty of nonbelligerence. He spoke about a planned trip to the Middle East, culminating in a visit to Israel. He promised, guardedly, that this time he would bring Israel an agreement of "almost peace" with all her neighbors. However, he demanded an advance commitment: IDF withdrawal from the October 24 cease-fire lines and removal of the noose around the Egyptian Third Army trapped in Sinai.

Dayan tried to cool Kissinger's enthusiasm, suggesting that he concentrate on achieving partial agreement with each Arab country separately. He tried to find an English idiom like "Don't bite off more than you can chew" to match the Talmudic proverb, "If you try to catch too much, you end up catching nothing." Kissinger understood the Hebrew original, but disagreed with Dayan's evaluation. "Now is the time to move ahead, in the wake of a war which gave no one a decisive victory, to strike while the iron is hot, and to bring all sides to the negotiating table and to an agreement," he countered.

As we were leaving his private office, Kissinger whispered to Dayan that he would shortly be meeting a senior Egyptian representative. The reference was to Foreign Minister Ismail Fahmi, who was coming to see him. Kissinger said that he would update Dayan later, and asked, "What are you planning for this evening?" Dayan gave him a wry smile and said, "I have plans similar to yours." They exchanged smiles and did indeed meet that evening to discuss the upcoming visit of the secretary of state to the Middle East, this time in light of information elicited from the Egyptian envoy.

On the way back to the hotel, Dayan bubbled with optimism about his two meetings of that day, and the one scheduled for that evening. "He will try to bring us peace treaties with seventeen Arab states, and will end up happy if he comes to Israel with Sadat's agreement to an interim arrangement or a partial agreement, which Assad might possibly follow." This was Dayan's appraisal of Kissinger's ambitious plans. It was Friday afternoon. I went to the Georgetown Kesher LeIsrael Synagogue for Sabbath eve prayers and on to the home of author Herman Wouk, who lived nearby, for dinner. Dayan spent the evening with Kissinger and learned that a new wind was blowing from Cairo. He told me about it Saturday morning, on our way to a meeting with Vice President Gerald Ford, who had just taken up his new office in the White House.

After the previous evening's session with Kissinger, Dayan felt there was a chance of improving relations with Egypt, leading to some kind of an agreement. He did not yet speak of peace in the offing, but he did believe that we – Egypt and Israel – had ended the state of war in our generation. "Much now depends on us, and I hope that this time we will not miss the opportunity," he said, in a clear reference to his interim agreement proposals that had been turned down by his cabinet colleagues in 1971, two years prior to the Yom Kippur War.

At the close of the Sabbath, we flew to New York for Dayan's public appearance at a United Jewish Appeal dinner. The following morning we returned to Washington to meet Defense Secretary James Schlesinger. That conversation was devoted to procurement of materiel. Dayan described the growing strength of Syria and Egypt, sustained by massive arms deliveries from the Soviet Union and Western Europe. Schlesinger listened attentively, almost without a word, except for his comment to correct the impression that he had been the one responsible for the delays in the airlift of vital materiel during the war. Later, on the Israeli Air Force cargo plane that carried us and military equipment back to Israel, Dayan expressed doubt about the credibility of both Schlesinger and Kissinger regarding their role in the dispatch of critical supplies: "How can I possibly know which of them is telling the truth?" he asked, with a bitter smile. At that moment, I believed that the only one telling the truth was President Nixon, who stated that he had decided on an urgent airlift of arms and ammunition on the third day of the war.

Nixon had won wide respect for his decision to help at a time of crisis. However, his status had been completely undermined by the Watergate affair, that cost him the presidency. Now we were to meet with the new president, Gerald Ford, newly sworn into office. Dayan was impressed with Ford's practical approach to the issues and hoped it would be possible to maintain an effective dialogue with him.

In breaks between meetings, Dayan allowed himself to nap for a quarter of an hour. Outside of those few moments of rest, he kept pacing the hotel room, constantly seeking to share ideas and analyses with his aides. Occasionally he would include Rachel in these deliberations. For the most part, however, he tried out his ideas on us, his staff, before presenting them to the Americans and, through them, to the Egyptians and Syrians. Thus, though we were not actual partners in the debates with his counterparts, we felt that we were active participants with an intensely emotional involvement in putting an end to bloodshed, both ours and that of our neighbors. We sat in the comfortable armchairs of an opulent Washington hotel and analyzed the moves that might expedite the return of prisoners and set the conditions for a stable cease-fire. In the back of my mind, I could still see the horrors of the war just past: carnage on the battle fields, bereaved parents, young widows, and orphans at open graves mourning their sons, husbands, and fathers. Our conversations in the corridors and waiting rooms of Washington gave me hope that perhaps, at last, we might be able to moderate the Arab enmity and put an end to the tragic cycle of wars that had held sway over us for almost a century.

The onslaught of reporters, American and Israeli, brought me back to the urgent demands of the moment. The Israeli reporters wanted to know what Israel would get in return for a separation of forces that entailed withdrawal from the October 24 cease-fire lines. Most of all, they wanted to hear about the chance of the return of our prisoners, the subject of greatest public sensitivity in Israel. The Americans wanted to know what Israel had been promised in terms of military equipment and financial aid as inducement for an agreement. I had to deal with these and similar questions at least four times a day, and it did not help to explain that these issues had not yet been addressed. Every time I opened the newspapers or watched a TV newscast, I came across reports of discussions, demands, and promises that were no more than figments of journalistic creativity. In analyzing the reports, it was clear beyond any doubt that no one from the inside was leaking information. The speculations were totally unsubstantiated and unrelated to the timing and content of the discussions.

Six days after our return to Israel, Kissinger arrived, at the end of his tour of several Arab capitals in the area. In Damascus he had tried to secure the release of Israeli prisoners in return for the Syrians held by Israel. Assad was holding tight to his trump card, the prisoners. He was well aware of Israeli public sensitivities and he wanted to use them to extort maximum territory in drawing the lines for the separation of forces on the Golan Heights. Sadat, for his part, interpreted separation of forces as unilateral Israeli withdrawal from territory conquered west of the Suez Canal, with no tangible Egyptian quid pro quo. In light of this, Kissinger sought to convince Israel that there was a need for more Israeli concessions.

Dayan was careful not to get involved in "private" negotiations with Kissinger, who courted him assiduously, probing for original ideas from Moshe to thaw the stalemate. In the guesthouse near Tel Aviv, I saw Kissinger time and time again draw Dayan into a private exchange. At one point, after a few whispered words with Golda Meir, Dayan returned to his corner in the conference hall, a glass of Scotch in hand, and nodded to Kissinger. Within a minute, the two were deep in conversation, with a hint of a smile on Dayan's face. When Dayan was leaving, I joined him and asked whether Kissinger had brought anything new. "Sadat is beginning to understand the new reality and, if he [Kissinger] continues at this pace, he will reach the idea of a partial settlement," he replied with a smile of satisfaction.

Coming out of the guesthouse, I encountered Kissinger, accompanied by his bodyguards, heading toward his car. As we shook hands, he commented with a smile, "I understood the Talmudic proverb in Hebrew. Now I also see it was indeed applicable. Moshe was right."

Kissinger's achievement on this trip was the convening of a Geneva conference, which aimed at bringing peace to the region. It was to continue until it reached its objectives. The opening date was set for December 21, 1973, but the practical discussions were postponed to January, after the elections in Israel. Syria did not take part in the conference because of Israel's refusal to sit with her delegates until they produced a list of the prisoners they were holding. Nevertheless, there was some unofficial dialogue. Almost all the discussions with Egypt and Syria took place in the Middle East or Washington. The aim of the Geneva conference was to serve as a framework for peace talks following agreements on the separation of forces, an aim that was not achieved until the Madrid conference of May 1992, opening a new page in the dialogue between Israel and its neighbors.

Once the election results for the Knesset were in and it was clear that Golda Meir would continue as prime minister, Kissinger renewed his initiative and invited Dayan to Washington on January 4, 1974, for another round of talks. As earlier in December, the talks centered on separation of forces between Israel and Egypt, between Israel and Syria, and on the exchange of POWs. After a two-week shuttle between Jerusalem and Cairo, Kissinger gained Egyptian agreement on the exchange of prisoners and the separation of forces, which was immediately approved by Israel, on January 18, 1974. This put an end to the sporadic exchange of fire on the front lines. Syria was still outside the negotiating circle. The road to official talks with Syria did not open until February 27, 1974, when Kissinger brought back a list of the sixty-five Israeli prisoners of war held there. The Syrians remained extremely stubborn throughout the negotiations. It took Kissinger three months to convince them that a separation of forces was to their advantage. On June 5, 1974, a document was finally signed, instituting the political and military reality on the Golan Heights that prevails to this day.

The talks held in Washington on cessation of Egyptian and Syrian hostilities did not diminish the ongoing protest in Israel. The Labor Party, headed by Golda Meir and Moshe Dayan, had won a majority in the election, but had lost 5.5% of its Knesset strength to the opposition. The government was compelled to come to terms with smaller factions in order to form a coalition with a Knesset majority. Golda and Dayan viewed the results as a renewed mandate. Dayan informed Golda that if the Agranat Commission, appointed to examine the circumstances of the war, should find fault with his conduct as defense minister, either before or during the course of the war, he would refuse to serve in that capacity in her new government.

The Agranat Commission, headed by Supreme Court President Shimon Agranat, had been established by a government decision on November 18, 1973, and was mandated to investigate the events leading up to the Yom Kippur War and the initial military moves to block the Syrian and Egyptian armies. Its findings were to be submitted to the cabinet within four months. On April 1, 1974, the recommendations were submitted. Chief of Staff David Elazar; Major General Shmuel Gonen, OC Southern Command; Major General Eli Zeira, Intelligence Branch chief; and three senior intelligence officers were all removed from their posts. However, the Minister of Defense, Moshe Dayan, was absolved of any guilt in carrying out his function. As for parliamentary responsibility, the Agranat Commission viewed it as beyond their mandate and left that issue to the politicians. In the eyes of Dayan and many others, the political decision had been taken inside the Labor Party, when it put together the list of candidates for the Knesset election, and by the public in the voting booths when it gave a majority to the Labor Party and its coalition partners. The members of these parties had been given a vote of confidence, which clearly included Golda Meir and Moshe Dayan.

Nevertheless, neither the election results nor the Agranat recommendations eased the public censure of the incompetence prior to and during the war. The one-man, day-and-night demonstration by

Captain Motti Ashkenazi, reserve officer, continued outside the prime minister's office. Dayan, seeking to get a true picture of this persistent lone demonstrator, invited Ashkenazi to a meeting in the Jerusalem home of Professor Natan Rotenstreich. I joined them at that meeting and heard the protests of this young officer, who had been commander of the "Budapest" stronghold on the northern sector of the Suez Canal, the only one not captured by the Egyptians. Ashkenazi described the situation that had prevailed among his men and pointed to a number of incidents that he labeled as serious blunders on the part of the army command. However, most of his criticism dealt with exaggerated social, economic, and political errors committed by the government which, in his view, had given rise to the blunders of the Yom Kippur War. I was convinced that no rational response to his protests would placate him. His demonstration continued for another two weeks.

Despite the demonstrations and denunciation at home, Dayan kept up his shuttle from Israel to the United States, interspersed among Kissinger's shuttles to the Middle East, in order to complete the separation-of-forces agreement. The one with Egypt was signed on January 18 by Golda Meir; the one with Syria was signed on June 5 by the government of Yitzhak Rabin, two days after he assumed the premiership, following Golda Meir's resignation on April 11.

In the midst of all the talks, the Syrians tried to improve their positions on Mount Hermon. The IDF had captured all of Mount Hermon before the cease-fire of the Yom Kippur War, including the pinnacle that controls the entire area. It had been left unmanned because of the harsh weather and deep snow in the winter months. In the beginning of April, as the weather improved, an elite Syrian force took control of the pinnacle. Dayan ordered the army to remove them and establish a fortified position. He would not rest until the vantage point was firmly back in Israeli hands. On April 13, an attacking Israeli force ousted the Syrians, who left their twelve dead behind.

Arriving shortly after the battle, Dayan and I found dead soldiers still scattered about the area. Our helicopter was forced to land behind a ridge, to protect us from Syrian mortar fire. We were picked up by an armored personnel carrier (APC) and slowly made our way toward the peak, while shells dropped within thirty feet of us. We decided to leave the APC and proceeded to climb the last stretch on foot, frequently dropping face down into the remaining patches of snow to avoid the shells. Nearby, I saw Dayan advancing rapidly. At the sound of an explosion, he spread his arms and dropped to the ground. I aimed my camera and captured his spread-eagled form on the snow for posterity. Near him on the snow, caught by my camera, were two major generals, Moti Hod and Avigdor Bengal. Upon arriving, we took shelter in a cave and Dayan proceeded to question the soldiers of the elite unit who had ousted the Syrians just two hours earlier.

On the way back from Mount Hermon, Dayan asked the pilot to detour to Kiryat Shmona, where we had visited just two days earlier, after three terrorists from the George Habash branch of the PLO had seized a building and killed eighteen people, eight of them children. The terrorists had arrived at 7:30 A.M. at a school, intending to take control and hold the children hostage. Upon finding the building empty, because of a school holiday, they broke into a nearby apartment building, shooting and throwing grenades in all directions, running from apartment to apartment, killing all who crossed their path. Finally an army unit overcame them and killed all three in a short battle. We found them still clutching their weapons in death when we arrived. One of them had apparently been shattered by an explosive charge he was wearing, set off by the impact of a bullet. Now, knowing that mothers and children who had escaped the carnage were still traumatized by the horror, Dayan decided to return to Kiryat Shmona to visit the injured and console the bereaved families.

One month later, we saw a similarly dreadful sight at the school building in the town of Ma'alot, near the Lebanese border. Three Arab terrorists had burst into a school where a group of students from Safed were spending the night as part of a two-day outing. The terrorists took the students and teachers hostage and demanded the release of convicted terrorists held by Israel. On their way to the school, they had broken into the home of the Cohen family and murdered the parents and their young toddler. By the time the IDF stormed the school and killed them, the terrorists had already murdered twenty-one innocent children and injured another seventy.

Initially, the government opposed an immediate military assault in order to give time to the French and Romanian ambassadors, the mediators chosen by the terrorists, to arrange for some quid pro quo. The terrorists would be flown to Damascus in return for the release of the hostages. Dayan flew to Jerusalem to convince the government that getting the hostages released by any sort of deal was not a viable option. He returned to Ma'alot with government approval for a military assault. The chief of staff, Motta Gur, who was in command, delayed the assault until the last possible moment before the deadline, six in the evening, awaiting a response to the terrorists' ultimatum.

I had found shelter behind a wall about two hundred feet from the school, and was trying to take pictures. I was sitting on the ground, leaning against the wall, when suddenly Dayan, his adjutant, and two bodyguards crawled to my vantage point. Dayan put field glasses to his eye and described what he saw through the windows: two mustached young men, one wearing a red shirt, the other black, both looking out of the window, each holding a Kalatchnikov rifle. He could also see the frightened faces of the children, and said aloud to himself, "Any additional delay will cost us dearly." However, he was not in command.

My hands shook. I could not operate the camera. I saw soldiers deployed all around the school building ready to leap forward at the command, and I was certain the terrorists could see them, just as I could. The assault was brief. When the shooting stopped, I raced forward right behind Dayan. Dozens of boys and girls and a few adults lay dead or wounded on the floor. Some were calling for help. The sickening sight took me back to the horrors of Auschwitz and Buchenwald thirty years earlier, memories which still haunt me. I stood there helpless, I felt my legs were about to fail me, and hastily sat down on the edge of a stone by the playground. A soldier passed by and offered me some water, which I gulped down; then I got on my feet again.

These two terrorist massacres at Kiryat Shmona and Ma'alot occurred after Golda Meir had announced her decision to resign as prime minister. The public outrage and pressure from party leaders, and even members of the cabinet, convinced her that she had lost their trust, and on April 11 she informed the Knesset of the resignation of the government. After discussions within the party, the premiership was given to Yitzhak Rabin; the Ministry of Defense to Shimon Peres; and the Foreign Ministry to Yigal Allon. Golda Meir and Moshe Dayan remained outside the new cabinet. Two days after the new government was sworn in, on June 3, it signed an agreement with Syria on the separation of forces on the Golan Heights. The two agreements, with Syria and with Egypt, which Dayan had initiated and for which he had worked so assiduously, along with the vigorous mediation of Henry Kissinger, paved the way for the peace agreement with Egypt, something Dayan energetically pursued as foreign minister in Menachem Begin's government, which took office three years later in June 1977.

29

RABIN-PERES RIVALRY

On June 5, 1974, the day that Yitzhak Rabin's new government was sworn in, all the key defense establishment figures crowded into the conference room to bid farewell to Moshe Dayan, the man who had headed the Ministry of Defense since the 1967 war. After a short toast in his honor, Dayan was presented with the latest model "Galil" assault rifle. He took it out from its impressive wooden case, checked the mechanism, put the telescopic sight to his eye, and said with his dry humor, "I have a number of good targets, but none are in this range." Back in his office, where he was gathering the last of his papers, I presented him with a personal memento: a thick-barreled pen with a broad ballpoint, the kind he particularly liked. "You're already expecting my memoirs," he thanked me with a smile. "Yes, and perhaps the signing of a peace treaty with the Arabs," I replied. We both smiled. Neither of us could possibly foresee that a day would come when he would pull that pen from his pocket to sign a memorandum of understanding with U.S. Secretary of State Cyrus Vance, following a ceremony on the White House lawn to herald the peace treaty with Egypt.

The struggle between Ben-Gurion and his old guard ministers carried over to the next generation, causing enmity and rivalry between Peres, Ben-Gurion's protegé, and Rabin, the choice of the old guard. They would never forgive Ben-Gurion and Peres for setting up a rival political party to contest their power. In an electoral confrontation, Rabin defeated Peres, but the margin was narrow. Rabin could not reconcile himself to the impressive performance of Peres at the party convention, but was unable to deny him the key post of minister of defense. Relations between the two men were fundamentally hostile, though both tried to portray an outward appearance of unity.

In addition to their personal rivalry, there were political and ideological differences between them. Rabin favored a territorial compromise on the west bank of the Jordan River along the lines of the Allon plan put forward earlier by Rabin's commander and mentor, Yigal Allon. This involved Israel's disengagement from Judea and Samaria territory on the west bank of the river, except for security strips along the Jordan Valley and along the pre-1967 eastern border called the Green Line.

Peres supported a functional compromise that Dayan had suggested earlier, whereby Israel would retain responsibility for security and foreign affairs, leaving all other functions in the hands of the local Arabs. Peres sought a peaceful coexistence with the Arabs that would not require withdrawal back to the Green Line.

On the day Peres took office, I told him that I had decided to leave my position in the Ministry of Defense. He was surprised and said it would be unfair to walk out just when he needed me most. I told him that even though we had known each other a long time and were friendly, I felt that my appointment by Moshe Dayan should not bind his successor. Peres urged me to continue and even added certain areas of responsibility to my position, that I could not resist.

From his first moment in the ministry, Peres worked without let-up. His main objective was to rehabilitate a defense establishment sorely damaged in the Yom Kippur War. Day and night he met with scientists, soldiers, and defense-industry executives to find answers to problems that came to light during that war. He pushed for new initiatives in weapon systems development, created new military formations, increased procurement of sophisticated equipment from the United States and Europe, and reorganized army installations and emergency warehouses. In this massive effort, he held his assistants and the IDF general staff to a regime that allowed no days off, no relaxation for many months.

He would often summon me from home to join him in a surprise visit to an army base or field camp in the dead of night. I would report at midnight to the air force base at Tel Aviv's Sde Dov Airport in order to join him to inspect some unsuspecting reserve store or installation. Invariably, the commanders knew only of the impending arrival of a helicopter, with no advance notice about its passengers. When we landed, the reception party would stare wide-eyed in surprise at the sudden appearance of the minister. Wasting no time on ceremonies, Peres would ask to inspect the installations and see for himself whether the pace of work was in keeping with the preset schedules. Then we would return home close to dawn, knowing that a new work day would begin promptly at seven in the morning.

Shimon Peres had grown up in the Ministry of Defense, first as its youngest director general, appointed by Ben-Gurion in 1953, and six years later as deputy minister. He was thoroughly at home in this ministry and slipped back into the security establishment as though he had never left. The only factor that made his ministerial performance difficult was Yitzhak Rabin's suspicious attitude, largely because Peres had contested the election for prime minister. Rabin signaled his hostility by the appointment of Major General (reserve) Ariel Sharon to a newly created position: the prime minister's adviser on security matters. This was interpreted in the ministry as an attempt to bypass Peres' authority and to indicate Rabin's lack of confidence in him.

Sharon came to the prime minister's office directly from political activities in the opposition Likud Party, where he had not succeeded in establishing himself. Peres understood Rabin's message but gritted his teeth and said nothing, whereas Rabin's associates did not refrain from spreading rumors that the minister of defense was undermining the prime minister's authority.

Peres, outstanding when it came to dynamic public relations, won a good press for his performance as minister of defense. By comparison, Rabin made a few unfortunate slips that aroused public opinion against him, sharp and even hostile criticism. Some of Rabin's assistants found opportunities to point a finger at Peres and at me as his spokesman and media adviser. I sometimes found myself in the middle of a conflict between the two rival leaders. During my work with Peres, I did my best to ease the tensions between the two. The newspapermen, who harassed me persistently at home and at the office hoping to catch some hint or comment that could be used to exacerbate the tension between Peres and Rabin, remained disappointed. A few of them grudgingly complimented me on the way I handled such a sensitive situation, despite the fact that I had given them no information.

One touchy issue that demanded cooperation and disregard of political rivalry between Rabin and Peres was the confrontation with the newly founded right-wing movement, Gush Emunim (Group of the Faithful), which held massive demonstrations demanding the establishment of Jewish settlements in Judea, Samaria, and the Gaza Strip, the historical and biblical heartland of the Land of Israel, in order to block the government's option to give these areas to the Arabs. This was in response to the rumor that Kissinger's shuttle diplomacy had raised the possibility of granting Jordan a land corridor from Jericho to Jerusalem.

Their first settlement attempt took place on June 5, 1974, the day that Rabin's government was sworn in at the Knesset. At dawn, a few hundred young people appeared at a site south of Nablus in Samaria, led by the octogenarian spiritual mentor of Gush Emunim, Rabbi Zvi Yehuda Kook, and accompanied by Ariel (Arik) Sharon, Geula Cohen, Zevulun Hammer, and Yehuda Ben Meir (the latter two represented the young faction of the National Religious Party). They brought along tents, field kitchens, beds, mattresses, sleeping bags, and other equipment needed to set up a pioneer settlement. They had selected a deserted Jordanian Arab-Legion camp known in the IDF as Horon. This was to be the first Jewish settlement in Samaria. Arik Sharon, who a short time later was to be appointed adviser for defense to the prime minister, maintained direct contact with Yitzhak Rabin in an effort to influence him to refrain from ordering removal of the settlement. Rabin consulted his ministers and advisers, with the result that the OC Central Command, Major General Yona Efrat, arrived at the settlement within hours with a demand that the settlers vacate the site. Rabbi Kook ordered the settlers to obey the army's orders. They were gone before midnight, without any confrontation with the IDF. A story promptly circulated to the effect that Sharon had Rabin's promise to allow a limited number of settlements in Samaria to create a Jewish presence in the area.

Another bid came in August 1974. The site was the abandoned railway station of the small town of Sebastia in central Samaria near Nablus. About one thousand people, including many youths on vacation from school, set up a prefab building and dozens of tents. The operation was carried out like a well-planned military move, exploiting surprise. The IDF forces and the police were ordered to remove the settlers, who again left the area without any confrontation. There were two more attempts to settle Sebastia. The last one took place in the second week of December 1974, during the Hanukkah school vacation. By the time the military command learned of the new settlement attempt, the scope of the operation appeared to make it difficult to evacuate the two thousand settlers without the use of force. The minister of defense requested an urgent consultation with the prime minister, a few other ministers, the chief of staff, and security personnel. Most of those present in Rabin's Jerusalem office were inclined to favor evacuation, by force if necessary, and to avoid any negotiation. The military men noted the mass of young people spearheaded by the right-wing youth movements in a confined space in which they had fortified themselves, fearing that there would be bloodshed. Chief of Staff Motta Gur suggested to the cabinet ministers that they fly with him in a helicopter over Sebastia to see for themselves what was going on. We were soon circling in a helicopter above the demonstrators in the old Turkish railway station. Luckily I had a camera with me to record the scene. None of my fellow-passengers on that gripping flight were aware that among the crowd below were my two sons, Shai and Benny, both of whom had joined our neighbors, the family of Professor Mordechai Chen, one of the leaders of the settlers.

Rabin looked through the window of the helicopter at the masses below who, in turn, were looking up at him. He did not utter a sound. Peres too kept his own counsel. The only one who spoke his mind was the chief of staff, who warned of possible bloodshed. Without anyone's saying so, it was clear to all of us that a compromise had to be sought instead of a confrontation by force. The diplomatic mission was assigned to Peres, as the minister responsible for the occupied territories and supervisor of the security forces. We returned the prime minister and his entourage, including the chief of staff, to Jerusalem and flew back to Sebastia, near Nablus. The helicopter landed a short walk from Sebastia. We entered a large tent to find the leaders of the demonstration holding a turbulent debate over coffee with poet Chaim Guri. It was hard to decide who was trying to convince whom. Guri understood the motives of the settlers and even expressed sympathy for their activities.

The settlers obviously enjoyed wide public support. My impression at the time was that the silent majority sympathized with them, realizing that the settlers' anxiety over security for the country was a reaction to the Yom Kippur War, just one year past. I tried to analyze my feelings and found myself torn between a personal logic that favored the settlement activities and a political logic that necessitated refraining from any action in the occupied territories that would negatively affect the dialogue with the Arabs, thus reducing the chance of reaching an agreement with them.

Early in this controversy, I had asked Moshe Dayan where he stood in this nationwide debate. He agreed that given the post-Yom Kippur War atmosphere, we needed to shore up our security in the West Bank, lest our existence be endangered. Dayan believed that civilian settlements in unpopulated areas were preferable to military bases scattered across the territories, causing constant friction with the local Arabs. "More coexistence between Jews and Arabs becomes possible if they are farmers, clerks, laborers, and merchants sharing common interests than can ever be achieved in a population divided between those governed and those governing." Though I shared his view regarding possible coexistence, we were both wary of mass movements creating precedents with political facts on the ground contrary to the government position and openly flouting its decisions. Dayan dismissed my evaluation that a spate of settlements would push the Arab leaders into a dialogue with Israel in order to prevent an irreversible reality.

There was a hubbub at Sebastia when the demonstrators noted the arrival of the minister of defense. Some shouted greetings while others hurled insults. I mingled in the crowd looking for my sons, and found them, their clothes covered with mud. They seemed happy to see me in this faraway place, but rejected my offer to take them home with me. "Until they promise us a place to settle, we won't budge from here," was their firm stand. In the tent, Peres was already discussing conditions for evacuation. Suddenly Moshe Levinger, one of the more extreme Gush Emunim leaders, appeared in the entrance and delivered an inflammatory harangue against evacuation, in the course of which he tore his jacket (an expression of mourning) as a symbol of protest against any decree removing a Jewish settlement from the Land of Israel. Levinger's words had the intended effect of adding fuel to the already overwrought crowd. We walked back to the helicopter, leaving my sons behind with the demonstrators, and flew on to a prior engagement at a civil defense conference in Nahariya, in northern Israel.

On our way back to Tel Aviv, Peres seemed preoccupied. Sensing his dread of violent confrontation with the Sebastia settlers, I suggested he try to talk with their leaders in order to find a solution without the use of force. I urged him to meet the leaders early in the morning, before giving any order for evacuation. He agreed, on condition that Moshe Levinger not be present.

It was already after midnight when I arrived home. After several futile attempts, I finally located the leaders at a private apartment in Netanya and invited them to a meeting in the minister's office at seven in the morning, stipulating that they must come without Levinger. At 6:45 A.M., entering the courtyard of the Ministry of Defense, I was surprised to find Moshe Levinger waiting for his comrades. I took him up to my room and then went to Peres' office with the other leaders for the fateful discussion on the future of Sebastia.

Peres was tense, unwilling to discuss anything other than voluntary evacuation as a precondition to a debate on the future of settlement in Samaria. There was a prior suggestion, favored by cabinet minister Yisrael Galili, a close associate of Rabin, to transfer the settlers temporarily to a military police base at Kadum, west of Nablus, until a solution could be found. The settlers demanded a promise from the prime minister that their concerns would be discussed within three months. In the prevailing atmosphere of dialogue, it was relatively easy to find an acceptable compromise. In a telephone consultation between Peres, Rabin, and Galili, it was agreed that the settlers would vacate the site voluntarily that same day, and that a few dozen could move into Kadum. Those moving in would receive a building with kitchen and other service facilities, and space to set up caravans. The settlers accepted the deal. To seal it, I brought a bottle of Scotch and some glasses from the bar in Peres' office and we all raised our glasses in a toast to the agreement.

Three months elapsed without any cabinet discussion on the settlement issue and the members of the government remained divided on the subject. Some ministers viewed the deal as a surrender to unacceptable pressure. Others welcomed it as preventing bloodshed and the possibility of internecine violence.

"Temporary" Kadum became the permanent settlement Kedumim, which today houses two thousand residents in buildings that could hardly be described as temporary. Throughout the years since December 1974, dozens of settlements have been created in the West Bank – Judea and Samaria – populated by over one hundred fifty thousand people. Indeed, the settlements served as an efficient incentive for causing a complete turnabout in the stand of the Arabs, who did not want to miss the train once again and finally did come to the negotiating table.

Within the Labor Party, criticism of the Kadum Agreement continued, and the prime minister's associates pointed an accusing finger at the minister of defense. From time to time the tension reached new heights. Important issues, such as municipal elections in Judea and Samaria and military procurement of defense equipment, suffered from the friction between them. Rabin and Peres differed on every one of these issues. Sometimes Minister of Foreign Affairs Yigal Allon would also be involved on one side or the other. He too was treated with suspicion by Rabin, who had been his subordinate in the Palmach and in the IDF. Despite his high-principled nature, Allon did express his bitterness to close associates.

The most heated argument between the three was over the interim arrangements with Syria and Egypt. Rabin's government had inherited the agreement on separation of forces and repatriation of POWs from Golda Meir. Now the arrangements had to be completed in Sinai and on the Golan, with the help of Henry Kissinger's seemingly indefatigable mediation. Initially, Rabin stubbornly dug in his heels, whereas Allon and Peres were more flexible. However, when the debate began on determining the border lines in Sinai, it was Allon and Peres who were more sensitive to the security considerations in the absence of an Egyptian commitment to nonbelligerence. They were insistent and uncompromising when it came to redeployment of IDF troops at the Jiddi and Mitle passes, which control the only passageways through the Sinai Mountain ridge running from north to south in western Sinai.

Discussions with Egypt were stalemated over a number of points. Kissinger often demonstrated a talent for double-talk, to bridge the gaps between the two parties. On one occasion, he raised his arms in apparent surrender and suggested that Rabin send, through him, a personal message to President Sadat. The prime minister asked his political adviser, Ambassador Mordechai Gazit, to draft a short note about the issue on the agenda. Upon his return, Kissinger reported that when Sadat received Rabin's note, he was very excited. Kissinger brought back only a verbal answer, giving Sadat's explanation that he could not trust any of his associates to transfer written messages personally to the prime minister of Israel. Kissinger believed that he could move the negotiations along this way, and begged Rabin to write another personal letter. Rabin stubbornly refused. Peres' intervention made no difference. The talks with Washington reached a crisis and Kissinger went home empty-handed. Consequently, President Ford announced a reassessment of United States relations with Israel, resulting in delays in the already-agreed-upon supply of military equipment, and the deterioration in day-to-day contacts between Washington and Jerusalem.

This situation sparked intense media interest in the relationships within the leadership. Leaks from closed cabinet sessions fed the press and obligated me to respond to questions, react to rumors, and confirm or deny details, while maintaining my own hard-earned credibility. It was an unnecessary and exhausting addition to the burden of dealing with a press corps constantly fed by reports from Kissinger's entourage. Kissinger augmented his negotiating skills by utilizing his unique and direct relations with the American correspondents who accompanied him. Every time his plane touched down, they could report on his reactions to new ideas, and particularly on his frame of mind. All these played a crucial role in his efforts to wear down our resistance to his positions on sensitive issues. Facing the deviousness of Kissinger's resorting to hiding behind the cover of "a senior official in his entourage," I had to come out openly and weigh every word without the cover of a "senior official, background-only" briefings, "not for quotation" and "not for attribution," and without the convenience of denying former statements, knowing full well that the media would continue to court him. The contest was sufficiently loaded against Israel without the added encumbrance of internal rivalry within the Israeli leadership.

In March 1976, the Arab municipal elections took place in Judea and Samaria under the auspices of the military government. The winning mayors and council members were mostly those recommended by the PLO. In spite of all that had been done for nine years to improve Arab conditions and to foster moderation and coexistence, Arab interests were once again eroded by the tendency of the masses to favor the most extreme leaders, whether by conviction or because of fear of reprisals. Prior to the elections, antigovernment demonstrations broke out in a few central towns: Nablus, Ramallah, Jenin, and Tulkarm. The correspondents zeroed in on the sight of youths burning tires. Smoke and fire attracted the TV cameramen, and vice versa. They were getting better shots than any film director could have arranged in a studio. The army authorities were unhappy with the free access given to reporters and cameramen. The contention was that the demonstrations were pre-planned for the media, and that the arrival of a TV crew or even a still photographer was the trigger that would immediately fan the flames of violence in that vicinity.

Accordingly, some cabinet ministers favored closure of the territories to the media. Rabin tended to that view. I told Peres that such an act would only increase wild and irresponsible reporting. The newspapers and networks would work with local stringers and there would be no control over the degree to which they could distort the facts. The damage to Israel's image would be severe. The minister empowered me to negotiate working arrangements with media representatives. With the help of the chief of intelligence, Major General Shlomo Gazit, I drew up a document that was duly signed by the local and foreign press. The gist of it was formalization of relations between the media and the army in the territories, allowing correspondents freedom of coverage, but without impeding the function of the security forces. Israel's image as a free country, giving unhampered movement to the media under almost impossible conditions, was respected and valued by editors and producers. They were well aware that our position was liberal, even by comparison with any of the Western countries that invariably censored news during their own security crises.

Entebbe Rescue

Between the daily handling of settlement issues, dealing with media coverage in the territories, and the new age that had dawned in the north with the opening of a gate in the security fence that separated Israel from Lebanon, I had to navigate cautiously in deciding what I would say to the media, whether for publication or as background only. The area was strewn with land mines that could explode the tense and tenuous relations between Rabin and Peres. There was almost no subject on which they agreed. When Peres supported the action of the OC Northern Command, Major General Raphael Eitan, in opening a free passageway between Israel and South Lebanon - called the Good Fence - because the Lebanese, as the major benefactors, found work and medical care on the Israeli side, Rabin had reservations. The reasoning of each was perhaps convincing, but the moment it reached the headlines, it became "grounds for dispute." This was true of the issue of procurement abroad and the diplomatic links that were involved. It was true of the settlement movement, which was daily growing in strength. No matter how I tried to defend each of them and find substantive reasons for each view, I sensed that personal rivalry was the determining factor in the opposing stance of each.

One example of the Rabin-Peres rivalry was their reaction to the hijacking of an Air France plane on a flight to Entebbe. On Sunday, June 27, 1976, I received an urgent phone call from an alert American television correspondent announcing that a French airbus, Flight 139 en route from Tel Aviv to Paris, had been hijacked by Arab terrorists. He knew nothing of the number of passengers, their identity, or the destination of the plane after it had been hijacked. When I called the prime minister's office in Jerusalem to report this news, the weekly session of the cabinet had already been informed. However, discussion continued according to the agenda, as though nothing out of the ordinary had happened.

I remembered the Sabena plane, hijacked by four Arab terrorists and brought to Ben-Gurion Airport a few years earlier. I had spent the night at the airport with Moshe Dayan, who pushed through the preparations for seizure of the aircraft and release of the hostages. The "Sabena affair" had been entirely in Israel's control. Now, the Air France plane was thousands of miles away, in hostile territory to which we had no access. An actual assault on the plane in Entebbe might be similar to Sabena, but the logistics involved were entirely different.

The information from Entebbe, arriving via French passengers who had been released and flown to Paris, was terrifying. The hostages were in the hands of a group of murderous Arabs and Germans, who had already held a "selection" to separate Jews from non-Jews and then another "selection" of Israelis only. It was hard for me to accept that four hours' flying time away from an independent and strong Israel, a "selection" could be made akin to what Jews had experienced on the railway platform at Birkenau, 1942-44, with life or death depending on the flick of a baton in the hand of the heinous Nazi Dr. Josef Mengele. It was difficult to accept such helplessness, now with a sovereign Jewish State, with an army capable of protecting its citizens. To their credit, the French air crew decided to stay with the Jews during the "selection," refusing to abandon their passengers. Though there were Jewish nationals of various countries among the hostages, none of those other countries were saying anything about safeguarding the lives of their Jewish citizens. Once again, Jewish lives seemed to be expendable in the eyes of the world. The only force that could change this shameful situation was the IDF, but the political echelon hesitated and faltered, and found it hard to make the bold decision needed to carry out a rescue.

The defense minister, Shimon Peres, had been convinced from the outset that there was no option for negotiating the demanded exchange of imprisoned terrorists in Israel for the hijacked passengers, half of whom were Israelis. He pushed ahead the military preparations for a rescue mission, even while he supported the government view that other means of gaining the release of the hostages must be explored. The prime minister, Yitzhak Rabin, preferred to negotiate a trade of hostages for convicted terrorists held in Israel. Rabin understandably dreaded the failure of a military operation, knowing that the responsibility would fall squarely on him as prime minister. He based his view on precedents in which Israel had occasionally succumbed to terrorist blackmail for such trades. By contrast, Peres contended that Israel should not surrender to terror and that the whole world would understand and support a military action to attempt the liberation of the hijacked passengers.

The government deliberated for seven days about the Entebbe hostages. Most of the ministers supported Rabin's view that Israel should begin negotiations. Peres also voted for this proposal, but made it clear that he did so only for tactical reasons. At the same time, the

IDF began to plan and practice an assault on a model of the Entebbe airport, even as the cabinet continued its discussions.

Peres received encouragement from senior IDF officers, foremost among them OC Air Force, Major General Benny Peled and chief of operations branch, Major General Yekutiel Adam, both of whom supported a rescue action. Eventually they took part in it as supervisors in the aerial-command-post plane, which remained in the air over Entebbe during the operation.

The families of the hostages demonstrated outside government offices, demanding that steps be taken to secure the release of the passengers. Public pressure was mounting, along with government jitters. A special ministerial team was set up to coordinate negotiations and other matters connected with the hijacking.

To gain time, Peres summoned the three IDF officers who had served as advisers in Uganda and were familiar with the country, with the military command, and with the ruler, Idi Amin. One of them, Colonel Mordechai (Burka) Bar Lev had assisted Amin in becoming chief of staff of the Ugandan Army and had also helped him stage the coup that brought him the presidency. Burka volunteered to call Amin in an attempt to determine how involved the Ugandan was with the terrorists, and to extract some missing critical information needed for a potential operation. He used my office phone to make his calls to Idi Amin. He worked hard to feed Amin's ego, promising him, "You will go down in history as one of the great leaders who saved hundreds of innocent lives." Amin loved the "message," returning day after day to speak to Burka and to brag about his part in the events at Entebbe Airport and about his plans to fly to Mauritius. This last item was particularly important, for nothing significant would happen at Entebbe in Amin's absence. Thus we could better assess the credibility of the hijackers' ultimatum and deadline for releasing their comrades in prison. It also gave rise to the idea of taking a black Mercedes to Entebbe similar to the one used by Amin, in order to deceive the Ugandan guards, who would assume that the advance units of the operation signified the return of Idi Amin and his escorts. This would provide the crucial few minutes at the start of the operation at Entebbe needed to get into the airport building undetected by the hijackers.

The minister of defense ran back and forth between debates of the special ministerial team and operational discussions with commanders, checking the possibilities for action. The OC Air Force suggested landing a paratroop force from the air, but the chief of staff dismissed his proposition as a fantasy. Peres was having difficulty convincing his cabinet colleagues that the only way to extricate the hostages was by means of a military operation. He was caught between the negative views of two chiefs of staff: Prime Minister Rabin, who was now his superior; and Motta Gur, who was under his political jurisdiction but independent in military considerations.

The reservations of the chiefs of staff were understandable, given the absence of hard intelligence from the field. Motta Gur feared failure. He called one of the options "a plan of charlatans," even though it was the one eventually executed. The prime minister's opposition was more surprising. Rabin had extensive military and political experience, and it would be reasonable to expect that he could correctly interpret the viability of a military action. Given the personal tensions, it is difficult to avoid the impression that Rabin's negative view might have been a reaction to Peres' initiative and dynamism in favoring a military solution from the outset. However, without the prime minister's consent, Peres could not proceed.

Peres turned to his old friend Moshe Dayan, to hear his opinion. Peres laid before him the details of the plan as it was, on Thursday, July 1, 1976. Dayan studied the details and stated emphatically, "I would go confidently with this plan."

Encouraged by support from the man whom he viewed as both a military and political authority, Peres began a campaign to persuade the ministerial team and his other cabinet colleagues, with most of his persuasive efforts concentrated on the chief of staff. Two hours after midnight on Friday, Peres finally got agreement and support for an operation to be staged on Saturday night. It was within his jurisdiction to approve the flight of the raiding force from central Israel to Sharm el-Sheikh, at the southern tip of the Sinai Peninsula. However, any departure from Israeli-controlled territory required government consent. In the early hours of Saturday morning, Rabin still hesitated. The minister of defense exercised his own authority to send the aircraft south, in order to save time in the event that the government would approve. By intense efforts and sophisticated diplomacy, Peres succeeded in recruiting the support of most of the special ministerial team. Finally he got Rabin himself to agree. By that time the Entebbe raiding force was already airborne and well on its way to Uganda.

Saturday night, July 3, 1976, we were gathered in the defense minister's office listening to the military radio communications of the force. It was eleven at night, the critical hour when the first plane was due to touch down at Entebbe. Among the men in the office tensely waiting for word were the prime minister; Shimon Peres; Commerce and Industry Minister Chaim Bar-Lev, whose son Omer was with the raiding force; Transport Minister Gad Ya'acobi; and the assistants of the minister of defense. The tension in the room was taut as a bowstring. No one broke the silence. A tray of smoked-meat sandwiches lay untouched. Rabin sat facing me, withdrawn, toying with a cigarette butt. Peres sat in his chair, both feet propped on his desk, a habit that for him indicated either extreme stress or total relaxation. There was no confusing the two extremes.

At three minutes past the hour, we heard the announcement that the first plane was safely on the ground. The black Mercedes quickly drove out of the belly of the plane. In the back seat was an Amin-sized soldier, his face painted black, dressed in what might pass as a field marshal's uniform. Two Landrover Jeeps escorted the Mercedes. To the Ugandans this was supposed to suggest Idi Amin, unexpectedly returning from Mauritius. Ten minutes passed before we heard Dan Shomron, the operation commander: "All proceeding according to plan." At 11:51 P.M. we picked up the code word "Mount Carmel," confirmation that the evacuation of the hostages was complete and the planes were safely on their way home.

Stiff facial muscles relaxed, turned into broad smiles. One after the other, the sandwiches disappeared from the tray. We walked across to the office of the chief of staff, where a number of senior officers were already analyzing the results of the operation. Here I learned about our two casualties: Lieutenant Colonel Yonathan Netanyahu mortally wounded, and Sergeant Major Hershko Surin paralyzed for life.

The chief of staff was very emotional as he reported the full results to those present. He pointed out the ability of the IDF to perform excellently, and mentioned some of the lessons of this successful operation that would find their place in the combat doctrines of the army. He then added: "It would be impossible to sum up the operation, even at this early stage, without mentioning the drive and influence on performance concentrated in one man, the minister of defense, Shimon Peres, who deserves the entire credit."

After we raised glasses of champagne in a toast, I returned to my office to find Burka still chatting with his friend Idi Amin. The conversation was taking place ninety minutes after the last of our aircraft had left the sky over Entebbe, and it was clear that Idi Amin still knew nothing about the operation. Burka tried to evade the subject and Amin couldn't quite follow the conversation. Peres entered and, hearing Burka's side of the conversation, burst into laughter. He wanted to share it with Rabin, who was back in his own office, waiting for the minister of defense to give him a complete report.

It was 1:30 A.M. of July 4, 1976, when the first media report of something happening at Entebbe arrived from Agence France Presse. Following a previous decision, I issued a communiqué, through the IDF spokesman, on the rescue of the hostages and crew, without giving any details of the operation. By three in the morning I was home, hoping to catch a short nap before going to the airport to greet the hostages and their rescuers. No sooner was I in bed than the phone began to ring, starting a two-hour marathon of answering media questions from the local press and from many countries abroad. I finally yielded to official duties, showered, dressed, and returned to my office, where telegrams of congratulation were piling up from Jewish communities, from organizations, and from individuals wanting to express their pride in being Jews – all because of the IDF rescue in Entebbe.

30

THE UPHEAVAL

Within a few months of taking office, Rabin's public image began to tarnish. His popularity declined rapidly, mostly because of his derogatory remarks about individuals, sometimes denigrating entire segments of the public. At the beginning of his term in office, he was the darling of the press, but his abrasive comments aimed in many directions caused a shift, and the press began to turn hostile. Ignoring the real source of the problem, Rabin looked for a scapegoat, attributing every negative news item or hostile article to the influence of Peres and to me as Peres' spokesman and media adviser, considered to have influence with the media. Rabin never bothered to check the veracity of these allegations. It was only years later that he admitted to me that his assistants had fed him false information.

In their attempt to improve his image in the press, his staff began to channel confidential information to selected reporters. Foreign Minister Yigal Allon's staff was doing the same, inundating the press with secret data on sensitive matters. Some of the correspondents who scored political or security scoops revealed to me the source of their material. When one paper printed a sensational item about Israeli contacts with the Soviet Union, Rabin's people placed the responsibility on the office of the minister of defense. Peres, knowing the identity of the source, confronted Rabin and demanded a thorough investigation. Both, the security service (Shin Bet) and the Israeli police were supposed to conduct the investigation. For some reason the task was undertaken by the police alone. The only people they interrogated were those on the staff of the Defense Ministry. The investigators were aware of the source of the leaks, but felt stymied in pursuing an investigation.

Shimon Peres displayed considerable staying power and adherence but was extremely bitter about the course of events. He felt that Rabin had not only stymied his political advance in the party but had interfered with the performance of his governmental responsibilities. Rabin lacked a sophisticated understanding of party apparatus and interparty relations. As a result, at the end of 1976, he walked into a political minefield from which he could have readily extricated himself by prudent maneuvering. However, he employed tactics that exacerbated the explosive situation.

The incident began with a last-minute change in the scheduled arrival of new F-15 aircraft that the United States had agreed to supply to the IAF for the first time. Peres had worked long and hard to finalize this deal, which would give the IAF the last word in new technology. Originally, the first group of planes was to arrive after the weekend. Peres was to attend the landing ceremony, reaping well-earned public credit for arranging the deal. Rabin, unhappy about Peres' growing prestige, advanced the scheduled arrival to Friday, prior to Peres' return from an official visit to the United States. Because of this last-minute change in schedule, the planes arrived just before the onset of the Sabbath, leaving no time for the official ceremony. Nevertheless, Rabin decided to go ahead with the ceremony, knowing full well it would violate the sanctity of the Sabbath. This triggered a crisis. The religious parties in the government protested the deliberate desecration of the Sabbath, in violation of agreed norms of procedure, and proposed a vote of nonconfidence. Instead of defusing the issue, Rabin dismissed the religious representatives in his cabinet, thus losing his majority in the Knesset. The government fell. The move, called by his supporters "a brilliant political maneuver," ended in the demise of Rabin's government and removed the Labor Party from power for years to come. New elections were set for May 17, 1977.

The rivalry between Rabin and Peres reached a new high in February 1977. When the Labor Party Central Committee met to prepare its list of candidates for the Knesset and to choose its leader, the atmosphere was tense. Despite Peres' greater public popularity, Rabin won a majority in the committee and was chosen to head the party list. However, not long after the vote, a bombshell fell into the political arena. Leah Rabin was found to have kept a bank account in Washington, in violation of Israel's foreign currency laws. Her husband, the prime minister, resigned.

Shimon Peres was now at the head of the Labor Party list, something he had sought for years. However, it came at the worst possible juncture. The Labor Party had been riddled with crises for three years, as revelations of corruption in high places kept shaking the country. In addition, relations between the withdrawing prime minister and Peres were at an all-time low.

In the months preceding the election, I saw Peres campaigning tirelessly. He worked day and night to achieve his goal to become the next prime minister. He visited every town, village, settlement, and kibbutz, while continuing to carry out his responsibilities as minister of defense. Unlike others, he ran a campaign free of insults and mud-slinging. But the party was at its lowest ebb and chances of winning were negligible. "I received a house in disarray, but I will not abandon it," Peres told me.

Indeed, his efforts would have been in vain except for an entirely unexpected event. At the height of the campaign, Begin, the Likud candidate, had a heart attack and had to be hospitalized. The Likud campaign managers were panic-stricken. They attempted to solve the problem by recruiting Peres to head their list. Ezer Weizman, the campaign chairman, sent mediators to test the idea on Peres' close associates. Among the messengers were Eliezer Zhurabin, a businessman responsible for the Likud's advertising, and David Kolitz, a personal friend of Weizman. They tried to convince Peres that his future was with the Likud, which was likely to win, and not with Labor, which would continue to embitter his life in the ranks of the opposition. Peres rebuffed the Likud approaches and put all his energies into attaining a Labor victory. His popularity continued to grow and the polls predicted a decisive victory over Menachem Begin's Likud Party.

Meanwhile, Begin recovered from his illness and resumed his campaign. His decisive move was a personal TV confrontation with Peres, who led the Labor Party. Their TV debate was to take place in a studio next to the Jerusalem Theater. Yossi Sarid was at Peres' side and Eliyahu Ben Elissar accompanied Begin. Each was responsible for his party's election propaganda. I sat with them in the control room following the debate.

Peres was well prepared and performed faultlessly. He had all the facts and figures at his fingertips and acquitted himself with honor, considering that he was facing Begin, a formidable opponent. Sarid was satisfied with Peres' performance. Ben Elissar felt that Begin had delivered a knockout blow to Peres. I was inclined to agree with Ben Elissar, but I was not betting on the results at the polls.

The election results, on the morning after May 17, 1977, marked a fundamental upheaval in Israel's political life. For the first time since David Ben-Gurion declared the establishment of the State of Israel, the Labor Party was defeated in an election. The Likud's blocking majority on the right convinced Yigael Yadin, head of a new centrist party, Dash, with fifteen MKs, that his only chance to influence events was to join the coalition with Begin's Likud, even though he would have preferred joining the Labor Party, had they been able to put together a majority.

While Menachem Begin held talks with potential coalition partners to form a government, I began clearing out my office, located one floor above that of the minister of defense. For seven years this office had been my second home. This office consumed more hours out of the twenty-four than my home and family did. I had gone through many crises there: the last days of the War of Attrition over the Suez Canal, diplomatic discussions with the U.S. and UN, the Yom Kippur War with its ensuing discussions and negotiations, Kissinger's diplomatic shuttles, the hijacking of the Sabena aircraft, Entebbe, and other terrorist actions. Now I was about to part from the tension and excitement of my seven years in this office, four years with Moshe Dayan and three with Shimon Peres, both wise and courageous men. I had enjoyed working with them and had learned much from each of them.

Ezer Weizman, who led the Likud's election campaign to victory, was slated to be minister of defense in the new government. A warm and hearty person, he brought many talents to the job. While waiting to be installed, he visited the office daily, joking and promising new appointments to the secretaries, some of whom had been there since Ben-Gurion's days as defense minister. No stranger to the ministry, he knew most of its employees personally. When we ran into each other in

Chaim Yisraeli's office, Ezer grabbed me by the hair and roared, "From now on you'll take your instructions only from me."

Standing near the door to his new office, Weizman, with a slap on my back, asked when we could meet to discuss my work in the ministry. I explained that, for all the affection and respect I had for him, I could not see myself adjusting to his stormy temperament and resorted to a white lie, stating that, according to my contract with the Ministry of Defense, I had to return to my job at *Ha'aretz*. The following day, Ezer phoned to ask me whether my colleague and friend from the newspaper, Dan Margalit, would be suitable for the job of spokesman. I was glad to give him a well-deserved recommendation. After clearing my desk, I called Gershom Schocken, owner and chief editor of *Ha'aretz*, to tell him of my desire to resume working for the paper. We set a lunch appointment for June 7, at the Dan Hotel in Tel Aviv, to discuss my position at the paper. However, two weeks before that date, Shimon Peres phoned to say that Dayan wished to meet me at his Zahala home. I did not understand why Dayan needed Peres as an intermediary. It was only a few days since I had last talked to him and nothing seemed urgent, but I joined Moshe that same evening, amid the archaeological relics in his garden, watching as he tried to fit together the shards of a broken Canaanite ewer.

"You won't believe this, but hear me out," he began. Menachem Begin had invited him to become foreign minister. Seeing my amazement, Dayan said he was perfectly aware of the public storm it would create. However, considering the chance of an accommodation with the Arabs in the immediate future, he was prepared to risk "the little personal popularity" he still had, if he could succeed in influencing relations with the Arabs. He did not talk about peace, but he did believe that he could contribute to a new chapter between Israel and her neighbors, particularly with the Arabs in the territories controlled by Israel.

The conditions that he had presented to Begin included no closing of options for negotiation by imposing Israeli sovereignty on the territories. Dayan said, "I see a very reasonable chance of steering the wagon in a desired direction," adding that "this opportunity cannot be allowed to pass." After that prelude, he made me a personal offer, "that you can't afford to refuse," to continue to work for him as spokesman and adviser, with whatever title I chose. "As your friend, I would not want you to miss this historic opportunity to be at the center of the action," he said. As we parted at the end of the evening, I asked why he had not called me directly. "Formally you still work for Shimon. Relations between the three of us are such that I would not want to do anything that could be construed as going behind his back," explained Dayan with a mischievous smile, as if to say that Peres too might be ready to accept some appropriate position within his new domain.

When I arrived at the Ministry of Defense the following morning, Chaim Yisraeli already knew about the Zahala conversation and that I had agreed to work in the Foreign Ministry, though I had not yet said a word to Dayan or anyone else. I went in to Peres' office and told him about Moshe's offer. Peres was obviously in favor of keeping Dayan's intention secret. Dayan ranked rather high on the Labor list of new Knesset members and was aware of the public storm that would erupt over his sudden Likud affiliation. Congratulating me on my new job, Peres expressed the hope that Dayan would indeed succeed in guiding Israel in the direction he had discussed with both of us.

For the ensuing ten days I did not exchange a word with Dayan. I was a man between jobs and used the opportunity to devote more time to my family. Our daughter, Chaya, had injured her knee during her army service and was about to undergo surgery. Between visiting her in hospital, driving to Jerusalem to see the boys, Shai and Benny, who were studying in high school, and my regular morning swim, I still found time for a little get-together given for me by my colleagues at the Defense Ministry, even though I had not yet officially taken leave of the outgoing minister.

The presentation of the new government to the Knesset was set for June 20. At seven that morning, Dayan phoned asking me to meet him in the Knesset cafeteria at 3:30 P.M., a half hour before the session, and to bring along my close friend Eliakim Rubinstein of the legal department of the Ministry of Defense, whom he had decided to appoint as head of the foreign minister's office. Since Eli had some prior commitment, I ended up driving alone. I met Dayan in the cafeteria, where we were joined for a few moments by his daughter Yael. She had come to congratulate her father, but also to be at his side through the anticipated opposition attack on him as a "deserter."

Dayan knew that a vicious storm would sweep the Knesset when Begin presented his government. He asked me to respond with restraint and to avoid being dragged into any personal denunciations. We agreed to meet the following day at the Foreign Ministry, where Dayan was to take over the ministry from his predecessor, Yigal Allon. Dayan and Allon had competed since the days when both were young officers under the command of Yitzhak Sadeh, one of the earliest senior Haganah commanders. The rivalry had continued into politics, when Dayan faithfully stood by David Ben-Gurion, and Allon joined his kibbutz comrades in Mapam and Kibbutz HaMeuchad (a left-wing unbrella organization of a number of kibbutzim).

The Knesset session was explosive. The opposition Labor MKs launched a concerted attack on Dayan, some calling him a traitor to the Labor Party, accusing him of immorally retaining his Knesset seat earned under the banner of the Labor Party. Pale but calm, Dayan sat at the government table to the right of Begin and answered his attackers, point by point, avoiding unnecessary rhetoric.

In the late morning of June 21, I arrived at the Foreign Ministry courtyard in Jerusalem. Ambassador Amos Ganor, head of personnel, was waiting to guide me to the suite of rooms allotted to the minister's staff, and to assist me with the preliminary administrative procedures.

Yigal Allon sat in his second-floor office waiting for Dayan's arrival. Seeing me chatting with Nitza and Techia, two veteran secretaries of the minister's office, he called me in. During the period that I had edited the front page news at *Lamerchav*, the newspaper of his party, we had become friends. He was a warm and sociable man, making everyone around him feel comfortable. In the few moments that we had before Dayan's arrival, he told me how much he regretted not having reached the foreign policy targets he had set for himself and had hoped to accomplish. Our conversation ended when Techia came in at precisely twelve noon to announce Dayan's arrival.

A pile of files that Allon obviously intended to discuss with his successor lay on his desk. Professor Shlomo Avineri's letter of resignation from his post as director general of the ministry was undoubtedly in the pile. The position was given to Ephraim Evron, who had been Avineri's deputy. Later, when Evron was appointed ambassador to Washington, Dayan brought in Yosef (Yossi) Ciechanover to replace him as director general. Yossi had returned from heading the Ministry of Defense mission in New York and was a long-time associate of Dayan, having worked with him in many previous positions.

While Dayan was closeted with Allon, discussing urgent and long-term matters under consideration by the Foreign Ministry, I took the opportunity to arrange office space for Eli and myself, the only newcomers, additions to the permanent professionals on the staff of the new foreign minister. We chose offices close to Dayan.

Our first working session with Dayan was set for 8:00 A.M. the following day. Eli and I, the only participants, listened as the new foreign minister discussed his ideas and plans. He mentioned that Prime Minister Begin had received an invitation from the White House, delivered two days earlier by U.S. ambassador Sam Lewis. From Lewis' words and President Carter's cabled congratulations, Dayan inferred that a diplomatic process was about to begin. His own sources and instincts told him that the thinking of certain Arab leaders had sobered. He believed that Begin's ascent to power would encourage the more moderate Arab leaders, who wanted to settle.

He spoke of the secret information conveyed by the outgoing minister, including: relations with Iran and the Shah; links with the African continent, particularly with South Africa and Mengistu's regime in Ethiopia; Central and South America; and the European Economic Community, all calling for immediate attention. However, Dayan would be putting his own major effort into relations with the Arabs, either directly or through the agency of the United States. Meir Rosenne, legal adviser of the ministry, was familiar with all the details of the negotiations since the Yom Kippur War. At Dayan's request, he prepared draft treaties for peace formulas with each of the neighboring Arab countries. Dayan put the drafts into his briefcase to study at home. Meanwhile, he discussed with us the possibilities that he could foresee.

He wanted to make his first move in the direction of King Hussein of Jordan, with whom he had held pertinent conversations in the past, leading to an understanding between the two. Dayan surmised that Hussein's position would not permit him to make the first move, yet the nature of their relationship gave the king of Jordan priority. He also remembered fondly the cable from Hussein in June 1974, when Dayan resigned from Golda Meir's government:

As you leave the Cabinet I would like you to know how
grateful I am for the pleasure I had of knowing you
personally in our efforts to attain a peaceful settlement
to the problems facing our two countries. I shall always
cherish the hours of discussion we spent together and I
shall forever admire your wisdom, your insight and
foresight, your imaginative, creative and constructive
approach to the problems facing us and the fact that
you have always had the courage of your convictions in
dealing with these problems. You have and always will
have my deepest admiration as a true and responsible
patriot. I wish to thank you once again for your many
courtesies. I hope our paths may cross again, until then
please accept my regards and sincerest best wishes.

"We must try Hussein first, even if there is no visible chance," Dayan said.

In consultation with Begin, it was agreed to start with Hussein. Upon Begin's return from his first meeting with President Carter on July 25, Dayan was supposed to meet King Hussein. For some reason, this was postponed for three weeks. Dayan was disappointed, but continued with his other initiatives. His relationship with Arab leaders in the occupied territories had been good when he had set the Israeli policy in his role as minister of defense. Now he tried to assess how willing they might be to serve as partners in a dialogue to seek a solution. None of them was willing to express an opinion in public, resorting to the slogan, "Only the PLO can speak in our name."

In keeping with his December 1973 prediction that Sadat would now prefer a settlement rather than war, Dayan directed his attention to Egypt. "Egypt, which led the Arabs in wars against us, can now lead in the direction of settlement and maybe even peace." To test the chance for talks with Egypt, Dayan went to distant India to meet Prime Minister Desai, who had influence with Sadat. Properly disguised for a visit to a country that did not recognize Israel diplomatically, Dayan left on August 14 for his encounter with the aging Desai, who promised to make every effort to bring the two sides together. No sooner was Dayan back from India than he was off again, this time to Teheran to talk with the Shah, Reza Pahlavi, who was also well connected with the President of Egypt. The Shah received Dayan with warmth and friendliness, as befits an old acquaintance, entertaining him as well as his entourage. The Shah promised to use his influence with Sadat and his "friend in the peninsula," the king of Saudi Arabia, whom he did not hesitate to condemn for his "corrupt regime."

On August 22, three days after meeting the Shah in Teheran, Dayan met King Hussein in the London home of a mutual friend, where Hussein had met with various Israeli leaders on previous occasions, including Moshe Dayan when he was minister of defense. Dayan found the meeting disappointing.

"The conversation was one-sided. I talked, and the king said 'yes' or 'no.' He barely contributed. He is a different man, not the one I knew in the past. It seems that the helicopter crash that killed his wife and his pilot, a faithful friend, so depressed him that he had no interest in the subject. We'll get no milk from that billy goat."

Dayan fared much better in his meeting with King Hassan of Morocco. Early in September, two weeks before Rosh Hashanah, a first hint came from Cairo, via the king of Morocco, about a possible high-level meeting with an Egyptian envoy. Hassan II invited Dayan to his summer palace in Fez in order to explore the chances of such a meeting. On September 4 Dayan slipped incognito into Paris and boarded the plane of the king of Morocco for a flight to Fez. This meeting laid the foundation for the Dayan-Tohami talk that eventually brought President Sadat to Jerusalem and culminated in the signing of the peace treaty between Israel and Egypt.

On September 15 Moshe met the Belgian foreign minister, who was chairman of the Foreign Ministers' Council of the European Economic Community, to discuss Israel's economic problems and associate membership. These matters, which were pending between Israel and the EEC, were overshadowed by the "Venice Declaration," wherein European ministers criticized Israel in clearly pro-Arab tones. Dayan also met General Alexander Haig, who was then commander in chief of NATO, based in Brussels. Moshe and Rachel Dayan, Eli Rubinstein, and I were due to fly on September 16 to Washington, where a meeting had been set with President Carter and his aides for September 19.

On our way to the Sabena plane that was to take us to New York, the security guards placed Rachel Dayan, Eli, and me in the car of our ambassador to Belgium, Eliashiv Ben Horin, and his wife. Dayan, traveling in another car, slipped out of the motorcade on the way to the airport and disappeared. The ambassador had no idea what was happening. We were met at the top of the steps to the aircraft by a beaming pilot, Reginald Levy, who had been captain of the hijacked Sabena in the early seventies, when Dayan had supervised the rescue operation.

The ambassador and his wife boarded the aircraft with us to take leave of Moshe Dayan. We mentioned to the pilot that we would be going without Moshe and told the Ben Horin couple that the minister could not be disturbed at the moment. The ambassador, a veteran in the foreign service, sensed that something strange was going on but asked no questions. He and his wife parted from us most courteously and left the plane.

While we were flying over the Atlantic, Moshe Dayan was in a small plane on his way to an airfield outside Paris, where he boarded another plane to Fez. Anwar Sadat's envoy was already waiting for him in King Hassan's summer palace. Dayan later described this first meeting between the Israeli foreign minister and Egyptian Deputy Prime Minister for Presidential Affairs Hassan el-Tohami, as an encounter between two different worlds. Dayan, always pragmatic, sought a practical basis for dialogue, but Tohami launched into a mystic lecture on religious matters and seemed to be floating between heaven and earth. Nevertheless, there was rapport between the two, aided by the occasional intervention of the king, their host.

Dayan suggested that Begin and Sadat should meet to explore the possibilities for continuing contacts. Tohami declared that as long as a single Israeli soldier stood on holy Egyptian ground, such a meeting was impossible. Dayan tried to enlighten Tohami about history and something concerning nations at war. Slowly Tohami got the message and agreed to pass it on to the president of Egypt.

Dayan was impressed, and believed that there were grounds for discussion. He was sure that the door had opened a crack. Before continuing to Washington where his entourage was waiting, he decided to return immediately to Israel and report to the prime minister. He also wanted to coordinate with Begin the positions that he would be proposing to President Carter, who was pressing for an international conference to resolve the Arab-Israel conflict. The meeting with the Egyptian envoy was, of course, top secret, though we could not judge what the Americans might know of it. The secret, so carefully kept, blew wide open on September 17, the day after Dayan's meeting with Sadat's trusted personal courier.

When we disembarked from the plane at Kennedy Airport, dozens of reporters and photographers were waiting. They pounced on Rachel Dayan, certain that her husband could not be far behind. To their disappointment, she was followed by Eli Rubinstein and myself. The mystery surrounding Dayan's absence took wings. The media recruited anyone and everyone who might be considered an expert in Middle East affairs to shed some light. Meanwhile we settled into the Regency Hotel on Park Avenue and tried to steer clear of reporters. I was trapped in the lobby by an old acquaintance, Arnaud de Borchgrave of *Newsweek* magazine, who questioned me, while expounding what he apparently thought was great familiarity with the understanding reached between Dayan and King Hussein at their meeting in a private villa near Paris. I overcame my urge to smile and made no comment. Two days later, I read a detailed account in *Newsweek* of a conversation between Dayan and a Saudi Arabian prince, who had promised to arrange a meeting with the king of Saudi Arabia.

The speculation over Dayan's absence ran wild for two days, until a report from Jerusalem noted Dayan's unscheduled return from a meeting in Morocco to report to Begin. The White House and State Department personnel whom we met on September 19, two days after our arrival, were taken by surprise by Dayan's side trip to Morocco. They wanted details about the purpose and results. In turn, we were surprised at how much they had been caught off balance by the Jerusalem announcement. There were indications that they did know something prior to the public report, but to this day I am not sure whether they were aware in advance that the meeting had been planned. Intelligence experts, including Americans who had watched Dayan's movements as minister of defense and foreign minister, had lost track of him on his way from Brussels to Paris in a small plane. It was only a phone call between the kings of Morocco and Spain, intercepted by certain intelligence services, that revealed to the Americans the secret of Dayan's disappearance.

31

CONFRONTATION WITH CARTER

In the early morning hours of September 18, 1977, an El Al plane brought Moshe Dayan to New York's Kennedy Airport. A few Israelis, including Rachel Dayan, Eli Rubinstein, and myself, had come to meet him. We had to penetrate a tight American and Israeli security cordon to reach him. An army of reporters had gathered nearby; I asked security to let them approach Dayan for a few minutes of questions in order to preserve good relations with the press. Dayan confirmed his visit to Morocco and his meeting with the prime minister in Jerusalem, but beyond that he said not a word, leaving the guesswork to the reporters.

From the airport we drove to the Regency Hotel for initial consultations. Dayan brought us up to date on the events of the forty-eight hours since we had parted in Brussels. Then we began to chart the course for the coming talks. Dayan wanted to know the mood in the White House and State Department. The picture sketched by Ambassador Simcha Dinitz and Chargé d'Affaires Chanan Bar-On was extremely bleak. They cited a position paper of the Brookings Political Research Institute in Washington, according to which Israel must withdraw to the June 1967 borders, with only very slight border adjustments. Israel must also permit the establishment of a "Palestinian entity" – the code name for a Palestinian state. The senior researchers of Brookings included Zbigniew Brzezinski, national security adviser to the president; and William Quandt, one of Professor Brzezinski's senior aides. This Brookings paper had become the guidebook in the Middle East policy of President Carter. Dinitz and Bar-On also pointed to a significant erosion of sympathy for Israel in American public opinion, on Capitol Hill, and in the media.

This visit was entirely different from all of Dayan's previous official visits to the United States, when he came as minister of defense in Golda Meir's government, with its solid respectability. Now he was foreign minister in Menachem Begin's Likud government. In American eyes, this new government and its leader appeared to be narrowly parochial and rigidly unrealistic in their attitude to the Arab world. Dayan was viewed as an outsider in the Likud. At this stage, even the American Jewish leadership harbored serious doubts about the Likud regime. Dayan was the only ray of hope. His credit was solid from his years as a senior member in the Labor government. It was from this difficult initial position that he was to begin talks in Washington. What made his task all the more challenging was the determination of the U.S. to start a radically new approach, one that appeared to hold grave dangers for Israel. The U.S. administration intended to steer toward a resumption of the Geneva Peace Conference. The Geneva conferees had met only twice since their initial meeting in December 1973, and the conference had since become defunct. Nevertheless, the U.S. administration was determined to reactivate a conference in this format before the year's end.

We were scheduled to meet the following day with Secretary of State Cyrus Vance, on the seventh floor of the State Department. Dayan was punctual to a fault, with no tolerance for people who were late, but he was also unwilling to arrive earlier than scheduled. Since we came a few minutes early, he asked the driver to circle for another four minutes before pulling up to the main entrance. When one of us started to suggest a last-minute idea for the coming talks, Dayan silenced him immediately, putting a finger to his ear by way of suggesting that our Cadillac limousine might be bugged.

At twelve noon on the dot, we were ushered into Secretary Vance's office, with which I was already familiar from previous visits with William Rogers and Henry Kissinger during the presidencies of Nixon and Ford. Without ceremony the two delegations introduced themselves. Ours, apart from Dayan, consisted of Ambassador Simcha Dinitz; Chanan Bar-On; Meir Rosenne, legal adviser of the Foreign Ministry; Eli Rubinstein; and myself. On the American side were Secretary of State Cyrus Vance; Sam Lewis, ambassador to Israel;

Philip Habib, Alfred Atherton, and Harold Saunders, assistant secretaries of state; Hodding Carter, spokesman for the State Department; as well as William Quandt, Michael Sterner, and David Koren, who spoke fluent Hebrew after having served in the Tel Aviv embassy.

The atmosphere was businesslike and cold. We did not feel that we were among friends with whom we could hold an intimate conversation and work out a common policy. We were led into the adjoining conference room, where the table was set for a kosher lunch according to the strictest precepts and under the watchful eye of a religious supervisor. After a number of jokes about Eli and me, the "culprits" responsible for the kosher meal, Vance toasted American-Israeli friendship (with kosher wine). Dayan responded with a toast of his own, referring to previous visits to this office, where understandings and agreements between Israel and the U.S. had been worked out. He expressed the hope that the present visit would also lead to growing cooperation between us.

Vance, a lawyer by profession, adopted a very practical approach, not letting tangential issues sidetrack the discussion. He began with comments on the draft of the Israeli peace agreement that Begin had presented to Carter at their meeting two months earlier. It was a document of several pages, titled, "Principles for Negotiation of Peace with the Arabs," and was now viewed against the background of the anticipated reconvening of the Geneva conference. From Vance's comments, plus the remarks of the national security adviser to the president, Zbigniew Brzezinski, it was clear that we were headed for a dead end. There was a momentary diversion when the Americans asked Dayan about his talks with President Sadat's envoy in Morocco.

Vance asked Dayan to describe the proposed security arrangements for peace treaties with every country involved in the conflict. Using a large wall map, Dayan traced Israel's security lines in the south along the Red Sea from Sharm El-Sheikh to Eilat and along the international land border from Eilat to Rafiah.

Brzezinski asked whether Israel would expect a defense pact with the United States as part of the peace treaties, since such a pact would be conditional on significant concessions of territory on any front where agreement was possible. From the Sinai, we moved on to discuss the Golan Heights, with Dayan explaining the government's position on security needs after reaching a peace agreement. Finally, we arrived at the subject of autonomy for Judea, Samaria, and the Gaza Strip, the status of Jerusalem and, more particularly, the status of the holy places.

Dayan was forceful in his presentation of Israel's position. From their questions, he understood the aims of the administration, which indicated what we might expect in our upcoming meeting with President Carter in the White House. It was difficult to shake the impression that the position, no less forcefully presented by the Americans, was essentially the Arab position. Our dialogue to reach agreement with the Arabs was being conducted with the Americans instead of the Arabs, who didn't participate because they refused to recognize Israel as having any legal status. This view precluded any meeting with them to discuss issues face to face. Our only consolation lay in the feeble hope that the Arabs might reject the Americans as being one-sided in acting as spokesman and advocate. Unfortunately, there seemed little prospect of that.

I studied both of the main American spokesmen, Vance and Brzezinski. Vance, who had earlier served under a Democratic president, a superb lawyer and experienced diplomat, tried to adhere to an agenda acceptable to both sides. In fact he would later prove to be an honest broker, often finding the right formula to resolve complex issues.

Brzezinski, on the other hand, projected an aura of a scholarly adviser who knew all the answers in advance, convinced that only his responses were correct. Somehow, he seemed to be attempting to follow in the footsteps of his predecessor and fellow academic, Henry Kissinger. Unlike Vance, Brzezinski kept shunting aside the professional diplomats, averse to hearing the views of the other side.

At 3:00 P.M. we were to meet with the president. Brzezinski had briefed Carter on our talks over lunch and was waiting for us at the White House. Vice President Walter Mondale invited Dayan into President Carter's office for an intimate chat, scheduled to last fifteen minutes. The conversation lasted for more than an hour. Mondale occasionally emerged to assure us that Carter and Dayan would soon rejoin their delegations for a larger meeting. At 4:15 P.M. they finally emerged. The two teams arranged themselves along opposite sides of a rectangular table. Carter greeted us and gave a summary of his talks with Dayan, including the points of disagreement, as well as a point of reluctant agreement regarding new Israeli settlements in the occupied territories.

For the Americans, the main purpose in inviting us to the White House was to reconvene the Geneva Peace Conference, which had opened in December 1973, after the Yom Kippur War. The conference was supposed to lead to peace treaties, or at least to nonbelligerency pacts, between Israel and its neighbors. However, once Kissinger began to deal with the realities of the Middle East, he found it necessary to retreat from this overly ambitious program and settle for more realistic goals, as Dayan had predicted from the start.

One of the belligerents, Syria, had refused to attend. Nevertheless, the Syrians did benefit from the negotiations that followed the convening of the conference, in that it resulted in the disengagement between the armies of Israel and Syria on the Golan Heights, as well as between the armies of Egypt and Israel in the Sinai desert. Secretary of State Henry Kissinger's prime aim had been to achieve such a separation of forces after a cease-fire on each front. After the separation of forces and exchange of prisoners, Kissinger began to shuttle between Jerusalem, Cairo, and Damascus, in order to reach interim agreements on both fronts, which were signed first with Egypt, then with Syria.

The Geneva conference had ceased to exist. However, it seemed to have endured in the minds of the American diplomats. Now it was the goal of the Carter administration to revive it. In fact, the Americans had already voiced their plans for Geneva when Prime Minister Yitzhak Rabin came for a visit in March 1977, and later when Prime Minister Menachem Begin paid his first official visit to Washington. In July 1977, Carter was intent not only on reconvening the conference, but also on inviting a Palestinian delegation to discuss the future of the territories where they lived under Israeli control. Begin had agreed to their inclusion in a "united Arab delegation" on condition that the Palestinians be actual residents of the territories and not representatives of the PLO.

At the time of Dayan's arrival at the White House, the administration in Washington was concerned with a new problem. The Americans argued that the placing of civilian settlements in occupied territory was illegal under the terms of the fourth Geneva convention and that they were an obstacle to peace talks. Prior to his trip to Washington, Dayan had proposed a formula to the cabinet in Jerusalem aimed at satisfying the Americans. He suggested that the six new settlements approved by the government should be declared army installations, populated by military personnel. The majority of Likud ministers, who looked upon Dayan as a Labor Party member inclined toward compromise and pragmatism, rejected the idea as a concession. But Begin agreed in order to reach an understanding with President Carter, who was adamantly opposed to the settlements. However, since the Geneva convention did permit construction of military facilities, there was no legal problem. Carter accepted this compromise, agreeing that it was the least damaging of the alternatives. He also accepted a formula, worked out with Dayan, for reconvening the Geneva convention, which Dayan had earlier coordinated with Begin.

The tension between the two sides of the table in the conference room was manifest. In their private session, Dayan had made no effort to hide his displeasure with Carter's proposals. Mondale, standing at Carter's side during their long private meeting, needled Dayan incessantly with caustic comments. Dayan reacted by ignoring the vice president. When the two of us were alone in the hotel, Dayan poured out his wrath. Mondale had been described by our people as a friend. "With friends like that," he vented, "we don't need enemies."

Dayan was visibly preoccupied and depressed. "We're going to have a serious confrontation with this administration. This man Carter sees himself as curing all the ills of the world. He is constantly criticizing and preaching to us and won't spare the rod to make us come to heel." I asked him whether it might not be prudent to drop the whole settlement issue from our agenda with the United States in order not to sour relations. After a minute of silence, he grinned chidingly and reminded me of my personal involvement in persuading the then-Defense Minister Shimon Peres to allow the establishment of the first two West Bank settlements, Kedumim and Ofra. At that time, 1975-76, in the aftermath of the Yom Kippur War and its implications for public morale, I could not accept the idea of making parts of Israel *Judenrein* (cleansed of Jews). Now, however, with an opportunity to negotiate with the Arabs, I thought we should not place obstacles in the path of the Americans, who wanted to initiate talks. Dayan concurred, but reminded me that the prime minister and his party were firmly committed to the settlement policy and could not be budged from it.

Early the following morning I phoned home to congratulate my son, Shai, who had been sworn in at a Western Wall ceremony that day, as a soldier in one of the IDF elite units, to let him know of my pride in him and regret that I could not be there in person. Immediately afterwards, we went to the *Washington Post* office at the invitation of publisher Katherine Graham, a longtime admirer of Dayan. On our way there, Dayan told me that he intended to speak out bluntly against the administration's machinations. Though I had stipulated with the editor in chief, Ben Bradley, that the conversation was to be strictly off the record, I was still concerned that there might be leaks on items of importance. I suggested that Moshe restrain his criticism, particularly of the president, as long as there was a chance to avert a rift. He entered the meeting radiating good humor and refrained from talking about our serious disagreements with the Carter White House.

From the office of the *Post*, Dayan went on to a number of meetings with senators and congressmen, mostly from the Appropriations and Foreign Affairs committees. In the evening, the Israeli ambassador, Simcha Dinitz, hosted Dayan at a dinner attended by government leaders, senators, members of Congress, Jewish leaders, and senior American media representatives. Henry Kissinger was among the guests and wanted to hear firsthand from Dayan, as well as to express his own views about the meetings with Carter and his administration.

Senator Ted Kennedy, greeting me with a big smile like an old friend, shook hands warmly. He wanted to know Dayan's reaction to the talks with Carter. Was there any truth to the rumor that President Carter was trying to "steamroller" us?

The next day was Yom Kippur eve. Our entourage had dispersed and I remained alone with Dayan and the security men. We were returning to New York that afternoon, following a meeting with senior Washington columnists. We landed at La Guardia about an hour before the start of the Yom Kippur fast. Traffic was heavy and I worried that we would not reach our hotel in time to eat the special meal before the fast. Dayan watched me out of the corner of his eye and suggested with a smile, "Why not ask them to turn on the siren?" The security detail complied immediately and we zoomed down the expressway at top speed. Within twenty minutes we were at the Regency, in time for me to eat the pre-fast Yom Kippur eve meal and even shower and shave before the commencement of the holy day. We walked to the Fifth Avenue Synagogue, escorted on all sides by a phalanx of security men. The synagogue officers were waiting for us at the entrance.

They seated us in the front row. Rabbi Emmanuel Rackman stood up before the Ark of the Law and welcomed the foreign minister of Israel, "visiting in America on a mission of grave concern for the Jewish State," and then launched into his sermon. Dayan leaned over and whispered, "Better he should pray. The sermon will not bring us redemption." He was curious about the surroundings. It was the first time in his life that he attended the *Kol Nidrei* service, which ushers in Yom Kippur, the holiest day of the year. In fact, he told me that he had never been in a synagogue during prayer. At Nahalal, where he grew up, he had not even had a bar mitzvah. I could sense his emotion, revealed by his tendency to shift from side to side in his seat when he was tense or moved. As the cantor began the haunting, traditional melody of *Kol Nidrei*, the opening prayer, we saw Leonard Bernstein, standing in a corner, wearing a big, white silk *kippa*, wrapped in a *tallit* (prayer shawl), tears flowing down his cheeks.

Dayan asked me to show him the right place in the prayer book. As I sat next to him, helping him find his way through the prayer book, I could not help but recall another *Kol Nidrei* in the Great Synagogue of Piotrkow, forty-two years earlier. My father was delivering his first sermon as rabbi of that community, and the synagogue was full. I sat behind Father, facing the congregation. I heard sighs and muted sobs as Father spoke. The atmosphere was charged with emotion. Now I was in the midst of a completely different congregation. In the pleasant and intimate Fifth Avenue Synagogue, the atmosphere was restrained and "correct" – a different mode of communication with the Creator.

I looked around at the congregants, some of whom would later become close friends during the four years that I would pray there as Israel's consul general in New York. They were intent on prayer, but from the stolen glances it was clear that they derived pride from the presence of Israel's foreign minister.

In this prestigious synagogue, I was also reminded of Yom Kippur at the Ministry of Defense and IDF general staff in Tel Aviv, the Yom Kippur of October 6, 1973, when Israel was caught unprepared by a surprise Syrian and Egyptian offensive. Services were held in a small hut, on the fringe of the general staff camp. One after another, during breaks in cabinet consultations and war-room discussions, ministers, senior officers, and soldiers came in for a few moments of prayer. After the *mussaf* service, when I entered Dayan's office, he gave me a somber look and asked if I had prayed for him too. The gravity of his question reflected the precarious situation of our troops on the front lines, critical at that juncture.

The Fifth Avenue Synagogue usually has an intimate atmosphere, but on this night it bustled with activity. Dozens of men, their heads covered with white skullcaps, were scattered in the main sanctuary and, surprisingly, in the gallery reserved strictly for women. Only the tiny earphones betrayed their security function. At the end of the service, the congregation was held back until we emerged and began to walk east along 62nd Street toward our Park Avenue hotel.

At the 62nd Street exit of the synagogue, a convoy of black limousines and a phalanx of American and Israeli security agents had cordoned off a segment of the sidewalk and street. The moment we emerged from the synagogue, two agents tried to lead Dayan straight to the open door of a vehicle for the 500-yard ride to the hotel. He brushed past them and walked with me; so did the agents. Some cordoned us inside a security ring while others ran ahead to block Madison Avenue so that we could cross it on our way to the hotel. Though not observant himself, Dayan was extremely considerate and respectful of the needs of his two orthodox aides, Eli and me, which sometimes prevented our riding with him or engaging in other activities that would involve a desecration of the Sabbath or festivals. As on this occasion, he did not mind a lengthy walk on a busy street, accompanied by a convoy of limousines crawling slowly alongside with a complement of anxious security men all around. Whenever possible, kosher meals were provided, even when he might have preferred something else. He never complained or even commented about accommodating our needs.

The next day Dayan stayed in the hotel and invited Simcha Ehrlich, minister of finance, to join him. Ehrlich was leader of the moderate Liberal Party faction in Begin's government and Dayan wanted to bring him up to date on the Washington discussions. I spent the entire day in the synagogue. At nightfall I returned to the hotel to find Dayan in low spirits, following a conversation with someone he referred to only as "an old friend in America who once held an important government position." I surmised that it was Henry Kissinger, although Dayan did not mention any name. The gist of the conversation was that Carter was hell-bent on coordinating with the Soviet Union a resumption of the Geneva conference, with emphasis on the resolution of the "Palestinian problem" based on Carter's views as conveyed to Begin in July. Dayan sensed that a confrontation with the Carter administration was now inevitable.

In Dayan's view, a conference, jointly chaired by the U.S. and the USSR, would force Israel into a trap from which it would be difficult to escape. He knew from past experience that at such a conference Israel would be forced to make far-reaching concessions without getting anything in return. He assumed that the Syrians would once again refuse to attend, as before, and that the whole peace discussion would degenerate into a means of pressuring Israel to give up Judea, Samaria, and Gaza, and maybe even East Jerusalem. From his talk with Carter concerning the six settlements that the government had decided to establish in the territories, he could see where the president was heading. Carter's anger over the settlements aimed at pushing Israel into a corner, making it easier for the U.S. to get concessions from Israel about convening the conference. "He won't hesitate to pressure us," Dayan predicted.

We felt that the Carter administration in 1977, like that of Bush fifteen years later, sought to weaken Israel's standing in American public opinion; that the president of the United States was trying to undermine the legitimacy of our claims vis-à-vis Arab demands. However, unlike Bush in the 1990s, Carter did not enjoy close cooperation with the Arab states. At this time the Arabs steadfastly clung to their stubborn refusal to talk to Israel, or even publicly to recognize its right to exist. This Arab attitude reduced Carter's effectiveness in applying pressure on Israel, and made it easier for us to stand up to the White House, thanks to the sympathetic press. It would only be after Anwar Sadat's visit to Jerusalem, breaking the united Arab boycott, that Carter could permit himself to bring increased pressure on Israel. Sadat's willingness to recognize Israel and speak openly with her leaders enlisted sympathetic public opinion for the Arabs, placing Israel on the defensive.

Rachel Dayan left to spend the evening with friends, and Moshe and I were left alone in our twelfth-floor hotel suite. He poured whiskey for both of us and began to think aloud about the counterattack he wanted to open against the pressures of the Carter administration. The media were willing to listen to Israel's side of the story. Begin's government was new and few editors and columnists knew much about its goals.

Curiosity, mixed with a desire to play fair with a little country that was under an American steamroller, opened sympathetic ears to us in the American press. On the other hand, Dayan had to navigate very cautiously so as not to exacerbate relations with the U.S. administration. Unsure as to how strongly to react, he left the initiative up to me.

The following morning, Friday, September 23, I began calling friends and old acquaintances in the American media with whom I had become friendly during my days as spokesman for the Ministry of Defense, at the time of the Yom Kippur War. I set up off-the-record meetings with Dayan at the *New York Times*, the *Wall Street Journal*, *Time*, *Newsweek*, and the three TV networks ABC, CBS, and NBC. In addition, I invited several editors, correspondents, and columnists to the hotel, among them, James Reston, Joseph Kraft, Marvin Kalb, Barbara Walters, Maggie Greenfield, Bruce Rothwell, and others who had presented Israel's views in their articles or programs.

The weakness of Israeli public relations greatly troubled us. Kissinger had tried to bring Israel to her knees during his shuttle diplomacy of 1974-76. Rabin, Peres, and Allon were then serving as a minicabinet of the Israeli government, negotiating with Kissinger the interim agreements with Syria and Egypt. They had not given in to his dictates and he, in turn, dubbed them "stubborn and lacking in understanding." Expressions like that had done much to erode the generally sympathetic public opinion of Israel.

On Friday morning, the day after Yom Kippur, while Dayan was meeting with a group of Jewish leaders and molders of public opinion in a hotel meeting room, a message came from Secretary of State Vance that a few of his assistants were on their way to our hotel for a meeting with Dayan. Harold Saunders, Philip Habib, Alfred Atherton, William Quandt, and Michael Sterner showed up. Saunders explained the urgency of their visit: to inform us of a pending joint American-

Soviet communique on the reconvening of the Geneva onference, which was completely different from the one that had been agreed upon a few days earlier in the talks in Washington with the president and the secretary of state. Dayan raised the eyebrow over his right eye, as if to ask in astonishment, "What caused the sudden shift?" There was no doubt that the draft of the Israeli-American version on reconvening the Geneva convention had been changed by the Americans to fit their joint announcement with the Soviets. Dayan rejected the new working paper of Vance and Gromyko.

Ignoring our obvious consternation and without waiting for a verbal response, Atherton proffered a stack of photocopies of the communiqué. Being the closest, I took the papers from him. Dayan ordered me to return them immediately: "We are not a party to this announcement." Turning to Vance's assistants he said sharply, "You did not ask us. You did not try to consult with us, even though it concerns us directly, and you heard our opposing views in Washington just a few days ago. I do not think such a joint statement serves to advance the matter under discussion. You would be better off without any such announcement and without bringing the Soviets back into the arena." I returned the bundle, but kept one copy for us to study later at our leisure.

Cyrus Vance later called Dayan to explain that without Soviet involvement it would be impossible to move the process, stalemated since 1973. He had met with Soviet Foreign Minister Gromyko and both had agreed on the joint announcement – with the blessing, and perhaps at the initiative, of President Carter. Dayan remained firmly opposed to the joint communiqué, which was a U.S. retreat from the understanding reached with the president and the secretary of state. He explained to Vance that the communiqué would retard the process. In his opinion, Egypt would also be unhappy at the resumption of the Geneva conference. Vance would later hear the Egyptian reservations from Foreign Minister Ismail Fahmi. But what angered Dayan most of all was the change in the original working paper already agreed upon with Prime Minister Begin. Now the Americans had unilaterally changed it into a version detrimental to Israel.

The tension developed into a crisis in our relations with the United States. In Jerusalem, the situation was even more acute. Prime Minister Begin was furious at the American double-dealing. Dayan's talks with

Carter on September 19 had implied an understanding between Jerusalem and Washington on how discussions would be conducted prior to the conference. "Presenting Israel with a fait accompli arranged by Gromyko and Vance has pulled the carpet from under our feet," said Dayan.

The president and his aides were well aware of Israel's angry reaction. The secretary of state took the initiative of inviting the Israeli delegation to dinner at his suite in the UN Plaza Hotel on September 26, 1977. It was the eve of Succoth, the Feast of Tabernacles. Eli Rubinstein and I had been invited to eat at my brother-in-law J.P. Lunzer's house on Manhattan's West Side. Now, instead of a holiday meal in a succah (a booth with a thatched roof in remembrance of the dwellings used during the forty years in the desert after the Exodus from Egypt) among friends and family, we found ourselves walking from the Regency Hotel to the UN Plaza Hotel. On the way, we passed a synagogue on Sutton Place. We made up the *minyan* (the ten-man prayer quorum) and were invited into the succah on the synagogue roof, where we recited *Kiddush,* the traditional blessings over the festive bread and wine.

Vance's suite, on the thirty-sixth floor, was next to the president's. The table was set for twelve. Two of the places were set with plastic instead of silver cutlery, along with TV-dinner kosher meal trays wrapped in cellophane. Eli and I did not have to be told where to sit. The rest of our staff found their places, with Dayan at the head. At the opposite half circle sat Vance and his aides. We finished our less than festive meal, hungry and frustrated. Vance insisted on going ahead with his joint communiqué with Gromyko. Dayan just as obstinately opposed it as a nonstarter.

That same night Dayan accepted my suggestion to appeal to American public opinion directly. The meetings already arranged with the important newspapers and national television networks were a convenient launch pad for our public information campaign. To follow his off-the-record briefings of media people in New York and of the leaders of the Jewish organizations, Dayan decided to extend his stay and tour the country. Appearances were arranged before local Jewish leadership in Chicago, Los Angeles, Atlanta, and New York. The campaign was to begin in Chicago on October 6 and end in New York on October 13. The arrangements were made by the United Jewish

Appeal and Israel Bonds, under the patronage of the Conference of Presidents of Major American Jewish Organizations. I informed a number of my media friends, with the result that a few newspapers asked to send reporters to cover the public information tour throughout the country.

Before the start of the tour, I summoned a few editors and correspondents to Dayan's suite. This time it was all for on-the-record attribution. Contrary to the advice we had been given not to use media big guns but rather to send signals to the administration from less important papers, I decided to start at the very top. Thanks to Dayan's confidence in my work, I had free rein to proceed. I set up a series of meetings with the top media people, resulting in sympathetic support in editorials in *The New York Times, The Washington Post, The Los Angeles Times, The Boston Globe,* and the *Wall Street Journal,* as well as the three popular news weeklies, *Time, Newsweek,* and *U.S. News and World Report.* Dayan made appearances on all three national TV networks, including the prestigious Sunday morning panel shows, which gave him the opportunity to present the Israeli stand in a straightforward way to the American public.

The widespread and favorable coverage in the press and Dayan's projected tour made the White House and State Department nervous. The press severely criticized the administration's plan to restore the USSR to the Middle East as an influential factor after Kissinger had successfully ejected them. In a period of four days, the Jewish community inundated the White House with thousands of telegrams and angry phone calls protesting the administration's negative policy toward Israel.

The newspaper reports of Dayan's tour during the following week made a huge impression in the media. *Time* and *Newsweek* both made it their cover story. *The New York Times* did the same, giving front-page coverage to the reports from their journalist who traveled with Dayan on the entire trip. *Time,* in its cover story, attributed Israel's sharp reaction to the U.S.-USSR communiqué to a "Holocaust complex." *Time* quoted a White House staffer: "They became hysterical. They read into that statement things that were never there. It's their Holocaust mentality." The magazine's Jerusalem bureau chief, Donald Neff, wrote: "The Holocaust complex, while it may be unrealistic, retains its hold on Israeli decision makers. . . . I wonder if Jimmy Carter truly appreciates this irrational side of the conflict."

Senators and congressmen showed an interest in the tour, and their requests to meet Dayan at his various stops added to the tension among the president's staff. On September 30, Vance requested another meeting with Dayan. Again we met in Vance's suite in the hotel at the UN Plaza. It was a Friday evening. The meeting continued late into the evening but produced no positive result. "I've made you miss another festive dinner," Dayan joked as he entered the car to return to the hotel. Eli and I walked again. We arrived an hour later, and sat down with Dayan to analyze the discussion with Vance and his assistants. "Nothing is going to move until the president himself gets involved," Dayan concluded. He assumed that following the media uproar, we could expect a call from the president.

Indeed, the call did come two days later. A meeting was set for Tuesday, October 4. Carter was scheduled to hold a reception for the chiefs of the UN delegations that same evening. However, he said that we would meet at his hotel suite at seven in the evening. He intended to sit with us, until there was an agreement.

In light of the positive influence of our media campaign, I suggested to Dayan that I would arrange a full-scale press conference to be held after his meeting with the president. Assuming that the meeting with Carter would last until close to midnight, I tried to reserve the pressroom at the president's hotel for that hour. The hotel management told me to talk to the president's aides. They in turn directed me to the president's spokesman, Jody Powell, who wanted at all costs to avoid embarrassing Carter in his own hotel. He put the president's chief of staff, Hamilton Jordan, on the line and they both quizzed me on why we needed the pressroom. I explained that the rainy weather would make it impossible for the foreign minister of Israel to answer the questions of hundreds of waiting reporters standing on the sidewalk outside the hotel.

"Are you convening a press conference?" Powell asked me. I replied that reporters were going to be around whether we invited them or not. Within the hour, Powell called back to say that the room would be at our disposal from eight o'clock on. Without making any formal announcement and carefully covering my tracks, I made sure that the message got to the reporters. The story spread that Dayan would be making an appearance late that night, with or without President Carter. The pressroom, designed to hold three hundred, was so full that there was standing room only. Each time I came down to see who was there, I found Powell and his staff anxiously surveying the crowd of reporters. Returning to the meeting room on the top floor, I could sense the shadowy presence of the media hanging over the discussions.

Carter received us with what seemed like a forced smile. Seating us around a glass coffee table in the center of the room, he chose a corner of the sofa for himself. Dayan sat at the other end of the sofa. Brzezinski, Vance, Atherton, Quandt, Saunders, Koren, and Powell sat on the president's left. Our team – Dinitz, Rosenne, Bar-On, Rubinstein, and I – sat on Dayan's right.

"What do you intend to tell the Jews on your tour next week?" Carter opened, then hurriedly rephrased, " the Jewish organizations."

"I will explain our position with regard to the political options that I can see in the Middle East, not only to the Jews, but to anyone willing to listen," responded Dayan.

"And why is it that you do not want our joint communiqué with the Soviet Union?" Carter persisted.

Dayan enumerated the negative aspects of the statement, contending that it would undermine the significant progress Israel had made in relations with some of her neighbors. Without specifying, it was clear that he was referring to the recent contacts with Egypt.

Carter continued to justify the Soviet involvement on the grounds that, if left out, the USSR would sabotage any progress toward a settlement. He also reiterated his belief that Palestinian elements should be brought into the negotiations. While not naming the organization, he implied that PLO representatives were to be included. Referring to his July 1977 discussions with the prime minister, Carter claimed that Begin had agreed to the inclusion of Palestinian representatives in a united Arab delegation. He said Begin's sole reservation was that "they should not be well-known PLO representatives." Dayan responded that the moment these representatives appeared at the peace conference, they would be "extremely well-known" PLO representatives. Carter laughed, saying that he had made the same point to Begin.

The conversation was at times strident, especially when Carter moralized that Israel's control over a conquered population in the territories was intolerable. He rejected the establishment of a

Palestinian state, but supported the creation of a national entity, which he refrained from defining. I sensed Dayan's growing impatience. He continued to treat the president with respect, but it was noticeable that the presidential sermonizing had strained his patience.

When Carter told him to believe and trust that he, the president of the United States, would not allow anything untoward to happen to Israel if she accepted his recommendation, Dayan sat bolt upright in his seat, looked directly into the president's eyes, and said, "Mr. President, I may have only one eye, but I can see very well the dangers threatening our existence as a nation if we accept your advice. As an individual, I am no coward. But as a Jew, I have good reason to be worried. In our times one catastrophe has already befallen us, and some of us [pointing to me] suffered the experience firsthand. So long as it is in our power, we will prevent an additional tragedy for our people."

It was a very emotional monologue. At times he turned his eye to us as if asking for help. Carter and his entourage sat silent, until one of the aides reminded the president that he must proceed to the reception he was hosting. Carter apologized for taking a break in the talks and promised to return in about one and a half or two hours. He left the chairmanship for the continuing dialogue to State Secretary Cyrus Vance and to Zbigniew Brzezinski, his national security adviser. "Carry on from where we left off, and I'll be back for the summing up," he told them.

Carter returned around midnight. "What are you going to say to the reporters waiting downstairs?" he asked. "What we agree on here," responded Dayan. Turning to his aides, Carter suggested drafting a press statement. One of them ventured that it should be only an Israeli statement. "In that case, we'll draft it ourselves," Dayan retorted. By then it was 1:30 A.M. and the president was beginning to show signs of fatigue and edginess. He asked Dayan over and over again, "What are you planning to say to your people on your tour?" Dayan looked amused, "We'll repeat whatever we say downstairs to the press."

Carter got the hint. He told his spokesman to take a few people from each side into the next room to prepare a joint press statement. Atherton, Powell, Bar-On, and I moved next door. Within a half hour we returned with a first draft, based on the original working paper regarding the convening of the Geneva conference as agreed upon in the initial Washington talks. There was some disagreement. Carter glanced at it once or twice, then told his aides, "I have to go. You are not to leave here until there's something we all accept." We revised the first version and finally arrived at a mutually acceptable document that effectively revoked the American-Soviet communiqué, which had caused us so much consternation.

The press statement became the American-Israeli "working paper" for a Geneva conference that would be reconvened, although no date had been set. Dayan justifiably considered the document an important achievement. Before presenting it to the press, he wanted to relay the contents to Begin, who was then in Ichilov Hospital in Tel Aviv.

At 2:15 A.M., Moshe Dayan and Cyrus Vance faced the hundreds of reporters who had been waiting for more than six hours. Jody Powell wanted to introduce me as the Israeli spokesman and have me read the announcement. I declined and asked Powell to introduce the two foreign ministers, so that one or both could read the statement and answer questions. The presence of Vance and Dayan together gave the announcement more weight, and the reporters understood that it negated the joint Vance-Gromyko communiqué on the convening of a peace conference with conditions unacceptable to Israel. In the diplomatic history of Israel this was an unprecedented achievement, whereby a press release became the official governmental U.S.-Israel document that canceled an official, signed agreement between the two major powers. Though the U.S.-Israel press release continued to be referred to as a "working paper," it became accepted policy. We had won this round.

32

SADAT IN JERUSALEM

Prime Minister Begin was unhappy with the working paper that Dayan had "successfully" negotiated with President Carter in New York. For Begin, acceptance of any document that determined procedures for reconvening the Geneva conference represented an erosion of Israel's position. He was also disturbed by the clause that agreed to the inclusion of Palestinians in the Arab delegation. However, Carter was adamant about their inclusion, and Begin himself had agreed to it in their first talks in July, making his agreement contingent upon the understanding that those Palestinians not be "well-known members of the PLO," even adding that Israel would not examine their credentials too closely.

Upon our return to Jerusalem, Dayan presented the document to a plenary session of the Knesset. He also appeared at a meeting of the Knesset Security and Foreign Affairs Committee. At both he was bombarded with provocative questions, mostly from right-wing MKs, all of whom shared the view that Dayan had spinelessly surrendered to Carter's demands. Political gossipmongers fed reporters with rumors about tension, perhaps even a rift, between Dayan and Begin. The reality was different. There was complete compatibility between them. Whenever I sat with Dayan, we were invariably interrupted several times by phone calls from Begin.

The ongoing contacts with the Americans were carried out between Dayan and U.S. Ambassador Sam Lewis in numerous meetings every week. Knowing the balance of power within the government, Lewis did not neglect calling on the prime minister from time to time.

Dayan was thorough in dealing with any topic. He overlooked no possible source to update, enrich, or expand his knowledge. He learned all aspects of a topic before relating to it publicly and it was a rarity for him to make a slip of the tongue. In preparation for a possible renewal of the Geneva conference, Dayan made trips to study firsthand every geographical area that might come under discussion. He enlisted academics who were experts on the different forms of government to help him formulate practical ideas for implementing autonomy for the Arab populace of the West Bank and Gaza.

After his talks in Morocco with Sadat's personal representative, Dayan believed the day was close for the opening of a serious dialogue with our Egyptian neighbors. The first signal that the day had indeed come was in a speech by President Sadat before the Egyptian Parliament on November 9, 1977, in which he expressed willingness to come to Jerusalem for talks with Israeli leaders. His remarks aroused astonishment and great hope in Israel. Even before the correspondents could get through to me with requests for the Israeli response, Dayan was on the phone from his home asking about the public reaction to the speech. I asked him for instructions regarding our policy: "Don't worry! Trust Begin! He'll know how to play it, and he will play it big," Dayan responded.

Sadat's surprise announcement of his intended visit to Jerusalem utterly astonished President Carter and his administration. On that day, three prominent leaders of the West Palm Beach Jewish community – Robert Lewinson, Irwin Levy, and Fred Singer – were at the White House at the invitation of Carter's adviser, Robert Lipshutz. On the agenda was a discussion of Jewish complaints about the president's changed policies regarding Israel. Their first session was to be with William Quandt. They were waiting for him when the news of Sadat's speech reached the White House. Lipshutz told his guests about Sadat's surprise proposal and about the White House reservations regarding it. According to Lipshutz, Quandt had been dispatched to the State Department to coordinate a joint statement expressing the administration's reservations about a visit by Sadat to Jerusalem without proper advance preparation. Shortly after leaving for the State Department, Quandt was recalled to the White House, which had decided to delay issuing the statement. Within an hour, the response was toned down to something more positive. Finally the president ordered a public announcement supporting Sadat's planned visit to Jerusalem. The confusion at the White House that day underscored the extent to which Sadat had gone to undercut Carter's determination to reconvene the Geneva conference under joint American and Soviet chairmanship.

The days that followed were devoted to the analysis of Sadat's intentions and the formulation of a practical response from Israel. In conjunction with political preparations for a possible visit, we began to work on the myriad organizational details and logistics – a job assigned to the Foreign Ministry. Responsibility for the media and public information aspects were assigned to me. The expected influx of hundreds of reporters and camera crews put us under considerable pressure. With the help of personel from the Ministry of Foreign Ministry Affairs, we recruited a staff with the necessary language and diplomatic skills, ranging from novices to ambassadors. They were to serve as briefing officers in the media centers set up in the Jerusalem Theater and the Jerusalem Hilton Hotel.

Media personnel from abroad had already reserved blocks of rooms in the Jerusalem hotels and had sent their advance men to make arrangements. Among the senior media people were many old acquaintances, including Walter Cronkite, Barbara Walters, Ted Koppel, and others with whom I had previously worked and had personal connections. Among others at one briefing just before Sadat's arrival were senior British reporters – Patrick Donovan, James Cameron, and Max Hastings – whom I knew quite well from previous encounters. One of them, tall, broadly built, and given to emphasizing his Oxford accent, spoke with a pipe clamped in the corner of his mouth. He enjoyed an authority among his colleagues on matters pertaining to the Middle East. When he rose to pose his question, I found myself tensing, prepared for a confrontation. But he tried to disarm me with a compliment for "always being in the right place at the right time," referring to our previous encounter during the 1973 Yom Kippur War.

Then he unsheathed the sting behind the compliment: "In the last war you were fighting hard to repel the Egyptians from a narrow strip of desert along the Suez Canal and you took heavy losses. Are you now going to give Sadat the whole of Sinai simply because he comes in a civilian plane and is greeted with an official ceremony?" His associates

The author and Chief Rabbi of Israel, Rabbi Israel Meir Lau,
in conversation with Pope John Paul II, 1995

With President of Hungary, Dr. Arpad Goncz, Chief Rabbi Lau
secretary-general of World Jewish Congress, Dr. Israel Singer, 1995

With TV star Barbara Walters, 1985

With the Executive Editor of the New York Times, Max Frankel

Joan Lau-Lavie with Mr. and Mrs. Cyrus Vance, 1985

With friends in New York; Mr. and Mrs.
George Klein and Yosef Ciechanover, 1985

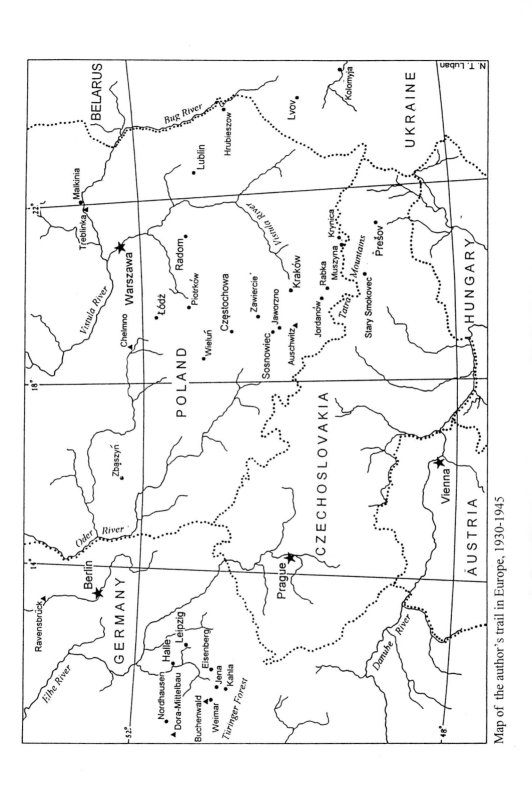

Map of the author's trail in Europe, 1930-1945

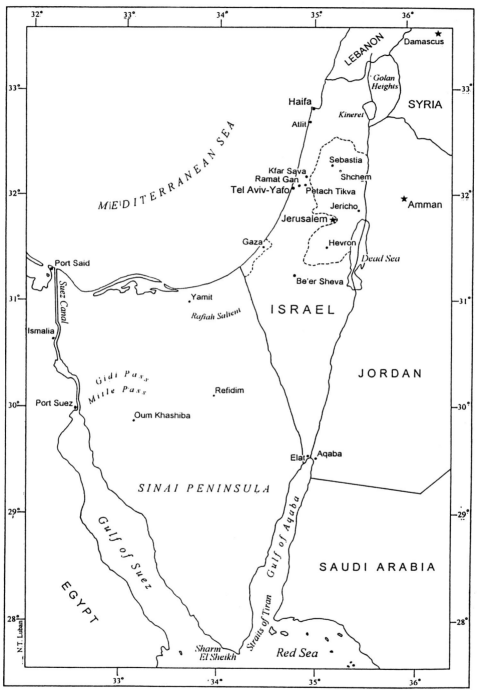

Map of the authors trail in Palestine-Israel, 1945-1995

With Prof. Elie Wiesel, Ambassador Moshe Arens
and Rabbi Yehuda Neidich at a memorial service for Holocaust
victims at Temple Emanuel in New York, 1985

The author bestows the award of righteous gentile
by the Yad Vashem Authority in Jerusalem
on Mr. Stanislaw Wyrwa, an American citizen
of Polish origin, for rescuing Jewish neighbors
during the Holocaust, 1983

With Prime Minister Shamir, Foreign Minister David Levy, and
Chief of Staff of IDF, General Ehud Barak, are welcoming
the Ethiopian immigrants arriving on the "Operation Solomon"
airlift, 1991

A panel discussion at the Tel Aviv library reviewing
the author's book in its Hebrew version "Am KeLavie", 1993

At the gravesite of his great grandfather, Rabbi Naphtali Halberstam,
in Chrzanow, Poland, 1994

wanted to know whether the game was still open or had it already been played and settled at Dayan's meeting with Sadat's representative in Morocco. In vain I tried to convince them that no deal had been made and that Sadat was trying to push us into a corner by means of an astute public relations campaign, without having received any prior promises. Unfortunately, I was prohibited from producing any of the secret protocols or documents to support my case.

Sadat's arrival was set for 8:00 P.M., Saturday evening, November 19, 1977. Special teams were set up in the prime minister's office and the Foreign Ministry to deal with all the arrangements. The previous day we waited at Ben-Gurion Airport to receive the very first Egyptian plane to land in Israel, bearing the Egyptian advance party to coordinate Sadat's visit with us. It was an emotional moment when the Boeing, painted in the Egyptian national colors, touched down in Israel at Ben-Gurion Airport. The reception party – Eliyahu Ben Elissar, director general of the prime minister's office; Ephraim Evron of the Foreign Ministry; and I – walked over to the plane. Rehavam Amir, our chief of protocol, introduced the Egyptian visitors to us; and his Egyptian counterpart, who had arrived on the plane, introduced us to them. We took them into one of the airport reception lounges to get acquainted over coffee.

My personal guest was Sadat's spokesman and adviser, Saad Zaglul Nasser, a newspaperman by profession. After our coffee I offered to drive him to Jerusalem. The others traveled by the old road, through the towns of Lod and Ramle. I chose to take the newer but still incomplete main road, which was shorter and much faster. My guest commented on the poor quality of the main road to the capital of Israel. I explained the history of this road, which had been under Jordanian control until the Six-Day War in 1967 and was now under construction as an expressway intended to become the major traffic artery: Highway One. He asked whether we were crossing "captured lands." I assured him that the president of Egypt would be crossing this same "captured land" the following day.

On the way to Jerusalem, I engaged Saad Zaglul Nasser in conversation, trying to understand Sadat's motive for taking this dramatic step. He replied that Sadat had long been thinking about taking some direct initiative, unrelated to any outside factor, even without the agreement of the other Arab states and without American coordination. According to him, Sadat was furious with the U.S. initiative to reconvene the Geneva conference in cooperation with the Soviet Union. Sadat saw it as an obstacle to dialogue rather than a favorable arena to promote regional interaction. He had concluded that it was possible to reach a positive dialogue with Israel without outside chaperones. Prior to his decision to fly to Jerusalem, Sadat had met with a number of regional Arab leaders, among them King Halled of Saudi Arabia, King Hussein of Jordan, and President Assad of Syria. He wanted to convince them that an understanding with Israel was necessary to pave the way to greater economic development, promoted by regional cooperation with all the Middle Eastern nations and with financial assistance from the international community, particularly the United States and the European Common Market. Sadat was in the habit of telling his close associates that the oil-rich kings and princes were mistaken if they thought they could rely indefinitely on the riches buried in their lands. He pointed to the oil boycott that the Arabs had used against the West at the end of 1973 and in 1974. The West took it as a warning to prepare reserves and alternatives to any future move of that kind. Furthermore, the Egyptian spokesman confirmed, Sadat had made it clear to the king of Saudi Arabia that the United States would never allow the Arabs to strike a fatal blow at Israel. As for the Soviet Union, it had proved unable to assist in reaching any resolution of the problems in the region. These were Sadat's reasons for deciding on the trip to Israel, with the assurance that he would protect Arab interests, including the maintenance of the holy places.

King Halled did not accept Sadat's reasoning; however, he voiced no threats regarding the visit to Jerusalem. President Hafez el-Assad of Syria reacted more strongly. Nasser continued, "Yesterday, President Sadat again visited Damascus in a last attempt to get at least tacit assent to the trip to Jerusalem. Assad refused to listen to any argument favoring such a visit. He even warned Sadat that the entire Arab world would boycott him because of this step. Sadat slammed the door behind him and left Damascus." In conclusion, Saad Zaglul Nasser implied that in the absence of any support from Arab leaders, Israel must make a grand gesture. He thought we should offer far-reaching concessions to justify the gamble Sadat had taken upon himself. This would permit him to accelerate the momentum in initiating a dialogue with Israel.

At the outskirts of the city, I asked him whether he would be interested in driving through the eastern sections of Jerusalem and seeing the holy places of the three religions. He inquired whether we would have to cross captured territory. Hearing my answer, he dropped the idea and we drove directly to the King David Hotel, where Sadat and his entourage were to stay.

Within the hour I reported my conversation with Sadat's adviser to Dayan, who was not surprised by the Syrian position. He hoped that the negative Saudi stand was not irreversible, but felt that it would depend largely on the degree of resolve exhibited by Washington. Dayan estimated that it was too late for Sadat to turn back the clock. "We have reached the point of no return," he said. He was not sure we could reach a peace treaty since, in his opinion, Sadat would avoid signing a separate agreement with us without resolution of the Palestinian issue. However, he believed that a nonbelligerency agreement was an attainable goal.

Aware of the influence this media event would have on world opinion, Dayan urged me to make sure that the briefing centers should be staffed with a number of well-informed Foreign Ministry people, qualified to speak effectively in whatever language was needed. Only then would we have a chance to come out of the anticipated controversy with a favorably disposed public opinion. "As for the negotiations in the meeting rooms, you can depend on Begin. He knows the rules of the game and won't need to take a back seat to Sadat in negotiating skill."

The big show began at eight the following evening, on the center tarmac of Ben-Gurion Airport. Everyone of importance, including opposition leaders, was there at this emotionally charged moment as Anwar Sadat's presidential plane rolled to a stop in front of President Ephraim Katzir and Prime Minister Menachem Begin. The entire country held its breath.

The Israeli jet fighters that had escorted the president of Egypt through our airspace as an honor guard, now flew low overhead and saluted by dipping their wings. The noise of their engines still echoed in our ears when the door of the plane opened. There, behind the Egyptian chief of protocol and the military aide-de-camp, stood Sadat, in a blaze of floodlights from TV and still-photographers. He cut an impressive figure with his erect posture and elegant, custom-made dark suit. A pathway had to be forged through the throng of photographers for the president of Israel to approach the stairway ramp to greet Sadat. Then came the historic moment, as the two heads of state shook hands and stood at attention during the playing of both national anthems.

The ceremony was dramatic. President Katzir led Sadat down the long line of notables. Sadat paused for a moment in front of Dayan, with a quizzical look on his face. When he reached Ariel Sharon, he stopped and commented with a smile that he had sought the general in Sinai and had somehow missed him, but now they could shake hands. Reaching Golda Meir, he bowed and pressed both her hands.

I took two members of the Egyptian entourage in my car for the ride to Jerusalem. They were impressed by the cordiality between us. "I feel as if we are the best man and bridesmaid at a wedding and don't know each other yet," commented Nabil of the Egyptian Foreign Ministry. "In our case, I think even the bride and groom don't know each other," I responded, to the amusement of my new friends.

The thousands of Israelis lining the roads through Jerusalem, cheering and waving Israeli and Egyptian flags at the procession of cars, deeply touched my passengers. They were impressed by the view of the city and the well-lit streets. They had anticipated a small neglected town. What they saw was entirely different. One of them admitted that they had imagined something like one of the holy cities in Saudi Arabia.

Later, in his hotel room, Dayan told us about his conversation with Boutros Ghali, the Egyptian minister of state for foreign affairs, on their ride from the airport. Ghali had been very reserved in his first encounter with an Israeli leader. Nevertheless, he responded courteously to Dayan's questions, saying, "The president has not come to sign a peace treaty with Israel without resolving the issues in dispute between Israel and the Arab world and particularly the Palestinian problem." Dayan had given his guest a comprehensive history of the conflict and the specific underlying difficulties that made it hard to reach agreement with the Palestinians. All of this was unrelated to the conflict between Israel and Egypt, which could be settled more readily. The safest way to proceed with all the disputed matters was by way of a bilateral agreement between Israel and Egypt. Such an agreement would encourage the other parties to the conflict to advance with practical discussions for resolving the dispute.

While Moshe was telling us about his exchange, Boutros Ghali reported Dayan's view to Sadat in the presidential suite of the King David Hotel. Ghali perceived that Dayan wanted a bilateral treaty with Egypt but declined talks about a comprehensive settlement. He was sure that Dayan was leading the government along this obstinate route against a comprehensive solution. We could see Sadat's reaction in the way he behaved toward Dayan, demonstrating disappointment. In his talks with an Israeli delegation that included Menachem Begin, Yigael Yadin, Moshe Dayan, and Ezer Weizman, the Egyptian president pointedly ignored Dayan's presence. It was Deputy Prime Minister Yadin who whispered in Sadat's ear that he really should converse with Dayan, the one man capable of advancing the whole debate to a fruitful conclusion.

Over breakfast in his room, Dayan said sorrowfully, "He expected a grand aristocratic gesture from us, that we should announce withdrawal from all the territories in response to his coming to Jerusalem." He analyzed Sadat's thought processes as somewhat naive and as an incorrect reading of the Israeli position. "On second thought, he is apparently trying to widen his corridor to Washington via Jerusalem," estimated Dayan. He was convinced that the move was aimed at the United States, even though Sadat knew that he was on a road from which it would be difficult to digress.

After Sadat's speech in the Knesset, there was a sense that we were on a treadmill, getting nowhere, and that Sadat would return to Cairo exactly as he had come, empty-handed. Contrary to his normal pessimism, which he viewed as realism, Moshe found a few points of light in Sadat's speech, which might possibly lead to some advances. He was encouraged by his conversation with Sadat at the banquet which Begin gave in Sadat's honor. Sadat was sitting between Begin and Dayan. From where I sat, opposite the trio, I could see that Sadat was trying to engage Dayan in conversation. From time to time he would turn his head toward Moshe but invariably it was at the same split second that Begin addressed him from the other side. Finally, Sadat leaned over and the two began a long discussion, which seemed more serious than just an exchange of polite pleasantries. After dinner, as the Israeli team made its way back to the sixth floor to continue the discussion with the president of Egypt, Moshe managed to tell me his impression: "There is someone to talk to and something to talk about."

As Sadat departed for Cairo, Ben-Gurion Airport was again the scene of a festive ceremony. We already felt a certain closeness to our Egyptian colleagues. Despite my mixed feelings as I assessed the outcome of the visit, I personally sensed that we had started on a good road from which I would not want to depart. Later, surrounded on all sides by correspondents who wanted to know the practical results achieved by the visit, I could tell them that parallel political and military committees would be meeting in Jerusalem and Cairo, serving as a framework for discussions on political and military matters between representatives at a very high level. The political team from Israel would be headed by Foreign Minister Moshe Dayan and the military team by Defense Minister Ezer Weizman. The Egyptian teams would be headed by their counterparts of the same cabinet rank.

Alongside Dayan in the political delegation were, from the Ministry of Foreign Affairs: Ephraim Evron, director general; Meir Rosenne, legal adviser; Ziama Divon, head of the Department of Middle East Affairs; Eliakim Rubinstein, bureau chief; and Naphtali Lavie, adviser and spokesman. In addition there were Brigadier General Ephraim Poran, the prime minister's military secretary; Professor Aharon Barak, attorney general; Major General Yehoshua Sagui, chief of IDF Intelligence Branch; and Mordechai Tzipori, deputy defense minister.

From this augmented delegation, the permanent core that remained throughout the peace talks with Egypt consisted of Meir Rosenne, Eliakim Rubinstein, and myself.

33

KADDISH AT BERGEN-BELSEN

I t was a cold, dreary, and depressing day when Foreign Minister Moshe Dayan and his entourage landed at Frankfurt Airport for an official visit to Germany on Sunday, November 27, 1977. The El Al plane taxied to a stop far away from the terminal and was immediately surrounded by a tight security cordon that sealed off the area. The heads of protocol of the West German Foreign Ministry and of the Hessian state awaited us alongside the landing ramp. Wordlessly but courteously they escorted us to the military Luftwaffe plane parked alongside our Israeli aircraft. We flew to the military air force base at Zelle, close to our first destination, the concentration camp of Bergen-Belsen.

As I ascended the steps to the German plane behind Moshe Dayan, the sight of the German cross on the plane struck me. This cross had been engraved in my memory ever since World War II, and my heart skipped a beat. I quickly recovered and found my seat. Next to me sat Herr Imhof and Herr Jochum, the two heads of protocol. Herr Jochum tried to carry on a friendly conversation with me, from which I gathered that he had read a dossier on my background. It took all my willpower to keep up a polite dialogue for the half-hour flight to the military runway. The reception party for Foreign Minister Dayan and his entourage included Dr. Ernst Albrecht, head of state of Niedersachsen; Herr Rutger Gross; and representatives of the local Jewish community. We boarded two air force helicopters that brought us ten minutes later to the entrance to the Bergen-Belsen concentration camp.

The entire area was covered with a gray-white layer of ice and snow. The cold froze our ears. The sight of hundreds of Jews who had come from Hanover to accompany us to the memorials, waving small Israeli flags, eased my anxiety somewhat. Dayan ascended the stairs to the central memorial and placed a wreath. He then turned to face the crowd and recited the *Kaddish*, his bald head covered with a black *kippa*. I stood opposite him, shivering from cold and emotion. When he finished, I detached myself from the crowd and turned toward the fenced-off areas marked as mass graves of Jewish victims. It was here that I wanted to say my own private *Kaddish*. My close friend Noah Klieger, a reporter for the Israeli newspaper *Yediot Aharonot*, rounded up a few more Jewish journalists to make up a *minyan* required for reciting the *Kaddish*.

After the ceremony, we were invited to the museum that displayed some of the evidence of Nazi horrors. I did not need to see these all too familiar sights. Instead, I studied Dayan and the other Israelis whose knowledge of the Holocaust had been relatively superficial. When they came out, their stricken faces and prolonged silence testified to a deepened, agonizing awareness, a soul-searing experience.

An hour later we again landed at Zelle and boarded a plane to Hamburg. On the plane, Dayan asked his official West German escort, sitting next to him, to exchange seats with me. Fixing his one eye on me he asked whether I had seen the museum exhibit. Learning that I had not, he gently chided me, "But you requested it." True. A month earlier, upon receipt of Chancellor Schmidt's invitation to make an official visit to Germany, Dayan asked me to accompany him. Since my liberation from Buchenwald, April 11, 1945, I had not set foot on German soil, except for a journalistic mission in 1963 for the newspaper *Ha'aretz*. My assignment had been to investigate and expose the scientific and technical activities of German scientists in advancing Egyptian war plans. Israel was especially concerned that the German contribution to the development of biological and chemical warheads, as well as missile-guidance systems, might enable Egypt to aim such weapons against us. I explained my reluctance to Dayan. Nevertheless he urged me to join him. I agreed to accompany him to Germany, provided he gave me a free hand in planning the itinerary. His only request was that I coordinate the details with our ambassador to Bonn, Yochanan Meroz.

I explained to Dayan that a public personality like him, representing the Jewish State, could not start an official visit to

Germany without first honoring the memory of the Nazi victims by coming to recite *Kaddish,* standing in solemn communion with those who had been murdered. Dayan asked no further questions. However, our ambassador feared an unpleasant German reaction if Dayan would come to Bonn straight from a visit to a place that focused on the Nazi period in Germany's history. There was no need to involve Dayan in my discussion with Meroz. We compromised by setting the departure from Israel to Frankfurt for Sunday morning. In that way, we could continue to Bergen-Belsen and then to Hamburg on Sunday. Thus our formal state visit would begin on Monday morning, when we would fly from Hamburg to Bonn.

A delegation of local dignitaries, headed by State Secretary Dr. Schulze and his wife, met us at Hamburg Airport. The Germanic fetish for order and precision was getting on my nerves, but in visits of this sort it had its advantages. We were taken in a procession of cars to the guesthouse of the president of the senate. In the evening, Mayor Hans Ulrich Close of Hamburg and his wife, who had been part of the welcoming delegation at the airport, were our hosts at a reception in the Hamburg senate building. They were a young friendly couple with whom I experienced no discomfort. Afterwards they took us to the elegant Senate Guesthouse on the banks of the Elbe River, where we stayed for the night.

Moshe and Rachel Dayan were assigned adjacent rooms, as usual, and I was given the Green Room on the same floor. Next to the Green Room were two rooms for the Israeli and German security men. The rest of the entourage was housed in the Atlantic Hotel. When we arrived at the guesthouse, Axel Springer was already there waiting for us, together with Ernest Kramer, editor of his chain of newspapers. After spending a good hour with them, we were joined by Bundestag member Erich Blumenfeld, a good friend of Israel among German politicians. These talks gave Dayan a clear picture of current German government thinking and public opinion, and helped him prepare for the discussions in Bonn.

At a late hour, overtaken by fatigue after the long and emotional day, we retired to our rooms for the night. An inner disquiet overcame me and I could not even think of sleep, in spite of fatigue. Nissan, head of the Israeli security team, was sitting with other team members in the entrance hall. I invited him to come with me for a short walk to get some fresh air. Nissan called a colleague and the three of us took a midnight stroll along the banks of the Elbe River, flowing beneath a thick sheet of ice.

I have rarely relished a soft, warm bed as much as I did after returning from that bitter-cold walk in twenty-three degrees centigrade below zero. However, even in this soft, warm bed, I still could not fall asleep. The physical comfort could not overcome the emotional turbulence reawakened in me. I lay in bed, my eyes focusing on the floral frost designs on the windowpanes. My thoughts strayed to the bunks of bare wooden boards that had served as my bed, mattress, and cover on the frigid nights that followed long days of forced labor in the quarries at Buchenwald, just like those we had seen earlier in the day at Bergen-Belsen. Now, in the guesthouse in Hamburg, they reappeared before my eyes.

Turning over in bed, I saw a thin beam of light emanating from the direction of the door. The door slowly opened and the silhouette of Moshe appeared. "Naphtali, you're not asleep, are you?" He came in and sat down on the edge of my bed. "How did you get out of there?" I didn't know what to say. He paused, and then began to talk. It seemed that he wanted to unburden himself rather than to listen to me. "How is it that we knew nothing of what happened there?" he asked.

He sat a long while, talking, asking me questions that I could not answer. Although he had, of course, been aware of what happened during the Holocaust, the impact of the horrors he witnessed during his visit now struck him with full force. The display at the museum distressed him during the rest of our stay in Germany and he did not hesitate to speak about it to the heads of government in Bonn. Three years later, when working on his book *Breakthrough*, we again talked about Bergen-Belsen and his late-night conversation with me in Hamburg. He asked for comments. I made none.

I learned a lot from Dayan's shocked reaction, which I compared to that of other sabras of his generation whom I had met in 1946-47 during my army training in the Hagana. Those sabras had displayed a pointedly superior attitude toward us, the newly arrived survivors, mocking us simply because we represented what was in their view a fundamentally negative value – attachment to life in the Diaspora. Had we left the Diaspora and come to Israel before the war, we would have avoided the Holocaust. Thus the atrocities of the Holocaust were of no relevance. It was almost as if we, the victims, had brought this tragedy upon ourselves. That was how they saw us and that is why they related to us in their haughty manner. Dayan's reaction, thirty years after the Holocaust, impressed me as being intellectually mature without the element of sabra superiority over those who came from "over there." The derogatory names that we heard – sheep, soapbar, and *musselmen* – have vanished from the vocabulary of today's sabras.

We flew to Bonn early the following morning, landing at the airport that served both Bonn and Cologne, then transferred to a helicopter for a flight to the official Venusberg Guesthouse. Our reception party was headed by the Acting Foreign Minister Baron Otto Lamsdorf, the economics minister, standing in for Foreign Minister Hans Dietrich Genscher, who was hospitalized with pneumonia. Lamsdorf received us in the guesthouse for light refreshments and our first official discussion. To Lamsdorf's left sat the director general of the Federal Foreign Ministry, Gunther Van Wehl, who would shortly be appointed ambassador to the United States. I was placed on Dayan's right, facing Van Wehl across the table. There was something disturbing about his sharp features and white hair that reminded me of a face that made me shudder. I was supposed to take minutes of the session but left the task to Meroz and Political Minister Edgar Ruppin. I simply could not concentrate on the discussion. Unthinkingly, I began to sketch the features of the man across from me, adding a black SS marine-type cap with its skull-and-crossbones insignia. Out of the corner of his eye Dayan noticed, and to my acute embarrassment pulled the paper away from me, scribbled something, and returned it. I looked down, to read: "Which of those facing us is that bastard?"

After lunch Dayan called me to his room. In front of him was the draft of a speech he was to give that evening at an official dinner in his honor. Meroz, one of the most experienced and wisest of men in our foreign service, had worked hard to polish the speech. Dayan went through it time and again, convinced that something was missing. "I have to tell them what's in my heart, not play diplomatic games. We must not forget where we are." In the margin he had written some expressions in Hebrew that he wanted to use in order to settle his own account with Germany's past. I softened his abrasive Hebrew to what I deemed a more suitable English and took the draft to Meroz. He predicted there would be an emotional reaction from the audience. He was right.

The following day, Dayan visited the office of Chancellor Helmut Schmidt, accompanied by Meroz and myself. Next to the chancellor sat Klaus Schuetz, German ambassador to Israel, and Gunther Van Wehl. Schmidt was very friendly. He was proud of his position as leader of the Social Democrats, which he saw as providing a clean break from his past as an officer in the Nazi air force. He kept holding a silver snuffbox in his hand, and asked very politely why Israel refused to grant the Palestinians the right of self-determination. Dayan did not answer immediately. He preferred to wait until Schmidt finished posing questions and offering advice. The chancellor then referred to Dayan's outspoken statements in the speech of the previous evening and asked how many generations must pass before Germans would no longer be reminded of that dark period in the past. Moshe Dayan stared at Schmidt, pointed to me with his finger, and said, "As long as they, their children, and perhaps even their grandchildren continue to ask why and how it could have happened, all honest men will remember and remind others."

As for self-determination for the Palestinians, Dayan explained that this would inevitably lead to the creation of a Palestinian state between Israel and Jordan, essentially determining the future of the Jews in their own land. Israel could not be expected to agree to that. In a deliberately aimed barb, he added that in our generation there were those who had attempted to determine the future of the Jews as a people, and we would not permit that to happen again. Schmidt did not take his eyes off Dayan during this monologue. At the end he responded, "I understand you very well, but a solution must be found."

Dayan expressed the opinion that Germany's sympathetic position toward Israel had eroded and was now playing a negative role among the foreign ministers of the nine countries in the European Economic Community. Schmidt protested that there had been no change in Germany's policy toward Israel, but France was trying to influence the West European countries to adopt a pro-Arab stance because of her own interests in the Arab world, particularly Syria and Iraq.

Dayan wanted to know why Schmidt had been putting off a standing invitation to visit Israel. The chancellor did not answer directly but implied that he feared a personal confrontation with Prime

Minister Menachem Begin. "I don't believe he would be too happy if I would come on a formal state visit to Israel," he said sarcastically. He left the invitation open for an appropriate occasion, without indicating when that might be.

Schmidt made an effort to convince Dayan that today's Germany was different from the one of the past. Part of the world still persisted in relating Germany to the Hitler era. He asked that Israel join those who recognize the new reality and view Germany not only as an important economic power in Europe but as a free and democratic society that had gained a respected place in the free world.

As we left the meeting, Dayan whispered in my ear his response to Chancellor Schmidt's request: "By your deeds shall you be known."

34

WITH THE SHAH IN TEHERAN

U pon our return from Germany we began to prepare for the Egyptian-Israeli Political Committee, which was to meet in Jerusalem in January 1978, with American participation. Meanwhile Dayan had accepted an invitation from the Shah to visit Teheran on December 27, 1977. Dayan and Menachem Begin had spent the two preceding days in Ismailia, on a reciprocal visit to Sadat. These two non-Christian leaders – Begin, a Jew speaking for the Jewish people; and Sadat, a Moslem speaking for the Egyptians – spent Christmas together. We had high hopes for the Ismailia meeting. Regrettably, there was no chemistry between them. We feared that our entire peace structure was about to collapse. Dayan was downcast when he emerged from the room where Begin and Sadat were now meeting alone. The only one radiating good spirits and optimism was Ezer Weizman. He spoke words of encouragement, resorting to Yiddish: *"Kinderlach* (children), don't despair. Things will work out very well." I asked Moshe on what Ezer based this optimism. "Ask him," said Dayan, shrugging his shoulders. "He has an answer for everything and every situation."

Within two hours of our return from Ismailia, on December 26, we were driven in unmarked cars to a remote runway of Ben-Gurion Airport to board an unmarked Israel Air Force Boeing 707. Dayan's small delegation included David Kimche, one of the leaders in the Mossad and later director general of the Foreign Ministry, Eli Rubinstein, and myself. We landed on a side runway at the Teheran Airport in darkness, and were whisked away with no welcoming ceremony to one of the Shah's palaces.

There was absolutely no traffic on the road from the airport to the city. Only when we approached the entrance to Teheran did we see a few cars on the road. We encountered army and other security forces everywhere but very few pedestrians. The entrance to the palace garden at the outskirts of the city was imposing, as was the garden itself, covered with a beautiful spread of leaves fallen from the trees. However, the appearance of the palace was disappointing, falling far short of my expectations based on descriptions and stories I had heard about the splendor of the palaces of the Persian Shah.

We sat in deep leather armchairs in a hall, with walls and floor covered with turquoise-blue carpeting that featured the peacock as the central motif. Servants dressed in long gowns served us cups of black coffee, cookies, and wafers on the low tables next to our chairs. Then we were introduced to Muchamad Nassiri, strongman of the Iranian regime who controlled even the most sensitive matters. He was holding the hand of his six-year-old son, who accompanied him everywhere. Over seventy, Nassiri headed Iran's security services and concentrated great power in his hands. No senior army or security officer could approach the Shah except through Nassiri. The regime's opponents were terrified of him. Later, after the Shah was deposed by the Khomeini revolution, Nassiri was among its first victims. The revolutionaries singled him out for "special treatment." First they shot him, then they hanged him, and finally dumped his body into a pool.

Reuven Merchav, the Mossad representative, and Uri Lubrani, our ambassador to Iran, painted a bleak picture of the Shah's situation. Both agreed that his regime was nearing its end, and differed only in their assessment of the time that remained for him to rule. His popularity had eroded significantly, as had his support in military circles. In addition, his cancer had already left its mark, and he was slowly losing control of himself and his kingdom.

Nassiri updated Dayan on matters likely to be raised at the meeting with the Shah. He sat on a sofa facing us, holding his young son on his knee. The boy, born to Nassiri at an advanced age, was meant to be living proof of his virility; in actuality, the father projected an image of a man tending to senility, whose peak performance had long since passed. Dayan questioned him about events in Iran, about relations with Iraq and the oil-rich Gulf States, and the Iranian army's needs for weapons and equipment. Nassiri seemed indifferent, barely responding coherently. On the other hand, he wanted to know about Israel's activities in Africa and advised us to make concessions to Sadat in order to reach an agreement. This bit of advice was the only sober and lucid comment he made, something he carried over from a previous meeting on August 19, 1977, when Dayan had asked the Shah to intercede with Sadat regarding an Egyptian-Israeli dialogue.

When we were alone, Dayan remarked that the Shah was in deep trouble if his personal security and kingdom depended on Nassiri. Senior army officers and politicians had apparently tried to warn the Shah about what was going on behind his back, not only in Iraq and France, where Khomeini was spinning his web, but even in Teheran itself. The messages got only as far as Nassiri, who saw to it that they never reached the Shah, the ailing king who trusted him and viewed him as his main supporter.

Israel's interests in Iran were wide-ranging and varied. Iran was one of the most important customers for our export of agricultural and industrial products, and especially military equipment. The growing cancer that had begun to threaten the Shah's regime sent strong warning signals that caused deep concern in Israel. Dayan's extensive conversations with the Shah covered Sadat's visit to Jerusalem, the Ismailia discussions, and the possibilities resulting from these meetings. But the main topic dealt with the relationship and quality of trade between Israel and Iran. They had a joint security project, a mutual interest in strengthening and widening the relationship. However, given the prevailing circumstances in December 1977, Dayan would have been prepared to settle for securing a status quo. In the end, he negotiated an agreement of far-ranging importance with the Shah. On the Iranian side, this agreement was to be implemented by General Hasan Toufinian, deputy minister of defense, who was in charge of army security and military equipment purchases.

According to Toufinian, both Israel and Iran were threatened by the Scud missiles that the USSR was supplying to Iraq. The U.S. Lance missiles would have served as a partial answer by posing a counterthreat to the Scuds, but the Carter administration refused to supply Lance missiles to either Iran or Israel. Consequently, the Shah and Dayan negotiated an agreement for security cooperation, a project for the development of long-range, ground-to-ground missiles.

While Dayan was talking with the Shah, Eli and I went for a short tour of the city guided by Carol Merchav, Reuven's wife. Without warning, a speeding car burst out of a side street and struck our car, almost overturning the vehicle. Eli, sitting next to the driver, was thrown backwards and ended up with a whiplash that plagued him for many months. Carol, to my right, was thrown on top of me. Her fur coat stopped the glass shards that otherwise would have penetrated us. We both escaped unhurt. The car was badly damaged and the security service had to drive us back to the palace in a different car. Our vehicle had no special markings, but it must have been identifiable as belonging to the palace. The culprit disappeared right after the collision. Both our own and the local security details suspected that this had been a planned assassination attempt rather than an accident.

In the plane on our way home, we had the distinct feeling that the days of the Shah's reign were numbered. Some thought he might hang on for another two to three years. Others thought it was a matter of months or maybe even weeks until the collapse of his throne. I asked Dayan which of the kings in our region would survive. "Hussein," he answered emphatically.

Ben-Gurion defined a strategic outer circle around Israel, including Turkey to the north, Iran to the east, and Ethiopia to the south. Now we felt that this circle had been broken irreparably. Ethiopia was dominated by a Marxist dictator whose policy toward Israel could best be described as extortionist. He made endless demands on Israel in return for the right of Ethiopian Jews to emigrate to Israel and for an Israeli presence in the area. Turkey was drawing ever closer to the European Economic Community and, deterred by the threat from Syria, located between her and Israel, had ceased to play any regional role that could assist Israel. The regime of the Iranian Shah, east of Iraq, was on its way out as a partner of strategic importance, not to mention the loss of an important client for our military industries. These political realities sharpened the sense of urgency for us to reach an understanding with Egypt. It would be a welcome break in the hostile barrier of Arab states surrounding Israel. An accord with Egypt, the largest of these states, would be particularly advantageous in influencing other Arab states to follow suit.

The chance of reaching such an agreement with Egypt seemed slim in light of Sadat's insistence that we return all of Sinai, down to the very last inch. On most of Sinai, including the strategic strip along the Gulf of Eilat, there was a reluctant readiness to concede territory for the sake of an agreement, but not on giving up the Rafiah Salient area, a prosperous, thriving area with fourteen agricultural settlements and the city of Yamit in its midst. (See map.) These settlers had come at the invitation of Golda Meir's government, according to a plan which had national approval. Israel saw the Rafiah Salient as a security belt facing the major approach from Sinai to Israel, and viewed these settlements as important for its vital security needs. This had been assumed to be obvious, regardless of any possible future agreement with Egypt.

The settlers formed a strong and forceful lobby, supported by wide circles of those who firmly opposed uprooting settlements for any reason. They suspected the government might make extensive concessions in the framework of a peace agreement. At the prime minister's request, Dayan and Sharon, minister of agriculture, visited Moshav Sadot in the Rafiah Salient. The representatives of the northern Sinai settlements were firmly opposed to any dialogue with Egypt that considered concession of their land. Among those present were representatives of the Labor Party's settlement organizations who jointly presented a demand, almost an ultimatum, for the government to remove the fate of their lands and homes from the agenda with Egypt.

At a public meeting with hundreds of settlers, Dayan tried to defuse the situation. His words could be understood to imply that the settlements in the Rafiah Salient would not be uprooted. However, at a later meeting with thirty of the leaders in the clubhouse of the village of Sadot, he expressed the possibility that, under certain circumstances, Israel would be compelled to make concessions even at the expense of existing settlements.

Back in Jerusalem, Sharon advised Dayan to establish another ten settlements as quickly as possible to augment the Israeli presence. My impression was that Dayan basically accepted Sharon's recommendation. In a closed meeting of a few ministers, chaired by Begin, Sharon was given a green light to set up a dozen "tower-and-stockade" settlements similar to those erected during the days when the British mandatory authority was trying to prevent Jewish immigration and settlement.

Sunday morning, January 9, 1978, I came to Dayan's home, ready to accompany him on an official visit to Italy. Minutes later, Ezer Weizman and Ariel Sharon, accompanied by their aides and by Cabinet Secretary Arie Naor, arrived. Sharon spread out a map on the Persian rug and pointed out the sites, already marked on the map, for new settlements in the Rafiah Salient. In response to Dayan's question, he said that each community would contain a hut and a wooden tower topped by a barrel of water. Each site would be surrounded by a barbed-wire fence and would be equipped with tall antennas to create the impression of a populated settlement. Weizman commented, "Those are dummies. Nobody will take them seriously." Sharon ignored the comment and asked Naor to confirm the fact that creation of these settlements had already been decided upon.

Dayan asked Weizman whether there was a chance of reaching an understanding with General Gamasi, the Egyptian minister of defense, on an exchange of lands along the international frontier between Sinai and the Negev, as some members of the cabinet had suggested, in order to allow the Rafiah settlements to remain. Weizman was not inclined to place any hopes on an Egyptian agreement to such an arrangement. Dayan conceded that it would be impossible to retain the Rafiah Salient within the framework of a full peace treaty, "The Egyptians will not concede, so there's nothing to be done about it."

This early morning discussion was inconclusive, and a number of settlements were erected in the Salient. Ultimately they were dismantled and evacuated together with the fourteen actual settlements that had been thriving sources of livelihood for hundreds of families, along with the town of Yamit, which was leveled to the ground.

On the way to Rome, Dayan was morose. He came from a farming background and sympathized deeply with the Rafiah settlers' ties to their farmlands and homes, which they had built with the hard labor of their own hands. Now they were being asked to allow themselves to be uprooted, relocated, to start all over again from the beginning. Sitting next to me on the plane, Moshe empathized, "It breaks my heart, but what can we do? We cannot just give up on peace." His mood remained somber throughout our visit to Rome and during his talks with the Italian prime minister and foreign minister.

For security reasons, our motorcade was driven into Vatican City by a roundabout route to avoid the crowds in St. Peter's Square. We were met at the entrance to the library building by the Vatican foreign minister, Monsignor Cassarolli. He took us into the library to view the collection of handwritten ancient Bibles, some in Hebrew, others in different languages. We also saw some of the earliest printed editions of the Bible, some with beautifully illustrated manuscripts. Then, accompanied by the Swiss honor guards in their colorful uniforms and carrying decorated javelins and flags with the special Vatican Guard insignia, we walked down long corridors to the pope's reception room. Pope Paulus VI came out, shook hands with each of us, and invited us to an audience in his office.

In the talks with the pope, Dayan avoided the subject of peace and its price. With the pope he spoke of the place of Jerusalem in the consciousness of the Jewish people as the capital city and seat of its government for a thousand years, starting from the time of King David, three thousand years back. In contrast, Jerusalem had a purely religious status among the Christians, who came to Jerusalem one thousand years later; and for the Moslems, who came to Jerusalem seventeen hundred years after the time of King David. It was a courtesy visit, with no expectations that the Vatican would change its attitude regarding Jerusalem.

Even on the Capaucci matter Dayan's comment to the pope received no response. Bishop Capaucci, of Arab origin, had been sentenced to a prison term in Israel for having used his position to smuggle weapons into Israel in his car and handing them over to Arab terrorists. In response to Vatican pressure, Israel released Capaucci on condition that he would not engage in any political actions against Israel. Nevertheless, said Dayan, Capaucci was continuing his political activities in violation of the agreement. He received no comment from the Vatican.

From Rome we flew in an Italian air force plane to Sicily, and from there in a helicopter to one of the most spectacularly beautiful places in all of Italy, the remains of the city of Agrigento in Sicily. Here Dayan regained his good spirits. We strolled through the relics of magnificent palaces of the Hellenic-Roman culture from the fifth century B.C.E. enchanted by the exquisite treasures, statues, mosaic floors, and marble pillars. Dayan searched for, and found in the local museum, beautifully hand-fashioned earthenware, from two-and-one-half millenia ago. The scene in the Valley of the Temples is breathtaking. There are six temples in all, some in ruins, others intact. The Concord Temple towers over the others and offers a magnificent view in all directions all the way to the horizon.

The many hours we walked in this charming place brought us back to the period of the great Roman Empire. The relics bear witness to its magnificent past. This was the empire that had, in those days, overcome the Israel we now sought to rebuild. While still roaming in the Valley of the Temples, Dayan observed, "These temples to Concord, Juno, Jupiter, and Castor displayed here do not afford me the same enthusiasm and pleasure that I feel at finding a Canaanite pot or a ruined Nabatean building in our own country."

By the time we returned to Jerusalem, we were prepared for the Egyptian-Israeli Political Committee discussions, headed by Dayan, scheduled to begin on January 17. The Military Committee, chaired by Ezer Weizman, would be meeting at the same time in Cairo. Weizman's Egyptian counterpart was General Gamasi, commander of their army during the Yom Kippur War and the current defense minister. The head of the Egyptian delegation to the Political Committee was their new foreign minister, Kamal Ibrahim, who had been ambassador to Bonn. His predecessor, Foreign Minister Ismail Fahmi, had resigned in protest against Sadat's visit to Jerusalem. Among the colleagues of the newly appointed Kamal were two outstanding and influential men: Boutros Ghali, minister of state for foreign affairs; and Osama el-Baz, trusted aide of future president Hosni Mubarak.

Both, the American delegation headed by Secretary of State Cyrus Vance, and the Egyptian delegation headed by Foreign Minister Kamal, arrived on January 16, one day before the scheduled opening. Dayan used the day to warm the atmosphere between the delegations. The Israeli leaders held detailed discussions with the United States delegation, since both were interested in assuring progress in the talks and avoiding diplomatic land mines that could stymie this opportunity, even before the talks got under way.

That day Dayan hosted the Egyptians for lunch in Shaul Eisenberg's suite at the Plaza Hotel in Jerusalem. He was masterful at creating a pleasant and friendly atmosphere, so much so that his guests watched him in wonder and admiration. To them he was still the war hero who had beaten them on the battlefield. Yet here he was, entertaining them with his folk wisdom in English spiced with Arabic. My neighbor at the table, a pleasant and friendly Egyptian who introduced himself as Amru Mussa, later the foreign minister of Egypt, said, pointing to Dayan, "He is wise and charming. With him we could make a deal."

On the first evening following the formal discussions, Menachem Begin hosted the three delegations at a festive dinner. Welcoming the two foreign heads of the delegations of the U.S. and Egypt, the prime minister referred to the Egyptian foreign minister as "my young friend." The Egyptian delegation was aghast at this "affront." They saw this reference to the relative youth of the head of their delegation as degrading and insulting. On my way down from the twenty-first floor in the hotel elevator, I overheard two Egyptian security men mentioning Ben-Gurion. I could not understand why the Old Man should be of any interest to them, until a companion who could follow the Arabic said they were talking about going to Ben-Gurion Airport to prepare for departure. In the lobby the correspondents were already spreading a rumor that the Egyptians were leaving that very night. Among other reasons given for their sudden departure was the allegation that the prime minister had insulted the foreign minister of Egypt. We attempted to clarify the situation with the Egyptians and were informed that they had indeed considered returning home that night, but were ordered by Cairo to remain.

The session of the political committee convened at the round table in the Hilton Hotel. One seat remained empty, that of the Finnish General Ansio Siilasvuo, the UN truce supervisor for the region. Under orders from Secretary General Kurt Waldheim, the UN representative boycotted the first real peace conference between Egypt and Israel because the two sides were talking to each other directly, without the mediation of the United Nations. The Egyptian delegation sat to our left, the Americans to our right. General Siilasvuo's empty chair faced us, as a constant reminder of the UN reservations about any understanding reached between two adversaries without its help. The United States stepped into the role of mediator acceptable to both sides. However, on that historic first day, the American "broker" was unable to prevent a breakup of the discussions because of a fundamental disagreement between the Israelis and Egyptians on the items to be included in the agenda.

The Egyptians left Israel that same night, with the talks deadlocked. The Americans also decided to leave. We escorted the United States delegation to the plane at Ben-Gurion Airport and returned to Jerusalem in a state of dejection, feeling that we had missed a great opportunity. Dayan consoled us, "This peace is not going to run away from us, but it will take a great deal of strength and wisdom to hold on to it."

In Cairo, at the Military Committee session, matters were simpler. On the agenda were communication arrangements between the two countries, as a means of avoiding future misunderstandings between the armies. This debate was to lay the foundations for much wider dialogues in the future.

35

THE LONG ROAD TO PEACE

The premature and abrupt departure of the Egyptian delegation from the talks of the Political (Israeli-Egyptian-American) Committee on the morning of the opening of discussions, brought about a pall of depression in Israel. Many feared that this once-in-a-lifetime opportunity had been lost. Others thought it more likely that the Egyptian strategy was tactical, a deliberate display of anger to sway world opinion into blaming Israel for the breakdown of the talks and thereby pressuring her to soften her stance. Thus, upon resumption of negotiations, Israel's position would already have been undermined.

The Israeli position was a willingness to trade Sinai for peace, with minor border adjustments that would allow Israel to retain the Rafiah Salient in exchange for other equivalent parcels of land along the international border. Egypt demanded much more: (1) Israel must commit herself to implement UN Resolution 242, which required withdrawal not only from Sinai but also from the Golan, Judea (including East Jerusalem), Samaria, and Gaza to the pre-June 1967 armistice lines; (2) Israel must award local autonomy to the Palestinians in Judea, Samaria, and Gaza for an interim period of five years, after which they would be given the right of self-determination to establish their own entity, in effect a state of their own; (3) Israel must stop all settlement activities in the territories during the five-year interim period. Though this tough line was only the opening Egyptian position, it had clearly won almost complete U.S. support, as well as that of world public opinion. The fact that Sadat had taken the first step by his dramatic visit to Jerusalem was exploited by the Egyptian propaganda campaign to push Israel into a defensive position.

To avoid further damage to our image, we exercised restraint and moderation vis-à-vis the Egyptians in our response to the Israeli and foreign reporters who filled the Jerusalem hotels and mobbed our communications center. After the Egyptian departure, U.S. delegation spokesmen remained in Jerusalem and made it their business to criticize our position as negative, as sabotaging the peace efforts. Combating them was my toughest assignment.

The gap between Israel and Egypt was wide indeed. Nevertheless there was hope that the Egyptian position was really a "fig leaf" to cover their desire for agreement on the evacuation of Sinai, while paying lip service to a demand for resolution of the conflict with the Palestinians. An Arabist expert in the American delegation confided to me: "The Egyptians fear accusation by the Arab world that they are betraying the wider Arab interests and Palestinian rights. This is what impels them to extremist positions." He tried to convince me that we must find a Palestinian formula to give them that "fig leaf." I passed these comments on to Dayan, who responded only with a smile, giving me the impression that he shared that view and believed that ultimately the discussions would result in a separate treaty, which would obligate a future solution for the Palestinians.

To persuade the Egyptians to resume meetings with the Israelis and Americans required five exhausting months of separate talks in Jerusalem, Cairo, and Washington, including visits of the Israeli prime minister and foreign minister to the U.S., and of Vice President Walter Mondale and Secretary of State Cyrus Vance to Israel. Finally, a joint Egyptian-Israeli-American two-day meeting was arranged for July 17-18, 1978, at Leeds Castle in England. The site was remote, away from the media, in a tranquil atmosphere conducive to allowing each side to clarify its position. The Israeli delegation included: the delegation head, Foreign Minister Moshe Dayan; the legal adviser to the government, Professor Aharon Barak; the Israeli ambassador to the U.S., Simcha Dinitz; the legal adviser to the foreign office, Meir Rosenne; bureau chief of the foreign minister, Eli Rubinstein; adviser and spokesman for the Foreign Ministry, Naphtali Lavie.

The six-man Egyptian delegation was headed by Foreign Minister Ibrahim Kamal; the ten-man U.S. delegation by Secretary of State Cyrus Vance.

In this beautiful old castle we felt protected and secure, surrounded by a water-filled, high-walled moat with a sparkling lake mirroring a group of swans swimming gracefully. The atmosphere was like that of a seminar held in comfortable and congenial surroundings. Each delegation was housed in a different wing of the castle. Dayan, accompanied by Rachel, was given a royal apartment with a huge four-poster bed. He asked for a more modest room with a regular bed, but our hosts were unable to comply. Eli and I were put in a room with two large beds buried under a pile of enormous square pillows and feather quilts. There was no bathroom. Putting his detective instincts to work, Eli found a large unfurnished room behind the straw door of a wardrobe. I inspected his find and noticed a latticework screen which surrounded an armchair standing on the highly polished parquet floor. It stood with a certain majesty in the corner of this room, empty except for wall bookcases. It seemed mysterious until we discovered a well-hidden lavatory bowl underneath the armchair. A long iron rod with a wooden handle protruded from the floor like the manual shift of a car. It turned out to be the toilet flush. The rumors of this indoor toilet spread, and within minutes the members of all the delegations gathered around our find. We asked for a volunteer to try out this unique service but no one accepted the challenge. After the crowd dispersed, the two of us tried out the "throne." It worked quite adequately.

After I had settled into my room, I went out to explore the extensive green grounds around the castle. The pastoral atmosphere was so soothing that it was easy to forget the decisive mission that had brought us here. It was not the first time that I felt myself at the center of history-making drama. In complete contrast to these tranquil surroundings, I remembered the experiences of the Yom Kippur War five years earlier, when I had witnessed the heartrending scenes of young men at the peak of their vitality being killed, one after another, in a desperate struggle to save our homeland. Now I was to sit face-to-face with emissaries of the enemy who had plunged us into that war. I felt the wings of history lifting me and I prayed in my heart that we would emerge from this encounter with results that would abolish further bloodshed on both sides.

On the eve of the first session, the U.S. secretary of state hosted a dinner for the delegations. We sat on richly-embroidered tapestry chairs around a mahogany dining table: ten Americans, six Israelis, and six Egyptians seated at random. The table was laid with Royal Crown Derby china, silver cutlery, and crystal stemware for wines and drinks. The decor lent a festive air that, for the moment, pushed the fateful discussions into the background.

Enjoying the regal setting, I was totally unprepared for the minor challenge that suddenly confronted me. The headwaiter came up and in an apologetic whisper asked me to follow him into the kitchen. Our American hosts had relied on English logistics, and the British in turn had felt compelled to ask the advice of our London embassy regarding kosher food for the three of us who required it: Eli Rubinstein, Meir Rosenne, and I. The Israeli embassy had consulted the chief rabbinate, which recommended a London Jewish restaurant famous both for the quality of its kosher food and for its steep prices. After thorough security checks, the restaurant was allowed to bring in the van with food and workers, including a kashrut supervisor, into the castle courtyard. The restaurant owners had widely advertised their role in "Operation Leeds Castle," but had neglected to supply the necessary kosher carving utensils.

With great embarrassment the headwaiter led me to a huge fowl lying on a wooden tray, intact except for superficial cuts and scars. The cooks had labored for some time to carve the bird using small plastic disposable knives, and succeeded only in breaking the plastic blades in the bird's flesh. In a state of complete frustration, the headwaiter called on me for help. I tried my luck and broke another four plastic knives. I was about to suggest that he call in Cyrus Vance, our host, whose job it was to solve all problems during our stay in Leeds Castle, when someone found a brand-new metal carving knife. I returned to find that my elegant plates, crystal, and silverware had vanished. A waiter approached me and, with an air of embarrassment, apologized for not having found a suitable quantity of kosher crystal, china, and silver. I had to make do with plasticware. I was a bit peeved about the restaurant's failure to rise to the occasion and meet the royal standard of this castle.

Immediately after dinner we had a chance to get acquainted more casually, strolling through the castle galleries and gardens. I struck up a friendly conversation with one of our counterparts, when we were interrupted by a footman in full regalia, who handed me a brown envelope. Not expecting to receive any communications in this remote location, I was surprised to read that some four hundred correspondents were waiting at a cinema hall in a nearby town, designated for a briefing on the conference. The note was from an old friend, Barbara Walters. Back in 1971 I had invited her to visit Israel, where she formed a firm friendship with Moshe and Rachel Dayan. Now she was here to cover the story for NBC. I sent my sincere apologies, pointing out that such a briefing would be a serious infraction of the rules we all had accepted.

The following morning formal discussions were opened under the chairmanship of Cyrus Vance, who was to provide impetus for getting us back on the long road to peace. Already during the first hour of discussions it became clear that we were still on the same treadmill, walking but making no progress. The Egyptians persisted in the position they had presented in Jerusalem. The only change was that they now raised another demand. They were no longer content with a freeze on new settlements, but called for the removal of all the existing settlements in the territories. Their most vigorous spokesmen were Osama el-Baz and Boutros Ghali, whose opening statements were highly aggressive. At times it seemed as though these negotiations were not between Israel and Egypt, but rather between Israel and the entire Arab world, especially the Palestinians.

The Egyptians kept reiterating the same demands, and Dayan finally asked whether they were prepared to discuss territorial compromise on the West Bank along the lines of the Allon Plan, or something similar. Ibrahim Kamal's response was that partition of the West Bank was unthinkable. Then Dayan asked directly whether they accept Israel's proposal for an accommodation with Egypt as we had presented it to them. If the Egyptian delegation was not prepared to discuss that, then Israel would view its proposal as withdrawn. The Egyptians had viewed Sinai as already in their pocket and clearly understood Dayan's tactic. To eliminate any doubt, Dayan rephrased his stand in sharper language, "Either we talk about peace, the future of Sinai, and the borders between us, or we drop the subject. Then we may talk all you wish about the Palestinian issue." The Egyptians were caught by surprise and uncertain as to how to deal with this ploy. They requested a recess for consultations. Vance looked at us with approval, signifying his appreciation of Dayan's move, in the hope that it would rescue the dialogue from deadlock.

In our own consultations Dayan said, "They won't give up the bird already in their hand" – an opinion we all shared. In about an hour, everyone returned to the conference table. The Egyptian foreign minister stated that his delegation was not authorized to respond to Dayan's question but preferred to continue the bilateral talks on Sinai along with a discussion of the Palestinian future. Dayan asked the chairman, Vance, for a ruling on the agenda. Vance promptly ruled that at this stage the debate would be on bilateral relations between Israel and Egypt, thus shelving the Palestinian issue.

On the second day, toward the scheduled end of the conference, a proposal was made to continue the discussions on board an American ship sailing the Mediterranean between Gaza and North Sinai or at the U.S. early warning station of Um Hashiba, the site of a forward IDF command post in Sinai during the Yom Kippur War. The secretary of state preferred Um Hashiba and promised to return to the Middle East within two weeks to carry on the discussions. In his opinion, the talks at the Leeds Castle conference had opened a positive channel for further negotiations. Dayan's initiative had cleverly funneled the discussion into a constructive direction, which justified holding the next stage of talks.

A consultation between the heads of the delegations resulted in a decision to brief the media. The improved atmosphere would be divulged but no details would be given. The Egyptian delegation was to be represented by Dr. Osama el-Baz; the American, by Hodding Carter, state department spokesman; and the Israeli, by me. The three of us sat in the car, ready to leave for the press briefing. As the driver turned the key in the ignition, el-Baz jumped out and pushed the spokesman for the Egyptian Foreign Ministry, Dr. Nabil, into the car in his place.

After waiting two days for something solid to report, the hundreds of journalists were starved for information. They wanted to know whether it had been a debate at a round table and whether the conference could be categorized as direct negotiation between the parties. The Egyptians tried to avoid that definition and contended that the discussions had been between each party and the United States delegation. When pressed, their spokesman repeatedly sidestepped the issue and refused to answer directly. When the question was put to me, I simply described the seating arrangements during the discussions, at meals, and in the lounges of the castle, leaving little doubt about the direct nature of the talks. When Nabil tried to correct the impression by explaining that these were only the social events, the correspondents chuckled.

An internal consultation of our own confirmed the general impression that this conference had broken through the Egyptian barrier against a separate agreement. The optimists thought they could see the light at the end of the tunnel. Actually, it would take another seven months to get the signature on a peace treaty in a Washington ceremony. It would involve two Camp David conferences, a four-week marathon at Blair House in Washington, and a lightning-speed visit by President Carter to Jerusalem and Cairo.

Dayan had taken another initiative at Leeds Castle that almost caused his dismissal from the government. When the discussions ran aground, he asked Vance for a personal meeting, taking along Professor Aharon Barak, legal adviser to the government. Dayan handed Vance a memorandum, which outlined his own personal position on three major issues: (1) Israel rejects a peace proposal based on withdrawal to the pre-June 1967 frontiers; (2) Israel will be prepared to discuss territorial compromise provided that a concrete proposal is submitted; and (3) if the other party will accept the Israeli peace proposal, then we will be prepared to discuss, after five years of autonomy, the question of sovereignty or permanent status of the territories.

When Dayan read us this memorandum from his scribbled notes, we feared that its publication would cause a rift in the coalition government and that the prime minister would be unable to accept it. Simply put, Dayan's memorandum went beyond the willingness of any Israeli government for a territorial compromise, in that it indicated a readiness to discuss here and now the nature of that future compromise. This was a position vigorously rejected by the government's central component, Menachem Begin's own Likud Party.

Upon our return home, Dayan went to Begin to report on the Leeds talks, including the personal memorandum that he had given to Vance. On the way to the prime minister's office he said, "This may well be my last act as foreign minister, for Begin will not be able to come to terms with my readiness to discuss territorial compromise now." Begin did indeed display displeasure. Dayan remarked that if a prime minister was not prepared to grant his foreign minister freedom to express a personal view during negotiations, then he should replace him. I accompanied Dayan to the subsequent cabinet session, assuming that this would be his last day as foreign minister. I was even more astonished than Dayan when Begin presented a report on the Leeds discussions which included Dayan's memorandum to Vance, and proposed to submit it for the approval of the Knesset. A number of prominent Likud cabinet members and MKs were furious at the prime minister's change of position and support for Dayan's memorandum. In a television appearance, Transport Minister Chaim Landau, Begin's right-hand man since the time of the underground struggle before independence, expressed bitter opposition to this shift in policy. The prime minister was disturbed by his comrades' dissension, but remained steadfast in support of Dayan.

Over coffee in the Knesset cafeteria during a break in the discussion, Dayan told me that he now felt secure in his stand, since this incident proved to him that Begin sincerely wanted to achieve peace. He claimed that, "If Begin were not truly interested in peace, he would have rejected my memorandum." Dayan felt that the handcuffs had been removed from his wrists and he began to show much more initiative in advancing the talks. He relied on Ambassador Sam Lewis as a go-between with Washington in a monumental effort to pull the wagon of peace out of the rut. In that role, Lewis was a daily and sometimes twice-daily visitor to Dayan's offices in Tel Aviv or Jerusalem and to his home.

Cyrus Vance arrived on August 6 to continue the momentum generated three weeks earlier in Leeds Castle. In his meetings with Dayan he found abundant ground to develop practical ideas, and returned to the United States with a message of his own to the president, urging him to increase his efforts to advance peace. Armed with an Israeli position that seemed reasonable to Washington, and which he estimated would be acceptable to Cairo as well, Carter invited Sadat and Begin to an open-ended summit conference at Camp David on September 5.

The format of the Camp David discussions was set by Carter himself. To assure that there would be a total media blackout, he asked both sides not to bring their spokesmen. Prior to leaving for Washington with Menachem Begin and Ezer Weizman, Dayan said he agreed to the request, and suggested that I come under a different title. I rejected the idea, concerned that, should there be a leak to the press, some parties might view me as an underground spokesman and the guilty party.

Carter used a steamroller on both parties. He hinted and sometimes openly threatened that if Begin showed no flexibility there would be a rift in U.S.-Israeli relations. A number of times the summit verged on disaster, and each time the delegates began to pack their bags. Finally, on September 17, after thirteen days of marathon debates in which Carter displayed admirable determination and dedication, the parties signed an agreement that laid the foundation for a historic turning point in relations between Israel and the Arab countries. It was an agreement that would become, within six months, a peace treaty between Israel and Egypt, the largest of our Arab neighbors.

Sadat had to abandon his stubborn stance over Israeli withdrawal to the 1949 lines, which included withdrawal from East Jerusalem, and the creation of a Palestinian entity in the territories. Similarly, Begin had to make peace with the concept that settlements in Sinai would be evacuated and dismantled, and the Sinai Peninsula would be handed over to the Egyptians in return for a peace treaty and normalization of relations. The redeeming formula that extricated the Camp David talks from crisis was full autonomy, which Begin agreed to grant the inhabitants of the West Bank and Gaza for an interim period of five years, after which the ultimate status of the territories would be resolved.

One last-minute crisis that almost stymied the agreement was over a letter that President Carter had sent to Sadat. After assuring Begin in the early morning hours that the United States rejected partition of Jerusalem, Carter that same day handed Sadat a letter that determined that East Jerusalem, in American eyes, was conquered territory, thus upholding the Arab view that East Jerusalem must be evacuated. When our delegation found out about Carter's letter, tempers rose. A letter was delivered to the president informing him that, under these conditions, Israel could not be a party to the agreement.

The president refused to retract his letter to Sadat, but finally relented and accepted a formula offered by Professor Barak. This formula enabled Carter to respond to letters from Sadat and Begin in which each presented his own view relating to Jerusalem. Carter's identical response to them was in very general and noncommittal terms, mentioning the U.S. position as expressed in the UN speeches of Ambassadors Arthur Goldberg and Charles Yost. This was the last obstacle to a positive conclusion of the summit.

The hardest part in finalizing the treaty was to commence one month later at Blair House and the Madison Hotel. It took a six-week dialogue to formulate the version of the peace treaty which would be signed at the end of March 1979, and then only after concerted efforts to move the parties from their entrenched positions. At the end of the Camp David summit, President Carter sent congratulatory letters to Sadat and Begin and suggested that the practical discussions of a peace treaty based on the principles of the Camp David "Accords" should begin on October 12 at Blair House in Washington. This was the day after Yom Kippur. We had to arrive two days earlier and observe the fast in the Madison Hotel, a forty-minute walk from the nearest synagogue.

On Tuesday morning, October 10, we arrived in Washington from New York, where Dayan had addressed the UN General Assembly and met foreign ministers and the UN secretary general. Upon arrival in Washington, Dayan was invited for a talk with President Carter and his senior aides, which lasted almost until the beginning of the Yom Kippur fast. We barely managed to gulp down a couple of bites of the prefast meal and rushed by car to the *Kol Nidrei* service at the Kesher Yisrael Synagogue in Georgetown.

This relatively small synagogue was filled almost beyond capacity – not only by the regular worshipers, but by numerous journalists who had gathered there. Dayan again asked me to sit next to him to help him find the appropriate prayers in the book. When he saw me removing my shoes, he followed suit. Ezer Weizman, knowing nothing about this custom, was amused and teased us about it. When he was honored by an invitation to open the Holy Ark for one of the prayers, he was about to ascend the steps with his shoes on. The beadle politely asked him to remove them. Ezer declined and had to return to his seat. When Dayan was so honored, he passed inspection but was unsure of what he was supposed to do. I accompanied him to the Ark, helped him slide open the velvet curtain and open the doors of the Ark, revealing the scrolls of the Torah. At the conclusion of the particular prayer, he confidently closed the doors and curtain of the Ark, and returned to his seat. At the end of the service, Rabbi Philip Rabinowitz rose to bless the important visitors from Israel and wished them success in their endeavor to bring peace to the Jewish people and their land. The congregation was visibly moved; so were we Israeli guests. When we came outside, we saw the procession of black limousines waiting as usual, surrounded by cars of the security details. At the open door of the Dayan limousine, I gave him the traditional wish for a *gemar hatima tova* (may you be sealed in the Book of Life) and an easy fast. We were still shaking hands when he said with a smile, "Yom Kippur obligates me too," and joined us in the long walk to the hotel, with the convoy of limousines and police escorting us at our pace.

Many correspondents, including familiar faces, were waiting for us in the hotel lobby. Dayan proceeded immediately to his room, where Boutros Ghali was waiting for a personal chat with him. I stayed below with the reporters, among them: Ted Koppel, Marvin Kalb, Diane Sawyer, and Bernard Gverzman. One reporter told me a "secret" from an Egyptian source, stating that no peace treaty with Israel would be signed without our giving autonomy to the Palestinians, as agreed at Camp David. I was aware of the psychological tug-of-war going on in the Blair House discussions, although it was hard to tell whether it was of Egyptian or American origin. I soon realized that within the next few days I would have to deal with a barrage of rumors meant to embarrass us or to provoke us into imprudent action. The Yom Kippur fast enabled me to decline unwanted invitations for a drink with correspondents. I walked upstairs to my room, slept until morning, and then walked back to the synagogue, where I stayed all day.

The following morning, we arrived at the White House for the official opening of the peace talks. The Egyptian delegation was headed by Defense Minister Kamal Hassan Ali, who would later become prime minister. The others on his team were already old acquaintances, the most prominent being Osama el-Baz and Boutros Ghali. Our delegation, led by Foreign Minister Moshe Dayan and Defense Minister Ezer Weizman, included Dr. Meir Rosenne, Ambassador Simcha Dinitz, Chargé d'Affaires Chanan Bar-On, Major General Avraham

Tamir; the prime minister's military secretary, Brigadier General Ephraim Poran; Ezer's military secretary, Colonel Ilan Tehila; Eli Rubinstein; and myself. We were joined later by Professor Barak. President Carter welcomed us with a short speech full of hope for a successful conclusion of the talks, for which the Americans had allotted two to three weeks.

After the responses of the two delegation heads, we walked across the street to our first session at Blair House. Cyrus Vance, the chairman, opened with an announcement that the United States delegation would be holding separate talks during the day with each delegation in order to ascertain the nature of their proposals. The plenary session of all three delegations would convene at the end of the day. We already had a draft of an American peace proposal, largely based on ideas previously presented by Israel and Egypt. Both delegations agreed that the U.S. proposal could serve as a basis for discussion, although each reserved the right to make amendments.

Late that night, I was invited for a drink by a friend who was the political commentator of an important American daily. Knowing of his access to good sources in the State Department and White House, I was curious to hear his assessment of the Blair House talks. He confirmed some items I had heard from members of the U.S. delegation, which made it clear that the American position had shifted toward the Egyptian side. Their justification was that Egypt must be bolstered in the Arab world in the face of the isolation imposed upon her by the other Arab states. Among other things, my friend told me of an imminent trip to Jordan by Assistant Secretary of State Harold Saunders, to answer the king's questions put publicly to President Carter. My friend also knew the gist of the American answers, which, he surmised, would cause Israel some anxiety. This was a clear deviation from the official American position promised us in the past on a number of controversial issues.

Dayan was furious when I told him of my conversation with that particular friend, whom he knew to be highly reliable. Our hosts had told us nothing about their plans to send a high-level envoy to Amman to respond to Hussein's questions broadcast on NBC. When I told Dayan some of the American answers, he became even angrier. There was a definite shift toward Arab demands on such sensitive issues as the status of East Jerusalem as "captured territory," the temporary nature of Jewish settlements on the West Bank, and the deployment of the IDF in limited sites agreed upon by all sides.

Although he knew and trusted the source of my information, Dayan found it difficult to believe that the Americans would go so far in their attempt to court Hussein. He did not believe that the king would join the talks. Sadat had confirmed this in a Camp David discussion when he described his own appeal to Hussein to join in the negotiations. Nevertheless, the Americans had decided to appease Hussein despite the promises they had given to Israel and despite the bitter reaction this would elicit.

Two days later Harold Saunders asked to meet Dayan and told him about his forthcoming flight to Jordan. Dayan voiced his opinion in sharp words to Saunders and Alfred Atherton, who was chairing the Blair House talks during Vance's absence in South Africa. They both sought to convince us that, with the Baghdad conference due to convene on November 1 to declare a general boycott of Egypt, the United States wanted to pull Hussein to our side in order to weaken the unity of the rejectionist front in the Arab world. Nothing they said changed Dayan's firm opposition to their plan. In the end, Saunders went to Jordan and returned empty-handed, as Dayan had predicted.

The talks at the Blair House conference, and more important unofficial communications between the three delegations, were marked by ups and downs according to the participants' moods. The crises that arose were defused in various ways. In some instances, the delegation heads initiated discussions with the president to find a way out. Carter often displayed hostility to our demands and expressed himself with such crudity that even his aides were shocked. During another crisis, Dayan asked for a recess so that he could go to Jerusalem to report to the cabinet and get decisions on further procedures. On yet another occasion, Ezer Weizman flew to Jerusalem to calm the ministers who were critical of the delegation at Blair House, claiming, "They're giving everything away in a clearance sale."

On the days that Dayan and Weizman were both in Israel and the pressure of work was substantially reduced, we were able to take in a little of the beauty of Washington in autumn, with the trees changing color and the golden leaves on the ground heralding the coming of winter. One evening we decided to see an Agatha Christie mystery movie being screened at a nearby cinema. We invited some of our friends in the Egyptian delegation to join us. Eight of us, Israelis and Egyptians of the rival delegations, sat together watching *Death on the Nile*. Our Egyptian colleagues volunteered interesting details about the sights on the screen. We ended up with a friendly get-together, as if peace were already an established fact.

At the hotel, after midnight, a pleasant surprise awaited me. As I entered the lobby, a man in his sixties rushed over and fell on me with hugs and kisses, as did his wife. "I saw you today on television and recognized you immediately. You have traveled a long way since I carried you like a dead weight on my back. Luckily for me, then you weighed only 85 pounds," he said. It was only when I heard his voice that I identified Leon Reichman, with whom I had shared a few stations on our odyssey through the Nazi concentration camps. Leon had emigrated to the U.S. immediately after liberation and settled in Washington, where he opened a wholesale liquor business. When he learned that I was in Washington as a member of the Israeli delegation, he rushed to the hotel, waiting four hours. He could not overcome his emotion at seeing me, the former *musselman*, participating in one of the most crucial developments in the history of the Jewish people.

The Israeli government had convened a number of times while Dayan and Weizman were in Israel. The cabinet decided to discontinue the settlement freeze in the territories at the end of the three-month period specified in the Camp David Accords of September 17. This was in reaction to the U.S. response to Hussein in which the president had ruled that the settlements were temporary and could be dismantled. When the cabinet decision was made public, I was again swamped with correspondents' questions. From their wording, it was clear that they had been carefully coached, and I had no doubt about the identity of the "coachers" in the State Department and the National Security Council in the White House. Both of those institutions were seething over the news that the freeze would end in mid-December. Numerous times a day I was compelled to respond, usually off the record but sometimes even for citation, in order to block the propaganda campaign waged against us.

On October 27, after a five-day recess, Dayan and Weizman returned from Israel, and the talks of the full delegations resumed. After some slight amendments, the Israeli cabinet approved by a large majority the seventh draft of a peace treaty written at Blair House. The

Americans were satisfied with the results of the mission, although they did not conceal the president's anger over the decision to end the freeze on settlements.

Barak and Rosenne worked on the legal draft of the treaty. At a critical stage they consulted the leading American international lawyers - Professors Eugene Rostow, Myres Smith McDougall, and Leon Lipson - and received full support for the Israeli position. When Carter heard about the support from American legal experts, he was furious. In an angry outburst, he suggested sarcastically that we turn the whole negotiation over to lawyers. Nevertheless, he respected the expertise of our lawyers, Barak and Rosenne, who were the ones who would contend with both the American and Egyptian attorneys on every detail in the agreement.

There still remained two obstacles. One was the existing Egyptian commitment in five mutual defense pacts with Arab countries hostile to Israel. We demanded that our peace treaty, when signed, should take precedence over Egypt's prior obligations in those pacts. The second obstacle was an Egyptian demand for linkage between implementation of the treaty and of Palestinian autonomy. The prime minister and other ministers were adamant in their opposition to such linkage at any price. Since both Jordan and the Palestinians had rejected the idea in principle and were unwilling to join the talks, it was unreasonable to link the validity of the peace treaty to the implementation of Palestinian autonomy. A series of clashes kept erupting among the delegations in their attempt to get around these obstacles. At one point the Egyptians even cut off contacts for two days, until Dayan took the initiative and invited the head of their delegation to his room.

Although we wanted to respond favorably to the positive turning point marked by Sadat's visit to Jerusalem, and made great efforts to bridge the differences between us, I still doubted the sincerity of the Egyptian intentions to come to terms with our existence and see us as a part of the Middle East. The embers of mutual suspicion were still smoldering, making it difficult to overcome disagreements that now may seem trivial, but at that time appeared as unbridgeable chasms.

Doubts remained about a number of topics, including the following security arrangements: Guarantees in the event of withdrawal and redeployment of our forces; the quality of normalization of relations between us; the political status of the Palestinians who would be given autonomy; the source of their authority to govern themselves; cancellation of the Arab boycott; and the status of Jerusalem as a united city. Sometimes it seemed that these were all stage props that concealed the underlying structure within which the two entities must learn to live together. I tried, in vain, to get my Egyptian colleagues to come to terms with our existence. Despite my feeling that Egypt wanted to get back Sinai without making any prior commitment to good-neighbor relations, and despite her lip service to the Pan-Arab position (with an alleged Israeli promise of a Palestinian state), I still saw the treaty as vital for the future of Israel.

I was sure that if we could break through the official hostility barrier with the largest of the Arab states, the road would be paved to treaties with other countries who would, ex post facto, reconcile themselves to our existence in the region. My faith was shared by all the members of our delegation. It made us persevere without letup to achieve a joint peace. We knew that we would have to pay a heavy price: the evacuation and dismantling of the town of Yamit and the fourteen Rafiah settlements, as well as the relinquishment of control over the Straits of Tiran and the air bases in Sinai. These would arouse stormy reactions at home. However, this was a historic opportunity to establish peaceful relations with Egypt, the country that had spearheaded the Arab coalition in wars against us. Now we hoped Egypt would lead that same coalition of Arab states on the road to peace.

36

CARTER IN THE KNESSET

We spent four weeks at the Madison Hotel in Washington, drafting a peace treaty acceptable to both Israel and Egypt. Crises kept arising, and though many were solved, at the end of the month we were still far from the signing stage. The new obstacles were mostly due to new demands by the Egyptians, who lacked the confidence to sign a separate bilateral agreement with Israel. The Arabs had excommunicated Egypt on November 1 at the Baghdad conference. Now she was afraid of what might happen at the forthcoming Riyadh conference. To avoid even harsher rebuffs, Egypt wanted the treaty to include a firm Israeli commitment to activate Palestinian autonomy within a set period of time.

As Arab opposition intensified, Egypt took more extreme positions. The Americans displayed sympathy for the Egyptian demand for more concessions. Against this background of contention, we now faced an additional crisis with the United States, this time with the involvement of Prime Minister Begin. He was returning to Israel from Canada and stopped off in New York for our meeting with the U.S. delegation at the airport. The meeting ended inconclusively. Begin and his entourage continued on to Israel, and we returned to Washington to wind up the Blair House conference, and head for home.

Carter did not permit the stalemate to persist for long. Ten days after we returned to Israel and after government discussions about the remaining differences, the prime minister received two letters, one from Carter and one from Sadat. Both urged the renewal of negotiations between the three sides. In mid-December, Cyrus Vance came to the Middle East to visit Cairo and Jerusalem. Upon his return to

Washington, he accused Israel of putting a stumbling block in the negotiations. Carter scheduled a meeting for the end of December in Brussels, which was to include Vance, Dayan, and Egyptian Prime Minister Mustafa Halil.

Following the discussions in Brussels, Carter invited the parties to a closed debate at Camp David, chaired by Vance, with the full delegations headed by Halil and Dayan. On Tuesday evening, February 20, 1979, we arrived at Camp David to find twenty inches of snow blown into huge drifts by a bitter cold wind. Dayan, Eli, and I were installed in one of the familiar three-room birch cabins, which had to serve as bedroom, office, and discussion room. A member of the U.S. delegation, who never missed a session, told us with a smile, "This time you won't stay long. You'll be happy to get back to your Middle East climate." Indeed, after four days of pointless discussions with neither side budging an inch, we packed our bags and left for Jerusalem.

During those four days we felt we were just treading water, making no real progress in resolving our differences on the remaining issues. This was particularly true of clause six, which dealt with the abrogation of Egypt's obligations under the previous defense pacts signed with Arab countries still in a state of war with Israel. Despite the lack of diplomatic accord, there developed an almost friendly social relationship. We ate together and spent whatever free time we had together, hoping that our mutuality might pave the way for a signed treaty and a new era between the two countries.

The American hosts also contributed to the pleasant atmosphere. Mindful of the approach of the Sabbath, they drastically reduced the number of discussions. The only scheduled meeting was one between Dayan and Halil, later joined by Vance. On Friday night we celebrated with a Sabbath dinner prepared by a kosher restaurant in Baltimore. Dayan asked me to recite the *Kiddush,* and lead in the rituals pertaining to the Sabbath eve meal. Our delegates and team of assistants from the Washington embassy joined in singing the traditional Sabbath melodies, to the accompaniment of enthusiastic hand clapping by our American hosts. The Egyptians chose not to participate in our Sabbath eve meal.

As we were leaving Camp David on Sunday morning, February 25, the delegation heads were invited for a discussion with the president at the White House. In an hour-long conversation, Carter pressed Dayan and Halil to settle all remaining differences, emphasizing that they had shrunk almost to zero and that we could not allow this opportunity for peace to fade away. The president knew that Dayan did not have the authority to make such a commitment, that he had to bring any change to the prime minister, who in turn had to take it to the full cabinet for decision. Nevertheless, knowing that Moshe had considerable influence in Jerusalem, the president was determined to persuade Dayan to stress the positive aspects.

Failing to enlist Sadat's participation, the president invited Begin and Halil for a meeting in Washington. Begin was insulted by the invitation and did not reply. To break the impasse, Carter invited Begin and Halil to separate meetings, in the hope of concluding the process that he considered close to completion. Begin met Carter on March 5 and reached agreement on most of the subjects in dispute. But the Egyptians were not quite prepared to give their approval. Begin and Sadat invited Carter to the Middle East to conclude the final draft of the treaty, ready for signature. On March 8, Carter arrived in Cairo and met with Sadat. Two days later he came to Jerusalem.

On Saturday night, March 10, we waited at Ben-Gurion Airport to greet the president of the United States. The entire "Who's Who" of the Israeli establishment was there to welcome him, as it had been sixteen months earlier to greet the president of Egypt. The intense emotion of that earlier meeting was absent, but again there was a feeling of history in the making. There were some who had high hopes for the success of the visit, while others were suspicious and concerned about the price we would have to pay.

Begin drove off with President and Mrs. Carter for a private dinner. Dayan and Weizman hosted the secretaries of state and defense with their assistants at an informal meal at the King David Hotel, and I entertained members of the American entourage. They could tell me nothing new, but I sensed a certain uneasiness among them, which I attributed to reluctance in confronting Begin with a demand for further concessions to Sadat. It was not until the following morning, during formal discussions, that we learned what points still remained to be settled. We were told in stages. First there was a ministerial discussion between Dayan and Vance, followed by a plenary session of the delegations. Carter presented the conclusions he had reached with

Sadat and requested a positive Israeli response, which Sadat would endorse by coming to Jerusalem to sign the treaty. The president stressed that he had to relay Israel's response to Egypt. However, Begin did not share Carter's enthusiasm for the formula worked out with Sadat.

He pointed out that the government had already decided to approve the understandings reached in Washington. Now Carter wanted to make further changes, under pressure from Sadat, reneging on decisions already agreed upon and, what is more, officially approved by the government. Begin was quite outspoken in his criticism of the U.S. collusion with Egypt's maneuvers, and rejected the proposed amendments to clause six. Two other matters were still unresolved: an Egyptian demand to appoint liaison officers in Gaza, given that Gaza would be the first area to receive autonomy; and Egypt's refusal to sell directly to Israel oil from the Suez Gulf wells that Israel had drilled. Begin stated that he could not respond to the president's request until he first referred the matter to the cabinet.

In the cabinet session, which lasted into the early morning hours, and in the joint sessions with Carter and his entourage, substantive progress was made. A verbal compromise acceptable to Carter was found for the problematic clause six. However, there was no progress on the other two issues. The two delegations sat together through the early hours of Monday, breaking up only when the time came for the Knesset to convene. The Knesset session was to be addressed by President Carter, Prime Minister Begin, and the opposition leader, Shimon Peres. It was a stormy session, in which members from the extreme right persisted in heckling, particularly Carter and Peres, until the Speaker was compelled to have the hecklers expelled from the assembly.

The members of the two delegations sat in the cafeteria or wandered about in the corridors of the Knesset, convinced that the crisis had deteriorated even further. We were told by the Americans that Carter would be leaving the country the following morning. Clearly, if he did so without reaching an agreement, Israel would be accused of blocking the way to peace. Dayan and Vance found a quiet corner and spent a half hour trying to work out a formula on the remaining two points that would be acceptable to both sides. When

Vance left, Dayan and I drove back to the Plaza Hotel, where we were staying. He seemed absorbed, deeply introspective.

At 8:00 P.M., he summoned me from my hotel room. I found him immersed in a bath, still looking preoccupied. He said, "I want to go to the King David Hotel to speak to Vance, but I think I should first tell Begin about it. What do you think?" he asked, as if thinking aloud. Wrapped in a bathrobe, he phoned the prime minister to tell him of his idea. He also suggested that Justice Minister Shmuel Tamir accompany him. From Dayan's responses, it was clear that Begin rejected the idea of Tamir's presence. Dayan had wanted the justice minister along because Tamir had been his partner in drafting a solution to the oil issue, but Begin preferred to leave the negotiation in the hands of Dayan alone. I phoned the King David Hotel but could not get through to Vance, who was apparently in Carter's suite. I left an urgent message and within ten minutes he rang back. Dayan invited himself over for a talk, specifying that Begin was aware of what he intended to say. Dayan suggested that President Carter invite Begin for breakfast in his suite, with the hope that by then he and Vance would have agreed on a final text for signature.

We arrived at Vance's room on the sixth floor at 9:00 P.M. Since Dayan decided to hold the meeting in private, with no written record, I went down to the lobby, where I could sense the low mood of the delegation members. The correspondents in the president's entourage and the Israeli reporters were spreading rumors of the failure of the president's visit. I was hoping that the conversation now under way on the sixth floor would cut through the stalemate and transform failure into success.

On the way back to the Plaza, Dayan was in a good mood. For the first time in days I saw him smiling. "I hope we've found the highway. Tomorrow morning Carter will host Begin at breakfast. Vance wants both of us to take part. If everything goes as we just agreed, we will have a treaty," he said.

Two and one half years later, Moshe Dayan died of cancer. I was consul general of Israel in New York and held a memorial meeting on the thirtieth day after his death. Cyrus Vance was among the speakers and talked of Dayan's contribution to reaching a peace treaty. He defined Dayan as a man of vision and yet a pragmatist without whom there would have been no treaty between Israel and Egypt.

When we arrived at Ben-Gurion Airport the next day, the media did not yet know of our breakthrough. Hundreds of reporters and photographers crowded behind the police barriers, waiting for the moment when Begin would part from his guest, the president of the United States. Most of them predicted that Carter would slam the door and leave Begin fuming. Few were optimistic. Some of my acquaintances tried to get a hint of what had occurred in Vance's room the night before and at Carter's breakfast with Begin. My only response was a smile. Some of them took the hint and immediately reported to their radio and television networks that a positive turning point had been reached on the road to peace. Others stuck to their gloomy evaluations and continued to broadcast "news" of the breakdown of the talks and the failure of Carter's mission to the Middle East.

On his way to the United States, the president landed in Cairo. A discussion between Carter and Sadat was enough to tie up the last details of the treaty. From his plane, Carter phoned Begin in his office to inform him of Sadat's approval of the final Jerusalem text. At noon on that Tuesday, March 13, 1979, torrential rain poured down from the overcast Jerusalem skies, but we were oblivious to the weather. The clouds that had hovered over us for so many months were lifting, letting the sunlight through. True, alongside the hope for peace was the anguish of having to evacuate the homesteads in Sinai, particularly the town of Yamit. We knew the price was high, both for the country and especially for the settlers who had chosen to live there and now had to uproot all they had planted and built. Only time would tell whether this peace would justify their sacrifice.

On March 22 the Knesset approved the peace treaty in a long and volatile session. Originally the signing ceremony was to take place in Jerusalem and Cairo. But since Sadat would not come to Jerusalem, the event was set for March 26 on the White House lawn in Washington. Three days earlier Dayan had arrived in the U.S. capital, with Rosenne, Rubinstein, and me, to finalize the draft of the Memorandum of Understanding between Israel and the United States. This document, which was to be signed by Dayan and Vance (in the latter's office) after the signing of the treaty, committed America to support the implementation of the peace treaty, to take steps against violations, and to give Israel military and economic aid.

The impressive ceremony, with President Carter seated between Anwar Sadat and Menachem Begin, was extensively covered by the world media. American politicians and visitors from abroad mingled with members of the negotiating delegations seated across the table from the three leaders, who cooperated in playing to the cameras. They shook hands and embraced after signing the three bound copies of the agreement. We, the members of the delegations, congratulated one another in high hopes that this would be the start of a new era in the Middle East.

The four of us – Dayan, Rubinstein, Rosenne, and I – followed Vance to the State Department to his seventh-floor office, where he and Dayan signed the Memorandum of Understanding and its annexes. No reporters or photographers were present to record this procedure for posterity, the pivotal event without which the peace treaty could not have been signed. I had a tiny Minox camera in my pocket, and was able to catch the intimate and emotional moment for which we had labored for sixteen months and traveled over four continents – Asia, Africa, America, and Europe – seeking a path to peace. It took considerable effort and resolve during those sixteen months to overcome the thirty years of suspicion and hatred between our two countries and peoples.

To celebrate the signing of the treaty, President Carter hosted a festive banquet in the White House to honor Begin, Sadat, their wives, and members of the delegations. Hundreds of guests were invited: cabinet members, senators, representatives, diplomats, the Washington social elite, and leading figures from the media and entertainment world. The organizers made sure that the American guests were seated among members of the Israeli and Egyptian delegations. I was placed between Sadat's daughter and Walter Cronkite, fully aware that I was privileged to sit there because of Dayan's invitation in June 1977 to join him at the Israeli Foreign Ministry, recalling his words: "I see a reasonable chance that we can move the cart in the right direction and I'm sure that my being involved will contribute. We must not let this opportunity pass. As your friend, I wouldn't want you to miss this historic opportunity." Dayan's words echoed in my ears as I sat at a round table in the White House, celebrating the peace treaty between Israel and Egypt together with hundreds of guests. This was indeed a moment of deep satisfaction.

A few weeks after the festivities, the practical work of effectuating the relations between the two states was under way. Although the exchange of ambassadors had already been agreed upon, we had an embassy but no ambassador in Cairo. It was my honor to accompany the first designated ambassador, Yosef Hadas, as he raised the flag of Israel over the building and I nailed the first *mezuzah* (a tiny scroll excerpt from the Bible attached to the doorpost as a symbolic guard of the house) and recited the prayer: ". . .Who has kept us alive to see this day." A few Jewish tourists and the staff and families of the embassy stood there, wiping tears from their eyes, proud to share in this historic moment.

For me it was the first opportunity to roam the streets of Cairo with Yosef Hadas, fluent in Arabic, as my guide and translator. But my most fascinating tour came a month later, as a member of Moshe Dayan's entourage on his first official visit as guest of President Anwar Sadat. A guided tour of the Pyramids, the National Museum, the Great Mosque, and other sites was a unique experience for me. But above all, I looked at the crowds along our route cheering the famous visitor from Israel and crying "Long live Moshe Dayan." I would never have expected such an enthusiastic reception for Dayan even in an Israeli city. Here in Cairo the masses were jumping up and down in admiration and joy. Then, on an impulse, Dayan, unconcerned about security, decided to visit the famous Khan Khalil Market. His guards had great difficulty opening a path for us through the shops. Crowds gathered on the rooftops, in the alleyways, and even on the roofs of vehicles in order to catch a glimpse of the man who for years had symbolized the unvanquished enemy and now had come to speak of peace.

From Cairo we were flown to the Valley of the Kings, where we visited the tombs of the Pharaohs, the city of Luxor, and the ruined Temple of Karnak. Here, too, the crowds ran after our cavalcade shouting their welcome to the visitor from Israel.

Later I exchanged letters with Vance about the peace treaty. He wrote about that crucial Monday, March 12, 1979, describing how he had returned to the hotel after a long day of fruitless discussions and saw that all of our efforts had failed. Describing Dayan's role that fateful day, he wrote:

I returned to the hotel very depressed to tell President Carter that the negotiations had run aground and we had reached a stalemate. I told my wife that the situation seemed hopeless and that only a miracle could save the day. Unexpectedly, Dayan phoned and asked to see me. I was very happy and told him to come over immediately. We sat down for a discussion that was to most fateful of the entire negotiation. After a few hours we had the formula that would extricate us from the stalemate. Dayan raised reasonable suggestions for resolving the problem of Gaza first and the appointment of Egyptian liaison officers, as the Egyptians were demanding, and for the supply of oil on a long-term basis. When I heard Dayan's suggestions, I knew that we had broken through. Dayan also suggested that President Carter invite the prime minister for breakfast. I approached the president and he agreed. After breakfast in the president's suite, I went with Dayan to complete the draft treaty. On the ride to Ben-Gurion Airport, Begin turned to Carter and said, "Mr. President, you have succeeded." That was how we ended the last stage before the signing of the treaty, which we would not have reached without Dayan's input and initiative.

Vance's tribute to Dayan's crucial role was not exaggerated.

37

FAREWELL TO DAYAN

Dayan returned in mid-July from a visit to Thailand and immediately checked into Tel Hashomer Hospital for tests. He had suffered abdominal pains while visiting a farm north of Bangkok. The tests revealed a growth in the large intestine. Within a couple of days, twelve inches of the large intestine were removed and found to contain malignant cells.

I visited him two days after the operation and asked for instructions about publicity, since rumors were already spreading. He advised, "Consult with Dr. Goldmann about the exact medical terminology and hide nothing about my condition." Ignoring his pain, he got up from his bed and walked to the window. The nurse saw this and immediately summoned the resident doctor. They checked his pulse and expressed concern that the strain may have been too much. Despite his deteriorating condition, he insisted on going home and was released one week after surgery. After one week's convalescence at home, he returned to the office.

On September 10, 1979, I joined him on a second trip to Bonn. This time it was after the peace treaty with Egypt had been signed. He met with various leaders, among them: Helmut Schmidt; his Christian Democrat rival, Helmut Kohl (who would succeed Schmidt as chancellor); and the former chancellor, Social Democrat Willy Brandt.

Dayan was still weak, his patience easily strained. In Bonn he anticipated an important diplomatic achievement. During his previous visit, Schmidt had promised to give economic assistance to Israel and Egypt when the peace treaty would be signed. Now, despite Dayan's reminders, Schmidt did not acknowledge his prior commitment, and proceeded to give us advice instead. Among other things, he asked why Israel "put all her eggs in one basket." He thought we should seek to open a dialogue with the Soviet Union instead of relying exclusively on U.S. support. Schmidt was critical of Carter's policy as it related to America's friends in Europe, and commented, "You will save yourselves some bitter disappointments if you find an alternative to the United States."

Foreign Minister Hans Dietrich Genscher explained that, when the time was right, Germany would give its share to the consolidation of Middle East peace, but aside from that vague statement he said nothing further about it. Dayan was disappointed with the German attitude and made that clear in a televised interview. Subsequently, the media would not leave him alone, pressing for exclusive interviews. He asked me to get rid of all "these nuisances" and talk to any member of the media I chose.

I appeared on one of the popular live TV talk shows. The interviewer posed a question in German and I responded in English. He asked that I speak German, contending that he knew I spoke German; why make it necessary to translate? I answered, again in English, that I preferred Hebrew or English. He persisted, and I politely declined.

The arrogance of his questions and his preaching infuriated me. I repeated the response Dayan had given to Schmidt on our previous visit and added a few reasons of my own to counter the Germans' right to lecture us. My interview left a very unfavorable impression. When Genscher escorted us to the helicopter that would bring us to the El Al plane, he commented to Dayan in his poor English, "Your adviser, Mr. Lavie, was very harsh on television." Dayan responded that he had not seen the program but, had he himself spoken, he undoubtedly would have been more forceful than I was.

On the flight from Frankfurt to Israel, Dayan asked me to sit next to him. Rachel sat by the window and I sat next to the aisle. It was during this flight that he first told me of his decision to quit Begin's government. Even before our trip to Germany, he mentioned an unpleasant conversation he had had with Begin. Dayan had headed the delegation to the talks with the Egyptians and Americans on the implementation of autonomy in Judea, Samaria, and Gaza according to the Camp David Accords. He fervently believed that the treaty and the peace depended on our following through on this understanding. Now he learned that this stance was unacceptable to Prime Minister Begin.

His assumption was that Menachem Begin had changed his mind and did not intend to implement autonomy in the form agreed upon at Camp David. During their "unpleasant conversation," Dayan told Begin that under these circumstances he could not see any possibility of continuing to head the Israeli delegation. Begin made no attempt to dissuade him and immediately mentioned Interior Minister Yosef Burg as a replacement. Hurt by Begin's attitude, Dayan decided to resign. He pulled a piece of paper from his pocket, showed me his draft letter of resignation, and then proceeded to rewrite it as we talked.

Dayan wanted to keep his imminent resignation a secret. There were a number of matters pending on his desk. Among them were some that he considered critical, requiring his input: relations with Iran following the downfall of the Shah and the rise of Khomeini; relations with South Africa; and the possibility of renewed dialogue with Mengistu, the ruler of Ethiopia, with a view to rescuing the Jewish population.

He viewed our situation in Europe as extremely serious, particularly in light of the frequent declarations by EEC foreign ministers. West Germany had to be the key, and Dayan thought that the Germans must not be allowed to default on their moral obligation to the Jewish people. I do not know whether it was a momentary inspiration or something that he had thought about previously, but suddenly he turned to me, and to my surprise, said, "You will go to Germany to replace Meroz."

Seeing my astonishment, he repeated the sentence. Yochanan Meroz was about to terminate his post as ambassador to Bonn. I explained that there was no way I could stay in Germany. My trip with him had been the limit of what I could bear. Undeterred by my resistance, he began to preach Zionism (duty to the state overriding personal wishes), saying that under the given conditions I could serve as an effective whip because of my past. He continued, "Diplomacy and polished language are not going to be adequate anymore." He noted my opposition, but was not ready to abandon the idea. Upon our return to Jerusalem, I discovered that the notion had caught on in the upper echelons of the Foreign Ministry. Chanan Bar-On, deputy director general and an experienced diplomat, tried to convince me to take the job. Chanan was highly regarded by all the foreign ministers under whom he had served as a clear-thinking and well-balanced diplomat. However, I could not bring myself to go along with the suggestion in spite of my esteem for him or for Moshe Dayan.

On October 2, 1979, Dayan submitted his resignation to Begin. The prime minister did not urge him to reconsider nor did he show any readiness to accept Dayan's opinion regarding the management of the autonomy talks. He only asked that the resignation be kept secret until the cabinet meeting that would convene after the festivals, on October 21. Two days after the meeting, on October 23, the prime minister announced to the Knesset that Foreign Minister Moshe Dayan had resigned from the government.

The Knesset session ended late that evening. Since my car was not available, Moshe drove me home to Ramat Gan. In the course of the hour-long ride, he spoke about some of the dramatic events in his public life and began to reminisce about work relations and close friendships he had established with some of his assistants and coworkers. He was unstinting in his praise of the loyalty and devotion displayed by a few of them. Turning to me, he said, "I have enjoyed working with you in the Foreign Ministry and before that in the Defense Ministry, even though it sometimes bothered me that I could not pester you on Saturdays and festivals. Your advice has often helped me and if I have any regrets, it is only about the suggestions that I did not accept." Without giving me time to wonder what suggestions he had in mind, he recalled a conversation we had had on Succoth following the outbreak of the 1973 Yom Kippur War. He wanted to know the public reaction to the heavy casualties, and upon hearing my report, shot back, "What do you suggest I do?" "Resign from your post as minister of defense," I replied.

Immediately after that conversation, Dayan did indeed go to Golda Meir and offered to resign. He told her that in view of negative public opinion, he was prepared to relinquish his post. Golda was shocked and said that under the prevailing circumstances it was unthinkable even to bring up such a thought. It would be a terrible blow to the people and would give a moral victory to the enemy. Moshe did not argue and carried on with his job. Ten days later in the Knesset cafeteria, Justice Minister Yaacov Shimshon Shapira called for Dayan's resignation, and Golda rebuked him in the presence of several ministers. "Why does he bring this up at the cafeteria tables? Let him come to me and I will give him an answer," she said to those around her. Shapira got the message.

Before dropping me off at the house, he grasped my hand and told me to stay on in the Foreign Ministry. "They did not put you in charge of the autonomy, nor did they take it away from you. Stay on in your job and we shall still meet and talk," he said.

Dayan stayed home and wrote a book summing up the path to peace that had begun with his entry into the Foreign Ministry two years earlier. From time to time he phoned and invited me over to refresh his memory on certain subjects. I could feel his sadness at not being able to complete the negotiations with Israel's neighbors in Judea, Samaria, Gaza, and East Jerusalem. He was pained by the knowledge that an opportunity within our grasp might be lost by mishandling, and often expressed concern that, in the absence of some resolution, the situation could regress into terrible bloodshed.

On one occasion, when I asked how he would proceed, he suggested granting autonomy unilaterally to a specific area. He thought the Gaza Strip was the most suitable place for self-rule by the inhabitants, with Israel providing acceptable security arrangements.

He began to appear on public platforms and write op-ed pieces for the papers to advance his ideas. The prime minister rejected all of his ideas outright, but that did not deter Dayan from publishing further articles. Eventually he decided, with a few supporters, to run for election to the Knesset on an independent ticket. His new party was called Telem (furrow), and its platform focused on the peace process and the prevention of stagnation. Public opinion polls projected up to twenty Knesset members for Telem, but the results were a bitter blow: Dayan won only two seats in the incoming Knesset.

Disappointed but adamant in his vision to extricate Israel from her political and economic morass, Dayan became introspective. In the summer of 1981 he had an infection that damaged his one eye, and he almost lost his sight. At that time I was Israel's consul general in New York. He phoned to tell me that he was coming to Mount Sinai Hospital for treatment. I met him and Rachel as they came down the ramp from the plane at Kennedy Airport and noticed that he was leaning on one of his bodyguards. He was happy that I had come and asked me to help him into the waiting car. It was only then that I realized he could hardly see.

That was September 10, 1981. On our way to the hospital Moshe wanted to know what was going on in the Jewish community now that Congress was in the throes of a battle over President Reagan's decision to supply airborne warning and control system spy planes (AWACS) to Saudi Arabia.

I brought him up to date on the mood of the Jewish leadership and on Prime Minister Begin's forthcoming discussions in Washington. Suddenly he blurted out, "I fear that we are headed for a war that we will greatly regret." He explained that Minister of Defense Ariel Sharon was leading the country into a war in Lebanon, a conflict that would be "a nest of troubles" from which we would emerge in much worse condition than when we entered. I asked whether he had discussed this view with the prime minister.

Dayan said, "Begin cannot be led anywhere against his will, but it is entirely possible that he does not grasp all the manifold complexities with which we are involved." I gathered from the response that Dayan had indeed spoken to Begin but the decision to go to war had already been taken.

After laser treatment, Dayan checked into the Lombardy Hotel on East 56th Street. He seemed very fragile after the treatment but continued talking about what bothered him: getting bogged down in the Lebanese morass, declining relations with Egypt in the absence of progress on autonomy, and a distressing decline in relations with the United States. When I left him, he said he would return to New York in December for another eye treatment. Three weeks later I was informed that he had died.

Moshe Dayan's departure from the landscape of our lives was a severe blow to me. He was not exactly a man with whom one easily became close friends. He was unbending and demanded much of himself and of his aides. His understanding and courage to speak from the heart, his sensitivity toward his fellow man, belied his stiff outer armor. His complex personality drew barbs from all sides. He was an easy target for many, but he knew how to rise above personal attacks and continue with what he thought right. If he found a better road, he did not hesitate to change direction and advocacy. His strength lay in his ability to predict at early stages the probable course of variable situations, and in his readiness to adapt to changes. Many interpreted these as forms of weakness and inconsistency. However, these very traits made him an unconventional leader who contributed more than all of his adversaries to the military invulnerability of Israel and to the achievement of peace with the largest of our neighbors. The seven years that I worked with him, in wartime and in pursuit of peace, gave me an opportunity to know the man and also the privilege of being closely involved in some of Israel's finest hours.

38

MISSION IN NEW YORK

When Moshe Dayan left the Foreign Ministry, I had a hard time finding a place for myself. Prime Minister Begin, who filled in for Dayan for three months, made exactly two appearances at the ministry during that period. On one of those visits he asked me, "Why are you rejecting the ambassadorship to Bonn?" I explained my motives, although he was well aware of my background. He then asked whether there was any other diplomatic post that I would prefer. I told him I was not interested in a diplomatic assignment, but would like to be involved in furthering Israel-Diaspora rapport. Within a week he informed me that I would be appointed consul general in New York, a post that was the link between Israel and the largest Jewish community abroad, as soon as the position became available.

Meanwhile I worked for about a month with Yigael Horowitz, the minister of finance, who asked for my assistance in organizing a public relations campaign around a new economic plan that he was about to announce to the public. When Yitzhak Shamir became foreign minister, he asked me to continue in the role I had filled for Dayan. Shamir was completely different from Dayan, but turned out to be an intelligent statesman, firm in his political views and strong in character. He placed full confidence in me, even though I was considered a "Dayan man." Without hesitation he consulted me about his speeches and even invited me to accompany him to top secret discussions with the prime minister and other important forums. Unlike Dayan, Shamir shunned the media. For the first three months, he empowered me to speak for him to the local and foreign media, and made no personal appearances before foreign correspondents. It seemed to me that, because he considered his knowledge of English to be inadequate, he avoided direct encounters with the English-language media. He was fluent in French and was obviously more at ease with French reporters. But in his fourth month as foreign minister he acquiesced to my request and held a press conference at the King David Hotel in Jerusalem. Two hundred foreign correspondents attended, including representatives from all of the Israeli television and radio networks. He did not captivate the audience as a public relations expert might have done, but he did draw attention to the forceful views that he intended to apply in the performance of his duties. He spent much time learning English and soon began conducting fluent conversations with visiting statesmen, politicians, and correspondents. His command of English and grasp of diplomacy in such a short time was impressive.

On September 1, 1981, I took office as consul general of Israel in New York. My area of responsibility covered New York, New Jersey, and Connecticut. The scope of activity included ongoing contacts with governors, congressmen, mayors, religious and labor leaders, people in the arts and other cultural circles, and, above all, the whole media spectrum. Beyond that I had to function as ambassador to the Jewish people through a range of organizational and congregational activities that took up most of my time.

Before leaving for America, I met with Prime Minister Begin and requested guidelines. He was extremely worried about the attitude of the American Jewish leadership toward Israel. One of his deepest concerns was the refusal of these leaders to stop the flow of aid to Soviet Jews who, after receiving exit permits for emigration to Israel, "dropped out" illegally at transit camps in Vienna or Rome. Begin contended that visas issued by the Soviet authorities were exclusively for Israel, within the framework of family reunion; that by misusing these permits, the dropouts were not only endangering continued emigration from the Soviet Union but dealing a blow to the Zionist goal, the ingathering of exiles to the Jewish homeland. He completely rejected the "freedom-of-choice" argument used by the Jewish leaders in the United States to justify financial support for dropouts. My assignment was to deal with this problem, to explore the feasibility of recruiting potential young leaders who would take a firmer stand in defense of Zionist goals.

I also met with Foreign Minister Yitzhak Shamir and with old friends Moshe Dayan and Shimon Peres, each of whom wished me success. One very helpful meeting was with Avraham (Abe) Harman, now chancellor of the Hebrew University, who had been the Israeli ambassador to the United States and a former consul general in New York. In his Mount Scopus office, Abe drew upon his vast experience and extensive personal contacts with leaders of Jewish organizations to explain the situation of the Jewish community in America and the problems of its leadership in relation to Israel, giving me valuable advice in my new role.

Three days before departing for New York, we celebrated the marriage of our son Shai to Varda Steinberg. Shai had been an officer in an elite IDF unit, and the wedding reception on the lawn at Bar-Ilan University reflected a wide mosaic of Israeli society. The guests were drawn from every facet of Israeli life: military, religious, social, and political. Among the guests were Foreign Minister Yitzhak Shamir and the opposition leader, Shimon Peres. Standing beside me under the *huppa* (ceremonial marriage canopy), Moshe Dayan commented in a whisper how moved he was at the sight of "such beautiful youth." Two days after the wedding Joan and I left for the United States, leaving behind the newlyweds and our son Benyamin, who was a Golani Brigade cadet at the IDF Officers' Training School. It was difficult for us to part from them; little did we know that within the year both sons would be in the thick of the fighting in Lebanon.

Before arriving in New York, I had established contact with American Jewish leaders who had expressed interest in what was happening in Israel. Through my work with Moshe Dayan, Yitzhak Shamir, and Shimon Peres, as ministers of defense or foreign affairs, I was already acquainted with many of the American Jewish leaders whom I would encounter in my first few days as consul. My first official acts were to call on two men to whom I felt uniquely indebted. One was New York State Governor Hugh Carey, who as a U.S. Army officer, had liberated me along with many others from concentration camps in Germany. Presenting my credentials to him as the representative of Israel, I took the opportunity to express my deep personal appreciation and thanks for his role in "Mission Deliverance." The second man, especially dear to me, was Hershel Shechter, rabbi of a congregation in the Bronx. At the end of the war he was the first "free

Jew" I beheld after liberation as he stood beside my hospital bed in Buchenwald, when I was recovering from typhus. Even though my mind was foggy from fever at the time, I cannot forget the image of the gleaming metal Tablets of the Law emblazoned on his military collar – the insignia of a Jewish chaplain. I could not possibly begin my new duties in New York without first visiting these two men to express my gratitude.

One week after our arrival I had my "initiation rite" with Jewish leaders, who at the time were being asked to support the Israeli effort to prevent the supply of AWACS surveillance aircraft to Saudi Arabia. According to the myth commonly accepted in Israel, the Jewish leadership in the United States wielded almost unlimited political influence. Some Israeli politicians believed that lifting a phone in Jerusalem and talking to a few Jewish leaders in America was all that was required to tip the scales of the U.S. administration in Israel's favor. When Jerusalem instructed me to enlist their support in opposing President Reagan's decision to supply the planes, I learned just how little power they really wielded. With a fair degree of justice and wisdom, one of them told me that it was not advisable to test the strength of the Jewish organizations vis-à-vis the president. "Such a test will expose the fallacy of the power of Jewish leadership, a myth that should be preserved." It took another ten years of close working relations with the Jewish community, first in New York and later in Jerusalem, for me to appraise realistically their political strength, their bond to Israel, and the limited extent of their willingness to engage in direct confrontation with the U.S. administration concerning Israeli interests.

Two weeks after I began my job in New York, Prime Minister Begin visited the United States. He seemed tired and somewhat sad as we drove from Kennedy Airport to the Waldorf Astoria, along with Ephraim Evron, our ambassador to Washington, and Yehuda Blum, our ambassador to the United Nations. He had read my report on the difficulties of enlisting the leadership against the AWACS deal once the president had thrown his full weight behind it, and now asked why I was so pessimistic about Jewish support for our cause. He was disappointed with my recommendation not to drag the American Jews into the fray, saying, "I know the American Jews very well and I am sure they will stand with us in any struggle for our survival." I tried to temper his enthusiasm by suggesting some private discussions with influential leaders. He agreed, and found that these discussions confirmed my misgivings about our ability to recruit the Jewish community to block the AWACS sale to Saudi Arabia.

Now that Israel had signed a peace treaty with Egypt and was about to evacuate the last strip of Sinai, her popularity soared. The administration and the media were pleased with us. It was comfortable for Jews to be on the right side, for a change. Virtually no criticism of Israel was to be heard among Jewish leaders, apart from a few left-wing extremists.

Israel's strongest and most trustworthy supporters in the Jewish community were the Holocaust survivors. They were the hard nucleus of committed, unhesitating, and unconditional boosters of Israel. Though their numbers were not great, their influence in raising the awareness of American Jews and their identification with Israel and Jewish communities in distress were extremely significant. This was a community that regarded the existence and success of Israel as its greatest consolation and source of satisfaction. I did not encounter any other group in the United States with such a deep-rooted empathy regarding Israeli issues. It was a personal joy to be part of this group and to be readily accepted within its ranks. They stood beside me throughout my service in New York, with evident pride that one of their own had been appointed as Israeli ambassador to the Jewish people. The leaders of this group unfailingly invited me to speak at every public function they organized, and especially their annual memorial assembly for Holocaust victims.

The first such assembly in which I participated was held at Temple Emanuel on Fifth Avenue. For nearly forty years I had relegated memories of the Holocaust to the lower strata of my consciousness. Now, speaking at this memorial assembly, I found myself having to retrieve these buried memories, relive them by sharing them with an audience numbering in the thousands. Yet I did it willingly, knowing the need for factual eyewitness accounts to offset revisionist calumny.

For the official consular reception marking my first Israeli Independence Day in New York, and the IDF Remembrance Day rally that precedes the celebration, I included in the guest list, along with the many Israelis living in New York, Jews from all walks of life, personalities from the media, representatives of the arts and culture in

New York, as well as politicians and representatives of the various ethnic communities.

As it happens, it was also a day to celebrate a joyous family event, the bar mitzvah of our youngest son, Amichai, born on Israel's Independence Day in 1969. For that occasion, observed partly at the Fifth Avenue Synagogue and partly at a small reception in our home, our older sons got leave from the Israeli army, and Joan's family arrived from England and Switzerland. It was a happy family reunion with an Israeli flavor in our official East Manhattan residence.

I used the first few months to strengthen contacts in the three states that comprised my area of responsibility. I visited governors, mayors of the larger cities, senators, members of the House of Representatives, newspaper editors, as well as television and radio producers. With greater exposure to the media came increased demands for appearances at organizations, institutions, community centers, and university campuses.

In addition, I began to organize an information system within the consulate aimed at various audiences, primarily the molders of public opinion, both Jewish and non-Jewish, for whom I wanted to issue a daily bulletin on Middle East events. With the help of information from Israel's Foreign Ministry, Defense Ministry, and the IDF, I gave editors and news-program producers exclusives on the Arab states, the Gulf emirates, and the royal courts of the various rulers — information not covered by conventional news services. The exposure of backyard events in the Middle East, sometimes remote from the context of the Arab-Israeli conflict, began to arouse interest in newsrooms, particularly in outlying towns. The media had been generally unaware of what went on among the Arab countries. Suddenly they realized that oil prices and instability in the region were influenced by factors beyond the conflict with Israel.

Following the positive reactions from editors and reporters, who often asked for clarifications and supplements to the daily bulletins, I added another information update. In a three-minute recording every morning, we broadcast to hundreds of subscribers to our access phone number a summary of Middle East news based on daily cables from Jerusalem. The time difference between Israel and the United States gave us a great advantage in transmitting news flashes before the regular news agencies sent in their communiqués.

This information system proved particularly advantageous when the war in Lebanon began in early June 1982. The media were being deluged with anti-Israel propaganda of unprecedented hostility. By now, the news editors knew that they had a source available twenty-four hours a day, for updates and answers to their questions. Thanks to this service, we were able to quell the onslaught of Arab propaganda, at least during the first few weeks of the war. National and local television networks and radio stations required a continuous flow of information. There were days when I was requested to grant as many as six ninety-second interviews in addition to the half-hour in-depth programs.

The first week of the war was a harrowing time. Each noon, I convened a press conference in the consulate conference room to report on the course of the battles and the objectives of the campaign. The correspondents were hungry for news from the war zone. But the censorship imposed by field security limited the news I could release. What I could give them was gleaned from personal stories from the front lines that I received via the broadcasts of IDF Radio, the army's own station. I marked progress each morning on maps of the area. Newspapermen spread the word among their colleagues that there was a news source in the Israeli consulate, and the conference room soon became too small to hold all those who came for briefings.

In the evenings and at night I was a regular guest in the newsroom studios. And there were evenings when the network crews broadcast interviews and updates from my living room. Some of the reporters with whom I had become friendly knew that I had two sons in the war and tried to penetrate my personal armor. During public appearances I tried to suppress my personal concern, which kept growing. During the first ten days of the war I heard nothing from or of my sons. My attempts to contact them did not succeed. The only reaction I allowed myself to voice to friends in the media was that this war, with my children in active combat, was far harder for me than any war in which I myself had participated.

On one occasion my armor did crack. At the daily noon meeting in the fourteenth-floor conference room, while I was explaining the procedure of the cease-fire that was to take effect on Friday, June 11, my capable bureau chief, Vera Golovensky, came over and whispered that Major General Moshe Nativ, chief of manpower in the IDF general staff, was on my office phone. I excused myself and, heart pounding,

pounding, ran up two flights of stairs to take Nativ's call. My first thought was that he had something terrible to tell me and had chosen to do it personally. I was sure that one of my boys had been hurt. It was only when I heard Moshe Nativ's voice that I realized my fears were groundless. What he wanted was that I should check with a certain source, who had good contacts in the Syrian government, whether it would be possible to get news of a few missing soldiers apparently taken by the Syrians.

I remained in the office late that Friday. The anxiety that had begun with news of Nativ's phone call would not leave me. When I asked him about the situation of a certain army unit, his only response was, "They took a very hard hit." At home, Joan and I waited anxiously for news. Every phone call made us jump. We turned into bundles of nerves ready to explode at any moment. For the following thirty hours I did not cross the threshold of the house, for fear of missing a call. I did not change clothes, wandered about the apartment like a restless, caged lion. It was not until two days later that we received the first communication from one of the boys.

During the siege and bombing of Beirut, Israel's public image began to decline. President Reagan himself contributed to the outcry against us when he pointed to a photo on his desk of a girl with four amputated limbs – a picture that Arab propaganda had succeeded in getting into the White House. When he discovered that he had fallen victim to a propaganda stunt by the Arabs, and that the photo had nothing to do with the war in Lebanon, the president apologized and tried to redress the injustice. But the damage had already been done.

Meanwhile, the State Department and National Security Council put pressure on the president to promote a dialogue between Israel and the Palestinians. In the wake of the PLO expulsion from Lebanon and the reduction of its power, the State Department hoped to generate a momentum between Israel and the local Palestinians to seek a solution to their problem. On September 1, 1982, President Reagan published his plan for resolving the conflict. But it deviated from the Camp David Accords and was promptly rejected by Jerusalem.

On September 12, I was invited to a dinner given by major New York contributors to the United Jewish Appeal, at the Helmsley Palace Hotel. The main speaker was to be George Shultz, who had recently replaced Alexander Haig as secretary of state. Shultz had served in

Nixon's cabinet and more recently as president of Bechtel, a large American firm engaged in construction work in Saudi Arabia. Having experienced the hostility of Secretary of Defense Caspar Weinberger, who had also been a senior executive at Bechtel, the Jewish leaders feared that United States relations with Israel were about to take a turn for the worse. When I heard about Shultz's imminent appointment, I contacted Irving Shapiro, president of Dupont, in an attempt to renew relations with Shultz.

I had met both of them in January 1978, after Sadat's visit to Jerusalem, when they made a brief visit to Israel on their way back from Saudi Arabia and Jordan. At that time Shultz had wanted to pass on to Moshe Dayan the gist of his conversation with the leaders of the Saudi court and King Hussein of Jordan. I met Shultz at the Jerusalem Hilton upon his return from Yad Vashem, the national monument to the victims of the Holocaust. During the few minutes that it took to drive him and Shapiro to the Foreign Ministry, Shultz expressed his shock at what he had seen in the Holocaust Memorial Museum, and mentioned in an aside that, "After seeing that, it is possible to understand the Israelis and Jews much better."

The meeting between Shultz and Dayan had been set for the afternoon. Dayan, just returning from a cabinet session, had been in a hurry to go home. I had prepared him for the meeting, telling him that Shultz, a former secretary in Nixon's administration, was carrying a message from Riyadh and Amman. Dayan was skeptical about the validity of its contents. "They know how to use the correct channels if they have something important to say to us," he commented.

After exchanging the usual courtesies, Dayan went straight to the point: "What's the message?" Shultz and Shapiro exchanged glances. Then Shultz said that at least two senior personages, including the commander of the Royal Saudi Air Force, had expressed the hope that something positive would come out of Sadat's initiative and that Israel would become a recognized and accepted part of the Middle East. The RSAF officer had even indicated the benefit that would accrue to Saudi Arabia from an Israeli-Arab peace. He had spoken of the dangers to Saudi Arabia from Iraq and perhaps even from Iran if the Shah were to be deposed and Khomeini's people took over. Shultz had concluded that the Saudis hoped one day to see Israel as a trusted ally. In the car on the way back to the hotel, Shultz had commented to Shapiro that Dayan did not seem convinced by the message.

Now, four years later, as consul general in New York, talking with both of them again, I recognized in Shultz an interested intellectual, willing to listen to another point of view without prior bias. On the basis of my impression, I cabled Jerusalem and suggested that they accord the new secretary of state the necessary trust. To the Israeli journalists who asked my opinion, I expressed confidence in Shultz and recommended giving credit for his mediation between us and the Arabs.

At the reception at the Helmsley Palace Hotel, prior to the banquet, I stood with two close friends: Larry Tisch, a major shareholder in CBS, and George Klein, chairman of the Republican Party Jewish Committee. Shultz stood about thirty feet away, surrounded by guests. When he noticed me, he strolled over and with a smile asked why Prime Minister Begin had rejected the president's proposed solution of the conflict. I explained that Begin saw it as a deviation from the Camp David agreement, particularly as it related to Jerusalem. One of the Jewish contributors standing close by intervened and criticized Israel for not putting enough trust in the Reagan administration. "It is the best there ever was in Washington, and Israel should not underestimate it. We Jews and Israel have the best man in the White House, and now we have the best and friendliest secretary of state." Shultz's response was a smile. He called over Assistant Secretary Richard Fairbanks and asked him to meet with me for briefings on the autonomy discussions with Egypt, which had come to a halt even before the outbreak of war in Lebanon. Given the task of reactivating these autonomy discussions, the assistant secretary visited me at the Israeli consulate on several occasions to learn about the complexities of the plan.

About one week after my conversation with Shultz, Lebanese Christian Phalangists massacred Palestinians in the Sabra and Shatilla refugee camps near Beirut. Before reliable news could arrive, the Arab propaganda machine spread the rumor that the Israelis had massacred hundreds of women and children. My first task was to allay the fears of the Jewish leaders, who were themselves led to believe that Israelis were responsible for the act. Some were taken in to the point where they even believed Israel had planned the massacre with the Phalangists.

On the morning after Rosh Hashanah, I met with members of the Conference of Presidents of Major American Jewish Organizations. They had received reports from their constituencies expressing considerable anxiety about the damage to Israel's image. The explanations I gave, based on trustworthy information received from Israel, persuaded them that our hands were clean. But the politicians and public wanted proof. I informed the Israeli ambassador, Moshe Arens, in Washington, about my meeting with the leadership and told him that I had given them my evaluation that Israel would initiate an inquiry into the events to prove that Israelis had not spilled that blood. Arens disagreed, arguing that Israel must not set up a committee of inquiry, which would invite putting the guilt on Israel unfairly. I could not accept his reasoning, even though he was my superior. At his request, the leaders reconvened at 3:00 P.M. that same day. Again, he repeated there would be no inquiry. Several leaders pointed out that an inquiry could not be avoided, and it would be better if Israel initiated it.

Upon my return to the office, I found an urgent request that I come to the CBS studios. Arriving at their West 57th Street building, I was taken straight into the newsroom studio. Anchorman David Marsh opened the bulletin with a live broadcast from the White House. President Reagan expressed his regret over the bloodshed and stated that he had ordered the U.S. Marines to return to their positions in Beirut. Marsh put me on camera to get my response. There was little I could say other than to welcome the decision to bring the marines back so as to restore law and order in Beirut and to express my regret that they had been removed too early, leaving a vacuum in which the Phalangists had been free to act. Asked whether Israel would hold an inquiry and take the necessary steps to punish any Israelis who might have been responsible, I answered in the affirmative.

Even before I got back to my office, my secretary was besieged with phone calls from Jews and non-Jews, reporters and politicians, who voiced their appreciation of my response and stated that it was a crushing weight off the chest. That evening I again appeared in a televised interview, this time in the *McNeil-Lehrer* Report on PBS. The format had Lehrer with the editor in chief of *Time* in the Washington studio, while Robert McNeil sat with me in New York. Again I was questioned about Israel's willingness to investigate the Sabra and Shatilla massacre, and again I explained that we would not attempt to protect those responsible for this atrocity, should there be any responsibility on our part. McNeil then embarrassed me by quoting Menachem Begin, who had spoken against holding an inquiry. For a moment I dropped the trappings of an official representative of my country and said that, as an Israeli citizen who knows his people, I was sure that Israel would investigate down to the last detail. At that time I was unaware of the pressure building up in Israel, demanding the inquiry. That same evening Ambassador Arens appeared with Ted Koppel on *Nightline* and rejected the idea of a commission of inquiry. To my surprise, there was not a word of complaint about my stand from any of my superiors in Jerusalem, neither from the foreign minister nor from the prime minister.

The war in Lebanon left deep scars on Israel's image. Even to our closest friends, who received their information from the Israeli press, it was difficult to explain the Lebanese quagmire, which was getting extensive media coverage. To deflect attention from Lebanon to other areas in the Middle East, I increased the flow of information about events in the Persian Gulf, the Iran-Iraq war, Syrian-inspired terrorism, Libya, and Iraq, and the blackmail of the world petroleum market by Middle Eastern producers.

In one Arab newspaper I found the transcript of a May 12, 1983, Paris meeting between U.S. Secretary of Defense Weinberger and his Saudi Arabian counterpart, Emir Sultan Ibn el-Aziz, with the participation of Emir Bandar Ibn Sultan, the Saudi ambassador to the United States. According to the July 17 edition of *a-Safir*, a Beirut daily, the U.S. defense secretary had made disparaging remarks about the president of the United States and had promised his Saudi companion a supply of aircraft and tanks, despite the difficulty of getting congressional approval. The Saudi defense minister complained about the delays in the arrival of twenty F-15s and two thousand M-1 tanks, and threatened to buy military equipment from other sources. Trying to appease the Saudi, Weinberger said, among other things, that the Pentagon could not submit the sale of aircraft to Congress before 1984, an election year for the president and many members of Congress; that President Reagan was not even aware of the Saudi Arabian request to buy the planes; and that the Saudi ambassador to the United States knew the reason for that: If this request were to be presented to the president, it might be leaked to Congress and the media, thereby sabotaging the plan to supply the promised planes.

The transcript revealed that the two ministers had also discussed the agreement between Israel and Lebanon, mediated by Secretary of State George Shultz in March 1983. The Saudi Arabian defense minister was aware of its contents, since Shultz had informed the Saudis about it. U.S. Secretary of Defense Weinberger praised the agreement, saying it benefited the Arabs.

Because of the importance of the transcript, the light it shed on the relationship between Secretary Weinberger and the Saudi establishment, and the attempt to bypass the president and Congress in Washington, I decided to publish the document in full, without any editing. A few of our regular subscribers called to express amazement over Weinberger's references to the president of the United States. In particular they wanted to know how reliable the Beirut newspaper was. The only reply I could give was that the story appeared in July, and until now, mid-September, two months later, nobody in Washington had denied its contents.

One subscriber to our service was Ed Koch, the mayor of New York. A wizard at public relations, he never missed an opportunity to get a headline in the printed press or on television. In his daily press conference he voiced sharp criticism of the secretary of defense for undermining the position of the president, basing his remarks on the protocol printed in *a-Safir*. The Defense Department spokesman in Washington was evasive in his comments to reporters who followed up on the published transcript. At first he claimed that *a-Safir* was not known to him and that no such meeting had taken place, either in Paris or elsewhere, and not on the date specified. When a reporter at the press conference stood up and identified himself as representing the Beirut paper, the spokesman seemed extremely embarrassed. Weinberger himself denied the content of the protocol, describing it as a "fabricated document," but Koch did not let up. He continued to attack the secretary of defense, achieving headlines both in the papers and in the electronic media. His comments generated further complaints in the Senate and the House. The result was confusion in the White House.

In his embarrassment, the secretary of defense resorted to activating the FBI. Bill Webster, the FBI director, appeared in Koch's office in New York to question him about the source of his information. In Webster's presence, the mayor phoned me to tell me of the investigation and asked whether he could reveal the source. I told him: "In the course of my duties as the representative of my country, I publish any legitimate material relevant to problems that concern Israel, as long as such material originates from known sources." I added that the newspaper that published the transcript appears in Beirut and is distributed in the United States and elsewhere in the world. If anyone felt hurt by something that appeared in this newspaper, he should take legal steps against the paper and its editor. I heard Koch repeat to Webster word for word what I had said.

It seems that my diplomatic immunity kept the investigators away from me. However, the secretary of defense sought every possible means to get an apology from me. At first his bureau chief contacted Meir Rosenne, our ambassador in Washington, to get him to influence me to write an apology to the secretary of defense. I informed the ambassador that I had no intention of doing so and that the proper person to apologize for a false article would be the editor of the newspaper that had published the fabricated transcript, if such it was.

Within a few days Leonard Garment, a close acquaintance of a number of presidents and Republican leaders, appeared at my office to invite me for coffee in a nearby cafe. In a "softening up" exercise, he explained the damage to Israel caused by the *a-Safir* story. He also claimed that the transcript was fake, and thus called for a letter from me to Weinberger to apologize for the distribution of the story from the consulate. Garment spared no effort to influence me. He even took out a piece of yellow legal paper from his pocket to use for the draft of my letter. I told him exactly what I had already told Ambassador Rosenne. Garment folded his yellow paper and left the table in a huff.

Two days later Garment phoned. This time he relied on my friendship with his wife, Suzie, an editor at the *Wall Street Journal*, to convince me of the need for compromise. I could see that it really bothered him, so I suggested that the secretary of defense write me a letter that denied the truth of the transcript. By way of reply, I would accept the denial and explain to him the nature of my assignment, which included distribution of news and articles from Arab press sources. I would be prepared to add my regrets at the embarrassment caused him by the publication.

On February 17, 1984, the Secretary of Defense wrote on his official stationery:

> *Dear Mr. Ambassador, I have been advised that comment with respect to the a-Safir story of July 17, 1983 continues to circulate. I would therefore like to restate for the record that the so-called "transcript" of my May 12, 1983 meeting with the Saudi Arabian Defense Minister, as published in the a-Safir, was a complete fabrication. Yours, Caspar W. Weinberger.*

That is how the matter ended.

In the summer of 1984, mostly at Joan's instigation, I decided to cut my tour of duty in New York from five to four years. We wanted our son, Amichai, now 15, to complete his schooling in Israel, before joining the army. During our home leave, I informed David Kimche, director general of the Foreign Ministry, of my desire to return home by September 1985. Kimche told me, on instructions from the foreign minister, that I was requested to stay on until 1986. I was not prepared to acquiesce; Joan and I had made plans. Upon our return to Israel, we would move from Ramat Gan to Jerusalem, where we had bought an apartment and where Ami would go to school.

Elections for the Eleventh Knesset took place in 1984, resulting in an even balance between the leading camps, Labor and Likud. As a result, the government called for Peres and Shamir to rotate the premiership. I had been on friendly terms with Peres for some years and admired his abilities and qualities as a statesman. However, my direct superior was Foreign Minister Yitzhak Shamir, and my loyalty and obedience would have to be to him. Already in those initial days I heard conflicting messages emanating from the prime minister and the foreign minister. I frequently found myself on the horns of a dilemma, having to explain the policies of the government when its two leaders took opposing sides. All this only strengthened my resolve to leave active government service and return to Israel at the end of my four years, in the fall of 1985. I had also decided to ask the Foreign Ministry for a long leave of absence. I did not have the faintest idea where or how to seek employment, but I was confident that I would not be unemployed for long.

Toward the end of 1984, I received a phone call from Prime Minister Peres, asking me to convene a group of major contributors and share with them the secret of "Operation Moses," a daring plan to bring to Israel thousands of Ethiopian Jews from the refugee camps in the Sudan. This operation was made possible by the personal involvement of Vice President George Bush, with Israel footing the bill. Peres also asked me to contact Foreign Minister Shamir, then in Los Angeles, to request that he appear at the meeting and share the secret with the small select group.

After setting up a date for this meeting with Shamir, I asked Stanley Horowitz, president and CEO of the United Jewish Appeal, to invite a few major contributors to a top-secret meeting the following day in my office, when I would reveal pertinent information. Eighteen philanthropists from the New York area gathered to hear Foreign Minister Shamir speak about the emigration of Ethiopian Jews. Of the $60 million that the UJA leaders guaranteed to collect within four months, $20 million were raised at that meeting. It was heartwarming to see elderly men, some in their eighties, listening to the challenge of absorbing Jews of whose existence they had never even been aware. Donors such as Joseph Gruss, Jack Weiler, Jack Reznik, Bill Rosenwald, and younger men were visibly moved as they heard the daring plan to save thousands of Jewish lives. Perhaps due to a sense of guilt about American Jewish inactivity during the Holocaust, or maybe a reawakening of nationalism as a result of the establishment of the State of Israel, whatever the motivation, their Jewish hearts responded generously. In my frequent appearances at UJA and Israel Bonds events, I was never so deeply affected by the willingness of Jews to help other Jews.

A few weeks later I was contacted by the leaders of the UJA: National Chairman Alex Grass; Chairman of the Board Robert Loup; and President and CEO Stanley Horowitz were offering me the directorship of the UJA office in Israel. After serious consideration, I accepted the offer. The farewell parties, both official and private, lasted some two months, including impressive ceremonies and the award of honorary doctorates from Bar-Ilan University and Yeshiva University of New York. On September 1, I returned to Israel with my family, and immediately began work as director general of the United Jewish Appeal office in Jerusalem. First I surveyed the operations and missions of the UJA in Israel, then I drew up a plan to reorganize the Jerusalem office. I saw as my main goal in this new position the tightening of the bonds linking American Jews to Israel, and the creation of a better mutual understanding between the two largest Jewish communities in the world.

39

BACK HOME

Since leaving government service and returning to Israel in September 1985, I had continued to steer clear of political involvement. However, I still maintained my many personal connections with the people in power, both directly as well as through mutual friends and colleagues. My new role as director general of the United Jewish Appeal in Israel demanded close contact with the Israeli government. Occasionally, in company with UJA leaders and sometimes alone, I met with the prime minister and his cabinet colleagues, particularly on matters concerning relations with American Jewry, aiming to bring about closer ties between American Jewish leaders and the Israeli establishment.

My involvement in government policy was limited to the relationship with American Jewry, but there was one exceptional case when I suggested a far-reaching change in foreign policy to then-Foreign Minister Shimon Peres. Although he did not make use of it at that time, he did adopt it as government policy nine years later, even though by that time the policy had lost some of the advantages that it would have had in 1987.

Through an American friend, Daniel Abraham, I became acquainted with a member of the U.S. Congress, Wayne Owen, a Democratic representative of Utah. The two men visited the Middle East frequently and had established personal contacts with leaders in both Syria and Israel. At the beginning of 1987, having just arrived from Damascus, the two Americans met me in Jerusalem. After listening to their report of talks they had conducted with senior government officials and political leaders, I got the impression that the time was ripe for a confidential Israeli-Syrian dialogue either through a third party or even directly. At that time the Syrian leadership had already realized and was just coming to terms with the fact that their dependence on Soviet military, economic, and political support would be coming to an end, since the Soviet Union was about to collapse. The only tangible alternative for Syria would be to join the Western camp and come closer to the U.S.

I was convinced that Syria could be brought to accept the good offices of Washington as an honest broker to work out an agreement with Israel. The broad outlines of an agreement could be built around several elements, which might include: an assurance by Syria to guarantee tranquillity on Israel's Lebanese border, enabling Israel to withdraw to its international border; a face-saving solution for Syria on the Golan Heights, by restoring Syria's sovereignty, yet ensuring Israel's security and water supplies; and finally, the opportunity for Syria to improve its relations with the U.S.

Syria has always been the toughest adversary of Israel, exerting a powerful influence and demonstrating a threatening attitude toward Israel's other Arab neighbors whenever they showed any sign of peaceful overtures. Thus it would be in Israel's interests to settle the conflict with Syria first, after our treaty with Egypt. Such a settlement could be expected to bear fruit in agreements with Lebanon, Jordan, and the Palestinians.

I enlisted the assistance of three close friends of Peres who had worked with him in the Ministry of Defense, two of them retired generals. One, a former chief of staff of the IDF; the other, a former chief of the intelligence branch of the IDF general staff. The four of us spent a few hours with Peres on March 16, 1987, at his home in Jerusalem, to convince him of the idea. But at that time Peres was preoccupied with the initial memorandum he was hoping to sign three weeks later in London with King Hussein. Nothing came of that Jordan initiative.

During the seven years that I served as the UJA representative, I endeavored to promote greater understanding of life in Israel among American Jews, and to deepen their involvement with and attachment to the Land and its people. During those years, some fifty thousand Americans visited Israel under UJA auspices, most in groups, others as individuals with their families. This program brought in close to $100 million to Israeli tourism, in addition to the favorable impression and goodwill of tens of thousands of American Jews, who learned firsthand about the State of Israel. I drew great satisfaction from my work with the UJA personnel. I saw in them and their guided visits to Israel the only program among American Jewish organizations that presented Israel in a tangible way, instead of relying on slogans, empty discussions, and superficial expressions of concern. This is not to say that every single visitor to Israel became a Zionist and a staunch supporter of Israel. Some visitors voiced criticism of Israel upon their return to the U.S., but they were a tiny minority. Those few were generally influenced by negative comments from escorting officials or guides who disagreed with the political decisions or management of projects and programs for which the moneys were collected. What the visitors saw for themselves of Israel's accomplishments generally impressed them far more than any criticism from disenchanted guides.

As a direct result of this program, there are many Jews in America who show an intense interest in Israel and take pride in the assistance they offer in support of various projects of the Jewish people. Many who came to Israel with the U.J.A. join the tens of thousands of dedicated people in the U.S. who, as a group, raise close to a billion dollars every year for projects in Israel (especially absorption of new immigrants), local philanthropic enterprises in their own communities, as well as for Jews the world over.

My scope of action widened with the sudden growth in the number of immigrants to Israel, and their varied needs. The mass immigration of Soviet Jews that began in 1989 demanded a special "Exodus" fund-raising campaign with a target of $420 million over three years, in addition to the regular annual campaign for $750 million. Even before Exodus was completed, the need arose for additional $130 million for "Operation Solomon" to bring the Jews of Ethiopia to Israel in May 1991. The waves of mass immigration enthralled all of us on the Jerusalem staff. We exposed the visitors to the dramatc scene of this immigration by enabling them to witness with their own eyes the planeloads of Soviet Jews and the airlift of their Ethiopian brothers.

Even the most hardened of Israelis, familiar with other such scenes, could not help but be moved by the daily arrival of hundreds of immigrants from the Soviet Union with bags, baggage, and pets coming off the planes. However, the most emotional scene still engraved deeply on my heart, took place the day when, at an air force base next to Ben-Gurion Airport, a fleet of Israeli transport planes disgorged more than 14,000 Ethiopian Jews over a twenty-four hour period. When told that the airlift was about to begin, I alerted the UJA leaders in New York and urged them to come at once and share in the historic moment. But by the time they had made arrangements to come, almost all the immigrants had already arrived. Seventeen UJA representatives arrived just in time to see the last plane land. Even that one plane made a strong impression, to the point where they willingly redoubled their efforts to raise the added funds needed for that operation.

On Friday, May 24, 1991, I stood on the tarmac with mixed emotions watching the landing of the air force transports, and could not refrain from dwelling on the fact that vast numbers of doomed European Jews could have been saved through such an airlift. I watched the hundreds of dark-skinned Jewish men and women, the aged and the children, as they sat on the floors of the Hercules and Boeing planes, scrutinizing us with their large eyes and wondering what their future would be. For fast identification in the confusion of embarkation in Addis Ababa, numbered tags had been stuck on their foreheads. Again I was thrown back to the memory of myself and my comrades in the dark days of the 1940s under Hitler, who had turned our people into numbered slaves awaiting their bitter fate. Every twenty minutes an IDF transport plane would roll to a stop. As the ramp dropped, we could see an ocean of numbered faces, a few hundred per plane, sitting quietly and waiting for instructions from their Israeli escorts. The welcoming party included the prime minister, cabinet members, the chief of staff, the air force commander, and many Knesset members. Suddenly I felt tears rolling down my cheeks. An old friend in the welcoming committee passed me a handkerchief. He too was moved, and murmured, "If only *then* we had had a State, an army, an air force, an airline, we could have saved hundreds of thousands." My feelings precisely, at that moment.

A common phenomenon before every election campaign is the establishment of new political parties with new suggestions, new solutions for the internal and external ills of the country. As the Shamir and Peres rotation government drew to its close in late 1988, a movement arose among religious Zionist circles with an intellectual bent and politically moderate views, concentrated around the personality of Rabbi Yehuda Amital, an educator and scholar who had established a *hesder* yeshiva (post-high school yeshiva including army service as an integral part of its program) in the Etzion Bloc between Jerusalem and Hebron. Rabbi Amital is one of the distinguished rabbis who has influenced a generation of Torah students as learned as the old-school yeshiva students, yet no less outstanding in their performance and devotion as combat soldiers of the IDF. To reverse the growing polarization among the youth of Israel, both religious and nationalist, Rabbi Amital resolved to initiate and bring into being a more moderate political force amongst religious Zionists, than the one in the existing National Religious Party. One of his supporters was Rabbi Danny Tropper, an orthodox rabbi born in America, who created a movement called Gesher (bridge) to span the abyss between religious and secular youth.

At the behest of Rabbi Amital, Danny came to my house to convince me to join the new political movement and to head its list for the Knesset. Even before reading their platform, I explained that I would not join any party unless, it acted to bring religious and secular Israelis closer together, even to the point of presenting a joint list for the elections.

The results of the November 1, 1988, election disappointed almost everyone. Neither the left-leaning nor the right-leaning major blocks received a majority, the balance between them being the *haredi* (extreme orthodox) votes. Many were disturbed by the sharply increased strength of the *haredi* parties, from eight to thirteen seats in the Knesset, which consists of one hundred and twenty members. These results showed the inadequacy of the democratic system in Israel. Whenever the two major blocks are closely balanced in strength, Israel's proportional representation system awards great power to any small party whose constituents and ideology permit them to join either major block. Such a small party can pressure the two major ones, Likud and Labor, playing one against the other to get exorbitant benefits (at the taxpayer's expense) and compromised principles. The closer the balance between the two large blocks, the greater the power of the small party and the higher the price it can exact.

Since the *haredi* parties held the balance of power in 1988, it was clear that they would demand, as a fundamental matter of principle, the amendment of the Law of Return, regardless of whether the senior coalition partner was Labor or Likud. This law provides that every Jew has the inalienable right to return to Israel and receive citizenship immediately upon arrival as an immigrant. To avoid confusion about who is a Jew, the religious parties wanted a qualifying clause stating that to be a Jew one must conform to the *halachah* (rabbinical law) definition of a Jew - one born to a Jewish mother or converted according to *halachah*. The addition of the words "according to *halachah*" aroused violent opposition among Jews in the Diaspora – where, in contrast to Israel, there are many Conservative and Reform congregations in addition to the Orthodox. According to the rabbinical establishment in Israel and the Orthodox rabbis abroad, conversions performed by Conservative or Reform rabbis abroad were not according to *halachah* and therefore not valid.

From my close knowledge of the Jews in America, I knew there would be great sensitivity on this issue. Americans understand that political issues in Israel must be decided by the Israelis in Israel. However, legislation that would affect the status of American Jews coming to settle in Israel was a different matter. It affected American Jews directly, thus making their intervention understandable and justified. In America, even among committed Jews who feel an obligation to Israel – and especially among their children – there is considerable social involvement with non-Jews and there is a high percentage of intermarriage, highly distressing to parents who want to assure the status of their grandchildren as Jews. A change in the Law of Return would undercut that status and be viewed by many as an insult to American Jewry.

From my conversations with leaders of the *haredi*, Likud, and Labor parties I realized that none of them was aware of the intensity of opposition such a change would arouse in the U.S. Jewish community. It seemed to me that on such a sensitive subject we could not ignore the position of those who want to be Jews, to be considered as Jews, and to be allied with Israel.

I cabled the UJA leaders in the United States, informing them of the probability that this time each of the major parties, Labor as well as Likud, was prepared to yield to the pressure of the *haredi* parties and add the controversial wording, "according to *halachah*," to the Law of Return.

The UJA and the Council of Jewish Federations dispatched a number of leadership missions to Israel. They met with party leaders, including Shamir and Peres, and with representatives of the *haredi* parties, in an attempt to prevent the inclusion of what had become known as the Who is a Jew? amendment. The dilemma of Shamir and Peres was evidenced by the frequently repeated scene of American Jewish delegations leaving the offices of Shamir or Peres only to be followed by leaders of the *haredi* parties presenting their own ultimatum.

The nonreligious Israelis felt uncomfortable about the growth of *haredi* power. The negotiating cards in the hands of the *haredi* rabbis stunned a public that feared the heavy price to be paid by either major party in setting up a coalition. Many Israelis showed hostility to the *haredim*, some of whose leaders criticized the irreligious government apparatus. Israelis, who had voted in a democratic election, were dismayed to find the balance of power with the *haredim*, while the major parties for whom they had voted appeared helpless in the face of *haredi* political tactics. Anger over the election results now changed to anxiety about what would happen when the two big parties began knocking on *haredi* doors and competing with each other in a bid to gain control of the government.

The day after the election, I happened to be in the prime minister's office and met Yitzhak Shamir. In a brief conversation referring to the public mood, of which he was well aware, I asked about his willingness to renew partnership with the Labor Party in a national unity government, despite past experience. He did not exclude the possibility, but remarked that it would not be a repeat of the previous format.

I put out feelers with some of his close associates. I spoke to Cabinet Secretary Eli Rubinstein, with whom I had worked under both foreign ministers, Dayan and Shamir; I also spoke to Yossi Ben Aharon, political adviser and director general of the prime minister's office; Knesset Member Ehud Olmert, who was politically close to Shamir; and other public figures from the ranks of the Likud.

I got the clear impression that Shamir was interested in a broad-based government with the Labor Party in order to avoid surrender to the pressure of the smaller parties. However, he had three preconditions: no rotation of the premiership, no international peace conference, and no national political role for Labor – which would rule out a portfolio in defense or foreign affairs for Shimon Peres in the new government.

That evening, Minister of Defense Yitzhak Rabin was hosting U.S. Secretary of Defense Frank Carlucci at a reception in the Tel Aviv Museum. During the evening I managed to recruit a few Labor Party leaders on behalf of a renewed partnership with the Likud. Outgoing Ministers Yitzchak Navon, Motta Gur, Yaacov Tzur, Chaim Bar-Lev, and Arik Nehamkin all agreed with me that everything possible should be done to establish a broad-based Likud-Labor government, thereby barring the small extreme parties from control over the affairs of state and controversial religious matters. But none of them was prepared to take the initiative.

Rabin, with whom I spoke at length that evening and the following day, rejected any overture under Shamir's conditions, particularly the denial of a ministerial function for Shimon Peres in the new government. Rabin thought that Shamir, required by the president to form a government, should take the initiative. I tried to convince Rabin that Peres would probably agree to accept the portfolio of minister of finance, which he would view as an important challenge, considering Israel's desperate economic situation. Rabin doubted whether the Likud would be prepared to give Labor two important ministries, such as finance and defense. I described the mood around Shamir regarding capitulation to the small parties' demands, given the fear that such a narrow-based coalition could not last long but would cause considerable damage to Israel's image overseas, particularly in the Jewish communities opposed to the 'Who is a Jew'? amendment.

That same weekend I asked Shamir's assistants about the possibility of his making the first move by inviting Rabin and Peres for a talk. Shamir was willing, but highly influential interests within his party took pains to counteract such a possibility and proceeded to build a narrow coalition with the *haredim*, the N.R.P., and the parties of the extreme right.

Over the next few days Ariel Sharon succeeded in getting promises of support from the *haredi* and far-right parties, which would give the Likud sixty-five votes in the Knesset, thus a majority of five. Internal party pressure in favor of such a coalition overcame Shamir's inclination toward a wider-based government. In any event, he made no overtures to Labor. Some Likud members asserted that Peres had caused the surrender to the small parties, since he himself had promised the *haredim* everything they wanted, forcing the Likud to follow suit.

By the end of November it appeared that a narrow government would be formed, composed of the Likud (forty), the *haredim* (thirteen), Religious Zionists (five), and the far right (seven). On Saturday night, November 26, in a last attempt to get a broad coalition, I went to talk to Shimon Peres in his home in Jerusalem. It was more than a year since I had last spoken with him. Nevertheless, a relationship of friendship and understanding remained between us from the time that I had been his adviser and spokesman in the Ministry of Defense.

He was alone at home. His wife Sonia, a woman esteemed for her integrity, modesty, and wisdom, who was always supportive, but kept a low profile, was out for the evening. We sat for a long while analyzing the situation after the elections. Peres was depressed. He foresaw a decline in Israel's status in the world, a multitude of economic and social problems, and a continued deterioration in Israel-Arab relations.

It was his gloomy forecast that impelled me to reiterate my plea for renewed contact with the Likud for a broad-based government. Peres, very sensitive about his prestige and status in the party leadership after losing his fourth election campaign to the Likud, could not contemplate any initiative when Shamir was already certain of his ability to form a government.

The tried and trusted tactic for a further attempt at a partnership between the Likud and Labor lay in the chance to put together a block of sixty votes that would prevent a Knesset majority of a narrow Likud government. Building that block would require switching one of the *haredi* parties with five votes from among those on which the narrow government of sixty-five depended. It seemed to me that the *haredi* five member Agudat Yisrael Party was the weak link in Shamir's chain. The Agudah obeyed the instructions of the Council of Torah Sages, which was composed of rabbis from the hassidic dynasties and the heads of yeshivas.

The council had instructed its party to recommend to the president of Israel that Yitzhak Shamir be given the task of forming a government, after Shamir had promised to bring before the Knesset the

'Who is a Jew' amendment to the Law of Return, as well as other far-reaching promises.

My family origins and personal relations with a number of the members of the Council of Sages had given me occasion to speak with them in the past, to understand their concerns and to receive their attentive interest when I brought up ideas that seldom penetrated into their sheltered lives. The senior members of the council had all known my father, who had been an active member of this party until World War II and had played an important role in its policymaking decisions.

Following my talks with Peres and his friends in the Labor leadership, as well as my conversations with Shamir and his friends in the Likud, I saw an urgent need to apprise some of the council members about the dangers of the extreme polarization and the growing hostility between religious and secular Jews over the demands of the *haredim*, who wanted to gain control over national resources and impose new legislation in religious areas of great sensitivity.

Two of the sages - one a hassidic leader from a distinguished Polish-Galician dynasty; the other, head of a yeshiva, respected for his scholarship by both *mitnagdim* (descendants of those who had opposed the rise of hassidism at its birth two hundred years ago) and *hassidim*, the two mainstreams of the *haredim* - accepted my assessment and were prepared to reconsider their earlier decision to support the Likud as the main party of a coalition. But the decisive power capable of bringing about such a change was a famous rabbi and head of yeshiva whose dynasty had led the Jews of Poland before the Holocaust and who still enjoyed a preeminent position among *haredim* in Israel. Rabbi Pinchas Menachem Alter, a charismatic leader who, as renowned rabbi of Ger, became known as the Gerer Rebbe, was a decisive figure in the Council of Sages. As children, we had played together in one of the famous Carpathian Mountain spas on the border between Poland and Slovakia.

I had a long conversation with the rabbi on Monday, November 28, and we agreed that he should meet Shimon Peres that same evening at my home. They talked for four hours, till 2:00 A.M. Peres despaired after all the effort he had invested. I saw it differently. To me it was clear that this wise and charismatic *haredi* rabbi, with his broad grasp of worldwide Jewish affairs, had in fact this evening undergone a revolutionary change in perceiving the circumstances, the economic and social problems confronting the new government, and recognized the national interest as superseding narrow, parochial party interests. Standing next to my car when I took him home, he told me that he understood the need to take a different stand.

The Council of Torah Sages reconvened on November 29. All the politicians of both right and left waited for the outcome of the council's deliberations, held behind closed doors in Bnei Brak, a center of *haredi* Jews. After seven hours, the council resolved to suggest to Agudat Yisrael that the party should reopen negotiations with Labor, with a view to creating a block against a narrow Likud-led government.

Over the following two days Agudat Yisrael negotiated with the Labor Party, and on Thursday, December 1, signed an agreement to form the block against a narrow government.

The switch of Agudat Yisrael from the Likud camp shocked that party leadership, particularly Yitzhak Shamir, who had undertaken to present his government to the president within a matter of days. Nevertheless, I had reason to believe that Shamir was satisfied with the imposed constraint that forced him to seek a broad coalition, since he was well aware of the pitfalls encountered in a narrow-based government.

Ministers Ariel Sharon and Yitzhak Modai, who had exerted immense efforts to assemble a narrow coalition without the partnership of Labor, again moved into high gear. Upon publication of the Agudat Yisrael reversal, they both sought meetings with influential members of the Council of Torah Sages. Using strong language, they even resorted to veiled threats about the future treatment of *haredi* Jews, particularly in relation to the exemption of yeshiva students from military service, if Agudah refused to return to Likud. Their softening-up process was effective. This time the Likud representatives brought with them proposals that were difficult to turn down. Agudat Yisrael demanded a written commitment signed by the candidate for prime minister. Shamir was compelled to put his signature to promises he had previously avoided, among them, a guarantee that he would furnish forty-three Likud right-wing votes in favor of the 'Who is a Jew' amendment. Together with the eighteen votes of the religious parties in the Knesset, the necessary sixty-one votes were assured.

Sharon and Modai claimed credit for the third Agudat Yisrael turnabout and for presenting Shamir with his Likud, Religious Zionist, *haredi*, right-wing (Techiya, Tzomet, and Moledet) government. The media were flooded with news items of the imminent creation of a narrow-based government, with its composition almost final. But Shamir, an astute and experienced politician, understood that he could not base a stable government on small coalition partners such as the Agudat Yisrael party. Many factors led Shamir to seek a broad-based government: the short life span of Peres' signed agreement with Agudat Yisrael; the extreme demands from the far right; an anticipated confrontation with President Bush and American public opinion over the U.S. dialogue with the PLO; and the rift with world Jewry over the *haredi* intent to amend the Law of Return. Reluctantly, but lacking a solid alternative, Shamir invited Peres and Rabin to discuss the creation of a broad-based coalition and renewal of the partnership with the Labor Party to form a broad and stable government.

Upon the establishment of the new government, I returned to my own affairs and family, keeping my distance from the political leaders. One month later, when my brother Lulek was installed as chief rabbi of Tel Aviv at an impressive ceremony at the Heichal Hatarbut, Prime Minister Shamir shook my hand warmly and, although nothing was said explicitly, I felt his appreciation of my initiative on behalf of a national unity government.

The installation of my brother as chief rabbi of the largest Jewish city in Israel took me back forty years. It was in 1944 when Mother deposited Lulek into my hands, two years after my father had charged me with the responsibility of putting him on the path followed by our ancestors through an unbroken chain of thirty-eight generations of rabbis. Feeling a need to express my personal gratitude and sense of fulfillment, I gave a reception in honor of Lulek at the King David Hotel in Jerusalem. Among the guests were rabbis, cabinet members, supreme court justices, university professors, MKs, and many other public figures, including the president of Israel, who made a speech lauding the new chief rabbi.

Rabbi Yisrael Meir Lau had acquired a reputation as a polished orator, but this time he was too choked up to share his feelings with the audience. He had just heard from me, for the first time, how our parents, each in turn, had placed him in my hands; and how our father charged me to see that our family tradition is carried on. It was also difficult for me to speak after fifty years of silence. Now, seeing our father's last will realized, our ancestral legacy sustained, enduring, I felt that a solemn responsibility had been gratefully discharged, a unique burden lifted from my shoulders. The scars branded into my being in my formative years - the personal torment, loss of family, decimation of our people - would remain with me as long as I lived.

Beyond the personal satisfaction over the accomplishment of the child I had carried in a sack on my back, the two of us together had overcome many obstacles in our lives. But this was a restorative moment: seeing my younger brother, now a person of stature, standing by my side, fulfilling our father's fondest dream as spiritual leader of a people that, despite Nazi efforts to obliterate us, "... as a lion doth he lift himself up" (Numbers 23:24) is deepening its roots as an independent people in its own homeland, gathering in far-flung remnants of Jewry. A redemptive moment indeed. My heart was filled to overflowing. But it meant much more than personal fulfillment. The heads of our family had perished in the death camps, but their seed, the three surviving brothers, had raised a new generation of fifteen sons and daughters and a third generation of several scores of grandchildren. We had left Europe and put down roots in Israel, from the north far to the deep south, and were bringing to fruition the dreams of millions whose ashes covered the fields of Poland and Germany. I never sought or knew the taste of vengeance. But if a person would ever need revenge for crimes committed against him, it seems to me that my revenge against Hitler and his accomplices has been fulfilled.

40

BROTHERS
WITHOUT BROTHERHOOD

L ooking back over fifty years of my personal and our collective struggle to survive, I am reminded of my father's parting words: "There are Jews of anxiety and Jews of tranquillity." On an October night in 1942, before going to his death with his congregation, this was his answer to a question that I posed several times as we were inexorably pushed down a blind alley. "Where are the Jews of the world? Why don't we hear them?" I asked him in the dark of night at the door of our home, just before we parted forever. Indeed, with maturity I also see two types of Jewish communities, those living in tranquillity and those facing anxieties.

Ever since that night, I have been plagued by the feeling that we who lived in terrible anxiety under the Nazis had been abandoned, "a people who live alone" (Numbers 23:9), while the Jews of tranquillity lived on in their secure havens watching from a safe distance as we, their brothers, fought for our existence besieged from all sides and finally overcome, at the mercy of our executioners. Unfortunately, the brotherhood expected from true brothers in emergencies was not to be found among our more fortunate kinsmen.

Today, fifty years later, the term "Jews of anxiety" is no less pertinent than it was in those dark days. The sovereign State of Israel, born from the ashes of the crematoria, is even now struggling for its existence in an ocean of enmity.

The arena may have changed geographically, but those who now take the role of vanguards of the State of Israel are at present the Jews of anxiety. The cries of anguish over the young lives lost while defending Israelis and Israel's borders have already reached the third generation. The Israelis who are constantly threatened by terrorist attacks do not think of opting out. They are there to stay and defend the Jewish State for all the Jews of the world. Their brethren in the Diaspora are proud of this state and its people, but following the slightest terrorist assault somewhere in the country, the Jews of tranquillity cancel their flights to Israel and their hotel reservations; and to au courant on the safe side, they watch the events from a comfortable armchair facing the TV screen.

It was my belief that, following the Holocaust, we could always depend on the Diaspora Jews to stand with us, particularly the Jews of the United States. I the light of Israel's national mission to open its gates to every Jew unconditionally, we assumed that the Jews of tranquillity, who enjoy social and political freedom in the midst of economic prosperity, would feel conscience-bound to come to the help of their brothers. Indeed, some fifty thousand to one hundred thousand American Jews (about one to two percent) do display a Jewish commitment and contribute $350 million a year for their brethren in distress; another few thousand Jews are active in lobbying the American government leaders. However, little has changed: About ninety-eight percent of American Jews are indifferent to the plight of Jews overseas, as were the American Jews of the 1930s and early 1940s, during the Nazi period.

American Jewish Leadership Prior to the State

Since the beginning of this century, as American Jews began to organize, their leaders labored to maintain a low profile and to suppress the unique nature of their Jewish identity. One example of this was the "establishment" opposition to the creation of an orthodox Yeshiva University in New York. Influenced by elements of Reform Judaism, the leadership opposed the project as a provocation to anti-Semitic groups such as the Ku Klux Klan. Even the moderate Louis Marshall voiced opposition to the establishment of Yeshiva University, on the grounds that it would create a Jewish ghetto. The Jewish leadership tried their utmost to hide their Jewish character and went to great lengths to demonstrate their community's loyalty to American values, way beyond what was actually expected of them. Jews participated in every Christian or ethnic function, even if it had no connection with Jewish interests. Late in 1939, when the Nazis were already murdering Jews daily in occupied Europe, the leaders of the United Jewish Appeal, specially created for the purpose of rescuing European Jews, announced a donation of $250,000 to a fund to commemorate Pope Pius XI. The money was transferred to Pius XII, to be distributed among Christian refugees in memory of his predecessor.

The small nucleus of involved Jews are warmhearted Jewish Americans, proud of Israel and quick to identify with the needs of less fortunate fellow Jews and to come to their help. Thousands of these American Jews, from different denominations and various organizations, visit Israel every year. Many bring their children. Some come for longer periods; others feel very much at ease in Israel and return "home" periodically. There is even a trickle of truly idealistic American Jews who have been making *aliyah*. Since the establishment of the state about eighty thousand American Jews chose to settle in the Jewish State out of their free will, thus contributing a great deal to the development of the country. These are the Jews who do not wait for leadership decisions in order to donate emergency funds or to take to the streets to demonstrate identification with Israel in times of dire need. They act on their empathy, and induce the leaders to follow. That is the way it was in May 1967, in the "waiting period" before the Six-Day War, when they demonstrated in the streets of New York as a sign of support for Israel and mobilized means for helping. That is the way it was during the Yom Kippur War, when masses of ordinary people initiated campaigns to help and to identify with Israel even before their leaders gave the signal for it. Nevertheless, all these caring people represent a relatively small percentage of American Jews.

Only once, on one particular occasion, close to two hundred fifty thousand American Jews marched in Washington, before Gorbachev's visit, on behalf of Soviet Jewry's freedom to leave Russia.

It is hard to assess the actual influence of American Jewry on the U.S. presidency, Congress, and public opinion. Before World War II, the Jewish leadership in the U.S. did not even aspire to affect administration policies. During the war, three Jewish congressmen chaired congressional committees, yet took no action to amend the rigid immigration laws that barred the entry of European refugees. With few exceptions, efforts of Jewish leaders to rescue European Jews in their darkest hour were feeble and low-profile. We now know how little influence they had on President Roosevelt and his administration. It was he who convinced American Jewish leaders to sit quietly and avoid any demonstrative action that might mark this as a "war to save the Jews," which would spark anti-Semitism and harm the war effort. During the 1940 German bombing of London, Congress voted unanimously to open the country's doors to tens of thousands of British children. A proposal to admit twenty thousand Jewish children living under the sword of Adolph Hitler never even reached the floor for debate in Congress.

After World War II, Dr. Chaim Weizmann was the first Zionist leader who attempted to recruit the American Jewish leadership to help in the campaign against the British Mandate's "White Paper," which limited Jewish immigration and settlement in Eretz Yisrael. After searching in vain for a man of prominence to approach the White House, he turned to Edward Jacobson, a personal friend of President Harry Truman, who had served with Truman in World War I and who had been his business partner after the war. Jacobson, a private citizen of Kansas City, succeeded in facilitating the historic meeting between Weizmann and Truman that led to United States' backing for the Zionist cause. Truman was the decisive factor on the international scene for the proposal to create a Jewish State. Jacobson, a modest Jewish merchant who had the president's heart and sympathy, had succeeded in paving the way for Weizmann to bring Zionism to the White House, whereas the well-known Zionist leaders, Rabbis Stephen Wise and Abba Hillel Silver, had failed.

David Ben-Gurion, who spent the early years of World War II in Britain trying to combat the mandatory government's hostility to the Jewish community in Palestine, went to the United States in 1940 to organize the American Jewish community against the British policy. According to his associates, Moshe Sharett and Eliahu Golomb, he felt that this community had an important potential that needed to be tapped and fostered. The scope of the Holocaust was then still unsuspected, but Ben-Gurion foresaw that support for the battle for the Land of Israel must be sought in America.

In New York, he met with Jewish leaders and Zionists in an effort to form a solid front of support for the Zionist movement campaign to carry out the promise of the Balfour Declaration to establish a Jewish national home in Eretz Yisrael. In his talks in the U.S. he spoke of the havoc the German air force was raining down on Britain, which he saw as being in the vanguard of the free world against Hitler. Ben-Gurion anticipated that the United States would eventually come to the aid of its embattled ally fighting for survival. In a conversation with Joseph Proskauer, an important Jewish leader who was chairman of the American Jewish Committee, Ben-Gurion asked whether Proskauer was willing to work on behalf of American aid to Britain. Proskauer thought for a moment and finally said no.

"Why don't you raise your voice on such an important issue?"

"Because I'm a Jew," Proskauer replied.

"Do you think such aid is in America's interest?"

"Yes," said Proskauer, "but I am first of all a Jew, and we Jews are a small minority. If it were to become clear after the war that so and so many Americans had been killed, they would contend that we Jews had pushed the United States into this war."

Ben-Gurion related that conversation on several occasions, once during the visit of the heads of the same organization to Jerusalem in June 1957, as recorded by Ben-Gurion's political adviser, Dr. Yaacov Herzog. Despite Proskauer's extreme caution and fear of inciting non-Jewish American public opinion, Ben-Gurion tried to recruit him, as well as figures like Louis Marshall, Jacob Blaustein, Felix Frankfurter, and others to his cause. Some were indifferent to Zionism, others downright hostile. The aid elicited from these non-Zionists was primarily humanitarian and philanthropic. Political support was difficult to obtain from these communal leaders, who were cautious about their "loyalty status" vis-à-vis a foreign, external element. They were unsure of their influence over administration policies or congressional legislation. But on a purely personal plane, individuals among them did use their contacts with influential government people, senators, and representatives, thereby helping to introduce the Zionist cause to the corridors of power in Washington and New York.

It was not until after World War II that many American Jews realized the enormity of the blunders made by their leaders, who had taken no steps to alert and marshal public opinion against the destruction of European Jewry. Now, a wave of sympathy and support materialized in the Zionist campaign against British Mandate policies in Palestine, especially the policy of denying entry to the remnant that had survived the Nazi horrors. The years between 1945 and 1949 were proud years for American Jewry. The same leaders who had failed their European brothers during the war, Rabbi Stephen Wise and others, now did an exemplary job in the struggle to open the doors of Palestine to Holocaust survivors and to affirm the Zionist movement's "Biltmore Plan" for the establishment of a Jewish national homeland. U.S. Jewry expressed its deep commitment to Israel in three areas: financial assistance, the creation of a supportive public opinion, and mobilization of aid from the U.S. administration and Congress.

The Dual Loyalty Dilemma

Before Israel reached its first birthday, Jewish leaders in the United States were already starting to worry about the future relationship between the American Diaspora and the new Jewish State. In an exchange between Prime Minister Ben-Gurion of Israel and Jacob Blaustein, president of the American Jewish Congress, a powerful Jewish organization that tended toward assimilation and a negation of Zionism, Blaustein expressed concern that Israel would begin to lure American Jews, thereby undermining the American orientation that the leaders sought to project.

Ben-Gurion ignored the Zionist leadership in the U.S. and concentrated on other communal heads. In his opinion, Zionists did not belong in the Diaspora and should "return" – that is, come to settle in Zion, the new State of Israel. His clash with Zionist leaders was exacerbated by his pragmatic acceptance of the partition of Palestine, proposed by the United Nations Special Commission on Palestine (UNSCOP) and endorsed by President Truman. The American Zionists under Silver's leadership were adhering to the 1942 Biltmore formula, with its eight clauses drafted by Ben-Gurion and Abba Hillel Silver. Ben-Gurion was at that time intent on whipping up impetus for the political campaign on behalf of a national home in Eretz Yisrael, but he did not feel bound by the specifics.

Ben-Gurion did not conceal his hope that large numbers of American Jews would consider immigration to Israel, which was now an independent Jewish State. He expressed it openly and forcefully.

Already in late 1949 he issued a call to American Jews to immigrate to Israel. Some of the communal leaders were upset by this and found it necessary to explain to themselves and to their colleagues that Ben-Gurion was not asking the Jews of America to swear allegiance to the Jewish State *instead of* to the United States. Proskauer sought to calm his colleagues' concern about dual loyalty. In his opinion, Israel would not demand any national identification from American Jewry. He explained U.S. support for Israel as being in the best interests of America, as well as of the UN, and not an action motivated solely by Jewish concerns – thus countering the dual loyalty charge.

Blaustein, a leading member of the AJCommittee, responded in much more specific terms to Ben-Gurion's call for Jewish immigrants from America, particularly the young and professionals. In the summer of 1950 he visited Ben-Gurion in Israel and the two men reached an understanding concerning relations between Israel and the American Diaspora. At a dinner given by Ben-Gurion in his honor, Blaustein read a statement declaring that the Jews of America regarded the United States as their country and their home; that they rejected the contention that they were Jews living in dispersion. In response, Ben-Gurion said that Israel does not speak or act for Jews other than her own citizens. Moreover, Israel respects the right of Jews living in different countries to contribute to the development of their own communities and institutions according to their needs.

Of all the Jewish organizations in the United States, the AJCommittee was viewed as the most important because of the connections of some of its leaders to the administration. However, with Eisenhower in the White House and John Foster Dulles in the State Department, this personal Jewish contact with the U.S. administration was lost. Organization leaders continued to function at the congressional level, the most outstanding among them being Sy Kenan. He virtually created a one-man Jewish lobby, which succeeded in getting through Congress its first decision on economic aid to Israel to the tune of $65 million. Years later, his lobby was transformed into the America-Israel Public Affairs Committee (AIPAC). It was not until 1953 that the umbrella organization of the Conference of Presidents of Major American Jewish Organizations, called the Conference of Presidents for short, was created. It speaks to this day for the entire Jewish community.

It was an American diplomat, Henry Byroade, assistant secretary of state and later U.S. ambassador to Egypt, pressured by the multiplicity of Jewish organizations, who had suggested to Dr. Nahum Goldmann the idea of creating an umbrella organization to represent all Jewish organizations. Together with Philip Klutznik, Goldmann set up the Conference of Presidents. Klutznik, a millionaire who had held posts in the U.S. administration, was president of B'nai B'rith, an organization that worked for the benefit of Israel. He was chosen chairman of the Conference of Presidents and became the community's spokesman to the administration. It was Klutznik who confronted Eisenhower's administration, when Dulles tilted U.S. policy in favor of the Arabs. He also formed a front of Jewish leaders to stand up to the White House and State Department when, after the 1956 Sinai Campaign, the administration was threatening to impose sanctions on Israel if it did not withdraw to the international frontier. However, Eisenhower ignored Jewish pressures. He believed that Jewish political power was negligible and flaunted that belief, even though he faced election to a second term in November 1956, at the close of the Sinai Campaign. The fact that he won a landslide victory in spite of his anti-Israel tactics only confirmed his belief that the Jewish forces' influence in the U.S. was only a paper tiger.

In June 1957, after the pressure from Washington had abated and Israel had withdrawn from Sinai, a leadership mission of the AJCommittee, led by its president, Irving Engel, arrived in Israel. It had two main points on its agenda for discussion with Ben-Gurion and his assistants: the status of Israeli Arabs, and the Law of Return. The leaders met with Ben-Gurion in two sessions that tended to underscore the gap between Israel and the Diaspora.

In a lengthy tour of Arab towns and villages in the Galilee and the Arab Triangle, between Petach Tikva, Hadera, and Afula, the mission attempted to learn about the attitude of the Israeli government toward its Arab citizens. Some of its members tried to wring out of their Arab hosts criticism of the government. In one case, the American Jewish leaders asked their Israeli escort to leave them alone with the Arabs, suspecting that the Arabs were afraid to be candid in his presence. At their second meeting with Ben-Gurion on June 24, mission members could not come up with a single Arab complaint. In fact, they complimented the government on its attitude toward the country's minorities. Asked what motivated their interest in the Arab minority, Engel responded that as an organization concerned with civil rights, the AJCommittee needed to know that the rights of Arabs were not being denied. He went on to note that there had been improvements in the Arab communities since his previous visit in 1949, though some problems still remained, relating to travel restrictions for local Arabs and land confiscation.

One member of Ben-Gurion's staff resented the patronizing attitude of members of the visiting mission, as if they had come to Israel to "teach us how to behave." Ben-Gurion was more patient. He explained to the mission that the military government still prevailing in the Galilee was necessitated by circumstance, but also served as a means to ensure the civil rights of the minority, as the state does for all of its citizens.

But the main preoccupation of the visitors was with the Law of Return. This law bestows on every Jew coming to Israel the automatic right to become an Israeli citizen, *if he so chooses*. Moreover, any Jew who establishes his residence in Israel automatically becomes an Israeli citizen after three years of residence, *unless he opts not to do so*. The chairman of the mission protested an expression used by Ben-Gurion in the 1953/54 Government Yearbook, that the Jews of the United States and other countries viewed the Israeli ambassador to their country as "our ambassador." According to Engel, the statement embarrassed the Diaspora Jews, who found themselves accused of dual loyalty. He reiterated his objection to the Israeli tendency to view all Jews as Israeli citizens, by virtue of the Law of Return, which he erroneously assumed forced Israeli citizenship on any Jew visiting the country, leaving him no choice.

Somewhat hesitantly, Engel handed Ben-Gurion a telegram that the AJC executive director, John Slawson, had received on June 16 from Dr. Eugen Hevesi, director of AJC External Affairs Committee in New York. It noted that the committee had submitted a memorandum to the National Platform Committee of Young Republicans, scheduled to meet on June 22, to draft the new election platform. The memo requested the National Platform Committee to adopt a resolution that the U.S. administration should:

1. reject the Zionist definition of Israel under which every Jew possesses Jewish   nationality;

2.press Israel to abolish the Zionist organization in the U.S.;

3.demand that Israel repeal its Law of Return and the Citizenship Law, which are based on the assumption that non-Israeli Jews hold certain national rights that are equal to those of Israeli citizens.

Hevesi added in his telegram that Edwin Lukas, AJCommittee director of political affairs, approached Republican leaders to persuade them against acceptance of the memorandum, pending clarification and identification of the person or persons responsible for its submission – in the name of the AJCommittee – to the Young Republicans as well as to the Republican Platform Committee in the U.S. Senate.

Babylon Facing Jerusalem

The American Jewish leaders seemed to fear that the centrality of Israel in Jewish life would overshadow the status of their community. These apprehensions spread to academic and religious circles, which began to emphasize the quality and achievements of the American Jewish community, a "Babylon facing Jerusalem." The allusion was clear: It was only thanks to the American "Babylon" that Jerusalem could exist and develop. They continued in their patronizing attitude toward Israel, even when it was noticeable that America's Jewish community was shrinking, both in quality and in numbers, while Israel's was growing and gaining strength.

The leadership in the "Babylon" of America tended to underestimate the significance of disturbing statistics about intermarriage – involving fifty-two percent of all American Jews. They also ignored the absolute decline in Jewish population. In 1945 there were, among 120 million Americans, 5.5 million Jews, about five percent. By 1990, the general population had almost doubled, reaching 245 million Americans without any corresponding growth in the Jewish population, thus reducing the ratio to about two percent. Based on the average growth rates in the United States, the Jewish population should have reached 12 million by 1990. Where had the missing 6 million American Jews vanished since World War II?

With a degree of justification, the involved Jews of the United States see themselves as the main benefactors regarding Jewish needs beyond their own borders. Aside from special emergency campaigns, the United Jewish Appeal (UJA) raises about $750 million every year. Two-thirds of the UJA moneys go toward the needs of local communities in the U.S. The remaining one-third is divided between the Jewish Agency, dealing with immigrant absorption and settlement in Israel; and the American Jewish Joint Distribution Committee, which is responsible for social aid and rehabilitation in distressed communities all over the world, including Israel. These funds come from some two hundred Council of Jewish Federation-affiliated communities and four hundred independent communities.

The professional fund raisers are well aware that the main motivation of the donors is a desire to help Jews in distressed countries and particularly to foster Israeli absorption of immigrants from all over the world, while developing a social and economic infrastructure. Emergency situations in Israel also influence the level of contributions. In 1948, of $205 million collected by UJA, $178 million (eighty-seven percent) was transferred to Israel, then fighting for her existence in the War of Independence. In 1992, the UJA raised $700 million, $210 million (thirty percent) going to Israel.

Israeli organizations and institutions raise funds in the United States to cover their own needs. The funds raised by American Jews for Israel amount to $350 million a year, apart from investments in Israel Bonds or in Israeli plants and companies. Though it amounts to less than two percent of the country's annual budget, this contribution to Israel should not be denigrated. Nevertheless, it cannot authorize the contributors to determine matters that affect the lives of the citizens and residents of the Jewish State.

Self-Appointed Ambassadors

The political involvement of American Jewry, their high voting rate, and their readiness to contribute to candidates' campaign funds have given them a political weight far greater than their numerical ratio would suggest. But that factor has its limitations. They are not prepared to confront the administration or public opinion on matters other than "American interest." President Bush's threats to the Jewish lobbyists who came to Washington on September 12, 1991, to urge approval of U.S. guarantees for loans that Israel was seeking on the world money markets left a bitter taste and some apprehension in the hearts of many Jewish leaders.

On the other hand, Israelis, in their attempt to enlist the intervention of the Jewish lobby in the United States, are doing an injustice to American Jews when they encourage confrontation with the U.S. government. A wise and farsighted Israeli leadership should avoid resorting to such political tactics in any clash with the president and his administration. The leaders in Jerusalem had grossly misjudged the situation when they thought that, with the aid of Jewish leaders, they could steer the government in a direction desirable to Israel and away from what the president and his government perceived as American interests.

A close study of the activities of Jewish leaders in the United States indicates that the scope of their support for Israel is strongly influenced by the attitude of the incumbent administration toward Israel. Whenever Washington smiles at the Jews, the Jewish leadership seems comfortable in its support of Israel. In stormier times, the relationship cools. As I recall the cautious and highly sensitive behavior of Jewish leaders in prewar Poland toward the government, I cannot escape the comparison between the two major Jewish Diasporas: the one in Poland before the Holocaust and the other, of our times, in the Unites States.

Nevertheless, the Jewish leaders do not hesitate to commute blithely back and forth between New York and Washington, presuming to speak in Israel's name on secret matters about which they know very little. Scores of such "ambassadors" vie for access to administration heads and elected officials, and hasten to impress their organizational colleagues with reports of their activities on Israel's behalf. They do not even bother to inform Israel's authorized representatives in the United States about their activities, nor do they seek guidance before setting up sessions in the State Department or with White House staff. As self-appointed ambassadors, they make pronouncements to the media about their talks with the administration, and send messages to the leaders of Israel about Washington's disappointments, expectations, and moods.

In the years before I became intimately acquainted with the Jewish community in the U.S., I believed that the Jewish leaders placed Israel's needs at the forefront of their objectives. On closer acquaintance with the community, I realized that some leaders were more intent on promoting their personal status and that of their organization. There are hundreds of Jewish organizations, only a few of which function in politics beyond their immediate locale. Most of these are linked through their membership in the Conference of Presidents. However, of the fifty member bodies, forty are without significant public membership, led by "generals" with no troops. It is convenient for Washington to relate to the conference as the official representative of the community, through which they can relay messages to Israel, in addition to the official channels of communication via the Israel embassy in Washington or the American embassy in Tel Aviv. Every U.S. administration, whether Republican or Democratic, is interested in gaining a foothold within the Jewish constituency. In times of political crisis, every candidate for elected office seeks the Jewish vote, which is concentrated in key states.

In courting votes and soliciting donations, candidates find the Conference of Presidents a convenient address. Israeli leaders visiting the United States also seek out that platform to state their opinions and needs, granting the conference an almost exclusive status in the community. In practice, however, the conference has its competitors, some of whom enjoy the encouragement of the Israeli government, which finds them helpful for its own purposes, while others serve the U.S. administration in softening bothersome or annoying Israeli positions. In the past, American Jewish leaders and organizations needed Israeli acceptance in order to win communal recognition. On occasion, they attempted to gain stature by voicing sharp criticism of Israel, sometimes even outdoing Washington. Whenever the U.S. administration has raged against Israel, there have been few Jewish leaders who dared to confront State Department or White House spokesmen. Statements defending Israel took up next to no space on the op-ed pages of prestigious American newspapers, whereas there was no shortage of prominent newspaper articles criticizing Israel.

The number of Jewish organizations, leaders, and executives keeps growing to the point where each becomes its own lobby, aspiring to speak for, offer advice to, and pass judgment on Israel. Any such leader who does not visit the White House or the State Department at least twice a year is consigned to oblivion by his peers.

For some reason, the leaders of Israel do not put these leaders and functionaries in their place. On the contrary, prior to every Israeli election, Israeli politicians send party fund-raisers to approach them, courting those who have no rank and file, thus short-circuiting their own sovereignty as leaders of an independent nation.

Unlike such self-serving operators, the authentic Jewish leaders and their grassroots constituencies of American Jews have strong pro-Israel sympathies. They commiserate with the country's pain and delight in its achievements. They are proud of Israel in general, not only when she wins a Six-Day War, or scores a spectacular triumph at Entebbe. They empathize with and love Israel unreservedly. Their names are engraved on hundreds of hospitals, educational institutions, forests, and public parks, which they helped establish. They have a place in the hearts of Israelis and the history of the Land, as do their predecessors, who came in the hundreds to stand together and fight together with us in 1948.

Today, apart from the extreme fringes – like the members of a classic Reform Judaism temple who disassociate themselves from Israel, or like some of the extremely orthodox sects in Brooklyn – the Jews of America who are involved in Jewish affairs are united in their bond with Israel. This is a link of great importance, both to Israel and to the American Diaspora, but it is not a safety belt to be relied upon in times of need. Far from being dependent on the Diaspora, Israel is a source of inspiration to Jews who are losing contact with the Jewish people and their spiritual identity.

Israelis need to understand the special situation of American Jewry, not to expect what cannot be given. The Jews of America should be seen as a Jewish community, most of whom wish to maintain their Judaism in whatever way they choose. We must reconcile ourselves to the fact that we live in a different milieu, that our objectives and priorities are not identical.

Israel is about to celebrate its fiftieth birthday. Now, numbering over five million people, it is seven times larger than it was in 1948. It has overcome its enemies, strengthened its economy, and consolidated its political existence. It will continue to be the nation of "Jews of anxiety" for as long as there are brethren in the world who need a haven, and as long as there are enemies lurking at her doors. For all the differences, there is much in common between the "Jews of anxiety" in

Israel and the "Jews of tranquillity" in America. Although their destinies are so different that it is difficult to define American and Israeli Jews as one people with a common fate, they share a common heritage and mutually yearn for a sincere brotherhood.

POSTSCRIPT

Soon Israel will celebrate its fiftieth birthday, its Jubilee year. In these five decades, dispersed Jews from all corners of the globe have been gathered into Israel to merge into one nation. The process has been long and painful. An independent observer from outer space would undoubtedly see a human effort unparalleled anywhere on Earth. Obstinately pursuing their objective in spite of formidable obstacles, the Jews of Israel have been attempting to create a new, integrated society. Envy and jealousy tend to undermine this new society-in-the-making, fragmented by economic hardships, political rifts, religious squabbles, and above all, a bloody conflict between two national entities locked in a struggle over one parcel of land. This is where Israel stands as it approaches the end of its fifth decade of sovereign existence.

From time to time a vexing question worries me: Are we really mature enough to create a new society such as we envision in our free and independent nation, in our own land? I also wonder occasionally whether we were destined from the start to face the challenge of persecution, being "anxious" rather than "tranquil."

Seeking answers to these gnawing questions, I felt impelled to return to places I had previously avoided and tried to erase from my memory. For the first time I invited my wife and four children to accompany me on a visit to my past. For seven days and nights we retraced my footsteps of close to fifty years ago. It was this visit that broke the lock on my heart, shattering me in the presence of my family. There was not a single building, not a hut, not a railway track, that could again arouse in me the terror I experienced in my Auschwitz-

Buchenwald days. Suddenly I came upon a bald, green patch in the heart of a thick forest with thousands of sharp stones pointing upward, as if pointing a finger at the havens. It was the site of Treblinka, where more than one million Jews, including my father and younger brother, had been murdered in cold blood.

I walked among the stones, on the surrounding pathways, and each grain of soil, each pebble seemed to be one of the burned bones. My family watched me with bewilderment and empathy, never having seen me like this. I resolved to come back to this place by myself, to be alone with my thoughts and my memories.

The following summer I drove north from Warsaw on the road to Bialystok. Near the small town of Brok, I turned east from the main road in the direction of Malkinia. The trees of the forest were already shedding their leaves, and a pastoral serenity prevailed in the villages. Here and there an aged farmer kept an eye on a few cows grazing by the roadside. Near the village of Poniatow stood an abandoned train complete with a long line of cattle wagons, like those "from that time." I parked the car near the rails and went to look for traces of the Jews this train had transported to their death. Looking into every wagon, with its broken and gaping doors, I could still see the families huddled on the hard floor, waiting for their doom. I searched for some last remnant of their lives, a scribbled message, a name, some forgotten item tossed in a corner, but I found nothing.

My next stop was at the entrance to Treblinka. Entering the forest, I turned toward the place I had seen on my previous visit. The silence of a cemetery hung over this place, accentuating the rustle of the leaves in trees that had sprung up over the last forty years from the ashes of the victims. No twitter of a bird broke the silence. I walked toward the memorial stones jutting out of the ground and stood next to a basalt slab inscribed with the name "Piotrkow." I lit no candle, recited no prayer, no psalm. I could not. I sat for a long while on a nearby stone, lost in thought, picturing the last moments of the multitudes put to death in this hellish place. My thoughts strayed back to the deserted train I had seen on my way here. Again I tried to reconstruct experiences and sights from those days of despair, until finally my imagination took me back home to Jerusalem, panic-stricken at the thought of "what if?" What if we lose our alertness, our vigilance, our balance, our sanity even for a single moment? Sitting on a memorial slab in Treblinka, seeing before my eyes the annihilation of one million of our people, brought home to me the danger still hovering overhead, whether from Scuds or other weapons of mass destruction. With all my might I tried to convince myself that a carnage like Treblinka could not ever happen again.

Looking back on a process begun half a century ago, from our state of utter vulnerability to our state of sovereignty, and looking ahead to assess the daunting obstacles still in our path, I cling to the fervent hope that we will ultimately achieve our national aspirations, our cherished goal of living in peace among nations.

Deep in my heart I still sense the stubborn resolve to survive, the injunction to "choose life" that helped us to survive *then*, amid the cinders, and now, surrounded by enemies who seek our destruction. The experience of our past has forged us and bolstered our collective resolve to pave a road that, I pray, will lead to a new Jewish society, self-reliant and just, with only minimal political, social, and religious tensions. As I survey my own experiences and the way the seemingly impossible became possible, repeatedly emerging from labyrinths that perplexed us, my certainty grows that we will find the strength to achieve our objectives: First and foremost, the guarantee of our continued national existence, and the creation of a healthy and prosperous society that will serve as a light to world Jewry.

This optimism is based on personal experiences. For fifty years I carried the responsibility passed on to me by my father before he went to his death in Treblinka. He placed in my care a weak child of five, who looked more like a skinny little three year old. For three years I served as father and mother, guardian, protector, and mentor to my young brother, Yisrael Meir, or Lulek as we called him then. I feel it was this mission, the mission to bring this brother to safety from the abyss of despair to the gates of hope - to the Promised Land - and thereby guarantee the continuation of our rabbinic dynasty, that kept me alive and gave me the will to fight for our lives rather than succumb to the fate that befell so many of us.

On the first day of the new month of Adar, February 21, 1993, I stood at afternoon prayer with this younger brother at the Western Wall of the second Temple in Jerusalem. It was the same spot where we had stood forty-eight years earlier, on our arrival in Jerusalem. Then, as a seven year old, he had gazed at the stones of the Western Wall without any appreciation or awareness of its significance. This time he was praying for divine guidance before assuming the highest post of any rabbi in Israel. My young brother, who had come forth from the ashes of the death camps, was shortly to be proclaimed chief rabbi of Israel. I looked at him with tears of pride and gratitude – and relief that my mission was at last fulfilled.

"Kaeith Yeamer L'Yaacov Ul'Yisrael Ma Pa'al E-L; Am K'Lavie Yakoom V'Keari Yitnassa."
In due time Yaacov and Yisrael are told what God has performed: Behold, the people shall rise up as a great lion, and lift himself up as a young lion.

Balaam's Prophecy (Numbers 23:23-24)

Appendix A

After our liberation from Buchenwald on April 11, 1945, we learned why we had been so heavily guarded by the *SS* while we worked in the stone quarry of Buchenwald. Shortly after liberation, U.S. troops of the Third Army discovered an extremely valuable treasure trove which the Nazis had hidden in two tunnels of the quarry. The Americans sorted out its contents and found vast quantities of gold ingots, currencies, coins, wedding rings, watches, diamonds, and other precious stones, as well as dental crowns, bridges, and fillings which the Nazis had looted throughout occupied Europe and confiscated from prisoners upon their arrival in Buchenwald.

On May 6, 1945, a convoy of six trucks escorted by armored military police vehicles left Buchenwald with a shipment of over twenty tons containing the trove. It was deposited at the Frankfurt Exchange Depository, where it was marked as Shipment 16.

SOURCE: Report of the U.N. War Crimes Commission, Nuremberg, 1946-7

Appendix B

The life expectancy of a concentration camp prisoner was calculated by the SS Economic Department to be nine months. The Economic Department supplied slave labor from the camps to German industries such as Krupp, Volkswagen, Messerschmidt, AEG, IG Farben, Rheinmetal, and Siemens, according to their request.

The SS Economic Department received six marks per day for every slave laborer. According to the calculations of the *SS*, as recorded in a document exhibited at the International War Crimes Trials in Nuremberg, the *SS* income from every slave laborer amounted to 1,631 marks for the 270 days of his service to the German war machine, after deducting food and clothing expenses, and including an additional income of 200 marks for the valuables, which were found on the body, as well as for the ashes and bones of the disposed body which were sold for fertilization.

SOURCE: Dr. Eugen Kogon: **Der SS Staat**, *Frankfurt am Main, 1960*

Appendix C

In April 1945, the supreme commander of the *SS*, Heinrich Himmler, issued an order to all the commanders of the concentration camps not to transfer the camps to the approaching troops of the Allied forces or the Red Army, and not to allow any prisoners to fall into enemy hands. They were ordered to evacuate all the prisoners to a safe area and to blow up the vacated camps; in most cases the Germans were unable to carry out this order.

SOURCE: Exhibit D-63 at the International War Crimes Trials In Nuremberg, 1946-7

GLOSSARY

Achdut Ha'avoda   Activist socialist party – merged with Mapai

Agudat Yisrael   Ultra-orthodox Party

Aliyah   Literally "ascending"; immigrating to the Holy Land (Israel)

Apellplatz   Assembly ground in concentration camp, where the daily
　　　　roll-call took place

Auschwitz (Oswiecim)   Extermination camp in Poland. Situated one
hundred sixty miles southwest of Warsaw, the camp was built in an
unfavorable location surrounded by stagnant ponds, smelly and
pestilential. It was opened in 1940, after the defeat of Poland, and later
was greatly expanded. Special installations were added, including
bathhouses used for gassing and corpse cellars for storage of bodies. In
1941 Heinrich Himmler inspected Auschwitz and gave orders to
enlarge the camp and drain the swamps, in order to set up a new camp
at nearby Birkenau. It is estimated that from one to four million
persons died in gas chambers and by a variety of other methods at
Auschwitz-Birkenau.

Beth Din   Rabbinical court

Beth Midrash   Study hall of yeshiva

Belzec   With Sobibor and Maidanek, one of the extermination camps
in the Lublin district of Poland. Originally a labor camp, Belzec was
founded by *SS-Brigadefuehrer* Odilo Globocnik, who in 1941 became
head of all the death camps in the General Government of Poland.

Betar   Right-wing Zionist youth movement

Birkenau   See: Auschwitz

Bnei Akiva   Religious Zionist youth movement

Brit Halutzim Datiyim   Union of religious pioneers

Buchenwald   One of the major concentration camps in the Third Reich. Buchenwald was one of three camps set up in 1937 to form the nucleus of a concentration camp system: Sachsenhausen in the north, Dachau in the south, and Buchenwald in central Germany. Buchenwald was located on a wooded hill four miles from Weimar, the shrine of German culture associated with names such as Goethe, Schiller, Herder, and Weiland. According to the report of a U.S. congressional committee, the means of extermination were starvation, beatings, torture, incredibly over-crowded sleeping conditions, and sickness. On April 11, 1945, Buchenwald was liberated by the U.S. 80th Division.

Chelmno (Kulmhof)   The first and one of the main extermination camps in Poland. After the Wannsee Conference of January 20, 1942, on the Final Solution, a killing center at Chelmno, in the middle of the Warta (Warthe) River region, was set up as a strictly local enterprise for the Jews of this area. Chelmno later became one of the more important killing centers in occupied Poland. There were no industrial activities in this camp, nor were there any non-Jewish inmates. The victims were brought to a large mill in the nearby village of Zawadki and then taken in small groups by truck to Chelmno, being gassed during their ride to the mass graves.

Dayan   Religious judge

Eretz Yisrael   The Land of Israel

Etrog   Citrus fruit, one of the four species used for Succoth

Etzel   Jewish right-wing underground movement in Palestine

Fedayeen   Arab militant terrorists proclaimed as suicidal warriors

Final Solution   The cover name of Hitler's plan to eliminate all the Jews in Europe. About six million Jews were annihilated during World War II by officials of the Nazi regime. The year 1941 marked a turning point in the anti-Jewish campaign. The German invasion of the Soviet Union on June 22 unleashed Hitler's sense of destructive nihilism.

Several million Jews were incarcerated in Polish ghettos. Emigration was costly. A project initiated in 1940 to expel the Jews to Africa had failed. Hitler decided on a drastic move. At this time the idea of a "final solution," or what he called a "territorial solution," began to form in his mind. The plan called for the complete elimination of European Jewry. Hitler's *idee fixe* would be implemented at long last.

At the Wannsee Conference held on January 20, 1942, the course of action was completed: "In the course of the execution of the Final Solution, Europe will be combed from west to east." Responsibility for the project was placed in the hands of Heinrich Himmler and his assistants in the Gestapo and *SS*.

Get   Jewish bill of divorce

Gestapo (Secret State Police)   A secret police force dedicated to the task of maintaining the National Socialist regime. Hitler deemed it necessary to protect the existence of the Third Reich by a political police that would track down and eliminate all dissidents, complainers, and opponents. He regarded any individual, no matter what his status, as a potential suspect. His Gestapo became a symbol of the Nazi regime of terror. The Gestapo organization extended throughout Germany and developed into the most important security organ of the state. It became autonomous and set up its own legal system, with power far exceeding that of any law court in the Third Reich, and began to exercise its right to assume control over the lives, freedom, and property of all Germans. In working for "the annihilation of the enemy" it could and did use any methods it deemed necessary.

During World War II it was instrumental in breaking down resistance in the occupied countries. Gestapo agents were active during the terror in Poland, in the execution of Russian prisoners of war, and in the arrest and slaughter of the conspirators of July 1944. It followed the German armed forces into occupied countries and used its own tested methods to destroy all elements hostile to Nazi rule. It was regarded as one of the cruelest police forces of modern times.

Gomel   Prayer of thanksgiving for escaping death

Hagana   Jewish underground organization in Palestine

Halachah   Jewish law

Halachic   Pertaining to Halachah

Hallel   Prayer in praise of God

Hanukkah   Festival of Lights

Haredi   Ultra-orthodox Jew

Hashomer Hatzair   Left-wing Zionist youth movement

Hassid   Member of a popular Jewish spiritual movement
         that originated in Eastern Europe in the 18th century
         and is characterised by its emphasis on mysticism,
         prayer, religious zeal and joy
Havdalah   Ceremony marking the end of the Sabbath

Herut   Right-wing party, preceded Likud

Huppa   Wedding canopy

I.D.F.   Israel Defense Forces

Jihad   Islamic holy war

Kaddish   A prayer recited by mourners for parents and close relatives

Kapo   Group commander in concentration camp

Kiddush   A blessing or prayer; differing in form according to the
         occasion, that is recited over a cup of wine on Sabbath,
         a Festival or other festive events
Kippa   Skullcap

Knesset   Israel's parliament

Kol Nidrei   Opening prayer of Yom Kippur eve

Kommandos   Work groups in concentration camp

Lechi-Stern Group   Extremist underground organization in Palestine

Likud   Union of Herut and Liberal parties

Mapai   Preceded the Israel Labor Party

Mapam   Radical left-oriented socialist party

Matzoth   Unleavened bread eaten on Passover

Mikve   Pool for ritual purification

Mincha   Afternoon prayers

Minyan   Quorum of ten adult men, required for communal prayers

Mitzvoth   Religious commandments

Mizrachi   Zionist religious party, later N.R.P.

MK   Member of the Knesset

Mossad   Israeli clandestine agency equivalent to C.I.A.

Mossad L'Aliyah Bet   Preceded the Mossad

Musselman   Concentration camp inmate, starved and weakened, and
with no will to live
N.R.P.   National Religious Party

O.S.E.   *Organisation Juive de Secours aux Enfants*

Palestine   Land of Israel named Palestine by the British Mandate

Palmach   Elite units of the Hagana

PLO   Palestine Liberation Organization; established by Arabs in 1964

Poalei Agudat Yisrael   Zionist faction within Agudat Yisrael

Poskim   Halachic authorities

Purim   Festival celebrating deliverance of the Jews from extermination in Persia 25 centuries ago

Rashi   Bible and Talmud commentator of 11th century

Ravensbrueck   Concentration   camp   for   women   inmates. Ravensbrueck was located 50 miles north of Berlin, near Lake Fuerstenberg. It was surrounded by swampland. Established in 1938, the camp became a place of internment for Red Cross nurses, Russian women captured on the battlefields, French nationals, members of the Resistance, and Jewish women. The main camp was supposed to accommodate some six thousand prisoners, but from 1944 on there were never fewer than twelve thousand and in January 1945 there were at least thirty-six thousand. About fifty thousand prisoners perished in Ravensbrueck. Women were subjected to transplantation of human bones in experiments carried out there.

Rebbe   Title of respect for the leader of a hassidic group

Rosh Hashanah   The Jewish New Year

Sabra   Person born in Israel

Seder   A ceremonial dinner held on the eve of Passover when the story of exodus from Egypt is retold

Sefer Torah   Parchment scroll of the Written Law

Shabak   Formerly known as Shin Bet, Israel's security service

Shacharit   The morning prayer

Shas   Ultra-orthodox Sephardi Religious Party

Shavuoth   Festival of receiving the Torah (on Mount Sinai)

Sherut Bitachon Clali   Internal secret service of Israel, also known as Shin Bet, or Shabak

Soapbar   A derogatory description used against survivors who arrived in Palestine (Israel) in the late forties, referring to the unconfirmed rumors that the survivors were destined by the Nazis to become soap after their annihilation

Sonderkommandos   Special units for removing the dead in concentration camps

SS **(Elite Guard)**   Originally the black-shirted personal guard of Hitler but later transformed by its leader, Heinrich Himmler, into a mass army on which was to rest the ultimate exercise of Nazi power. *SS (Schutzstaffel)* literally means "defense echelon." The name was universally abbreviated to *SS*, not in Roman or Gothic letters but written as a lightning flash in imitation of ancient runic characters. The *SS* was known as the Black Order.

The *SS* served as a political police and was later assigned the duty of administering concentration camps and extermination camps. It was widely regarded as a limb of the Nazi Party. Shortly after Hitler became chancellor in 1933, the *SS, SA,* and Stahlhelm were all authorized to act as auxiliary police units. Under the leadership of Heinrich Himmler the SS was designed to find, fight, and destroy all open movement, and bring about "our racial resurrection." Himmler formed an *SS* economic empire that controlled business and manufacturing enterprises, which exploited the looted property, and personal belongings of the *SS* victims.

Taharah   Purification for burial by washing the dead body

Tallit   Prayer shawl

Talmud   Books of Jewish law

Tefillin   Phylacteries; scriptual passages contained in small black leather boxes, which are bound to the forehead and the upper arm as part of the morning prayers, except on Sabbath and Festivals

Teheran children   Jewish children rescued from Poland during World War II, who arrived in Palestine via Teheran in 1944

Tisha B'Av   The ninth of Av, commemorating the destruction of the Temples in Jerusalem, 586 BC and 70 AD

Tosefoth   Talmud commentators of 12th and 13th centuries

Treblinka   Extermination camp located at Malkinia Gorna, on the Bug River in Poland. With Chelmno, Belzec, and Sobibor, it was one of the four main Polish camps used as receiving centers, primarily for Jews. Treblinka was almost exclusively a death center. At first, inmates were killed by exhaust gas from internal combustion engines of captured tanks and trucks, which were often faulty. Zyklon-B gas was utilized. Mass expulsion of Jews from Warsaw began on July 22, 1942, with one train a day bringing five to six thousand Jews to Treblinka. Some of the prisoners were diverted from Sobibor. After being unloaded from trains, the prisoners were told they were to be taken to the "bath houses," where they were sprayed with gas instead of water.

UNRRA   United Nations Relief and Rehabilitation Agency

Yeshiva   Institute for Talmudic studies

Yom Kippur   Day of Atonement

Youth Aliyah   Organization to aid children to immigrate to Israel, to escape Nazi-dominated Europe

INDEX